Memoirs of
American Jews
1775-1865

In Three Volumes

Volume One

Memoirs

1955 — Philadelphia — 5715

# of American Jews

1775-1865

Jacob Rader Marcus

Director, American Jewish Archives;
Adolph S. Ochs Professor of Jewish History, Hebrew Union
College—Jewish Institute of Religion, Cincinnati

Volume One

The Jewish Publication Society of America

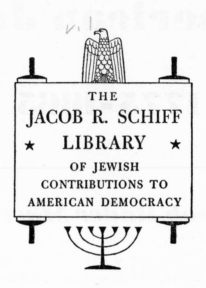

THE
JACOB R. SCHIFF
★ LIBRARY ★
OF JEWISH
CONTRIBUTIONS TO
AMERICAN DEMOCRACY

To Nettie

Preface

AMERICAN JUDAISM is now observing its three hundredth anniversary. In commemoration of the event, the American Jewish Archives has prepared this collection of memoirs.

The prime purpose of the Preface is to explain the editorial rules which were employed and to thank the many institutions and individuals who so graciously aided and encouraged the editor in his task. The nature and significance of the autobiographies and memoirs are explained in the detailed Introduction which follows.

The personal recollections and autobiographies which follow the Introduction are, on the whole, printed as they were written or originally published. Wherever it was necessary to edit them, the University of Chicago Press *Manual of Style* has been followed. The punctuation and paragraphing are the editor's, but the spelling and grammar have not been touched. For whatever mistakes in spelling, grammar, or fact appear in the text, the original author is responsible. We have not supplied *sic* whenever an author nodded, lest the pages be pock-marked and the reader be annoyed by the too frequent interruptions. Transliterations from foreign languages made by the original writers have been retained as they appear in the original, even if the reader is confronted by two or more spellings of the same Hebrew word. Those made by the editor follow modern accepted forms. In transcribing Hebrew words, the practice of *The Jewish Encyclopedia* has been followed, but diacritical marks have been omitted. Notes interpolated by the editor can be easily recognized, for they appear in square brackets. The Index to this work, which consists of three volumes, will appear in the last volume.

Now I turn to the pleasant task of thanking those who have aided in the preparation of these volumes. Mr. Thomas Jefferson Tobias of Charleston, S.C., and Mr. and Mrs. Albert M. Cohen of Wynnewood, Pa., have been most gracious in making their family papers available. E. P. Dutton & Co., Inc., New York, have kindly granted permission to reprint excerpts from *Seventy Years of Life and Work* by Samuel Gompers, copyright, 1925, by E. P. Dutton & Co., Inc., renewal 1952, Mrs. Gertrude C. Gompers.

I wish to express my thanks to the American Jewish Historical Society for permission to reprint "From Peddler to Regimental Commander in Two Years: The Civil War Career of Major Louis A. Gratz," by Jacob R. Marcus, which appeared in *Publications of the American Jewish Historical Society*, XXXVIII (1948), 33-44.

The following archivists, librarians, historical societies, and state libraries have generously supplied me with information and materials: Marie B. Owen of the Department of Archives and History of the State of Alabama, Montgomery; Allan R. Ottley of the California State Library, Sacramento; Isidore S. Meyer, Librarian-Editor of the American Jewish Historical Society, New York; Joshua Bloch, chief of the Jewish Division of the New York Public Library; George P. Hammond, director of the Bancroft Library of the University of California in Berkeley; Bertha L. Heilbron of the Minnesota Historical Society, St. Paul; Lilla M. Hawes of the Georgia Historical Society, Savannah; Edna L. Jacobsen of the New York State Library, Albany; David C. Adelman of the Rhode Island Jewish Historical Association, Providence; and the staffs of the National Archives, Washington, D.C.; the Library of Congress, Division of Manuscripts; the Virginia State Library, Richmond; the Virginia Historical Society, Richmond; the Howard-Tilton Memorial Library, New Orleans; the Historical Society of Pennsylvania, Philadelphia; the Southern Historical Collection of the University of North Carolina Library, Chapel Hill; the Wisconsin State Historical Society, Madison; and the Hebrew Union College—Jewish Institute of Religion Library, Cincinnati.

The preparation of this work has been made possible by a gift from the Eda K. Loeb Memorial Fund, whose trustees made the original grant to the American Jewish Archives and are, therefore, in large measure responsible for the appearance of these volumes. Future historians will be thankful to them for their devotion to cultural matters and for their farsighted generosity.

I am very grateful to my staff at the American Jewish Archives for the many courtesies they have shown me. Jeanette Weiss, my editorial assistant, has been most helpful; Etheljane Callner, my secretary, prepared the typescript; and Emil Oberholzer, Jr., served as my editorial aid in the preparation of these volumes. My colleague, Rabbi Abraham I. Shinedling, has carefully scrutinized the typescripts, read proof in his usual meticulous fashion, and prepared the Index. It is always a joy to acknowledge my gratitude to the Rabbi, my old classmate and friend of many years. To the aforementioned, my most heartfelt thanks for their conscientious labors.

There are many others who have made suggestions and who have volunteered information. Though I shall not mention them by name, I am thankful to them for their kindness. If large works are published today, they owe their appearance not only to the efforts of the editor, but also to the splendid co-operation of a host of workers in the republic of letters. Long may they prosper!

JACOB R. MARCUS

Cincinnati, Ohio
January 1, 1955

Contents

PREFACE   vii

LIST OF ILLUSTRATIONS   xiii

INTRODUCTION   1

THREE GENERATIONS OF COHENS   27
Memoirs of a Pennsylvania Family

MORDECAI SHEFTALL   40
Revolutionary Patriot of Georgia

DAVID SALISBURY FRANKS   45
Eighteenth-Century Soldier and Courier

CAPTAIN MORDECAI MYERS   50
Veteran of the War of 1812

URIAH PHILLIPS LEVY   76
Stormy Petrel of the Navy

MORDECAI MANUEL NOAH   117
Ebullient Politician

RAPHAEL JACOB MOSES   146
A Southern Romantic

JOSEPH JONAS   203
The Jews Come to Ohio

ALFRED MORDECAI   216
Brilliant West Point Cadet

ELLEN MORDECAI   232
Life on a Virginia Farm

JOSEPH LYONS   239
Random Thoughts of a Sick Soul

CLARA L. MOSES   261
War Days in Old Natchez

xi

REBECCA GRATZ   272
    The Idol of Her Generation

ROSA MORDECAI   281
    The Oldest Jewish Sunday School

HAIMAN PHILIP SPITZ   289
    A Pioneer Merchant in Maine

WILLIAM FRANK   302
    Pilgrim Father of Pittsburgh Jewry

LOUIS STIX   309
    Honesty Is the Best Policy

JESSE SELIGMAN   343
    The Making of a Financier

HENRY SEESSEL   353
    Typical German Jewish Immigrant

AUGUST PICARD   368
    Militant Artisan

List of Illustrations

After page

HENRY COHEN OF PHILADELPHIA   16
   Courtesy of Mr. and Mrs. Albert M. Cohen, Wynnewood, Pa.

PHILADELPHIA IN 1856—CHESTNUT STREET, EAST OF FIFTH   16
   Courtesy of the Library of Congress

DAVID SALISBURY FRANKS   48
   Courtesy of Mrs. Clarence I. De Sola, Montreal

MAJOR MORDECAI MYERS   48
   Hannah R. London Collection

NEW YORK CITY IN 1839   80
   Courtesy of the New York Public Library

MAJOR RAPHAEL J. MOSES   80
   *Reproduced from "The Jews of South Carolina" by
   B. A. Elzas*

JOSEPH JONAS. FIRST JEW IN CINCINNATI, 1817   112

CINCINNATI IN THE LATE 1820's   112
   *Courtesy of the Historical and Philosophical Society of Ohio,
   Cincinnati*

MAJOR ALFRED MORDECAI   144
   Hannah R. London Collection

WEST POINT FROM ABOVE WASHINGTON VALLEY—1834   144
   Courtesy of the Library of Congress

NATCHEZ, MISSISSIPPI, IN 1840   176
   Courtesy of the New York Public Library

BOSTON IN 1840   176
   Courtesy of the New York Public Library

PITTSBURGH IN 1849   208
   Courtesy of the New York Public Library

After page

Louis Stix   208
    Courtesy of Mrs. Carl Stix, Cincinnati

Cincinnati in 1848   240
    Courtesy of the Cincinnati Public Library

Jesse Seligman   240

August Picard. In His Uniform as an Officer in the
    Lafayette Guard   240
    Courtesy of Mrs. Simon Mendelsohn, Cincinnati

Memoirs of
American Jews
1775-1865

Volume One

Introduction

WHAT ARE MEMOIRS?

MEMOIRS have been defined as "a history or narrative composed from personal experience and memory; often, especially, an account of one's life, or of episodes in it, written by oneself." This description is broad enough to include practically all the material in the following collection. Some of the narratives presented here are not formal memoirs. They include travel notes, diaries, pension records, court-martial proceedings, and apologiae of an autobiographical nature.

Many of these memoirs are published for the first time from the original manuscripts. A very few of them, however, are already known to the historian. The greater part of them have been collected by the American Jewish Archives after years of careful search and investigation.

SUNDRY STATISTICS

A few statistics may be of interest. Of the eighty-odd memoirs available, fifty-nine were selected. Most of the originals were in English, or what purports to be English. Others were in German or French. Adolphus S. Solomons ascribed Yiddish phrases to Lincoln, but that was poetic license on the author's part. Mr. Solomons was just trying to be cute.

Thirty-eight of the chroniclers were immigrants, including twenty-nine Germans. Some of the twenty-one American-born Jews who wrote accounts of their experiences were already fourth- or fifth-generation Americans; three or four of those who wrote were related. Forty-nine memoirists were men, and ten were women.

Approximately two dozen of the authors were either born in the South or lived there. This very striking and significant fact is explained by the cultural and economic importance of that region in the pre-Civil War period. Forty writers touched on the period of the war; only four memoirs cover the decades prior to the nineteenth century.

1

Less than one-third of the relators told their story as the events unfolded themselves. Of the forty-one who recalled their adventures from memory, twenty-five wrote at least thirty-five years after the incidents they described had taken place.

There were few states and territories which did not play some part in these memoirs. The writers ranged from Bangor, Maine, to the ephemeral Florida boom towns on the Gulf of Mexico. Moving westward, they wrote of the Minnesota Territory, of Kansas, and of Texas. Jews had already reached the Pacific Coast via the Isthmus of Panama.

Over thirty of the fifty-nine writers were peddlers, clerks, and merchants. Among the rest were housewives, artisans, bankers, soldiers, politicians, teachers, rabbis, lawyers, surgeons, a sailor, and a communal worker.

MOTIVATIONS FOR WRITING

What prompted these men and women to keep a diary or, in their old age, to rehearse the stories of their lives? The motivations that induced them to write are almost as numerous as the narratives themselves. Some wrote to inform, to advise, and to warn their children. Sons and daughters, by that time grown and mature men and women, were exhorted to profit by the experiences and mistakes of the past. One brilliant businessman warned his son against speculation in stocks. (We may rest assured that this sound advice was blithely disregarded before 1929.)

An admiring niece wrote to save from oblivion the memory of her gifted Aunt Rebecca Gratz, "one of the brightest ornaments of society." Others were thrilled by the consciousness that they had lived through a great historic period and aspired to catch the rhythm of it and to put it down on paper. It was during their lifetime that the United States had passed from an agricultural to an industrial economy; their lives spanned the first appearance of the steamboat, the telegraph, electricity, the rotary press, the sewing machine, the reaper and thresher, anesthetics, and Wall Street! Few, if any, believed that they were making a substantial contribution to history; a number of them were eager to express themselves, to solace themselves, to talk to themselves, or to see themselves on paper. Besieged in their old age by admiring and flattering children and grandchildren, successful businessmen sat down—with or without the benefit of ghost writers—to recount their rise from peddler to merchant-prince. Most of the memoirs were written during the decades when millions of people were reading the success novels of Horatio Alger, Jr. What is more truly American than the rags-to-riches theme?

LIGHT ON AMERICAN HISTORY

Many of the great events in American history are touched on and illuminated in these personal chronicles. From 1775 to 1865 the panorama of war unrolls before us; there are pages on nullification and secession, and detailed accounts on almost every phase of commerce, trade, and transportation. American culture and social life are reflected in nearly every paragraph. It is very doubtful whether any of the memoirists makes a single statement which will in any degree modify the basic outlines of American history. But almost every writer makes the great events of the past live because of his personal relation to the events that he recounts.

The story of how the Democrats under Aaron Burr drove the Federalists out of power in New York State was set forth by Captain Mordecai Myers. That veteran of the War of 1812 also described how his soldiers marched barefoot in the dead of winter, leaving the imprints of their bleeding feet in the snow.

Major Raphael J. Moses told the story of what was probably the first Florida land boom, in the 1830's, when cotton truly was king, when village lots sold for $5,000 apiece, and when "water was scarcer than champagne." Those were the days when the cotton towns of the Old Southwest began to mushroom and when railroads first appeared, although it still took fourteen days to travel from Hamburg, S.C., to Mobile, Ala., by stage and river steamboat.

Although the first railroads were rude affairs and depots were "hogpens," their importance was fully realized. The disgruntled Rabbi Isaac M. Wise—disgruntled if only because a station agent refused him a pass and threatened to pull a gun on him—sensed that rapid transportation would revolutionize civilization. "The superstitions between nations," he said, "are *railroaded* and *steamboated* away."

It is a joy to live in the past with these chroniclers and adventurers. We can ride with John Brown against the Border Ruffians in Kansas, hang murderers with the Vigilantes in California, and explore the upper Mississippi, where three houses constituted a "city." Those were the days when Charles Blondin crossed Niagara Falls on a tightrope, and when the gullible, suspicious Americans felt cheated because he did not carry the Prince of Wales over the falls on his back. It was an age in which every smart American wanted

125 cents of value for the dollar, but was prey to every chance humbug. And let there be no doubt as to what humbug is: Max Maretzek has defined it as "exhibiting a fly through a microscope and passing it off as an elephant to one who pays."

THE SOUTH

For the memoirists of the ante-bellum generation there was never a dull moment. It may be something of a surprise to read that people were already experimenting with pre-fabricated houses and electric lights. The Millerites were predicting that the world would come to an end in 1843 or 1844, fire engines were studded with jewels, and bedbugs were universal. It was a day when industrial America was just beginning to flex its muscles, when Canal Street was the end of town in New York, when Charleston, S.C., was a city of "bananas, books, and oysters," while New Orleans was a great "emporium of wine, women, and segars."

Compared to comments on the Civil War by Southerners, the Northern writers had relatively little to say. The men and women who retold the fortunes of the South had much to say on slavery, the War, and their beloved Robert E. Lee. For the student who desires to know how a Southern gentleman, albeit a private, spent his time between battles, there is more than ample material in the journals of Eugene H. Levy. Other memoirists provide a mine of information on the fighting, drinking, and horseplay of the real Johnny Reb. Here is the story of war, real war, of men who marched and countermarched through mire and slush and snow.

Civil War supply? One could write a book on that alone. Here are narratives of smugglers, who risked their lives to bring back goods, quinine, and gold. Food? Let Philip Sartorius tell about the tasty Texas steers they ate: "They were so poor, two men had to hold them up while the butcher knocked them down." Hungry? Forage for yourself like brave Lewis Leon: "We got to one house and there was no one at home, but in the yard there were two chickens which we captured, for we were afraid they would bite us." Commissary Raphael Moses had more trouble than Leon. The latter, a buck private, had to feed himself only; Moses, like his ancestor in the wilderness, had to feed an army, to supply all of Longstreet's corps—84,000 hungry souls.

For the Southern boys in Yankee prison camps the menu was often mule meat, supplemented by a diet of rats. A Savannah nurse of an aristocratic family (her reminiscences are not published in this collection) has given us a contemporary recipe for preparing rats. Epicures reported that they tasted better than squirrel meat.

It is doubtful whether one can find a better picture of the last days of Richmond than in these accounts. Here is the story of the abolition of slavery and the end of the old order. Ambivalence tore the heartstrings of master and slave; affection and resentment crossed and crisscrossed. It was difficult for both white and black to accept the realities of emancipation. The Negroes will yet feel the "slavery of their freedom." Gleefully a resentful Virginian reported this soliloquy of a Negro on freedom: "Dis what you call freedom! No wuk to do, and got to feed and clothe yourself."

THE JEWISH NOTE

Beyond the fact that these vignettes are reported in the reminiscences of Jews, what is Jewish about them? They *are* part of the Jewish experience in this land. The division between general history and the history of the Jew in the United States is frequently arbitrary and artificial. Every aspect of Jewish life here is part of American life, even the perennial hustling of Rabbis Leeser and Wise to create new Jewish congregations. These volumes of autobiographical narratives describe in detail the realities of immigration, of business life, of emerging Jewish communities, of a changing Judaism, of the subtle processes of acculturation and integration. These happenings are of the essence of nineteenth-century American history—and they are the heart of the Jewish experience. American Jewish history is the story of *all* that happened to the Jew as an American. (The motivation for its study may be pardonable filiopietism or the desire to create a new American historiography which will more truly reflect the growth of the American people. The final decision, whatever it is, will not be uninfluenced by apologetics.)

THE JEWISH IMMIGRANT

Who came to these shores? Young, aggressive, eager, able young people—and some near failures and utter failures. They were German, English, French, Polish, Hungarian, and Russian. In the 1850's, the little village of San Juan Capistrano had a Polish Jewish and a Russian Jewish shopkeeper. Most of the immigrants, however, were German. Emily Seasongood has painted for us the picture of the quaint Bavarian background of some of the newcomers. The old Bavaria was a world passed by with its dear Uncle Fechheimer, the village Jew who had studied some English and greeted visiting American relatives with "good-bye" and shouted after them the cheerful farewell: "how-de-do."

Why did they come? Some left their old homes for purely personal reasons: they had made enemies and could not remain. A few wished to evade military conscription. Most of them left because of anti-Jewish prejudice, political disabilities, hard times, and the lack of economic opportunity. What Europe lacked, America offered: the youngsters hoped for a real chance to make money here; they wanted to help the old folks. The boys in their teens thought they were going on a picnic; lads like August Bondi and Jacob Hirschorn lusted for adventure. At seventeen, Hirschorn was one of the "Forlorn Hope" that stormed the citadel of Chapultepec.

The final incentive to migrate came from a relative, often a brother, who had gone ahead. At times a family moved as a whole; occasionally the father went ahead, leaving his wife and children behind until he made a place for them. Most typical was the gradual breaking up of the European family as first one son, then another, then the sisters, and finally the old folks deserted the village homestead. It was not unusual for a group of youngsters to leave together from the same district. Julius Weis and Philip Sartorius both sailed in the "Taglioni" from Havre in September, 1845. About twelve young men, six girls, and a family—all Jews?—were in the party. Certainly, Weis and Sartorius were friends, and surely their paths crossed in this country, but they do not mention one another by name in the memoirs which they wrote. Weis died in New Orleans, probably a millionaire; Sartorius died in Vicksburg, probably a poor man.

THE PEDDLER

Both of those men began as peddlers; most of our memoirists did. Nearly all the itinerant merchants told the story of their first beginnings, and it is for this reason that these chronicles are without doubt the best source yet published for the study of the American Jewish peddler.

There were city peddlers and country peddlers. The former sold notions, cigars, stationery, and jewelry; the packs of the latter, as a rule, contained clothing and dry goods. At best, the foot peddler was a beast of burden. He staggered under a heavy load that was never less than forty pounds, often through rain and storm, blizzard and mud. At times he walked as much as twenty-five miles a day; farmers and even planters refused him shelter; in some counties the

high license fees set by the storekeepers froze him out of business.
He could speak little English; he was homesick and footsore, miserable, bitter, and disillusioned: "I cannot say whether America has
misled me," wrote Abraham Kohn, "or whether I misled myself."
Some of the peddlers, men of some refinement and culture, were
broken in body and in spirit. They cursed the day they had left home.

Writing in 1842, Kohn proposed to solve the problem of the Jewish peddlers in this country by colonizing them. Apparently his project called for a close settlement with a farming hinterland. There
would be ample room for workers and craftsmen, and through their
labors there would arise a new Jerusalem.

The diary of Kohn, an articulate and forceful man, reflects the
struggles of a Jewish hawker in Yankee Massachusetts. In the South,
most of the peddlers found life easier and business more lucrative.
Natchez was a well-known center of such itinerants, with local houses
to supply their needs if they did not care to replenish their stocks
down the river at New Orleans. Because white men were at a premium in ante-bellum Mississippi and Louisiana, they were welcomed
in a land of black slaves. The Southern plantation owner was richer
than the Northern farmer; there were fewer industries, and crossroad stores were scarcer in that part of the country. The peddler
was needed more in the South than in the North. Consequently, when
he rode up to the plantation or poled his boatload of goods up a
bayou, he received a hearty welcome from the planter on the balcony
and the grinning servants on the lawn.

A study of these chronicles and journals of the early American
businessman will demonstrate that peddling was not so much a type
of permanent occupation as a transitional occupation during the
immigrant's economic adjustment to the American scene. It was the
initial step in Americanization whereby the European newcomer
acquired the language and mores of the land, as well as the indispensable capital needed to engage in another form of business. Henry
Stern of Milwaukee had money but became a peddler the sooner to
become an American!

Peddling was the first rung in the ladder of the commercial hierarchy. Peddlers frequently paired off in order to pool their pitifully
meager resources. The next step was to start a store even though
they continued peddling. The wife or the partner tended store, sometimes with the aid of a nephew or a brother who was encouraged to
come from Europe. (Jesse Seligman, one of eight brothers, was in
charge of a country store at the age of fifteen, and had clerks under
him!) Next, the country storekeeper moved to a city to open a re-

tail dry goods store. Jobbing, wholesaling, manufacturing, and even banking were higher echelons in the scale of economic success. But let this be quite clear. A handful ascended to the top rung of the ladder: Julius Weis, Jesse Seligman, Louis Stix. Thousands of others reached up, lost their grip, and perished at the bottom.

THE PEDDLER MYTH

Some historians of the American scene maintain that the Jewish peddler was a cultural force. This contention is not sustained by the evidence of these autobiographical narratives. It is true that Germany and France were, on the whole, culturally superior to the United States, and that individual peddlers were intelligent men; some of them had even enjoyed a relatively good training in the schools of their native lands. But most of them were humble men of modest attainments. They were foreigners who spoke little or no English; they were frequently miserably unhappy. What cultural values could they bring to the Mississippi planter or to the successful Massachusetts farmer who subscribed to three or four American newspapers and magazines?

The peddler was culturally superior to the poor whites of the South and to the plantation slaves, but he did little business with these. And the language barrier still persisted. Of course, he peddled and purveyed gossip, and in many places he was certainly welcome; but he was essentially a bird of passage, both geographically and chronologically. He remained in one place just long enough to make enough money to get out of peddling. Only the failure and the near failure remained in the business, and his cultural impact was of doubtful value. At most, through the goods which he supplied, the peddler helped maintain and possibly further the American standard of living. He served a useful purpose as a purveyor of goods, not of ideas.

THE JEWISH BUSINESSMAN

Though many Jews were peddlers, there were few fields of economic activity in which they were not represented. As the memoirs reveal, Jews were or became lawyers, doctors, farmers, schoolteachers, importers of finished goods, auctioneers, tailors, clothing and cap manufacturers, workers on "Singer's [sewing] machine," cigar makers, plumbers, carpenters, and the like. In 1851, Raphael J. Moses shipped peaches from Georgia to New York by stage, steamboat, and railroad and got $30 for his first basket. Toby Rosenthal, destined one day to become a famous artist, sold newspapers on the streets of San Francisco till he improved himself by becoming a fruit buyer for a grocery store. At fourteen, sturdy, squat Samuel Gompers was a full-fledged member of the Cigarmakers' Union, Local No. 15.

Some individuals were many things in one. August Bondi's father was peddler, brickworker, cigar maker, and furniture factory worker. Bondi himself was a barkeeper, clerk, storekeeper, farmer, stock raiser, Jayhawker, soldier, and all-around adventurer.

Five-foot, one-eyed Morris Shloss rode shotgun on a California stagecoach that carried gold dust for an express company. Once he worked in a San Francisco gambling house as a musician. His hours were from seven to ten, for which he was paid $16 a night plus a "grab" for overtime, a handful of silver from the monte table.

It is a relatively safe generalization that almost all Jews were engaged in some form of trade. These memoirs are particularly rich on this subject and offer much material for the study of the sedentary merchant in the first seven decades of the last century. As merchandisers, Jews were in dry goods and wearing apparel; a few were in wet goods (the liquor business) and in groceries. Ample evidence proves the important fact that Jews manufactured clothing as early as the 1840's. One of the memoirists listed the occupations of the six Jewish families in Bangor, Maine, about 1850. Two were in the dry goods business; one was a clothing merchant; three were peddlers.

The petty merchant—the typical merchant, if you will—sweated it out for a long time before he ever got his foot on the second rung of the ladder of success. Fires, floods, defaulting creditors, panics, crooked or irresponsible partners, and frontier desperadoes were some of the hazards he had to face. Michael Kraszewski, who lived in a village in southern California, barely escaped assassination at the hands of a gang of fugitives from San Quentin. Philip Sartorius of Mississippi had trouble with Sam Rothschild, his partner. Sam gambled away the firm's money, then sold the peddling boat and stock to a flatboat man for a Negro girl, took the girl to New Orleans, and traded her off for a load of tobacco. By that time the Sartorius family caught up with Rothschild and seized the tobacco.

For the run of the mine businessman, the way to make money was to save it. Money was made as much by thrift as by profit. Wives and sisters, parents and children, pitched in to work at the store and to help make the living. Mrs. Lazarus Straus (mother of the Strauses of R. H. Macy & Company), of Talbotton, Georgia, had an allowance of $20 a month for her family of seven and a slave or two, and managed very well. Her vegetable garden was the best in town. About the same time a Jewish memoirist living in California was able to make from five to six thousand dollars in a few weeks—and to lose it overnight in a disastrous fire in a city where insurance was not to be had.

America was the land of opportunity—for brilliant and exceptional and lucky people. Only two years elapsed between the time that Louis A. Gratz went hungry as an unsuccessful pack peddler and the day when he assumed the command of a regiment of cavalry in the United States Army!

MOBILE MERCHANTS AND EXPANSION WESTWARD

The peddler had no desire to peddle; he wanted to settle down, and when he found a likely spot at a crossroads, a busy county seat, or a bustling river town, he and his partner opened a little store. Few villages of any size or promise in ante-bellum America did not at some time shelter an ambitious Jewish merchant. Wherever the advancing farmers and immigrants went, the Jew went along. Sometimes he was there first, for he had laid out the town. Theodore Wiener, Bondi's buddy, laid out Wienersville in Kansas. Frequently a shopkeeper did not remain long in one place. Either the village failed to show promise or the merchant began to look for greener fields beyond the mountains. In about a decade, Samuel Kline's father lived and did business in Baltimore, Cincinnati, Jerseyville, Illinois; Leavenworth, Kansas; Central City and Denver, Colorado; and Montana.

The developing railroads carried Jews to the ever-expanding and advancing Western frontier. The more restless and adventurous traveled to the railhead and then pushed on by ox and mule team to the next likely town. It took a Leavenworth, Kansas, family twenty-five days to make the trek to Denver. (One of the casualties they suffered in that town was an encounter with a polecat. When the skunk moved into the cellar, the family moved out from above.) And in those days children went to school on snowshoes improvised from floor board and leather thongs, and the danger of an Indian massacre was still a dread reality.

Some Jews went West just to make a stake, intending to return, but stayed and built many of the great Jewish communities of present-day America. Beginning in the 1820's with Cincinnati, the "Queen City of the West," new congregations rose everywhere in the trans-

Allegheny country. Heine's smart-alecky remark, made in 1823, that a time would come when Jews would be munching unleavened bread on the banks of the Mississippi, became more fact than fiction, and before that poet died in Paris, in 1856, Jewish communities spanned the continent from New York to San Francisco and from St. Paul to Houston.

EDUCATION

It would be hazardous to make any generalizations about the educational attainments of the Jewish immigrants whose fortunes are portrayed in these memoirs. In one respect at least they were not typical immigrants, for they were "literate." They had the urge to sit down and write the stories of their lives; they were different. Some of the newcomers received relatively little education at home; others had the advantage of attending excellent German secondary schools. It is probably safe to say that the ordinary German Jew who came over before 1865 was as well or as poorly educated as the ordinary American Jew. Further studies may show that the scale was weighted in favor of the Europeans. Some of them were bilingual, speaking German and French, and many of them had enjoyed a few years of schooling in Hebrew. All of them had respect for learning. Young Samuel Gompers had quit the Jews' Free School in London at the age of ten, but in this country he continued his studies at night. He was "fairly quivering" in his "intense desire to know."

Some of the native Northerners were well-educated. Mordecai M. Noah had made a good job of teaching himself, and became an exceedingly clever writer. In the course of his active life of public service he was a reporter, dramatist, journalist, editor, and politician. Rebecca Gratz was sent to non-Jewish private schools and improved herself by reading widely and by engaging in extensive correspondence. She read the best in the English literature of her day and moved in the circle of the Gouverneurs, the Ogdens, the Fennos, and the Clays of Kentucky. Washington Irving was an intimate friend.

It is the Jewry of the South which stands out during this period. More and more the evidence indicates that culturally, religiously, and possibly in other directions as well, the center of gravity in American Jewish life during the first quarter of the nineteenth century was located in Charleston, S.C.

The children of the better-class Jewish families of Charleston went to the best private schools, some of which were conducted by Jews.

From 1808 on, for a decade, the Mordecais of Warrenton, N.C., operated one of the best-known female academies in the South.

The cultured Charleston Jew played a musical instrument, wrote poetry or drama, knew the English classics, and read Greek, Latin, French, and Spanish. Not many of the natives studied German. The Georgia Revolutionist Mordecai Sheftall mentioned casually that he spoke the language of one of his captors, a Hessian officer. It is possible that Mordecai, Georgia-born, had picked up German from the Salzburgers at Ebenezer on the Savannah River. It is far more probable, however, that he spoke to the Hessian in the Yiddish which he had learned from his German-born parents.

Music was widely cultivated by most American Jews of that day. Perchance that was a German heritage. The standards in music which were characteristic of Americans in that generation are portrayed brilliantly, if irresponsibly, by the impresario Max Maretzek. His description of the musical taste of the *nouveaux riches* is clever but caricatured. But his ironic indictment of the cultural attainments of the Americans of the 1850's may well contain a large measure of truth. The Astor Place Opera House and the Academy of Music, as the caustic Austrian pointed out, ended up with performances by learned dogs and trained horses.

Certainly, the more substantial citizens among the German immigrants appreciated the arts and encouraged their children to study music, dancing, and painting. Toby Rosenthal, the son of a Prussian tailor, finally succeeded in sailing for Europe to continue his art studies. It was in rough-and-tumble San Francisco that he first learned his craft from a Spanish-American teacher whom he assisted in painting "black eyes" with flesh-colored paint.

The American Jew of the first half of the nineteenth century was not a well-educated person. In most of the larger Jewish communities attempts were made to establish "parochial" or all-day schools, teaching general and Jewish subjects. Jews preferred their own schools because the public schools were Christian in character and educationally inadequate. In their travel letters Isaac Leeser and Isaac M. Wise mentioned the Jewish schools but generously declined to say how bad they were. (They were certainly no worse than many of the public schools.) When Leopold Mayer came to Chicago in 1850 and proposed to establish a school, the president of the local congregation naively inquired what he intended to teach.

Because there were so few schools to instruct Jews in their religion, Rebecca Gratz, in 1838, founded the Jewish Sunday School. The pattern she followed was taken over from the Christian Sunday schools of Philadelphia, and was soon adopted by most American Jewish communities. Two of the memoirists described her pioneer undertaking. There were Bible readings, Hebrew hymns, a recitation of Watts's metrical version of the Psalms, and a liberal recourse to Christian textbooks. These books of the Christian Sunday School Union were handed over to the children after the distinctively Christian passages had been carefully pasted over! Textbooks were not taken home but were studied in school. At the annual examination, classes and groups recited only that portion of a book which they had conned, and the gifted pupils were presented with prayer books. All children were rewarded with an orange and a pretzel at the final session.

The Jews in the big cities were fortunate, for they had at least their own Sunday school. Those in small towns were less fortunate. Down in Talbotton, Georgia, the Straus children had no formal Jewish training. Their father, Lazarus Straus, a student of the Hebrew Bible, explained the meaning of difficult passages to the Christian ministers, but he did not instruct his children in Judaism, nor did he forbid them to visit the Christian Sunday school. Apparently they were none the worse for the training they received. The absence of religious institutions, synagogues, and schools induced many Jews to desert the towns where they were making a good living. They moved to the nearest Jewish community in order that their growing children might receive a Jewish education and marry into their own group. Those who remained behind frequently intermarried and were lost to the faith.

THE JEWISH RELIGION

That Orthodox Judaism in the United States would be dead by 1883 was the prediction of Joseph Lyons. Maybe it would have died in his circle, for he and some of his friends were increasingly hostile to traditional practices and beliefs. When Lyons, a cultured Charlestonian, made his sour forecast in 1833, Isaac Leeser, then a young clergyman, was still new at his job in Philadelphia, and Rabbi Isaac Mayer Wise was still a student in Bohemia. As the memoir-like reports of both these leaders reveal, they organized the religious life of American Jewry and established it on the firm foundations on which it stands today.

Originally the commonly accepted rite in America was the Sephardic. It is interesting to note that in Cincinnati, in the 1820's, that pattern was followed, in part, even by the non-Sephardic Jews.

But as more Germans and Poles entered the nation, a "German" and a "Polish" order of worship dominated, until these, too, were in turn modified by new, reformistic liturgies.

The dissatisfaction of many Charlestonians with traditional Judaism was already manifest in the 1820's. Joseph Lyons noted with disapproval that Raphael J. Moses kept his store open on the Sabbath, but the same Lyons absented himself from services on the Day of Atonement and did not hesitate, in the intimacy of his diary, to sneer at some of the Bible stories. The Charleston community was willing to educate a young American for the Charleston "rabbinate," but no one was interested. Intimations of disregard for the ancient practices, of spiritual unrest, and of the coming conflict between Reform and Orthodox are found in a number of the autobiographies. We can detect the beginnings of the alignments which produced mid-nineteenth-century Orthodoxy, Conservatism, and Reform. Some of the traditionalists were opposed to the Christian-like Jewish Sunday schools. When Louis Stix had a runaway accident while pursuing his business on a Jewish holiday, his observant father said it was God's judgment.

Conscious of the growing dissension and centrifugalism, Isaac M. Wise called for an Americanized national Jewish community organization to control education, philanthropy, and religion. This bold idea was hundreds of years ahead of the times. It was all part of Wise's grand design, for he was a man with a "plan." World salvation was of the Jews! Within a generation, Wise said, the rational ethical monotheism of enlightened American Reform Judaism would be accepted, in principle at least, by the American people. Then, after American political liberalism had revolutionized Europe, the gospel of Reform would spread across the Atlantic and sweep over Europe, too. Born in 1819, Wise was a child of the Enlightenment of the eighteenth century. He never surrendered his dreams.

SOCIAL LIFE

It is pleasant to peek over the shoulders of the autobiographers and to relive with them the joys and heartaches of love and courtship, and to read, through the rosy spectacles of recollection, of plays and dances and Purim parties. Those were the days when metropolitan Cincinnati still boasted a town crier and "toesmashers." Sweet Emily Fechheimer, as a child, believed that there was some terrible ogre who ran after little boys and girls and smashed their toes with an iron rod.

Down South, on the Mississippi, Sartorius celebrated the Fourth of July with his neighbors. Back in Milliken's Bend, on the eve of the Civil War, someone fired a cannon, and Sartorius' expensive newly bought mule bolted and was drowned in the river. One hundred and seventy-five dollars down the drain dampened Sartorius' enthusiasm!

In those days, a half century before the first flicker of the cinema, almost everyone went to the theater. Phillip Goldsmith courted his Sophia there. They feasted on an apple which he divided into two halves. Papa and Mama had given them permission to go to the German theater. They went also to an English performance, but without asking her parents. At sixteen she married Phillip, or Papa, as she loved to call him. He was then all of twenty-one. And when she moved into her modest little apartment she found a mother cat with a litter of five little ones. "I was as happy as a child to play with them."

Sophia said yes without too much hesitation when her Phillip asked her to marry him. Fanny Levy was more hesitant when August Picard laid siege to her heart. Like all virtuous girls of her time, she distrusted all men, and above all, Frenchmen. (Picard was an Alsatian.) But let them speak for themselves:

August: How wrong you are judging me, Miss Levy! All men are not alike. Read more deeply into my soul. . . . Do I need to tell you that I love and respect you? . . . Your beloved image has not left my heart nor my memory. I will love you forever, Miss Fanny. . . .

Fanny: Mr. Picard, I will be very happy and very proud to be your wife. . . . And I hope you will not deceive me.

ACCULTURATION AND ASSIMILATION

The American Jew was not ghettoized. He was not separated by an act of state from his fellow-men. He desired to be an American in spirit. Concerned for integration, he sought it and attained it, either wittingly or unwittingly. Immigrant Louis Stix took a girl to a party, but he neglected to take her home. The farmer father came after him with a pitchfork. Stix never made that mistake again. He was learning to be an American—the hard way.

During his first year in this country, 1861, the Posen peddler, Louis A. Gratz, was interested in Jews and associated with them. But when he became a regimental commander and a corps staff officer he stopped mentioning the word "Jew" in his letters home. In a period of about three years he completely de-Germanized himself and learned to write and to speak English almost faultlessly. He became an American, as he conceived it, the fast way.

Most immigrants made no conscious effort to become one with their neighbors. Time and circumstances effected the almost inevitable change. A Milwaukee immigrant who learned to love this land and what it stood for named his three sons Franklin, Jefferson, and Madison. Down in Natchez, Jacob Mayer finally became John Mayer, but the customs and practices of Judaism were not forgotten at home. His older children bore European-influenced names like Emma, Simon, and Theresa, but his youngest son, born in 1864, in the midst of the War, was called Joseph Eggleston Johnston Mayer.

The Mordecais of Warrenton, N.C., were probably the only Jewish family in their part of the country. Since they were living in a village and later on a farm, removed from the influence of a Jewish community, the pull was inevitably toward the common Christian culture. In all likelihood, however, the father, Jacob Mordecai, kept some sort of kosher home, and certainly ate no pork. At night, this Orthodox Jew sat in front of the blazing hearth reading aloud the latest Waverley novel to his eager children. How thrilled they must have been as he read them the story of Ivanhoe and the beautiful Jewess Rebecca!

Mordecai, native American and loyal Jew, consciously resisted the inroads of an assimilatory process that would have swamped his Jewish consciousness. Rabbis Leeser and Wise urged deculturation upon unwilling German immigrants who were loathe to surrender the German language, which gave them a sense of security and well-being. Both of these religious leaders opposed German as the language of instruction in the Jewish parochial schools. Germany, the land of tyranny, said Wise, was synonymous with subjection. To be an American meant to have self-respect! But the immigrants surrendered their beloved German reluctantly. It was their mother tongue, and the educated German Jew held on to it, believing that the culture which he had brought from Europe was superior to the culture which he found here.

Leeser and Wise wanted English to be the language of instruction in the Jewish schools and synagogues. They wanted the Jew to accept Americanization without repudiating Judaism in the process. In 1849, when the old-line Jews of New York City sponsored a concert on behalf of the newly arriving immigrants, Leeser voiced his approval of the worthy project. If he was disturbed by the fact that

HENRY COHEN OF PHILADELPHIA
(see page 31)

PHILADELPHIA IN 1856—CHESTNUT STREET, EAST OF FIFTH

Note Levy Store at the Extreme Left

the concert was held in a Christian church, he said nothing. But he was unhappy that the program was limited to Italian opera. He wanted some Jewish note to remind the patrons of the rock whence they were hewn.

The assimilatory process was not slow in middle-nineteenth-century America. Back in the 1850's, Jews were already trading Christmas gifts. (No wonder their grandchildren cannot understand why twentieth-century rabbis make such a fuss about Christmas trees in Jewish homes!) Intermarriage occasionally was a threat in the cities. When an attractive Gentile started making eyes at Sophia Heller, her parents shipped her off to Chicago. In the smaller towns and villages intermarriage and conversion were widespread. No wonder immigrants were warned against the small town, where there was no established Jewish congregation. Some Jews refused to admit that they were children of Israel. With disgust and contempt, Bondi reported that some Jews in his company during the War denied their origin. A few of the writers represented in these volumes sedulously avoided any identification of themselves as Jews. The word "Jew" never occurs in their autobiographies; some even make religious references to Christianity. None of this was accidental. Within a few years some Jewish immigrants ran the gamut from open and automatic identification with their coreligionists to a complete denial of their Jewish past.

Young Salomon de Rothschild, traveling in this country on the eve of the Civil War, was very much impressed by the high social position enjoyed by Jews, especially those who had intermarried. He had in mind some of the people he had met: August Belmont, Judah P. Benjamin (later Secretary of State of the Confederacy), and Lieutenant Governor Henry M. Hyams of Louisiana. But Jews did not have to intermarry or to convert in order to be respected and accepted in American society. American tradition, encouraged by the philosophy of the Enlightenment and by the absence of an established church, made for tolerance. There was considerable social interplay between Jew and Christian. Because he was secure in his feeling as a Jew, and unhindered in the practice of his American citizenship, Philip Sartorius did not hesitate to mix with the Christian clergy and, on occasion, to attend their services of worship. Even in a Mississippi village, he was not threatened in his Jewish beliefs. Gentiles were present in large numbers at the dedication of the Touro Synagogue in New Orleans in 1850, and generous Christians (together with some politicians) made liberal contributions when they attended Jewish charity balls. As early as 1834, the Chris-

tians of the small western community of Cincinnati demonstrated
their interest in their Jewish neighbors. Fifty-two men of the Christian faith each gave $25—no mean sum—for the first synagogue
building in the trans-Allegheny West. That was the American way
of life.

ANTI-JEWISH PREJUDICE

The fact that the different groups in this country learned to live
together does not mean that there was no prejudice on the part of
Gentiles against the Jews or that there were no Jews who looked
askance at Gentiles. (Though markedly unsympathetic to certain
Christian doctrines, none of the chroniclers in these volumes mani-
fests any prejudice against his non-Jewish neighbors.) Prejudice
against the Jew has always been present in American society, but
only rarely has it degenerated into violence. As far back as 1658,
in Dutch New Amsterdam, an attorney turned to a Jew and said:
"You are a Jew, you are all cheats together." In later centuries, when
the German Gentile immigrants landed on these shores, they did not
shed their prejudices with their first bath. Isaac M. Wise ran into
Judaeophobia the first hour he landed on the dock, because he
stopped the German hackmen from cheating his fellow-travelers.
During the Civil War, Aaron Hirsch of Arkansas watched helplessly
as the Germans in the Federal cavalry raided his store. Hirsch was
not only a secessionist; he was also a Jew. That was a double indictment.

By using the phrase "Jew store," Louis Stix's competitors attempted to "smear" him. The Christian ministers' association in
Albany did not consider Rabbi Isaac M. Wise a clergyman and refused to certify him as a minister so that he might lead the state
legislature in prayer.

Anti-Jewish prejudice was not simply a distaste for the uncouth
immigrant of foreign brogue. Its deep roots are revealed in the
memoirs of two of America's most famous Jews, Mordecai M. Noah,
the publicist, and Captain Uriah P. Levy of the United States Navy.
Both men were fifth-generation Americans, descendants of Dr. Samuel
Nunez, who arrived in Georgia just a few months after General
James Oglethorpe founded the colony. President James Madison and
Secretary of State James Monroe removed Noah from his office as
consul at Tunis, primarily because of his religion. Levy ran into
trouble when he attempted to rise in the hierarchy of naval office.
He survived six courts-martial and two courts of inquiry, and there
is ample evidence that one of the prime faults of which he was guilty

was being a Jew. Both Noah and Levy met with hostility when they sought or exercised power and authority.

During the Civil War public attacks on the Jews, particularly in the press, became more frequent. The older motivation of religious bigotry was then supplemented by economic envy. A generation of German Jews had grown up in this country and had begun to make money. Rapid transportation brought not only immigrants, but also the latest notions in anti-Jewish propaganda. In Cincinnati a placard was posted that the Rothschilds were willing to spend millions at the 1860 Democratic National Convention to buy a President of their choice. (Behold the malevolent "international Jewish banker.")

In *The Presidents I Have Known,* Simon Wolf dwelt at considerable length on the attacks against American Jewry during the Civil War. The Jew was a rebel, a coward, a blockade runner, a Democrat (a traitor or Copperhead). Understandably, these assaults were very disturbing to the Jews. But even the German-born memoirists who complained of prejudice were conscious that conditions here were better than abroad. And after his return from Tunis, the native-born Noah became a political power in New York City politics as Grand Sachem of Tammany, while Captain Levy survived his enemies to become a commodore in charge of the Mediterranean fleet. The American liberal tradition was still sound.

The very writers who reported incidents of prejudice managed to maintain their emotional balance. Though they were deeply hurt and conscious of the significance of their own experiences, there was not the slightest doubt in their minds that the United States was still the most enlightened nation in all the world.

SECESSION AND SLAVERY

As we have noted, there is a great deal of material in these narratives touching on the Civil War. The War was a catastrophe, particularly for the South, where the battles were fought, and the importance of the conflict is reflected in the contemporary literature of the South. Behind the appeal to arms were at least thirty years of political, economic, and cultural tension, forming an effective emotional preparation for the War. These memoirs throw light on the developing sentiment which eventuated in conflict. The regional loyalties of cultured South Carolina Jews were already manifest in the Nullification controversy of the early 1830's. Joseph Lyons went out of his way to sport a palmetto button, the symbol of his native state, on a visit to the North in 1833. The romantic and sentimental

Southern Jewish gentleman was one with his many Gentile fellow-citizens in emphasizing the differences with the North. But it is also well to remember that one of the most distinguished of all Southern Jews, Colonel Philip Phillips, of South Carolina, Alabama, and Washington, D. C., was a Unionist.

Some aspects of the impending conflict are reflected in the attitude towards slavery. Dyed-in-the-wool abolitionism was rarely to be found among Northern Jews. As early as 1846, Louis Stix lost friends because he ate at the same table as the colored help, but he was no radical; he wanted a gradual emancipation with indemnity for the slave owner. On the other hand, August Bondi helped slaves to escape and fought with John Brown, but lost the confidence of the great abolitionist because of his moderate views. Down in Texas, Bondi was out on the Trinity River when a young man deliberately emptied a load of buckshot into his slave because the Negro thoughtlessly scared a flock of wild ducks. When Bondi bitterly reproached the young Texan for his brutality, the local Methodist Episcopal minister turned on Bondi with these words: "We have no use for Northern abolitionists, and only your age protects you from deserved punishment."

As might be expected, Southern Jews defended the slave system; individuals among them were among the institution's most vigorous apologists. Aaron Hirsch, an immigrant who began his career as a peddler, spoke up for slavery because the plantation owners had been kind to him. Julius Weis, who also owned slaves, recounted realistically the chase after runaway Negroes, who were tracked down and brutally rounded up with the aid of bloodhounds. It was left for a cultured Southern Jew to document the extremist point of view in his diary. When the report was bruited about that the South would emancipate those Negroes who fought against the North, this Southerner objected with impeccable logic, pointing out that the war was being fought to keep the Negro enslaved! And when the slave emerged a free man in 1865, this diarist, embittered by the attitude of the Negroes, wrote: "The extermination of this race is a necessary consequence of this state of affairs."

THE CIVIL WAR AND THE JEW

Although a number of Civil War diaries and memoirs were written by Northern Jews, few accounts of actual battle experiences have survived, in spite of the fact that about a half-dozen brevetted generals were of Jewish birth, and that several thousand Jewish soldiers and officers served in the Union armies. Probably Bondi's mother was not the only woman who said to her son that as a *Jehudi*, a Jew, he had a duty to perform, to defend the country "which gave equal rights to all beliefs."

A dramatic story of a deserter is recounted in the reminiscences of Simon Wolf, Jewry's unofficial representative at Washington. Eager to see his dying mother and apparently denied a furlough by his superior officers, a Jewish soldier deserted. He was arrested, convicted, and sentenced to be shot. At two o'clock on the morning of the day of execution, Simon Wolf was admitted to the office of the President and pleaded for the life of the unfortunate young man. Lincoln reprieved the soldier, who was restored to his command and died fighting at the battle of Cold Harbor. This is a true story, though it has all the earmarks of fiction.

The memoir-like letters of Salomon de Rothschild, with their analyses of the causes of the coming conflict, may well be considered documents of some historic significance. This visitor's opinions merit study because of his economic interpretations and because of his relationship to the powerful English and French banks bearing his name. It was his belief that the ultimate cause of the War lay in the attempt of the agricultural South to emancipate itself from the manufacturing North, and in the equal determination of the industrial North to preserve its lucrative and indispensable Southern markets.

Some Southern Jews, as we have already noted, were particularly fervent in their advocacy of slavery and of the rights of the South. In defense of a cause that was holy to them, they were willing to sacrifice their lives—and they did. Two other brothers fought with the diarist Eugene H. Levy in the armies of the Confederacy, and one died at Shiloh. Raphael Moses, a very successful Georgia lawyer, entered the war at the age of forty-nine. His three sons also enlisted; one of them died of wounds received in battle.

The apogee of patriotism was reached by the Southern women, including Jewesses. The journals of the two Carolinians, Eugenia Levy Phillips and Eleanor Cohen Seixas, are worth reading for an understanding of the romantic devotion shown to the South by its cultured women. Mrs. Phillips' diary and memoirs offer excellent insights into the life of a sentimental, flamboyant secessionist who lived in Union-held towns. Her belligerence often merged into the hysterical. A reputed Southern agent, she was twice arrested and imprisoned by the Federal authorities, those "crawling reptiles." And Eleanor Cohen Seixas, with true Carolina bravura, reported that the Union flag "carried loathing to every Southern heart."

There were other Jewesses who were not implacable in their hatred
of the North. Mrs. Jannette Mayer, of Natchez, did not prevent her
daughters from smuggling clothes through the Union lines to nearby
Southern soldiers. Nor did she desist from inviting Jewish Federals
to her hospitable home. Two of these Jewish Yankees stayed on to
become her sons-in-law.

Certainly, the South had the capacity to fire its devotees with
the most glowing ardor. Jewish immigrants but a year or two off
the boat volunteered for military service and were prepared to die
for the Confederate cause. (Or were they caught up in the mass wave
of hysteria to which they responded emotionally, because they, as
immigrants, were welcomed as friends? Those Jews had finally come
home. They had a sense of belonging.) Lewis Leon, son of a New
York German immigrant and in all probability foreign-born himself,
refused to admit that his beloved South was doomed until he had been
imprisoned for eight months in a Northern stockade. It was not until
January, 1865, that he wrote sadly: "I fear that our cause is lost."
And even after the surrender at Appomattox, Eugene H. Levy still
hoped that another rebellion would bring independence to the re-
surgent South.

TYPES AND PERSONALITIES

If some of the chronicles in these volumes are in any sense typical,
then they are historically significant, for they reflect the life and
fate not only of the writers but of many others. Types emerge: the
romantic female sentimentalist of the Old South, the ardent and cultured secessionist, the happy-go-lucky Jewish Johnny Reb, the embittered Northern peddler, the complacent Southern peddler, the
unsuccessful Jewish petty merchant, and the businessman who had
made good and was tempted to doff his hat every time he spoke of
himself. To gauge the career and the significance of these types is to
understand the history of an interesting era.

Not every Jew who wrote his memoirs was a "personality." Still,
had they not had a sense of self-importance or ego, they would not
have written at all. One of the chroniclers, Philip Phillips, a truly
notable figure, deliberately played down his career, for he did little
to betray the inner workings of his mind and heart. Many of the
memoirists were striking individuals, and their accounts of themselves help us to understand the men and women who were not without importance in the history of American Jewry.

Uriah P. Levy comes to life as he defends himself at courts-martial.
At ten he was off to sea as a cabin boy, and before he was twenty

he was captain and part-owner of a boat. During the War of 1812, he volunteered to fight for his country, ultimately rising to the highest rank in spite of the implacable opposition of small-minded men. The rejection which he experienced never turned him against the land that gave him birth. When Emperor Dom Pedro of Brazil offered Lieutenant Levy the command of a sixty-gun frigate, the young officer replied "that he would rather serve as a cabin boy in his own service than as a captain in any other service in the world."

That salty character, August Bondi of Kansas, could kill a butterfly at twenty-five yards with an old-fashioned pistol. (If you think that is easy, try it yourself with a modern precision firearm.)

Ike Hermann was a French immigrant who threw in his lot with the South he loved. One day he was unjustly arrested, and jailed in a guardhouse, and was about to be disciplined in a most brutal fashion. Unaided, he beat off a sergeant, disarmed one soldier, and drove eleven others out of the guardhouse. The Three Musketeers, his countrymen, would have loved Hermann! To the last day of his life, that unreconstructed Southern gentleman with the Vandyke beard, Raphael J. Moses, carried a calling card reading: "Major Raphael J. Moses, C. S. A." And there is something heroic in the sturdy honesty of Moses' fellow-townsman, Lazarus Straus, of Columbus, Ga. In 1865 he went to New York, years after he had contracted his antebellum debts, debts that had been forgotten and wiped out, and paid every cent he owed, because his conscience left him no other choice. And we catch a fleeting glimpse of little Charley Stix, whom the family had taken with them to Europe, to a great spa. When he saw the majestic Empress Elizabeth of Austria, he ran up to her with his outstretched dirty paws and cheerfully hailed her: "*Guten Morgen, Frau Kaiserin*." Here was a real American democrat in the making.

SUMMARY AND CONCLUSION

In a general sense these volumes of autobiographical materials are source material, throwing light on a developing America. They treat of the country's growth and of its expanding nationalism up to the very end of the Civil War. Here one can trace the Westward movement, the occupation of the Mississippi Valley, and the spread of the Anglo-American settlements in California. Above all, this literature reflects the coming of the immigrants and the part they played in the economic life of the land. Southern particularism, nullification, secession, slavery, and the Civil War are the themes of many of the annalists whose writings are now published for the first time. Their works, their thoughts, their prejudices, are facets of the social and cultural life of an emerging America ending with the close of the Civil War in 1865. The broad outlines which they followed are not new, but the details of their personal experiences give flesh to the bare bones of history.

The majority of the memoirists were immigrants, men who came as strangers with different backgrounds and training. Because they were intelligent as well as literate, and because they were articulate, they were able to portray the land, its institutions, its culture, and its peoples critically. And because their approach was critical, their opinions are frequently of value.

This body of material is the largest collection of sources yet published for what is the least known period of American Jewish history, the decades from about 1790 to about 1860. With one or two notable exceptions, those seven decades have hardly been touched by Jewish historians. The first forty years of the nineteenth century are years of almost complete silence, for the first Anglo-Jewish news magazine did not appear until 1843. Here, in these memoirs, is the story of the Central European Jewish immigrant: the Alsatian, the German, and the German Pole.

The economic historian will reap a rich harvest from these writings. Here are the details, the facts, that explain the daily lives and problems of the peddler and the shopkeeper. As historians have suspected, most of the ante-bellum Jews were engaged in the sale of some sort of merchandise. And here is the evidence that by the 1840's numbers of Jews were engaged in the apparel industry. Unfortunately, there are no details, but a study of the mercantile directories and of the newspapers of New York, Boston, and other seaboard cities may add to our knowledge of the beginnings of the Jew in the American clothing industry.

These Jewish traders were, as these sources reveal, mobile men. Eager for opportunity and fired by ambition, they were constantly shifting their base of operation in search of the good fortune which often eluded them. Their cultural life, with its secular and religious aspects, is here revealed. There are some data on the old-established Tidewater towns which stem from colonial days; there are hundreds of pages explaining the rise of the new German Jewish communities in every corner of the expanding country. Out of a multitude of stories and incidents there emerges a picture of the complex process of Americanization, the acceptance by the Jew of America. Its rejection of him by individuals of high and low estate is the continuation of the age-old story of prejudice, bigotry, and envy.

The study of these records will broaden our knowledge of the men who helped to create the American Jewish community of today. The picture is not always clear and simple. They were a diverse group, for they came from different parts of the United States and from a half dozen different lands of Europe. They ranged from the most cultivated of men to the little shopkeeper whose literary attainments were in inverse ratio to his ability to express himself. Fortunately, even the most humble were, on occasion, men of striking personality, whose courage and charm command our admiration and affection.

Without doubt one of the significant conclusions to be drawn from this material is that the Southern Jew was the most cultured Jew in the ante-bellum period. The acculturation pattern that he developed was to be followed a generation later in the other parts of the United States. He was the pacemaker. The identification of him as the cultured American Jew par excellence, however, must not obscure the fact that he was also a regional type, for frequently, though not always, he was first a Southern particularist, and only secondly a citizen of the United States. After all, he could not escape his environment; the pattern he followed was the pattern of a host of Southerners.

As far as the native American Jew was concerned, there were— to use my own terminology—probably two types: the Southern, and the National-American. (The immigrant, too, conformed to the prevailing mode.) The National-American includes the Northerner and the Westerner, who ranged from the Alleghenies to the Pacific Coast. He, too, was a type, but because of our lack of perspective, we find it difficult to envisage him, for he is the source of our common national type of today. He is the present-day American. The core of the differences between the Southerner and the National-American lies in their attitudes toward free and slave labor, and in the conflicts between the dominant plantation economy of the South and the farm and urban economy of the North. The struggle between the two types of Jews was ironically foreshadowed in a Jewish boarding-house in New York City in the spring of 1861, when a Jew from the South pulled his revolver from his pocket and threatened to shoot a Jew from the North in defense of slavery and secession. (That these two types of Jews are but reflections of the other Americans among whom they lived is obvious.)

Those readers who are not enamored of the more formal works on history will turn to these personal narratives with pleasure. They give connotation and meaning to the generalized statements of the historian who is concerned primarily with ideas and movements.

No conventional historical study can ever hope to pulsate with life like a good memoir. The attractiveness of the detail and the challenge of the personality make the period live. This is the virtue of this class of source material, but its virtues should not blind us to its faults and its dangers.

The reader, like the trained historian, must exercise care and caution in reading these narratives. They must be treated like all other documents which often are not accepted at face value. One must apply to these accounts the canons of methodology employed by the critical historian. Some of the biographies read so smoothly and interestingly that the unsuspecting reader is swept along by the impetus of the writers, who had close relations to the men and events they describe. The chroniclers wrote in all sincerity and integrity, but the facts are not necessarily as they describe them.

The diaries and travel reports are contemporary records. Their authors attempted to tell what they experienced or witnessed, and yet the impressions which they recorded are purely subjective. The diarists reported what they thought they had seen and most frequently they were right and accurate—but they could well have been wrong or utterly prejudiced.

Most of these memoirs were written many years after the events they chronicled. In one case, a very old woman dictated the story of an experience that she had lived through three generations earlier. People do forget; they romanticize; they rationalize after the events; they are influenced by a public opinion that crystallized in the generation after the incidents they describe. Some writers report what their parents told them; others put down what they saw as children, when their critical faculties were not awakened. It must be borne in mind that these memoirists were not trained historians.

The historian will, of course, check these personal chronicles against each other and against independent, established sources. Some details may well be wrong, but the bulk of the material will stand. The sobriety of many a paragraph is the surest guarantee of its authenticity. There is a consensus in the data that makes for the acceptance of the over-all picture of the era.

Three Generations of Cohens

Memoirs of a Pennsylvania Family

Some time in the 1760's, Joseph Cohen (1745-1822), a German Jew, came to this country via England. For a while he clerked with B. and M. Gratz, the Philadelphia merchants, and then went back to England to marry. Years later, in the 1790's, he returned to work for a famous colonial entrepreneur, Joseph Simon, of Lancaster, Pennsylvania, the father-in-law of Michael Gratz.

Family tradition has it that Joseph Cohen was the "household rabbi" for the Simon clan. In 1798, he served Shearith Israel Congregation of New York as shohet, and later moved to Charleston, South Carolina, where he became a "Hebrew clerk" (a beadle?) in Congregation Beth Elohim. He finally returned to London, no doubt to be near his first-born son, Solomon, who had become a successful pencil manufacturer. It was there that he died in 1822.

In the next generation, no later than 1837, Solomon's son Henry arrived in Philadelphia, where he started a stationery business. His Uncle Lewis was already a well-known stationer in New York City, and Henry may have served a short apprenticeship with him. In the course of time, he became a wealthy manufacturer of envelopes.

Henry Cohen was recognized as a leader in the Jewish community of Philadelphia within two or three years after his arrival in the city. He was active in its important Jewish philanthropic agencies and, at the time of his death in 1879, was parnas of the aristocratic Mikveh Israel Congregation. A member of the Union League and widely known as a highly respected citizen of the larger general community, Henry started a tradition of participation in the civic life of Philadelphia which was continued by his son, Charles Joseph Cohen (1847-1927). The latter Cohen served as president of the Fairmount Park Art Association and of the Philadelphia Chamber of Commerce. After Henry Cohen's death, he succeeded his father as president of Mikveh Israel.

Memoir materials cover the lives of these three generations of Cohens. Judith Cohen, old Joseph's daughter, recounted the story of her father's experiences in colonial and early national America in a letter to her nephew, Solomon L. Cohen, of New York. This letter is the first of the two items which follow. Charles Joseph Cohen wrote several memoir fragments dealing with his own career and the life of his father, Henry Cohen. These diverse materials, consolidated into a running story, constitute the second section below. Copies of these chronicles are found in the American Jewish Archives. The originals are in the possession of Mr. and Mrs. Albert M. Cohen, of Wynnewood, Pennsylvania.

JOSEPH COHEN

EIGHTEENTH-CENTURY IMMIGRANT

M Y DEAR NEPHEW:

I am about to accede to your oft repeated request that I would commit to paper some incidents of my lamented father's (Joseph Cohen's) life, but am somewhat puzzled where to begin.

He was born in the year 1745 in a village of Westphalia, and nothing of interest occurred until his fourth year, when his father died, leaving him the eldest of three children. After a widowhood of five or six years, his mother contracted a second marriage and became the mother of a second family. The high spirit of Joseph Cohen being unfitted to support the rule of a stepfather, he left home at the age of ten, rambled through the country for three weeks, but was compelled to return home until a year or two after, when he adopted the German mode of "finishing his education." [He] travelled from town to town and from village to village until, at the age of thirteen, we find him located in a farmhouse where he is described as buying a soldier's coat in which to make his debut in being called to the law, *bar mizvah* ["confirmand"]. After much traveling and many hardships, he arrived in London at the age of nineteen, alone and friendless. He obtained a situation in a shop, [with] Mr. Solomons of Duke St., and, having received a good education, was anxious to acquire the English language, to accomplish which he joined an English class in the evenings, with a Mr. Saul Gelindah [Galindo?].

His next employ was in the house of a widow, named Mrs. Moses, whose overweening affection for him caused him to relinquish his situation, where he had been foreman and factotum. His poor mistress . . . in despair followed him to Portsmouth (where he was detained by contrary winds) in the vain hope of persuading him to return and relinquish his project of embarking for America. To no purpose, however. His resolve was taken and he sailed for the Western Continent and arrived there in safety [about 1768]. His first engagement was as foreign clerk in the house of Gratz Brothers. Traveling and collecting for an established house, his savings became considerable and enabled him to gratify his yearning desire to behold once again his old mother.

He, with six others, embarked on board a "condemned" vessel
which sprung a leak in Antigua Bay. This detained him some time
in the West Indies, where he had a glimpse of colonial life, the
vessel requiring some repairs ere it could proceed to England.
There he arrived in safety and proceeded to Biederfeld [Germany].
Arrived in the vicinity, his chief anxiety was for the safety of his
mother, whom he recognized. But it was in vain he presented himself to his mother. Years had so altered him that she refused to
believe his identity until repeated appeals to memory brought to
mind the mark of a mouse on his left arm, which freak of nature
eventually brought happiness to the misled family, for his stepfather being dead, nought remained to impair their felicity. The
"rich American" was sought on all hands by matchmakers and—
can we doubt it?—by managing mothers, but Cupid was not pro-
pitious, and he took leave of his native land heart-free.

Rose Barnet, shortly after his return to London, succeeded in
captivating his affections, and in the year 1781 he was married
in the Hambro' Chule ("synagogue"), settled in No. 3, Crown
Court, and supported her and his son Solomon, by traveling. After
eleven years of marriage he lost his wife in a consumption consequent on careless exposure to cold. After her death things went
wrong, and he opened a shop in Duke St. A second marriage had
been arranged and was to have taken place during the following
week, when one night he was sent for by the chief rabbi, Dr. Hir-
schel's father, who informed him that the reports current about his
intended bride were sufficient to prevent his performing the ceremony. [In reality, the chief rabbi at that time was David Tevele
Schiff or Moses Myers.] Shortly after this contretemps he contracted a marriage with Hannah Moses, by whom he had three children: a son stillborn, Judith, and Rachael.

Misfortunes in business then determined him on returning to
America. After a voyage of eleven weeks from the Cove of Cork
[Queenstown] to New York . . . he found the yellow fever . . .
raging with such violence that he was advised on all hands to quit
the city. But as neither his means nor his faith would yield to circumstances, he accepted the hospitality of Isaac Moses, a friend of
old times, in whose house, ten days after his arrival, his third
daughter was born. She lived but fourteen months, dying at Lancaster [Pennsylvania] in 1799, shortly before the birth of his son
Lewis (Levy). Her burial was performed in the fields adjoining his
house by his own hands, a ceremony that was only surpassed by his
performing on his newly-born son the rite of circumcision, a cir-

cumstance of peculiar difficulty from its occurring on the Ninth day of Aav [when he was weak from fasting and], when he was suffering from the loss of a nail on his thumb. [The circumciser used his thumbnail to help perform the circumcision operation.] This he supplied with a piece of silver of the same form and, in the presence of the doctor, successfully performed the operation, immediately after which he yielded to overwrought nature and swooned away. . . .

THE COURTSHIP OF HENRY COHEN

As Told by Charles Joseph Cohen

My father, Henry Cohen [the grandson of Joseph Cohen], came to America in 1834 and lived in New York for a few years, being associated in business there with a relative, but finally came to Philadelphia in 1837, and was successful in business, the importation of stationery from England and France. He was an attractive young man of fine build, good appearance, with an excellent singing voice, and was always a welcome visitor.

The mothers with marriageable daughters, the sisters with marriageable sisters were confident that he would select one of their set as his partner in life. But while this was pending, he went to Europe on business, landing at Liverpool, and, meeting by chance at the synagogue service, [on] Sabbath Hanukah, Miss Matilda Samuel, the daughter of Lewis Samuel of Liverpool, he asked permission to visit her, and became infatuated with her intellectual and musical accomplishments. But before the engagement would be recognized, a letter was written to the brother, Morris L. Samuel, living in New York, who was engaged in the watch business. Mr. Samuel came to Philadelphia (something of a journey in those days) and visited the store of Henry Cohen (the prospective bridegroom), situated at that time on Fourth Street just north of the old Merchants' Hotel.

Inquiring for some articles of stationery, the clerk explained that they were in the wholesale business only, and that the firm would be glad to accommodate him with any article that he might desire for immediate use, since they were glad to show courtesy to a stranger. This made a favorable impression, and Mr. Samuel, ascertaining that Abraham Hart [of Carey and Hart, publishers] was the leading man in the Jewish community, called upon him, stating the object of his errand. . . . [He] received from Mr. Hart a very flattering description of Henry Cohen's character, build, trustworthiness, and steadfastness, notwithstanding the fact that a relative of Mr. Hart's had been one of the ladies to whom Henry Cohen had been attentive and who, it was generally expected, would have been selected as his bride before his departure for Europe.

Mr. Samuel gave an accurate description of his visit, and the family in Liverpool, being entirely satisfied, sanctioned the engagement. And the marriage took place in 1844, the bridal couple reaching Philadelphia during the spring of that year. But at first there was not a cordial feeling on the part of the women of the various households toward the bride, which, however, disappeared, since my mother's qualities of mind and heart soon made their proper impress.

It had been a matter of pride to Americans visiting Europe for a series of years to make comparison between the military aspect that existed in European countries, and the entire absence of military display that prevailed in American cities. And Henry Cohen had not been backward in advancing this particular claim in dwelling upon the advantages of a home in the new world. The astonishment was therefore the greater when, on the arrival of Henry Cohen and his bride in Philadelphia, it was found that the city was under marshall [martial] law. Cannons were placed at the corners of the principal streets, armed troops paraded at stated intervals through many sections, and it was evident that great excitement existed. This was in April, 1844, and the occurrences were the Anti-Catholic riots, for which there was not the slightest reason, and which resulted in great loss of life and property, very much to the disgrace of the community. It is not desirable to follow [dwell] on this unpleasant feature, but it may be noted that opposition to immigration in that day was upon religious grounds, for which there was not the slightest excuse or apology, since the descendants of those immigrants are today among the most valued citizens of our country. And it might be fittingly added that some of the diatribes and animadversives that are hurled at the present immigrants from the South of Europe will result in succeeding years in the same termination, viz., that the descendants of those who are now looked upon as undesirable will become the bone and sinew of our country.

During the following year [1845], Abraham Hart, who then

lived on the west side of Fourth Street just above Spruce, kept open house on the eve of Purim, and my father desired to show his appreciation of Mr. Hart's endorsement by an act of courtesy which he carried out in this manner: in my mother's trousseau was a handsome, white crepe shawl which my father carried under his disguise, since he was dressed as an Eastern Pilgrim, and of course masked, which was the custome in those days. Mr. Hart would not admit anyone to his home unless he was assured of the person's name, not for publication nor general knowledge, but only that he might be assured that the visitor was worthy of association with his other guests.

This was disconcerting, since the visitor's desire was to remain incognito, but he had to declare his name to Mr. Hart in the vestibule, whereupon he was immediately admitted, and participated in the frivolities of the occasion, finally presenting to Mrs. Hart this beautiful shawl. . . .

In the year 1844, my revered father [Henry Cohen] . . . returned from a visit to England, his native country, accompanied by his bride, my mother. They became congregants of Mikve-Israel [Synagogue], then worshipping in Cherry Street above Third Street.

Henry Cohen in the course of time became a member and then, successively, *gabay* ("treasurer") and parnas ("president"), serving as the last named until his demise in 1879. In the autumn of that year I [Charles Joseph Cohen] was elected as his successor, and the Reverend Dr. [Sabato] Morais called at my office to offer congratulations on my accession to the distinguished position, and to add a caution as to the possible enthusiasm of youth proceeding to an enlargement of activities leading to radical changes, most undesirable to be advocated by the authorities of our conservative congregation that had stood for more than a century as a bulwark of traditional Judaism. . . .

CHARLES JOSEPH COHEN

EDUCATION, SECULAR AND RELIGIOUS

I [CHARLES J. COHEN] was born on the twenty-first of September, 1847, in the house on the south side of Chestnut Street above Broad, known as No. 2 Clinton Square, where the Land Title Building now stands. On the eighth day after birth, at the commemoration of the ceremony of the covenant [circumcision], Miss Rebecca Gratz became my godmother and was a potent factor in confirming the home influence toward religious education and the proper moral standards of living. As is known, Miss Gratz was a woman of great celebrity, having been chosen by Sir Walter Scott as the impersonation of his heroine, Rebecca, in the novel of *Ivanhoe*.

At the age of seven I went to school at Miss Drake's. . . . One circumstance occurred during my stay at this school which made a deep and lasting impression. Returning from school with a new lead pencil, my sister Edith promptly claimed it as hers, she having had one with the same maker's name upon it. I vigorously defended my rights to its possession, stating that one of the boys had given it to me; his name I could not remember. And when my father accompanied me to the school the next morning and stated the matter at issue to Miss Sarah Drake, she appealed to the assembled scholars, asking the boy from whom I had received the pencil to rise. Not one moved, and for an hour my father and the teacher plead[ed] with me to acknowledge my supposed fault and to tell the truth. I still adhered to my first statement, and the teacher returned to the classroom, making another appeal to the boys to clear my character. The boy, one Jennings, arose and said he had given it to me, and that he had been too frightened to speak at first. He was a son of Napoleon Jennings of M. Thomas & Sons, the noted auctioneers. I have quite lost sight of him. My father and mother were naturally pleased with the outcome, and I have in my papers a letter from my father, expressing his joy accompanying a suitable present to mark the occasion.

In 1858 I entered the Classical Institute of Dr. J. W. Faires, beginning in the fifth Latin class. . . . I recall a declamation about the year 1861. It received commendation from Dr. Faires, who wrote: "Charles' recitation today I can highly commend. J. W. F., and his associate teachers," the subject being the address by Hamlet to the players, beginning: "Speak the speech, I pray you. . . . Nor do not saw the air too much with your hand thus." There were about fifteen lines in the address, and my parents, who were Shakespearean students, drilled me most thoroughly. I remember the cordial reception the presentation received.

In 1861, at the time of the breaking out of the Civil War, the boys subscribed for a handsome flag and pole. Its erection was a joyful occasion, and the martial spirit thus begun was followed by an enlistment in a corps of cadets that was raised by Mr. Hlasko and taught by an old soldier by the name of Reckendorfer. We were drilled with muskets as infantry and with sabres as dismounted cavalry. In 1862, the corps gave a gala performance at the Academy of Music. I was one of the guard of three ordered out to shoot a sentinel who had been caught sleeping at his post. Happily, a reprieve arrived at the last moment, so that the life of the young soldier, Koecker, was spared.

I was a fair scholar, very industrious, but not having a good memory, I had to work hard to keep my place in the class. Faires' first class indulged in many pranks that were tolerated by the principal, which, if carried out by one of the lower classes, would have met with severe criticism and punishment. One instance was the opening of the entire collection of umbrellas that had been deposited in the basement, as was the custom on rainy days, and the difficulty can be imagined on the part of the hundred or more students obtaining their individual possessions. This adventure was not repeated, since grave criticism followed from the parents of many of the younger boys, whose umbrellas had been injured or entirely destroyed. . . .

From early childhood I had accompanied my father to the regular Sabbath and holiday services. Our seats were in the second row of the circular benches to the left of the *tebah* ["reading desk"] (the late Hyman Gratz being seated immediately in front), so that the discourses in English were readily absorbed. . . . We were expected to give a brief account of the intent of the sermon on our return to the parental roof, especially if some member of the household had been unable to attend service. This requirement led in early youth to a careful absorption of the sermon, a habit that continued during the ministration of Dr. Morais, who was revered by every member of our household.

As a seat holder in the congregation, my next recollection is of my confirmation (*bar-mitzvah*), which occurred in September of 1860, it being the second one after the opening of the building on Seventh Street above Arch. At that time it was not customary for the minister to make an address or appeal to the confirmant, but I recall that it was done at the time of the confirmation of my two sons, following in the years 1894 and 1896. . . .

TRAVELS AND EDUCATION ABROAD

In the spring of 1862 my health failed as a result of typhoid fever the preceeding autumn, so that my parents decided to send me to school in England. I left New York on the eighth of May, 1862, on the steamer "Persia" of the Cunard Line, a fellow-passenger being Mr. Henry Owen of Sheffield, England, who was resident in New York as agent for Joseph Gillott & Sons, the celebrated steel penmakers. Steamers in those days were not fitted as they now are. The lamps in the saloon were fed by oil, and as the ventilation was imperfect, the odor was objectionable. There were no saloons nor rooms of any kind on the upper deck; the only resort was in the lee of the great central smokestack. The saloon and staterooms were in the stern, the section of greatest motion, the machinery being in the centre, since those were the days of paddle wheels.

We arrived in Liverpool in ten days, a fine run, and I was domiciled with my aunt, Mrs. Caroline Samuel (my mother's sister), a widow lady of culture and refinement. The family consisted of herself, two sons, five and ten years my senior, one daughter of my own age, and a niece and nephew some years older. I was anxious to see the great international exhibition in London, then in progress, so I proceeded thence and was hospitably received by my aunt, Mrs. Magnus (my father's sister), and remained with her for some weeks, subsequently taking a room near the exhibition grounds for the purpose of economy of time; the terms were a guinea per week with breakfast ($5). I was delighted with London and with the exhibition and with all the attractions of a foreign city: Madam Tussaud's wax works exhibit in Baker Street, the Tower of London, Windsor Castle, and many others. I had brought with me from America a tin sandwich box lettered on the outside "Noonday Exercises," a most convenient method of serving luncheon in a crowded city. Great was the amusement of friends and onlookers when the box was opened and its contents discovered.

Returning to Liverpool, the family moved to New Brighton, a neighboring seashore resort noted for its donkey rides and delightful sea air, but the summer temperature was a novelty since I wore the same thickness of clothing as during the winter. I had worn, on my arrival, the grey clothes of the military cadet corps, but my aunt declared this to be the garb of young serving-lads in England (pages, as they are called), [and] promptly superseded them by a suit of black broadcloth, at that time universally used in England for lads of that age. I also had to wear on Sabbath and state occasions a tall or high silk hat, quite the correct thing in England, but I was mobbed on Chestnut Street by the boys when I wore it on my return to Philadelphia at the close of the following year.

In the autumn of 1862 I entered the Carlton Terrace School, conducted by Dr. W. Ihne, who had been a tutor to the members of the royal family of Prussia, classical master at the *Gymnasium* ["high school"] of Elberfeld, later headmaster of the Liverpool Institute High School, and author of classical literature, especially researches into the history of the Roman constitution.

Dr. Ihne was not only an accomplished scholar but an able instructor, and with the groundwork received at the Faires School, rapid progress was made in my Latin and English studies, to which were added French and German, drawing, and music, . . . the last named being in the form of private lessons on the violin, in which some proficiency was acquired. And, although many of these branches of education were not continued after entering into a business career, they left their impress in a love for classical matters which has been a great delight through all these years.

Attendance at a gymnasium for athletic development was required several evenings in the week, so that time was fully occupied with the preparation for the lessons of the following day. The only opportunity for recreation being at the close of the week, when cricket was played with trips to places such as Rock-Ferry, Birkenhead, and New Brighton, all on the other [south] side of the River Mersey, also Waterloo and Bootle, on the Lancashire [County] side.

ENGLISH REACTION TO THE CIVIL WAR

During my residence in Liverpool, the Civil War in America was in progress. The sympathy of the better class of people was entirely with the South, the British government being urged by their influence to recognize the Southern Confederacy so that the port of Liverpool could resume its importation of cotton and the export of British-made goods to the Southern states, the interruption of this trade having been a serious blow to its commercial interests.

On the other hand, blockade running was assuming great proportions since vessels of light draft, sailing from England, would enter the ports of the British West India islands, where they would refit and make a dash for the Southern ports, where entry might be obtained notwithstanding the vigilance of the Federal blockade. This was a profitable undertaking and fortunes were amassed. The sympathies of merchants continued to be entirely pro-Southern, and I can recall the incident of the fitting out of the [Confederate raider] "Alabama" at the shipyards of the Lairds.

During these critical months I would rise early so as to get the morning newspaper before the family demands would arise, so as to be properly informed for the wordy battles that always ensued during the breakfast and dinner hours, as well as during the school sessions.

At this time the students were instructed to prepare a composition, the subject being "The Present Civil War in America." My paper has not been preserved, but it may be stated that it was the only one read to the assembled students, since assurance was given that it treated the subject in an accurate manner. Most of the papers talked of North and South America without the least knowledge of the geographical conditions obtaining in our country.

During my residence in Liverpool, the game of chess, which I had acquired at home in Philadelphia, was developed and musical and theatrical diversions indulged in at weekends and holidays. . . .

During my stay in Liverpool an invitation from my aunt, Mrs. Kate Samuel Yates, to be her guest for some weeks was accepted; the old lady had an excellent memory and was always interested in recounting incidents of the family history. Her daughter, Clara, became the wife of Edwin L. Samuel, a banker of Liverpool, not a relative although bearing the same surname. Mr. and Mrs. Edwin Samuel made their home in London, Mr. Samuel establishing with his brother the banking firm of Samuel, Montague and Company which has obtained a wide celebrity, now being carried on by the present Sir Stuart M. Samuel. His brother is the Right Honorable Herbert L. Samuel, recently High Commissioner for Palestine in the development of the Holy Land, former British Secretary of State for Home Affairs, and postmaster general in an earlier Cabinet. He is an accomplished statesman and man of letters as also an author of distinction, especially on economics.

RETURN TO PHILADELPHIA

In the autumn of 1863 I returned to Philadelphia and, since my father recognized that his advancing years and imperfect health necessitated a relief from arduous duties incident to a commercial life, I entered his establishment to learn the rudiments of the business with the proviso, required by my mother, that "Charles should continue the study of literature and the arts," opportunity being given from time to time. This encouragement was a potent factor during my early manhood, so that, on the occasion of my next trip to Europe in 1873, the opportunities of visiting the picture galleries both in Great Britain and on the Continent were eagerly availed of.

Several times during the week [during the year 1863] the Company [of Home Guards] would drill and my father would remove his office coat on such occasions, put on a blue coat with gilt buttons, and join in the drill. After a laborious and anxious day at business, this was no small tax upon his physical qualities, but his interest was so keen and desire so great to set a proper example, that he persevered until there was no longer an occasion [need for drilling]. The musket used was one of the old pattern muzzle-loader and stood for many years in the corner of his bedroom in Rittenhouse Square, as a proper threat against the midnight marauder, since it is well known and well remembered by those of that period that dread was felt by all citizens that dire results would follow the disbandment of approximately a million men at the close of the Civil War in 1865. Greatly, however, to the honor and credit of the American nation, there was not the slightest indication of moral or physical disturbances.

In 1865, at the close of the war, many of the troops returned through Philadelphia, and marched down Chestnut Street. At the first call of the bugle the rear door on Crocketts' Court [where our business was located] was locked, and we all went over to greet the returning soldier[s], and stood with uncovered head, expressing from time to time our word of appreciation of the sacrifice that had been made by the defenders of our homes.

Mordecai Sheftall

Revolutionary Patriot of Georgia

Mordecai Sheftall was the outstanding Jew of Georgia in the eighteenth century. His father, Benjamin, a German, had come to the colony in 1733, but a few weeks after General James Oglethorpe's arrival.

Mordecai, born in 1735, quickly achieved a considerable degree of success as a businessman. Like many other Georgians of his generation, he was active in a variety of commercial enterprises: he was a farmer, rancher, tanner, sawmill owner, shopkeeper, and shipper.

With the beginning of the Revolution, Sheftall became one of the patriot leaders of Georgia, in spite of the fact that most of the inhabitants were either Loyalists or indifferent to the Whig cause. Sheftall became the chairman of the committee to further the revolutionary cause in Christ Church Parish (County), which included Savannah, the colony's largest city. The Loyalists were well aware of his zeal, and Governor James Wright denounced him.

In 1777, Mordecai Sheftall was appointed Commissary General of Purchases and Issues to his state's militia. In the following year, General Robert Howe appointed him Deputy Commissary General of Issues to the Continental Troops in South Carolina and Georgia, an office which carried with it the rank of colonel. His son Sheftall Sheftall, then only sixteen years of age, was already an assistant deputy commissary of issues, serving as his father's deputy.

In the same year (1778), the British determined to capture Savannah and to sweep north through the Carolinas, hoping thus to wipe away the shame incurred in the preceding year by Burgoyne's surrender at Saratoga. Late in December, Lieutenant Colonel Archibald Campbell landed near Savannah, found a way through the swamps, and routed the smaller force of defending American militiamen under General Robert Howe. Both Mordecai Sheftall and his son were among those captured when the city fell on December 29, 1778.

Sometime later Mordecai Sheftall sat down to recount the dangers to which he and his son had been exposed during their first few days in captivity. The account, reproduced below, was published in the Reverend George White's Historical Collections of Georgia *(New York: 1854), pp. 340-42, and was subsequently reprinted in the* Publications of the American Jewish Historical Society, *XVII (1909), 176-78.*

Father and son remained prisoners until about June, 1780, when they were permitted to go to Philadelphia on parole. After the War, Mordecai Sheftall continued his mercantile career in his native city of Savannah. He played a leading part in the reorganization of the Jewish congregation and was widely known and highly respected in the larger Gentile community, holding minor civic appointments until his death in 1797.

In the Hands of the British

THIS DAY [December 29, 1778] the British troops, consisting of about 3,500 men, including two battalions of Hessians under the command of Lieutenant Colonel Archibald Campbell of the Seventy-first Regiment of Highlanders, landed early in the morning at Brewton Hill, two miles below the town of Savannah, where they met with very little opposition before they gained the height. At about three o'clock P.M. they entered and took possession of the town of Savannah, when I endeavored, with my son Sheftall, to make our escape across Musgrove Creek, having first premised that an intrenchment had been thrown up there in order to cover a retreat, and upon seeing Colonel Samuel Elbert and Major James Habersham endeavour to make their escape that way.

But on our arrival at the creek, after having sustained a very heavy fire of musketry from the light infantry under the command of Sir James Baird, during the time we were crossing the Common, without any injury to either of us, we found it high water. And my son not knowing how to swim, and we with about 186 officers and privates being caught, as it were, in a pen, and the Highlanders keeping up a constant fire on us, it was thought advisable to surrender ourselves prisoners, which we accordingly did. And which was no sooner done than the Highlanders plundered every one amongst us, except Major Low, myself, and son, who, being foremost, had an opportunity to surrender ourselves to the British officer, namely, Lieutenant Peter Campbell, who disarmed us as we came into the yard formerly occupied by Mr. Moses Nunes.

During this business Sir James Baird was missing, but on his coming into the yard, he mounted himself on the stepladder which was erected at the end of the house and sounded his brass bugle horn, which the Highlanders no sooner heard than they all got about him, when he addressed himself to them in Highland language, when they all dispersed and finished plundering such of the officers and men as had been fortunate enough to escape their first search. This over, we were marched in file, guarded by the Highlanders and [New] York Volunteers who had come up before

42

we were marched, when we were paraded before Mrs. Goffe's door
on the Bay, where we saw the greatest part of the army drawn
up.

From there, after some time, we were all marched through the
town to the courthouse, which was very much crowded, the greatest
part of the officers they had taken being here collected and indis-
criminately put together. I had been here about two hours, when
an officer, who I afterwards learned to be Major Crystie, called for
me by name and ordered me to follow him, which I did, with my
blanket and shirt under my arm, my clothing and my son's, which
were in my saddlebags, having been taken from my horse, so that
my wardrobe consisted of what I had on my back.

On our way to the white guardhouse we met with Colonel Campbell, who inquired of the major who he had got there. On his nam-
ing me to him, he desired that I might be well-guarded, as I was
a very great rebel. The major obeyed his orders, for, on lodging
me in the guardhouse, he ordered the sentry to guard me with a
drawn bayonet and not to suffer me to go without the reach of it,
which orders were strictly complied with until a Mr. Gild Busler,
their commissary general, called for me and ordered me to go with
him to my stores, that he might get some provisions for our people,
who, he said, were starving, not having eat[en] anything for three
days, which I contradicted, as I had victualled them that morning
for the day.

On our way to the office where I used to issue the provisions, he
ordered me to give him information of what stores I had in town
and what I had sent out of town, and where. This I declined doing,
which made him angry. He asked me if I knew that Charlestown
[South Carolina] was taken. I told him: "No." He then called us
poor, deluded wretches, and said: "Good God! how are you deluded
by your leaders!" When I inquired of him who had taken it, and
when, he said, General [James] Grant, with 10,000 men, and that
it had been taken eight or ten days ago, I smiled and told him it
was not so, as I had a letter in my pocket that was wrote in Charlestown but three days ago by my brother.

He replied we had been misinformed. I then retorted that I found
they could be misinformed by their leaders, as well as we could
be deluded by ours. This made him so angry that when he returned
me to the guardhouse, he ordered me to be confined amongst the
drunken soldiers and negroes, where I suffered a great deal of
abuse and was threatened to be run through the body or, as they
termed it, "skivered" by one of the York Volunteers, which threat

he attempted to put into execution three times during the night, but was prevented by one Sergeant Campbell.

In this situation I remained two days without a morsel to eat, when a Hessian officer named Zaltman, finding I could talk his language, removed me to his room and sympathized with me on my situation. He permitted me to send to Mrs. [Abigail] Minis, who sent me some victuals. He also permitted me to go and see my son, and to let him come and stay with me. He introduced me to Captain Kappel, also a Hessian, who treated me very politely.

In this situation I remained until Saturday morning, the second of January, 1779, when the commander, Colonel Innis, sent his orderly for me and [my] son to [go to] his quarters, which was James Habersham's house, where on the top of the step I met with Captain Stanhope, of the "Raven," sloop of war, who treated me with the most illiberal abuse and, after charging me with having refused the supplying of the King's ships with provisions, and of having shut the church door, together with many ill-natured things, ordered me on board the prison ship, together with my son. I made a point of giving Mr. Stanhope suitable answers to his impertinent treatment and then turned from him and inquired for Colonel Innis. I got his leave to go to Mrs. Minis for a shirt she had taken to wash for me, as it was the only one I had left except the one on my back, and that was given me by Captain Kappel, as the British soldiers had plundered both mine and my son's clothes.

This favour he granted me under guard, after which I was conducted on board one of the flatboats and put on board the prison ship "Nancy," commanded by Captain Samuel Tait, when the first thing that presented itself to my view was one of our poor Continental soldiers laying on the ship's main deck in the agonies of death, and who expired in a few hours. After being presented to the captain with mine and the rest of the prisoners' names, I gave him in charge what paper money I had, and my watch. My son also gave him his money to take care of. He appeared to be a little civiller after this confidence placed in him, and permitted us to sleep in a stateroom, that is, the Rev. Moses Allen, myself, and son. In the evening we were served with what was called our allowance, which consisted of two pints and a half [of water?], and a half gill of rice, and about seven ounces of boiled beef per man. We were permitted to choose our messmates, and I accordingly made choice of Capt. Thomas Fineley, Rev. Mr. Allen, Mr. Moses Valentonge, Mr. Daniel Flaherty, myself, and son Sheftall Sheftall.

David Salisbury Franks

Eighteenth-Century Soldier and Courier

David Salisbury Franks was a member of a widespread family which played an important part in eighteenth-century American Jewish history. He was a native of Philadelphia who moved to Quebec with his parents and later settled in Montreal.

Like many other English-speaking merchants in Montreal, Franks was eager to secure representative government for the province and joined in a petition asking for this. Unlike his fellow-Canadians, however, he was ready to break with the mother country when the crisis came in 1775. He was one of the few residents of Montreal who dared to show sympathy publicly for the colonists south of the border, who were then in a state of revolt. For a brief period, in May, 1775, he was imprisoned for his Whig sentiments, and when the Americans invaded Canada, he fortified those sentiments with purse and deed. It was quite clear, therefore, that when the invaders were driven out, he, too, would have to go.

Franks was among the Continentals by 1776, and for the next eleven years was engaged in the service of the new republic, fighting with its armed forces. He probably attained the rank of lieutenant colonel. Toward the end of the conflict, he was detached from military duty and sent on special missions to Europe and North Africa. His ability to speak French, no doubt acquired in Canada, served him in good stead.

Franks returned to the United States after the Revolution, eager to remain in the service of his country. Selling merchandise, his original occupation, had lost its charms for him. He enjoyed military life; he wanted a public career and yearned for government service. Apparently, he never attained his ambition.

In 1790 Franks was given a minor position in the ill-fated Scioto Land Company, but it is doubtful whether he ever left for the Ohio country with the French settlers whom he was expected to accompany. A year later he held a small post with the Bank of North America, in Philadelphia. He died shortly thereafter, in 1793.

Soon after Washington's inauguration in the spring of 1789, Franks wrote to the President and asked for a government position, hoping to be appointed consul general in France. With the petition for his appointment, he enclosed the following autobiographical account of his career. It is filed in the Library of Congress, Division of Manuscripts (U. S. Applications for office under Washington, May 12, 1789). A transcript was published by Oscar S. Straus in the Publications of the American Jewish Historical Society, X (1902), 102-5.

According to tradition, Franks was president of Montreal's congregation Shearith Israel in 1775. As far as our records show, that was his last official association with any Jewish community. After he became a public figure, so to say, he appears to have lost interest in his ancestral faith and in his fellow Jews.

My Military Career

Early in the year 1774, I settled in Montreal, with a small capital and a considerable credit as a merchant, and was successful in business. In the spring of 1775, I suffered a short tho' rigorous imprisonment on account of my attachment to the cause of America.

As soon as the troops under General [Richard] Montgomery took possession of Montreal [November 13, 1775], I did everything in my power to promote their success, and at one time advanced nearly to the amount of 500 half johanes [a Portuguese coin] in goods and money, which was afterwards paid to me in depreciated paper. In 1776, soon after the unfortunate attack on Quebec, General [David] Wooster appointed me to the office of clerk of the checque, or paymaster to the artificers of the garrison of Montreal, in which capacity I was indefatigable in forwarding the public works, and again advanced considerable sums of money at times when there was not a farthing in the military chest to satisfy the demands of the workmen.

When the Northern Army retreated from Canada, I joined it as a volunteer and continued attached to that army with some little intermission until the reduction of General [John] Bourgoyne [in 1777]. In 1778, after the evacuation of Philadelphia by the British Army, and on the arrival of Count D'Estaing, I procured letters of recommendation from the Board of War, from Mr. [C. A.] Gérard [the French minister] and Mr. [Silas] Deane, who came with the Count and joined him off Sandy Hook [in New York Bay]. I continued with that admiral until he arrived at Rhode Island, when, on the failure of that expedition, I returned to Philadelphia, where my military duty called me.

In 1779 I went, a volunteer, to Charlestown [South Carolina] and was an aid-de-camp in General [Benjamin] Lincoln's family till I was recalled to attend the tryal of General [Benedict] Arnold. In 1780, I was in Arnold's military family at West Point until his desertion to the enemy, when a court of enquiry, which I had solicited of the commander in chief, made the report, which his Excellency [General Washington] was pleased to accept and approve. [Franks was exonerated from any complicity in Arnold's treason.]

MY DIPLOMATIC CAREER

In 1781, the Superintendent of Finance [Robert Morris] sent me with dispatches to Mr. [John] Jay, at Madrid, and to Mr. [Benjamin] Franklin, at Paris. I continued employed in Europe until the next year, when I returned home with the approbation of our ministers, as well as of Mr. Morris, for my conduct while abroad. At my return, I found myself deranged from the line of the army, but on application to Congress, I was reinstated for one year only. When Mr. [Thomas] Jefferson was going to Paris [as] one of the commissioners for making a treaty of peace, he took me into his [official] family. We waited a considerable time at Baltimore for an opportunity to go to sea, a British squadron then guarding the Bay of Chesapeak[e]. Congress, in the meanwhile, received information that a treaty was already signed, and this precluded the necessity of Mr. Jefferson's embarking. I then solicited the Secretary for Foreign Affairs [Robert R. Livingston] for an appointment in the consular line and procured a recommendation from some of the most eminent merchants of my native place [Philadelphia]. Mr. Livingston mentioned me in a particular manner to Congress. . . .

In the winter of the year 1784, Congress dispatched me to Europe with a copy of the ratification of the definitive treaty [of peace] which I had the honor of delivering to our ministers in Paris, where I remained ill of a fever, which prevented me going to Holland in consequence of orders received from the Superintendent of Finance. In 1785, I went at a considerable expense to Marseilles, to which place Mr. [Thomas] Barclay [an American special agent] had named me vice consul. I resided there till my little stock of money was nearly exhausted, and in the spring of 1786, I returned to Paris. For my first voyage to Europe, as well as the second with the ratification of the definitive treaty, and for my residence at Marseilles as vice consul, I never received any emolument whatever.

In the fall, 1786, Mr. Barclay was commissioned by our ministers for making a treaty of peace and commerce with the Emperor of Morocco, and I was appointed his secretary. Previous to our departure for Africa, it was judged necessary to send a confidential person to London to get the proper instruments signed by Mr. [John] Adams [United States minister to Great Britain] and to fix the mode of drawing bills of exchange, etc., with that gentleman.

Charles Wilson Peale

DAVID SALISBURY FRANKS

(see page 47)

Pencil sketch of a portrait by John Wesley Jarvis

MAJOR MORDECAI MYERS

(see page 52)

I offered myself and executed what depended on me, in the two journeys I made to London, with zeal and dispatch. After Mr. Barclay's return to Spain from Morocco, where he had compleated a treaty with the Emperor, I was sent by him with it from Madrid to Paris, and from thence by Mr. Jefferson to London to get Mr. Adams' signature to it. In the month of March following, I embarked by order of our ministers for America, bearer of the Treaty of Morocco, and had the honor of delivering it to Mr. Jay [who had succeeded Mr. Livingston as Secretary for Foreign Affairs] at New York in the month of May. With me I also brought testimonials of the approbation of our ministers abroad as appears by their public dispatches.

Thus I have devoted eleven years of the best part of my life to the service of my country, in all which time, I am bold to say, that I have ever been actuated by a disenterested zeal for her honor and prosperity.

Captain Mordecai Myers

Veteran of the War of 1812

Mordecai Myers was born in Newport, R. I., in 1776, the son of Loyalists. His father was a learned Hungarian Jew who may have been known as Myer Benjamin.

Young Mordecai grew up in New York City where, it would seem, he made his living as a merchant or auctioneer. He was active in the Spanish-Portuguese synagogue, Shearith Israel, served as one of its trustees in the first decade of the nineteenth century, and voted against a raise in the rabbi's salary. (Apparently, he wasn't doing so well himself.)

When the War of 1812 broke out, Myers, who had served as an officer in the militia, took up arms and became a captain in the Thirteenth Infantry, United States Army. As he wrote to his friend, Naphtali Phillips, then the editor of what Myers facetiously termed a "kasher" newspaper: "Sum must spill there blud and others there ink." Myers belonged to the former category, for he almost died of wounds received in the Battle of Chrysler's Field, on November 11, 1813.

Most of his life Myers was busy with politics. In the 1820's he represented the city of New York in the State Assembly and, when eighty-four years of age, attempted unsuccessfully to win a seat in Congress.

In the 1850's, while he was mayor of Schenectady, N. Y., and at the age of seventy-seven, he wrote his memoirs in the form of letters to a son. In view of his age, and inasmuch as he wrote from memory, it is not surprising that he confused names, dates, and other data. These memoirs, therefore, must be used with caution; they are interesting recollections of an old man, but can hardly be considered as a reliable source.

After the War of 1812, and his marriage out of the faith, Myers drifted away from Judaism and no longer played a part in the Jewish community. The memoir material, edited after his death, betrays no relationship to his religion. The word Jew does not occur in it; the name of the writer's father is not even mentioned. Myers' de-

*scendants of today are represented in some of America's distinguished
Christian families.*

*After the major's death (his title of major is probably of postwar
militia provenance) the Schenectady* Times *(in an issue of January,
1871) wrote:*

Major Myers was in many respects a remarkable man. He was
possessed of a clear mind, strong will, and the fact that, with all
the hardships incident to the life of a soldier in [the] War of 1812,
he lived to be nearly ninety-six years of age, is proof that he possessed a strong and robust constitution. His physical appearance
was striking. No stranger ever met him or passed him on the street
without noticing his appearance; he was of very large proportions
and had a clear and keen black eye, giving evidence of the strong
intellectual power of the man. As Mayor of this city he added dignity to the office, and brought all the power of his common sense
and an indomitable will to bear against wrong, and in favor of
right and justice.

The following extracts are taken from Reminiscences 1780 to 1814
Including Incidents in the War of 1812-14 . . . Written by Major
Myers, 13th Infantry, U. S. Army to His Son *(Washington, D. C.,
1900). Some of the material has been rearranged to ensure chrono-
logical continuity.*

My Dear Son:

In accordance with your expressed wish, I will give you a condensed outline of the events of my long and varied life, beginning with a short account of family affairs. My father was a Hungarian, and my mother an Austrian by birth. They sailed from Helvoetsluys, in Holland, and arrived in New York in the year 1750. They soon after removed to Newport, where I was born on the thirty-first of May, 1776, two months before the signing of the Declaration of Independence. My father spoke and wrote all the living languages, and, at Newport, he became the friend of the Rev. Dr. [Ezra] Styles [Stiles], afterwards President of Yale College. In November, 1776, before having reached his fortieth year, my father died, beloved and respected by all who knew him. [If the above account is correct, the father was thirteen years of age when he arrived in this country, a married man!]

The British evacuated Newport in 1779, and, in 1780, my mother decided to return to New York. The winter of this year was known long after as the "hard winter." The snow was deeper than it had ever been known to be before on the continent; and I have seen nothing like it since. The Bay of New York was so firmly frozen over that the British marched troops and removed heavy guns on the ice to Staten Island.

We lived quietly in New York until 1783, when Great Britain was compelled, by her own necessities and by the persevering bravery of the Americans, to acknowledge the American colonies to be free and independent states. Preparations were being made to withdraw the forces, and the British, in common justice to those Americans who, unfortunately for themselves, had embraced the British cause, offered homes in Nova Scotia to all who would sign [had signed] Articles of Association [joined the companies of Associated Loyalists to fight the Continentals]. My mother agreed to this, and early in May we left New York in a British ship for our new home. We spent several happy years in Nova Scotia, where a pleasant society was formed. Our nearest neighbors were Captain Richard Lippincott and his wife, a Quaker. He had been a captain in the British Army, and, as such, he was ordered, sometime in the year 1782, to exchange the American Captain Huddy, then a prisoner at New York, for a British officer of equal rank, who was to be delivered to him on the Jersey shore at, or near, Bergen Point; but, on the way, he landed at Gibbet Island, and ordered his prisoner to prepare for death.

Huddy considered it a jest, and endeavored to laugh it off; but Lippincott directed his Negro servant to prepare a halter, and Huddy was actually hung to a limb of a tree. Lippincott then returned to New York, of course without the British officer whom he should have brought in the place of Huddy. [Huddy was hanged in retaliation for the hanging of New Jersey Loyalists by the Americans.]

Great excitement was felt in New York, as well as in the American camp. Lippincott was arrested and imprisoned, and General Washington demanded his delivery to the Americans, but was answered that the trial would take place under British law. All expected the condemnation and execution of the criminal, but, at about this time [1783], the treaty of peace was signed and ratified whereby our independence was acknowledged, and Lippincott was either acquitted or pardoned, when he went to Nova Scotia.

There was a story current at that time about the notorious Benedict Arnold. He had become a merchant in St. Johns, and, in connection with Monson Hoyt, had imported largely from England, not knowing what would be required in the new country. Consequently, he accumulated a large quantity of unsalable goods, which were, however, highly insured in England. It is said that he hired a woman, for a new dress, to set fire to the building in which his goods were stored. But the plot was discovered at the trial for the recovery of the insurance, and Arnold was obliged to leave the country.

In 1787 we returned to New York. On the voyage we stopped at New Haven, where we received an additional passenger, Captain John Paul Jones. I remember him as a man of medium height, rather stout and well-set, with dark hair and eyes. In conversation, free and easy; and in manner, rather bombastic. He seemed to me to look more like a German than a Scotchman. At New Haven, I saw a young man tied to a post and publicly whipped for horse stealing.

I had seen, when in New York, Hessian soldiers run the gauntlet, and a man under the "mild and humane" British laws, standing in the pillory, cropped and branded for stealing a loaf of bread from a baker's window.

In New York we took a house owned by the excellent Mr. [Robert Richard] Randall. He had begun life a poor sailor boy; but, by his own exertions, he became a very rich merchant. He had been aided by a seafaring man, and he amply returned the favors by leaving the bulk of his fortune to be used for the founding of an institution for the benefit of disabled and superannuated sailors. That fund forms the basis of the Sailors' Snug Harbor on Staten Island.

At this time, in the year 1787, New York contained 33,000 inhabitants. The city was still in rather a dilapidated state, not having, as yet, recovered from the effects of the war. The country was governed under the old Articles of Confederation formed during the Revolutionary War, merely to establish a union of force and action without defining or limiting the rights or powers of the general government of the states. Our commerce, both foreign and domestic, was very small and much embarrassed. A vessel and cargo going from one state to another was compelled to clear, enter, and secure duties. Each state had its proper currency which would not pass in the adjoining states; every kind of property was low and money scarce. . . .

POLITICS IN OLD NEW YORK

The new constitution of the United States had been agreed to in convention, but had not, as yet, been adopted by all the states. The French Revolution had burst forth, and party spirit ran high. Two great political parties were forming. "Commodore" Francis [James] Nicholson was the first president of the Democratic Society, and Thomas Jefferson was its great leader. Alexander Hamilton lead the Federal party. Jefferson and the Democrats were jealous of the power of the President by the new Constitution, and they considered the office nearly equal to that of king. They feared the establishment of a concentrated, luxurious, and extravagant government; a great, controlling, political institution; and a union of Church and State. They believed that [the Federalists] General Hamilton, Timothy Pickering, Oliver Wolcott, and others were trying to introduce a limited monarchy in disguise.

Among the propositions made to the convention, General Hamilton suggested that senators should be elected for life, and that the President should choose his successor. Mobs and riots were common, the Democratic printing office of [Thomas] Greenleaf was attacked, and the type scattered in the street. But after great and long excitement, the Constitution was ratified by most of the states. The convention of this State (N. Y.), having peace and the public interest in view, met at Newbury [Poughkeepsie?], and, after long debates, ratified the Constitution. At the same time, a declaration of reserved state rights was made, a copy of which may be found in the Assembly documents of 1833, placed there at my request, I having found the original in the office of the Secretary of State after long search.

George Washington was elected President of the United States, and all the states elected congressmen, who now assembled at the old City Hall in New York; it stood on Wall Street, where the Custom House now stands. I recollect seeing Chancellor Livingstone [Robert R. Livingston] administer the oath of office to General Washington on a Bible, which is still in a state of good preservation and in the possession of St. John's [Masonic] Lodge, No. 1, New York, where it is held as a relic of times past. . . .

The State Convention having ratified the Constitution of the United States accompanied by an instrument signed by all its members, and known as the Reserved Rights of the State of New York, both parties united in getting up a pageant such as had never been seen in New York. The corporation invited all the mechanical, civil, and charitable societies to appoint committees to make arrangements for a general procession. Each was allowed to make its own preparations, which were done on an extensive and brilliant plan. Early on the day appointed, each society assembled at the Battery [1788].

The governor, both branches of the legislature, the judges, the members of the bar, the officers of the courts, officers of the army and navy, the mayor and corporation, and other city officers, took part in the procession. All the mechanical trades were represented by men engaged at their respective occupations in cars mounted on trucks. The ship carpenters contributed a miniature frigate of thirty-six guns, completely rigged, armed, and manned. She was called the "United States," and commanded by Commodore Francis Nicholson. Her crew consisted of young lads dressed as sailors, her sails were loosed and sheeted home, and her guns were loaded and fired. This attracted great attention. During the day, the streets were crowded with people, and the houses were decorated with flags.

In the evening, Colonel Sebastian Bowman, a Prussian officer of the Revolution, and soon after appointed first postmaster of New York by General Washington, prepared extensive fireworks at the old fort, Bowling Green, and at other places. This was, I believe, the first exhibition of fireworks in New York. All places of amusement were opened and thronged. Most of the houses and public buildings were illuminated. It was near morning before the streets were again quiet. Thus was consummated the foundation of our excellent civil government, and the great Republic of thirteen free and independent United States.

Distraction to the brain that would conceive the idea of a separation of the Union, and palsied the hand that would break one link of this Heaven-wrought chain! [This sentence was directed against the secessionists of the 1850's.]

The following few years of my life were spent in New York, and in Richmond, Virginia. During my residence in Richmond, I made many valuable acquaintances, among whom was Judge [George] Wythe, one of the signers of the Declaration of Independence. He, and all his family, were poisoned by one of the household servants, a black boy, who had been treated rather as a pet than otherwise. The younger members of the family recovered, but the old gentleman died. The boy was hung; he prayed, and sang psalms under the gallows, and said that he had always been well-treated by the family, but that the devil had prompted him to do the wicked deed; and (as frequently happens in such cases) his Savior had appeared to him the night before, and pronounced his pardon. [This account is garbled.]

I became an active politician just before the election of 1793 [1800?], which put a period to the despotic reign of John Adams (the elder) and placed Thomas Jefferson in the presidential chair in the following year. The Federal party was composed in part of the old Tories of the Revolution, and the rich merchants and traders, who boasted of having all the wealth, talent, and respectability of the American people. Congress, under the Federal[ist] administration, had passed several oppressive laws, abridging the public rights. The Alien and Sedition Laws were particularly objected to by the Democratic Party. The President had power to transport or imprison, without trial, any suspected person, and he actually did imprison many valuable citizens, for speaking disrespectfully of him as an individual. Several of these were editors.

The warm partisans of the dominant party would neither deal with [n]or employ those who differed from them in politics. All the offices from highest to lowest were held exclusively by the Federal Party. Many of the merchants stooped so low as to discharge clerks, cartmen, and others who differed with them in politics. The measure of wrongs was filled to overflowing. The parties, numerically, were nearly equal; but the wealth and patronage were against the Democrats.

One evening three gentlemen met at the house of Brockholst Livingstone [Livingston], in Broadway: Mr. Livingstone, General Morgan Lewis, and Aaron Burr. The wrongs of the people was the subject of conversation. Mr. Burr said: "We must, at the next election, put a period to this 'reign of terror.' " The others agreed that this was desirable, but saw no way to bring it about. Mr. Burr said: "We must carry the city, and that will give us the majority in the legislature, and the state of New York being Democratic, will carry the Union, and transfer to the Democrats all the power and patronage of the government."

The other gentlemen thought this a brilliant plan, but did not see how it would be possible to gain the ascendency in the city. Mr. Burr took pen and paper and made out an Assembly ticket, heading it with the names of Gov. George Clinton, Gen. Horatio Gates, Col. Willett, Henry Rutgers, Brockholst Livingstone, Ezekiel Robbins, Aaron Burr, etc., making the whole ticket eleven members. Mr. Livingstone observed that many of these gentlemen would not agree to serve, and that, if they should, it would not be easy to get them nominated and elected.

Mr. Burr requested the gentlemen to discuss the question in a week from that night; but he said: "Mr. Livingston, you and I can agree at once. I will agree to serve my country on this occasion, and I am sure that you will not refuse." He answered: "No; if the rest will serve." The party separated, feeling great ardor in the cause.

In the course of the week, Mr. Burr called on all the other gentlemen and, with his usual eloquence and argumentative powers, induced them all to serve. At the end of the week, the three gentlemen met according to agreement, and Mr. Burr reported the assent of all. He next proposed to call a general meeting at Tammany Hall, and said: "As soon as the room begins to fill up, I will nominate Daniel Smith as chairman, and put the question quickly. Daniel being in the chair, you must each nominate one member; I will nominate one; and Fairley, Miller, Van Wyck, and others will nominate, and Daniel must put the question quickly on the names, and, in this way, we will get them nominated. We must then have some inspiring speeches, close the meeting, and retire. We must then have a caucus, and invite some of our most active and patriotic Democrats, both young and old, appoint meetings in the different wards, select speakers to address each, and keep up frequent meetings at Tammany Hall until the election. We will put down the monster Federalism, and bring the country back to pure Democratic principles." The whole plan succeeded, and the civil revolution was brought about.

I give you an account of what took place at Mr. Livingstone's as it was related to me by Gen. Morgan Lewis, and of the after proceedings, on my own authority, I being one of the actors. I accompanied Aaron Burr to several meetings which he addressed. I was

one of those selected to address the people at Tammany Hall and
in the wards. The general election was carried on with great energy
by both parties.

Our organization was completed by dividing the city into small
districts with a committee appointed to each, whose duty it was to
canvass its district and ascertain the political opinion of each voter
by going from house to house, seeing and conversing with as many
as possible, and enquiring the politics of such as we could not see.
The district committees reported their strength at the ward meetings,
the names were called off with marginal notes stating whether good,
bad, or doubtful, so that at the general meeting, we could determine
very nearly what would be the result in the city; and the result of
the election destroyed the hydra-monster, Federalism. . . .

RECRUITING IN 1812

At about this time [about 1801], I joined Captain John Swarth-
out's artillery company, in which I served for six years. I was then
appointed lieutenant of infantry in Captain James Cheatham's company, and was, at the next meeting of the council, promoted to the
rank of captain in Colonel Van Buren's regiment. I became senior
captain of the regiment and had command of a battalion; but before
the commissions were made out for the promotions (major in my
case), I left the regiment. At the particular request of D. D. Tompkins, then governor, I became a student of military tactics, etc., under
Colonel de la Croix, and remained under his instruction for about
two years, until I was appointed captain in the United States Infantry. . . .

In 1812, the storm of the war was gathering and I decided to ask
for a commission, as I was prepared by study for the military profession. I applied for a commission in the army, referring to the
Vice President [George Clinton] and several congressmen from this
state. And, in a few days, I received a captain's commission and was
assigned to the Thirteenth Regiment of U. S. Infantry commanded by
Colonel Peter P. Schuyler.

I now entered the army with rank far beneath what I might have
had, as my friend, Governor Tompkins, told me, if I had asked the
assistance of my friends. I said that I thought my rank as high as
it should be on entering, and that I should prefer to gain my promotion by service. He told me that I would find very many above me
who would be more fit to obey than to command; and so I found
it, for great ignorance of military tactics prevailed in the new army,

and the old one was not far beyond us in field duty. However, things soon took a better aspect, for we had some educated and scientific officers, and all soon improved who were capable of improvement.

I approach, with diffidence, a sketch of my military career, as I cannot extend it so as to give a general account of the war, but must confine myself to the movements in which I myself took part.

At an interview with Colonel Schuyler, he said: "The state of New York comprises five recruiting districts; four of these will be commanded by the field officers of the regiment, and I appoint you to the command of the fifth." He then asked me if I knew of any young officer of talent who would make a good adjutant. I was pleased with the opportunity to recommend my young friend, Joseph C. Eldri[d]ge, who had been appointed an ensign, and was very desirous of being attached to my company.

I knew that a regimental appointment would, in a measure, separate us on duty; but it would place him in a more prominent position, and, perhaps, promote his interests. Eldrige was appointed. This occurred on Tuesday, and the colonel said that my instructions would be ready on Thursday, when he wished me to proceed to Charlotte, on Lake Champlain, open my orders, and proceed as directed therein. On Thursday I buckled on my sword to advance to my station to begin duty as one of the defenders of my country.

I went up the [Hudson] River accompanied by Lieutenants [Daniel] Vale and Curtis, attached to my command, and several other officers going to different stations. We arrived at Troy, and took the stage to go north, but at Skenesborough we were obliged to exchange into open wagons on account of the bad state of roads.

We went on at about the rate of one mile per hour until we arrived at Charlotte on the east bank of Lake Champlain. I now opened my orders, and found my headquarters to be at Willsborough, five miles from the west bank of the lake, which was still frozen over; but the ice was not strong enough to cross on. We stayed with Judge McNeal for two days. The judge was an old-fashioned-looking old gentleman, and rather amusing. He said that, though he had taken no part in the Revolution, some called him "Toryish," as he expressed it, but they did not trouble him much. He said that he was not very "cute" at the law, but they made him a judge for want of a better person.

On the second night that we were with him, the old judge knocked at my door, and said I must get up and go down to the lake to see the ice break up. I did as he desired, hearing a noise like that of hundreds of mills grinding. When we reached the lake shore we found all the ice in motion. It was still stuck, but jambing [jam-ming] and breaking to pieces. The noise continued all night; but, in the morning, there was no ice to be seen. Though the wind was blowing down heavily from the mountains on the other side of the lake, we had the ferrymen prepare their boat to try to pull us across. I was induced to take the helm, and by dint of luffing in the squalls, managed, at length, to get over safely.

There was a clergyman in the boat who had traveled with us from New York. He was much alarmed in crossing the lake, and in the squalls he clung to my arms, which interfered with my steering. I several times requested him to desist, but he had no command over his muscles, and could not help it. Coming up from New York, he had entered into all our amusements, but he often called us "wicked fellows." On this occasion, I told him that he would be in bad com-pany in case we should capsize while he was clinging to such a "wicked fellow."

After crossing over we had much difficulty in finding horses. At length a fine-looking young man said to me: "Sir, I am making a journey, but you may take my horse to Willsborough if you will send him back to me immediately; I will wait here until the horse is returned." I thanked him and asked: "Isn't your name McNeal?" He said: "It is." "I thought so," said I, "for I have thus far found the most obliging people in the neighborhood bearing that name."

Leaving the other gentlemen to follow, I rode to Willsborough, a little village situated on a small river. It contained a post office, a mill, a forge, a distillery, a tavern, and ten or twelve small houses. I took quarters for myself and officers at Jones's Hotel, which ap-peared quite comfortable compared with other things I saw. Vale and Curtis joined me in the course of a day, and it was soon known in the neighborhood that our party had arrived, and many people came to call upon us. Recruits came in even during the first week. I en-listed eight men, a drummer, and a fifer. Other officers soon reported for duty, and I established thirteen recruiting stations in my district under captains and lieutenants who did not know much about their duty, having just entered the service.

One of the men introduced himself as Captain [Willard] Trull, and said that he commanded a company. He was a little lame, and I told him that I thought he would find it difficult to make long marches. He replied: "I will show you how I can march," and, hold-ing his cane before his right eye, he stepped off, "dot and carry one," in good style, as he supposed. I, of course, approved. He finally, after two days, went off to his station in good spirits, leaving his liquor bill unpaid. It was brought to me, and I found that he had consumed no less than thirty gin slings. I shall have occasion to speak of Captain Trull hereafter; also, of Captain Blachley [Moses Blachly], from Long Island. The latter made a requisition on me for uniform and side arms. I told him that the arms and ammunition had not, as yet, arrived; and there was no provision for clothing and arming officers, that they had to supply themselves. He said that it was very hard, and that he would be obliged to go home and sell his little farm to raise the necessary funds. He said that it was better to do this than to resign, and requested fifteen days' leave, which I gave him. At the expiration of that time he returned armed and equipped; and, being assigned to a station, and receiving his instructions and supplies, he proceeded to duty.

In Command at Plattsburg

On my arrival at Plattsburgh, I was ordered to take charge of the arsenal and all the batteaux built on the lake. About forty were delivered to me and secured in the small harbor at the mouth of the Saranac River.

Lieutenant Curtis was there, under my orders, recruiting. I found Plattsburgh a pleasant station compared with Willsborough. The citizens were much pleased at my coming to take command, and complained that Curtis had annoyed them by marching his recruits about the streets with music at unseasonable hours of the night. This was immediately discontinued on my arrival. I received clothing and supplies from Colonel [Isaac] Clark at Burlington. I had both infantry and artillery recruits, and arms and ammunition for each. Tents were erected for the infantry; I took barracks for the artillery, and began building both.

Curtis had enlisted a man who was an excellent drummer, but a very hard drinker, and I found it difficult to keep him sober even at drills and parades. I tried many ways, but to no effect. One day I directed my first sergeant, George Helmbold, to have one hundred stones as large as a fist collected and placed three feet apart, and a basket three feet from the first stone. I then ordered him to select a man for me to pick them up one by one and place them in the basket, all within forty-five minutes. He considered a moment, then (as he had been directed) recommended Jordan, the drummer. It was after morning drill; I ordered Jordan to be called and asked him if he could do this. He said: "Yes, sir; in half the time." He began, and got on well for a time, but not quick enough to do it in the specified time. I said: "If you are behindhand, it must be done again." He now kicked off his shoes.

When he finally accomplished his task he threw himself on the ground, quite exhausted. I then asked him if he knew why I had ordered it done. He said: "No," and I told him that it was for drinking too much. He said that it would cure him, for he had rather be shot than do it again. He had walked nearly six miles, and had stooped to pick up and deposit the stones in the basket 200 times. It did cure him; at least, he became quite a sober man; and I afterwards found this to be an excellent mode of punishment. I never knew a man to do it more than once. When the army assembled, it was generally adopted as a very severe punishment.

I remained at this station from June to September, and sent 330 well-drilled men to Greenbush [near Albany]. Many singular incidents occurred in recruiting. I used to have the men practice firing at the top rail of a fence. On one occasion, I noticed that one of them went through all the motions of loading, etc., but that he did not fire. I called him to the front and ordered him to fire off his piece. On doing so, he was wheeled about, his shoulder badly bruised, and his musket flew out of his hands. He was never after afraid to fire one charge after having fired three, all at the same time. The defence of the port and public property being left to me, I organized guards, patrols, countersigns, etc. Colonel [Stephen] Thorn soon arrived with a regiment of militia.

I furnished the militia commandant with the parole and countersign, and all went well until the arrival of a large detachment of militia, of which Gen. [Benjamin] Mooers took command, but continued to quarter at his house on Cumberland Head, three miles distant. I was, one night, called by the officer of the guard, and, on going to the guardhouse, found it full of prisoners, among whom were Gen. Mooers' aids-de-camp. I released them and passed them beyond my sentinels. On the next day I was served with an order from the general to strike my tents and remove my men half a mile off, and to desist from giving out parole and countersign. I addressed the general in writing and told him that I was placed there on special duty, being ordered by the War Department to take charge of the public buildings, etc., that I should obey his orders under protest. And I requested him to appoint some officer to take charge of the public property and to attend to my other duties, recruiting, etc., as I declined to do further duty except under special order from the department.

I, however, removed my men to the place assigned. But, in the afternoon, the general called upon me, and wished to come to an understanding. I told him that I presumed that he acted under the article which says: "If the officers of the regular army and the militia meet on the march or in quarters, or on duty, the one holding the highest commission shall command the whole." He said yes, that he did.

I told him that this rule did not apply in our case, as I was on special duty, and that he was ordered to defend the frontier; that he had nothing to do with my command, and that I had no right to abandon my duty or post. I told him that I deemed a guard, etc., necessary to secure the public property, and that he had no guard established. If he would remove his headquarters to the town and establish a well-regulated guard, it would answer the purpose; or if he would authorize an officer in the village to receive the parole and countersign, I would furnish them every day. The general acknowledged that he was wrong, and wished me to resume my old station, and proceed with my duties as before. I told him that I could not do it informally, as I had obeyed his order, and answered it in writing, and both order and answer were recorded in my orderly book, and it required a written revocation of the order to be likewise recorded. This he sent me and thus the matter ended. . . .

REMINISCENCES OF THE YEAR 1812

In March, 1812, Lieutenant Valens accompanied me from New York to my recruiting rendezvous of the fifth district at Willsborough, in Essex County.

He was a fine, young officer and amiable in disposition, but he knew nothing of military tactics. I appointed him my adjutant. He was desirous of acquiring a knowledge of his duty, but when speaking of it, he used to sigh and say: "It will be of no great service to me, for I have a strong presentiment that I shall be killed in the first engagement." I used to ridicule the superstition, and endeavor to convince him of the folly of entertaining it. But it so happened that Valens was attached to the Second Battalion of the Thirteenth, and at the battle of Queenstown [October 13, 1812], when crossing from Lewiston to the attack, he was heard to be in prayer in the bow of the boat; and it was not twenty minutes after landing that he was shot down by an Indian and scalped.

George Helmbold, my first sergeant, had the same presentiment. He was of the party that crossed the Niagara River below Black Rock to storm the British batteries. At first, he supposed that he must be killed in accordance with his presentiment, but he soon found his error, for he was brave and he did his duty manfully, and he was not killed, but taken prisoner. He soon returned on parole, with others, and, being a printer, I allowed him to work in the printing office at Buffalo until exchanged. [Helmbold had been editor of the Philadelphia *Tickler*.]

At the time, the officers of the navy boasted of their exploit in taking the two British brigs from the protection of Fort Erie. The movement was made under Lieutenant Elliot [J. D. Elliott] of the navy, but the force was made up equally of soldiers and sailors. Helmbold wrote and published a paragraph giving each corps equal credit for the part it took in the exploit, and signed it, "a young soldier." Midshipman [Josiah] Tatnall called at the office to see the editor. He was absent and Helmbold was in charge.

Helmbold inquired the midshipman's business. Tatnall said: "I wish to know who is the author of a piece signed 'a young soldier.' "

"What is your object, sir?"

"Why, if he's a gentleman, I will treat him as such; and if not, I will treat him accordingly."

"Please state what, in your estimation, would entitle him to be considered a gentleman."

"Why, if he is a commissioned officer he is one, of course."

"But suppose, sir, that he is but a warrant officer like yourself."

"There are no warrant officers in the army."

"You are in error; all sergeants and corporals have warrants, and I have the honor to hold one as orderly sergeant of Captain Myers' company; and I fear, sir, if you were to know the name of the 'young soldier,' you could not treat him as a gentleman, and you must not meet him until he is promoted, and then, acting on your own principle, he will decide whether your rank will entitle you to his notice."

Tatnall went off in anger, and the matter ended.

When I joined the army at Greenbush, in September, 1812, I found the officers too democratic in their intercourse even for me, bred, as I had been, in the democratic school of Jefferson. They used to enter one another's tents, order the servants as though they were their own, and make free with the pens, ink, paper, and drinks. In fact, it was "hail fellow well met." My idea of military etiquette and politeness revolted at such a mode of life. I stated my views to a number of the most gentlemanly officers, who accorded with me in opinion. We agreed to establish a suitable system of gentlemanly etiquette and immediately put it in operation. This added greatly to our comfort, but much to the disappointment of those who had supposed that all was to be in common. But in a short time, all were pleased with the change.

The day the army moved from Greenbush, we merely crossed the river at Albany and encamped on the first night near the first turnpike gate on the road to Schenectady. During the night one of our soldiers stole from a countryman's yard an ox chain, and, at a halt on the following day, sold it. Before we reached Schenectady, one of his comrades stole it again. In fact, the chain was stolen and sold seven or eight times before the regiment reached Buffalo.

One night we chanced to encamp near a fine poultry yard. During the evening the men cooked their rations over their respective company fires. One man carefully boiled something in a camp kettle, and a man from another company, seeing feathers on the ground, suspected that fowl were cooking, and procuring a kettle from his own company, he hung it over the same fire. When the proprietor of the fowl was out of the way for a moment the man exchanged the places of the kettles, and when requested to take his rations to his own campfire, he went off with great docility, taking the kettle filled with the fowl and leaving his own filled with water.

One night, while encamping near Utica, some of the officers applied to Colonel [John] Christie for permission to go to the town, but their request was refused. In revenge, they persuaded all the soldiers, officers, and men to shave their mustaches, to the great annoyance of Colonel Christie, who had particularly desired that they should be worn.

When in command of the fifth recruiting district of Plattsburgh in July, 1812, a large body of militia came in. Two of the officers had a difference. A challenge was given and accepted, and the parties were to fight in the lake to avoid the law which disfranchised those who sent or accepted challenges in the state. The parties met according to agreement, but their friends had ingeniously arranged to load with blood instead of ball. At the given word, they fired. One of them fell and was taken out of the water by his friend, covered with blood. It was some time before he could be convinced that he was not mortally wounded.

One night, while encamped at Flint Hill, three miles from Buffalo, I had just lain down in my tent on some straw covered with a buffalo skin, the whole resting on muddy ground (for it was in October, 1812, and everything was wet on and about us, as it had been raining more or less for ten days) [when] I was called to meet the captains and subalterns of the brigade on the right of the line. Captain [George Mercer] Brooke (now General Brooke) addressed the un-

lawful assemblage nearly as follows: "Gentlemen, and fellow soldiers: we all came here to fight and to conquer the enemy, not to
remain here suffering every want and privation, under the orders of
General [Alexander] Smyth, useless to ourselves and to our country.
Six weeks I have been on the lines. My friends expected to hear from
me before this. What can they hear, but that we are living inactively
in our tents at Flint Hill in rain, mud, and want, eating grass seed
and beef without salt, wearing soiled shirts for want of soap to wash
them, and without candlelight?" Here someone observed: "Brooke,
you have no fortitude." "Have I not?" said Brooke, and putting the
forefinger of his right hand into the blaze of the company fire before
us, he held it there until it was deeply burned.

"Now, gentlemen," said he, "I propose that each captain take full
command of his company, and that the senior captain of the brigade
lead us to, and across the river, that we may take Fort Erie by storm,
proceed to Chippeway, and thence to Fort George and take that; and
leave General Smyth to sleep the night out in his snug quarters."

All, for different reasons, agreed to this. The paymaster of the
Fifth said: "Gentlemen, General [Thomas] Parker, my relative, is
in camp, and I have no doubt that, if a deputation calls upon him,
he will join us and lead us on to glory."

Accordingly, Brooke, three others, and I were appointed. We
moved towards his marquee. But a private message was sent to
General Parker to inform him of what was going on. The general
received us very kindly, approved of the plan, and ordered refreshments. The effect of good, old brandy was to make the gentlemen
very drowsy. They drank freely, and soon the whole mutiny and expedition were forgotten; and General Parker, an excellent man, never
mentioned it, I believe, and it passed off harmlessly. . . .

One night we encamped in a swamp. Lieut. J. C. Eldridge and I
mounted a barrel of whiskey back to back for a lodging. In about
an hour I heard a noise, and, looking around, I found that the men
were pulling Eldridge out of the fire. It appeared that when we were
both asleep, I overbalanced him and he fell into the fire. Fortunately,
he was not much burned.

When encamped at Cumberland Head, Lake Champlain, I was
walking on the bank one morning and I saw a soldier lying in a fire
on the beach. I jumped down about eight feet and pulled him out,
a little burned. He was not entirely sober, but he thanked me and
walked off. Some years after he came to my office in Wall Street,
New York, related the circumstance, and said that I had, no doubt,

saved his life. It is a great happiness to have it in our power to
save a life.

I had a soldier named Clark who was a noted thief. While encamped at Northfields, near Champlain, Clinton County, he robbed
the sutler of the Fourteenth Regiment of all his goods, valued at
$1,400. He gave away most of the goods. He was detected, tried, and
condemned to have his pay stopped to make good what he had taken;
and when the paymaster was paying the men, he would come to me
with tears in his eyes and beg me for a dollar. I always gave it to
him. He was an excellent soldier in all other respects, but he was by
nature a thief. Poor, weak human nature! We require discipline and
firmness to resist our natural propensities.

It would naturally be supposed that, if any class of men is free
from superstition, it is sailors and soldiers; but, as a rule, I have
found the latter to be much under the influence of it. I had in my
company a young Irishman whose bravery was never doubted; but
while I was commanding the cantonment at Williamsville, in the
winter of 1812, a report was one morning current that O'Bryan had
seen the devil, when on post at the sally port leading to the graveyard. Fearing that others might feel alarmed on going on the same
post, I sent for O'Bryan and said to him: "It is said that you saw
the devil last night when on post." He turned very pale and said: "I
do not know whether it was the devil, but something black, about the
size of a horse without a head, came rolling towards me. I challenged,
but received no answer. It was light, and I plainly saw it still approaching. I sighted my piece to fire, but lost my strength and fell
back against the cantonment, where the relief soon after found me."

I said: "Are you afraid to go on the same post, at the same hour
tonight with me? Perhaps we may find that there was no devil, but
your own fear of spirits." He said: "Sir, I have never known fear,
and I am willing to go with or without you, but I should prefer to
have you go with me." I went, and we remained on post two hours.
But the black devil in the shape of a horse without a head did not
renew his visit, and my having been on post with O'Bryan was known
to all the command, and it satisfied all that they might go on that
post without meeting "His Satanic Majesty."

At the formation of the American Army of 1812, there was a great
rush for appointments. Many desired to join it from high-minded notions of national honor, or patriotism; others from motives of pride
and love of military show and splendor, and many for employment
and pay. Many were recommended by members of Congress without
much regard to their qualifications for command; so that at the re-

cruiting service, and the assemblage of the troops at Greenbush, in the autumn of 1812, we found a gathering of heterogeneous characters bearing commissions, men taken from every grade of society, from the highest to the lowest. But all felt the same pride. The most ignorant were the most jealous of their honor, so far, at least, as to take offence at the least circumstance or even word that seemed to them to reflect on their courage.

Challenges to single combat were of frequent occurrance. There are, occasionally, insults offered, or injuries inflicted for which the law affords no satisfaction; and it then becomes necessary for a man to take the matter into his own hands. But in most cases, duels are fought for trifling wrongs, or imaginary offences, and promoted by injudicious friends of the parties, from false pride and a desire to become conspicuous in such matters; when in ten cases out of twelve the affairs might be amicably adjusted by well-disposed friends, and so save the lives and the honor of well-meaning but hot headed men. It was my lot to be engaged in several affairs of the kind both before and after I became an officer in the regular army, and I look back with great satisfaction at many differences amicably arranged between those who, without a friend so disposed, would have lost their lives in silly combat, or have taken the lives of their opponents.

But in some few cases of aggravated controversies, I did not succeed in making settlements, and duels resulted. . . . In a few cases challenges were refused, and the person refusing was justified by the whole army.

When the army lay at Fort George, Upper Canada, in 1813, Lieut. Col. Winfield Scott was ordered out with a command of men to the head of Lake Ontario to take or destroy the British public stores at Burlington Bay, in which enterprise he was particularly successful. Colonel Homer Milton considered that as he ranked Scott, the command belonged to him. A correspondence took place which resulted in a challenge from Colonel Milton. Scott declined in words to this effect:

"I have no personal difference with Colonel Milton. If a command has been given to me in preference to him, he should apply to the commanding general who directed his adjutant general to give me the order. But if the colonel desires to test my courage, I prefer to show it to him in the face of the enemy when we are at the head of our respective commands." . . .

ON THE NIAGARA FRONT

We passed the winter of 1812-13 camping at Flint Hills, and marching to Buffalo and Black Rock and back. The troops suffered very much for want of provisions and clothing suitable to the climate. We built comfortable log barracks, but we lost by death through the winter some 300 men. My company and that of Captain Morgan marched to and from Buffalo twenty times during the winter. Old Colonel [Moses] Porter, known as "Blow hard," commanded. He frequently dreamed that there was an attack on Buffalo, and we were ordered to march from comfortable cantonments at Williamsville, eleven miles from Buffalo. And when there after a march, the tracks of which could be traced by the blood from the feet of the men (for they were nearly all barefooted), we were compelled to encamp in the streets, being unable to procure quarters.

Early in April [1813], the whole army was marched to the [Niagara] River to perform drill in order, first, to keep the militia from rebellion, and second, to storm the batteries on the British side of Niagara, both of which were effected. A brigade of Pennsylvania militia was mutinous, and even threatened to take General Smith [Alexander Smyth], our commander, out of camp. We formed [a] line of battle, on one occasion, expecting an attack from them. We soon left Camp Rock and returned to the cantonment at Williamsville. We remained there for a few days; then the whole force marched to Black Rock across the Niagara River and stormed the batteries on the British side. I was ordered to General Smith's quarters, where I found a number of officers assembled.

The general stated that we were to cross in three divisions, at twelve o'clock, and storm the batteries on the margin of the river. He asked me how many men I reported for duty. I answered, eighty. He said he would give me seventy more and an additional subaltern, and I was to have three boats. The general [a Virginian] remarked: "Virginia will not complain tonight." Most of the officers present were Virginians, and he thought me to be one also by my name. We were dismissed and we found our respective commands; but the boats were full of ice and water, and deficient in oars. It was near daylight before we moved. We stormed the batteries with a small loss, and took a number of prisoners. But, the enemy having received a large re-enforcement from Fort Erie, we were compelled to recross the river, leaving a small detachment behind, which was captured.

Among those taken was my first sergeant, George Helmbold, who had separated from my command in the bustle of retreat. He had a presentiment that, he should be killed in the first engagement, and he told me afterwards that finding, after a few shots had been exchanged, that he still lived, he gave up his superstition, and was ever after a brave man. After our return, General [William H.] Winder was ordered to cross with his brigade, but the fire was so brisk that he could not effect a landing. The prisoners taken from us were marched to Fort George and examined by Colonel Myers of the British Army. Helmbold had held prisoner, during the night, a British sergeant, and imprudently, as well as unmilitarily, had taken his sword and belt. The sergeant was missing, and it was reported that Helmbold had killed him, while a prisoner, and taken his sword and belts. The colonel asked him his regiment, and the name of his captain. Helmbold said that he belonged to the Thirteenth Regiment, and Captain Myers' Company. The colonel enquired particularly about the size, complexion, and appearance of his commander, and then said: "I know your captain; he is a British deserter, and I should like to see him." The sergeant replied: "Perhaps, sir, you may meet him by and by"; and so he did, for at the taking of Newark and Fort George, Colonel Myers was wounded and taken prisoner.

A few days after the battle, in company with some of the officers, I visited the British prisoners. The moment my name was mentioned, Colonel Myers related the above, and said: "I expressed a wish to see you, but not under the present circumstances. I am mistaken; you are not the deserter." Then he said: "Your sergeant is a brave fellow. He would have been condemned to be shot, had it not been for the wife of the missing British sergeant who, hearing the charges against Helmbold, came down to Fort George to say that her husband was wounded and taken to a hut, where he then was; but that he had not been ill used by Sergeant Helmbold further than having been deprived of his side arms and belt. This saved Helmbold's life."

The expedition thus ended, we marched to our cantonments at Williamsville. . . .

Wounded by a Musket Ball

Our line of battle was soon formed, and the battle of Williamsburg, or Chrysler's Field, began [November 11, 1813]. . . . Being senior captain, my command was in the rear nearest to the enemy and the field of battle. In a few minutes, Col. N. Pinkney, aide to General [James] Wilkinson, who was at that time sick on board of his vessel, directed me to form my guard and march to the field. I immediately formed, eighty-six strong, including one of my pilots who volunteered (a fine fellow he was).

When we approached General [John Parker] Boyd near the field, he said: "Rush on, my 'jolly snorters,' you are wanted." Before forming into line, I halted a moment to let my men go into action coolly.

Giving them a few directions, I marched them into line. We met Colonel [Jonas] Cutting with his regiment helter-skelter, just broken out of line. "Colonel," said I, "where are you going?" Said he: "My men will not stand." "But," said I, "you are leading them." They went off to the boats, and I took the place of the regiment with my little detachment of eighty-six. I soon saw Major [Richard Montgomery] Malcom and got permission to take position in a field on the enemy's right flank, where my "buck and ball" told well. My position was within 200 yards of the right flank; my men kneeled on the left knee behind a stone wall about two feet high. I was already wounded by a musket ball passing through my left arm two inches below the socket. I received the wound while advancing, and, no doubt from excitement, believed it to be a chip that struck my arm. Both armies made several attempts to charge bayonets; but, as is almost always the case excepting when storming batteries, when one side charged the other fell back, and vice versa.

At the beginning of the action, we had two pieces of field artillery under Lieutenant Smith on the river road on our left. They were taken by the enemy, and Smith and his men all killed. I did not know that they were taken until the battle was over, although I saw a detachment of dragoons wheel up to them, fire their pistols, wheel again, and retreat on receiving a fire. I supposed it to be a British attack, but found, afterwards, it was an attempt to retake the pieces by Lieut. Col. [Lt. William Jenkins?] Worth; but it was a complete failure. Our line was now out of ammunition for a short time, sixty-four rounds having been expended. The enemy formed in line and gave my little detachment a galling fire until again diverted in front. The ground was well-contested for four hours on plain, open ground, then the firing ceased on both sides.

There were 1,500 Americans against 2,200 of the enemy. [Actually, 2,000 Americans and 800 British.] My wound being very painful on account of the pressure of my coat on the swelling arm, I gave the command of my sixty-three men, twenty-three having been killed, to my First Lieutenant [William, Jr.] Anderson. Our troops were returning to the boats, the enemy having fallen back. Believing the field pieces before mentioned to be in the hands of our people, I

walked towards them, intending to return to the boats by the road;
I was very near when I discovered the British uniforms. I immediately turned and walked leisurely towards the retiring troops. They
did not fire at me or pursue me until I rose from a ravine; they then
fired, and one shot was returned by my servant, Williams, who was
seeking me at some distance among the dead. He did not suspect
that it was I, as he had heard that I was among the killed. It was
with great difficulty, with the use of only one hand, that I got out
of the ravine. I fell in with a man who had a horse and a keg of
ammunition; I took the horse, and finally reached the boats. The
horse was led part of the way by a camp woman. The loss in killed
and wounded on both sides was not less than 800, about equally
divided. The result is not generally understood by our people, and it
is as often called a defeat as a victory. . . .

This put an end to the campaign. We encamped at the junction
of Salmon Creek and the St. Lawrence for some time. The place is
now known as Fort Covington, named for General [Leonard] Covington, who was killed at Chrysler's Field.

I was invited to take up my quarters at the house of Dr. Mann.
I procured a horse, which was led by my faithful servant Williams.
When we arrived at Hitchcock's Tavern, we met a small party at
dinner, among them Miss Charlotte Bailey of Plattsburgh, your
mother, who was then visiting her uncle, Dr. Mann. I finally reached
Dr. Mann's house, where I had a comfortable room, and was shown
every attention by the family. General Wilkinson and several other
officers stopped at the doctor's house for a few days on their way
to Malone.

My wound had been neglected, and I had taken a severe cold by
remaining on duty. A fever ensued, and I suffered everything but
death. At one time, the doctor feared that he could not save me. The
army fell back on Plattsburgh early in December, and in March
[1814], I was so far recovered as to be able to follow.

In this month I was married to Charlotte, daughter of Judge William Bailey. I was then under orders to proceed as a witness before
a court-martial sitting at New York for the trial of General [Edmund
Pendleton] Gaines. When at New York my order was extended at
my request, by Governor [Daniel D.] Tompkins, allowing me to go
to Washington to settle my recruiting accounts. I returned to Plattsburgh in the beginning of April [1814]. . . .

We went into winter quarters and spent the winter of 1814 in
tents. In the spring [1815], General [Jacob J.] Brown told me that
I was entitled to promotion, that he would send me to New York on

special duty, to return by way of Plattsburgh, at which place I was
to take command of the companies of the Thirteenth and march them
to the regiments. On my arrival at Plattsburgh, I reported to General
[Alexander] Macomb. He said that he would add a company to the
two of the Thirteenth and give me the command as a battalion. But
he suggested that I might like to go to Franklin County for a time,
as my wife was there visiting Dr. Mann, and I could procure valuable information there respecting the intended movements of the
enemy in that direction, and in Upper Canada. I went there and frequently rode to St. Regis and over the line, and I procured much
valuable information at the risk of a halter for a neckcloth.

I returned to Plattsburgh and reported to General Macomb. His
battalion was not yet formed, and I remained there in camp until
the news of peace was received [February, 1815]. The men enlisted
to serve eighteen months and, therefore, during the war, were to be
discharged. But no money had been provided to pay the armies.

They were mutinous, and many of the companies refused to obey
their officers. Among them, the two companies of the Thirteenth
claimed their pay and discharge, and when ordered to unstack arms,
they disobeyed their officers to a man. I was called upon to address
them. I reminded them of their services, and called on them not to
tarnish the honor they had won by duty and discipline. I told them
to continue to obey orders and to keep up the usual discipline for
which the regiment had been noted, and that as soon as funds were
received by the paymasters they should be paid, and such as were
entitled to it should receive their honorable discharge.

I now gave the word: "Unstack arms." They complied, and I
marched them over to the artillery, who were under arms. We there
drummed out of camp all who disobeyed the orders of their officers,
and many of those who regretted their disobedience were restored
at my suggestion. In June, a board of officers was formed at Washington to reduce the army to a peace establishment, and a rule was
made that *none but effective officers should be retained*. All who had
been wounded or disabled should be discharged with an allowance
of three months' gratuitous pay, reversing [the] common sense and
common justice rule that all who had been wounded or disabled
should be retained to form skeleton regiments, which could at any
time be filled with recruits.

Many of the officers petitioned to be retained, and some were
retained and reduced one grade. Many of us met and determined,
after debate, that as we had seen service and done our duty, we
would neither petition to be retained, nor accept with reduced rank.

At the request of the colonel, I remained on duty with my regiment until September. I then went to Washington to close my accounts. Paymaster General Brant [Robert Brent] refused, at first, to pay me beyond the fourteenth of June. After considerable difficulty, I obtained pay to the tenth day of September, in Pittsburgh banknotes, which sold at eleven percent discount at New York. So I lost eleven percent on eleven months' pay. Thus were we rewarded.

A New Start in New York

I now returned to private life at the age of thirty-eight. After having settled my accounts at Washington, I returned to Plattsburgh and procured board for my wife and child (my daughter Henrietta) at John Palmer's. I then went to New York with about $100 to begin the world anew. After several weeks, and with much difficulty, I became engaged in the auction business.

I was aided by a friend for whom I had laid the foundation of a fortune which he had realized during my absence. My prospects looked encouraging, when a former lieutenant of my regiment, Charles Mitchell, called upon me for aid. He was destitute of means to pay even his board. I gave him what help I could, promising to pay his necessary expenses until he could procure a situation. He repaid me by robbing me and forging my name for three checks, two of which were on the Manhattan Bank. They could not determine whether the checks were forgeries or not. I had great trouble, and nearly lost my reputation, always dearer to me than money.

Mitchell, to divert my attention from himself, wrote me threatening letters, saying that he had once been in my power and that I had tyrannized over him, that I was now in his power, and that he had robbed me, forged three of my checks, would forge more, would ruin me, and perhaps take my life. He forged checks of Dr. Silas Lord, was detected, confessed all to me, and was sentenced by Judge Radcliffe, a friend of his family, to leave the state and never return.

The discharged soldiers were continually calling on me for advice in respect to their claims for back pay, pensions, and bounty lands. Several agencies commenced the business, and I among the rest. I arranged to co-operate with Col. Joseph Watson, who opened an office at Washington, and we did a large business together in that way. I went on quite prosperously, and in 1817 took and furnished a small house in Walker Street, went to Plattsburgh, and brought down my wife. We lived there for some time, then removed to the corner of Canal and Mercer streets; we remained there two years, then removed to a three-story house in Canal Street, where we lived until 1825, when I bought the house number 45 Mercer Street and remained there until I bought Judge Vanderpool's place at Kinderhook.

I was elected a member of the Assembly at New York in 1828, re-elected in 1830 for '31, again for '32, '33, and '34 (in '29 I was not elected). I was once nominated assistant alderman, and once alderman of the eighth ward; I declined both nominations. The year after I removed to Kinderhook [Martin Van Buren's home town] (1834), I was elected president of the village. During the time of my office, I received and addressed Martin Van Buren when Vice President, and again [in 1841] on his return at the end of his term as President.

I have now brought this sketch of the principal events of my long life to a period from which you are all acquainted. I have been as brief as possible, though sufficiently tedious to those not personally interested. I have omitted a great variety of incidents arising out of the events of the war, as not material in this sketch of my life.

I have no memoranda to aid my memory, and this accounts for the omission of particular dates.

Uriah Phillips Levy

Stormy Petrel of the Navy

Uriah P. Levy (1792-1862), the son of a Philadelphia merchant, a fourth- or fifth-generation American, ran away to sea at the age of ten. Before he was twenty, he was master and part owner of a ship. When the War of 1812 broke out, he joined the United States Navy and started to work his way to the top. Before he died he was a flag officer, a "commodore," in charge of the Mediterranean squadron. At that time, there was no higher rank in the United States Navy.

The task of making a career for himself in the American Navy was by no means easy. Rising from the ranks, he was resented as an interloper. Later on, as he acquired money, his wealth was held against him, and there were many of his associates who did not want him on board ship because he was a Jew.

Levy was not the man to go out of his way to placate his fellow-officers. He was a hard-bitten sailor, independent, sensitive, vain, prepared to fight at the least provocation. Many times he was miserably unhappy, snubbed or ignored by the officers in the ward-room. The trouble he experienced is reflected in the grim fact that between the years 1818 and 1857 he was court-martialed six times and faced courts of inquiry twice.

In 1857, when he appeared before the second Court of Inquiry, he was fighting for his official life, seeking to be restored to the navy lists from which he had recently been dropped. In 1855, he and dozens of other officers had been rather unceremoniously dumped by the navy. Levy was convinced that, in his case, the reviewing board had been motivated by anti-Jewish sentiment. There is no question that some of the men on the "Board of Fifteen," which sat in judgment on him in 1855, did not like him. Some no doubt were anti-Jewish, but the evidence is insufficient to prove that he was dropped from active service solely because he was a Jew.

Levy was doggedly determined to remain in the navy and as a man of wealth was able to hire the best of counsel. Two of his lawyers were men of national repute: Benjamin F. Butler, of New York, a member of President Andrew Jackson's cabinet, who must not be confused with "Beast" Butler of New Orleans fame, and Philip Phillips, the famous Washington lawyer, a Jew. The fighting captain won his appeal, was reinstated, and soon celebrated his victory by marrying a very young girl. The groom was then over sixty!

In spite of the fact that Levy led a most adventurous life, he wrote no autobiography. In his defense before the court in 1857, however, he found it advisable, on occasion, to tell the story of his life. Those autobiographical portions in the manuscript proceedings of the Court of Inquiry, now in the National Archives in Washington, have been excerpted and published below, having been compared with typed and printed copies of the record. The latter appeared as the Defense of Uriah P. Levy, *etc. (New York, 1858). One interpolation has been made: the material on the "tar-and-feathers case" has been taken directly from the records of the 1842 court-martial, not from the recapitulation in the proceedings of 1857.*

Levy's career is fascinating, as the record reveals. He was a man of great energy and ability. During the years that he was without a ship and on the inactive list, he made a fortune, part of which he used to pay homage to his beloved hero, Thomas Jefferson. Levy bought and improved Monticello, Jefferson's old Virginia home, and gave to the United States government a fine statue of the great democrat, which had been prepared by the French sculptor, David d'Angers.

In spite of the fact that Levy was court-martialed for what was considered "scandalous and cruel conduct" toward a sailor, he was a consistent opponent of flogging in the navy. Before he died, he left testamentary instructions that the following inscription be carved on his tombstone: "Father of the law for the abolition of the barbarous practice of corporal punishment in the Navy of the United States." Historians may well question the accuracy of the epitaph which Levy himself dictated, but there is no question that he strove to accomplish the abolition of flogging in the naval service.

His career illustrates the difficulties which not only he, but others of his faith, as Jews, were to encounter in the armed services of their country. It is unfortunately true that he was frequently the victim of religious bigotry. What is equally true is the fact that, in his case, the authorities at Washington helped him surmount that prejudice. This is not only a tribute to him, but equally a tribute to the spirit of democratic Americanism and fair play, which animated Presidents, Congress, and the majority of his superior officers.

INTRODUCTION

M R. PRESIDENT AND GENTLEMEN OF THE COURT:

I rejoice, for you as well as for myself, that you have at length reached the last stage of this long and wearisome investigation, and I thank you, in all sincerity, for the close and deliberate attention you have already given to my part of it. This has necessarily covered a large tract of time, and included a great number of details. For, as the testimony of the government goes back more than forty years, and seeks from this early date to impeach my character and conduct, personal and professional, so I have been compelled, in self-defence, to spread before you the history of my whole life, and to present to your view every feature of my character. It was impossible to do this without making heavy draughts on your time and attention. For the readiness and good will with which these demands have been met, I again tender you my thanks. . . .

THE TRAINING OF A SEAMAN

I was born in the city of Philadelphia, and my earliest recollections are connected with the waters and the shipping of that port. Impelled by a strong passion for the sea, I sought and procured, in 1802, and before I had completed my eleventh year, the place of cabin boy on board a coasting vessel, and in this capacity, but in different vessels, I continued for two years; and, I am sorry to say, without the consent, and except as to the general fact that I had gone to sea, without the knowledge of my excellent parents. Returning to them at the age of twelve, they yielded to my wishes to become a sailor by profession and, to ensure proficiency in my calling, my father apprenticed me, in 1806, for four years, to Mr. John Coulter, a most respectable merchant and shipowner, in one or other of whose vessels I sailed at different times between 1806 and 1810. A great part of my apprenticeship was passed under the eye of Captain James Maffet, than whom no man in the profession stood higher.

In 1808, during the embargo [because of the Napoleonic wars],

78

Mr. Coulter's ships were unemployed, but I had so far secured his good opinion that he placed me in the best naval school in the city. I attended it for nine months, studying not only navigation, but drawing and other kindred branches. When the carrying trade was partially opened, I again went to sea, and continued in active service until the expiration of my indentures [of my apprenticeship] in 1810. I was then second mate of the brig "Polly and Betsey," belonging to Mr. Coulter, and commanded by Captain John Silsby, also an experienced commander.

Having served out the full term of my apprenticeship, I was employed for five voyages as first mate of the brig "Five Sisters" and saved enough from my wages and from small ventures on my own account to purchase, in October, 1811, one third of the schooner "George Washington," of which I took command as master. I had thus passed through every grade of service: cabin boy, ordinary seaman, able seaman, boatswain, third, second, and first mate, to that of captain before the completion of the twentieth year of my age.

In the "George Washington" I continued as master until January, 1812. In that month, being on shore on the isle of May [Scotland] and my vessel lying in the open roadstead with $2,500 in Spanish dollars and fourteen casks of Teneriffe wine on board, she was piratically run away with by a part of my crew, the mate and one of the mariners being the ringleaders in the crime. I was left penniless, but succeeded in reaching the United States, where I obtained the requisite documents and material aid to return to the West Indies in pursuit of my vessel. After going from one island to another, I at length heard that one of the seamen had been murdered by the mate and his accomplices, that the vessel had been scuttled, and that the survivors, the two ringleaders and the cook, after dividing the money between them, had fallen into the hands of the local authorities of St. Lucia.

I found them there and caused them to be arrested and conveyed to the United States. Being first brought into the district of Massachusetts, the two principals were indicted for their crime at Boston, and on the testimony of the cook and other corroborating circumstances, were convicted and sentenced to be hung. One of them was pardoned by President [James] Madison; the other suffered the extreme penalty of the law. . . .

In numerous instances in the course of the evidence, references were made by the witnesses to the minuteness and perfection of my nautical attainments, as evidently showing that I had been a practical seaman before I entered the navy. The testimony of Lieutenants

[Peter] Turner, [Edmund] Lanier, and [J. N.] Maffit abounded with such references. In view of the testimony above cited and of the many proofs of my professional experience and knowledge which have been laid before you, I shall not, I trust, be charged with vanity, when I say that by means of my ten years' experience and instruction afloat and ashore, I had become familiar with every part of my profession, from the sculling of a jolly boat to the navigation of the largest vessel, from the boxing of the compass to the taking of the magnetic altitude of the sun, from the splicing of a rope to the fishing of a mainmast, from the holding of a reel to the heaving of a ship in a gale of wind. . . .

ON ACTIVE DUTY

I entered the Navy of the United States at the age of twenty as a sailing master, my warrant bearing date October 23d, 1812. In the preceding month of June, war had been declared by the United States against Great Britain. From my long service on shipboard, I was no stranger to those acts of lawless violence which forced us into the conflict. I had been an eyewitness of more than one of those outrages upon men, bearing the protection, and sailing under the flag, of the United States, which, at length, aroused the nation to the necessity of waging the second war of independence.

In 1809 I was, myself, for about a month, a forced and most unwilling victim of this insolence and oppression, having been taken by the press gang of a British sloop of war, while lawfully employed on shore, in the island of Tortola [Virgin Islands], and directly transferred to that ship, on board of which I was kept until I succeeded in getting my case before Admiral Sir Alexander Cochrane. This distinguished and noblehearted commander, on inspecting my protection and the duplicate of my indentures, which were fortunately in my possession, ordered me to be released and to be paid for my services.

Thirteen years afterwards, being in Paris, a lieutenant in the Navy of the United States and bearer of despatches from my government to its minister at the Court of France, I had the opportunity of meeting him in that city and of renewing to him the expression of my gratitude for the justice he had rendered to an American youth, who, but for his interposition, might perhaps have been compelled to drag out toilsome and joyless years in the service of his oppressors, or even to shed his blood in battle against his countrymen.

In the general desire of the American people to avenge, on the

NEW YORK CITY IN 1839

(see page 74)

MAJOR RAPHAEL J. MOSES
(see page 148)

highway of nations and in sight of mankind, the wrongs we had suffered, and to vindicate, in the same theatre and presence, the rights of our citizens and the honor of our flag, I largely participated; and to this object I resolved to dedicate whatever of physical prowess and of professional experience and knowledge I possessed.

Feeling properly qualified for the post of sailing master in the navy, I solicited, at the earliest practicable moment after the breaking out of the war, an appointment to that post, and on furnishing to President Madison the requisite proofs of my fitness, received shortly afterwards my warrant. I sought this particular position, in the belief that my nautical education and experience would enable me to render greater service to my country in this post than in that of a midshipman, the grade in which the naval service is usually entered.

The latter was the more conspicuous and attractive place, and it presented the only sure prospect of early promotion. But a sailing master is indispensable to the equipment of a ship of war, and in battle he is as much exposed as any other officer or man. I feel, therefore, that in thus giving up, in the hour of public danger, an eligible position in the merchant service for one in the navy, affording little prospect of promotion, and none of gain, I furnished the best proof my circumstances permitted of love to my country and of zeal in her cause. My appointment to this responsible post by President Madison at a juncture so critical would be, in itself, were no other evidence before you, conclusive proof of my fitness for its duties, physical, mental, professional, and moral.

My first public service was on board the sloop of war "Alert," in the harbor of New York, where I remained until June, 1813. I then joined the brig "Argus," under the command of Captain William Henry Allen, of Rhode Island, and sailed in her to France with our minister, Mr. [William H.] Crawford. During the voyage, I had the good fortune to gain the confidence and friendship of this eminent and most upright man, of which, in after years, I received many valuable proofs. Having landed him at L'Orient [France], the ship, in pursuance of the orders originally given to her commander, immediately began her memorable cruise in the British and Irish channels.

My service on board of her, from the time of our departure from New York, was full of interest and afforded the best possible opportunities of instruction. Her commander was in the freshness and vigor of early manhood, accomplished in his profession, and one of the bravest and most generous of men. His first and second lieutenants, William Henry Watson, of Virginia, and William Howard Allen, of New York, in professional skill and every manly virtue were his fit associates. Three nobler spirits were never banded together in the service of their country, that service to which each of them, at his appointed hour, yielded up his life.

I was not the regular sailing master of the ship; that post was filled by Sailing Master Hudson. Preferring active duty at sea to harbor duty, knowing that the cruise of the "Argus" could not fail to be a stirring one, and hoping that she might meet the enemy in such circumstances as to permit a battle, I sought and obtained permission to join her as a volunteer. When about two weeks out, Captain Allen appointed me an acting lieutenant, and in this latter capacity I served during the remainder of the cruise.

I had not the privilege of taking part in the fatal but glorious conflict of the fourteenth of August, 1813, in which the "Argus" was overcome by a vessel much her superior, her commander being mortally, and her first lieutenant severely, wounded, because on the preceding day I was placed with a prize crew in command of a British ship and cargo, whose great value induced Captain Allen to entrust her to me, in the hope she might be run into one of the French ports. The attempt failed, the prize being soon fallen in with and recaptured by a British frigate. With my crew I was, therefore, soon after reunited to my surviving comrades of the "Argus" and detained with them in England more than sixteen months, as a prisoner of war. In December, 1814, we were sent home in a cartel [prisoner-exchange] ship. Our voyage was a very long one; before our arrival at Norfolk [Virginia], news of the peace had been received, and the survivors of the "Argus" were deprived of all further opportunity of active war service.

All the officers of the "Argus" capable of speaking of the manner in which I performed my duties on board that vessel have been long dead. But from the known character of Capt. Allen, it may safely be inferred that they were performed efficiently and to his satisfaction, or he would not have appointed me, as already mentioned, an active lieutenant. At any rate, [he] would not have retained me in that post, as he did, during the cruise in the British seas. In this capacity it was my special duty to board and destroy the prizes captured by the "Argus," and in a majority of the cases, this responsible, and in many instances difficult and sometimes dangerous, service was actually performed by me. Still less would my commander, in the single case in which, under the discretion given to him by his orders, he attempted to send a prize ship into port,

have placed me in command of her, had not the confidence implied
in such a trust been fairly won by my good conduct and efficiency. . . .

MY PARENTS WERE ISRAELITES

In 1816, I was assigned to the "Franklin," seventy-four [guns],
as second sailing master, and in that vessel and capacity I served
under Commodore [Charles] Stewart until March, 1817, when I was
appointed a lieutenant, still, however, remaining in the same ship.
My conduct in her in both capacities received, as you know from his
testimony, the approbation of my distinguished commander. My
promotion to a lieutenancy was mainly founded on the strong recommendations of Commodore Stewart and all the officers of the
"Franklin." . . .

This promotion, though not in the ordinary course, was authorized
by a standing resolution of the Board of Navy Commissioners then
in force, in the following words:

Masters of extraordinary merit, and for extraordinary services,
may be promoted to lieutenants.

It was under this resolution that I obtained my promotion. Being
first recommended by the Navy Commissioners to the Secretary [of
the Navy Benjamin W. Crowninshield], I was by him named to the
President [James Monroe], who thereupon, by nomination to the
Senate, and with the approbation of that body, appointed me lieutenant. I refer with conscious pride to this part of my history. It
shows that my transfer from what is commonly a permanent position
to the line of regular promotion was not the gift of blind patronage
or of irresponsible power, but the intelligent and discriminating
reward of my superiors.

The commissioners who gave me this testimonial were John Rodgers, Stephen Decatur, and David Porter. In this place, it were needless to dilate on their character or services. Their fame is the boast
of their profession, a cherished portion of their country's glory.
Perfectly acquainted with the necessities of the service, thoroughly
devoted to its interests, jealously sensitive to everything connected
with its honor, elevated far above the approach of undue influence,
and incapable of favoritism, the action, in my case, of these great
commanders must be taken as the spontaneous and impartial tribute
to what they, at least, thought "extraordinary merit" and "extraordinary services." In my eyes, at least, it gives additional value to their
recommendation, that two of them had risen to their high places

in the navy and in the admiration of their countrymen from the same humble grade in the merchant service in which my own career was begun.

Sailing Master Trent was promoted to a lieutenancy at the same time with me; he was placed by the department at the head, and I next to him, of the list of lieutenants appointed with us. This distinction, though most grateful to my feelings as the fair reward of my services, increased the disfavor with which certain officers in the navy looked upon my promotion. And with the prejudice generated by the promotion itself, there was also mingled another of earlier date and greater intensity, and to which, as it plays a most active though at times a concealed part in my personal history, it is necessary I should now refer.

My parents were Israelites, and I was nurtured in the faith of my ancestors. In deciding to adhere to it, I have but exercised a right guaranteed to me by the Constitutions of my native state and of the United States, a right given to all men by their Maker, a right more precious to each of us than life itself. But, while claiming and exercising this freedom of conscience, I have never failed to acknowledge and respect the like freedom in others. I might safely defy the citation of a single act, in the whole course of my official career, injurious to the religious rights of any other person.

Remembering always that the great mass of my fellow-citizens were Christians, profoundly grateful to the Christian founders of our republic for their justice and liberality to my long-persecuted race, I have earnestly endeavored, in all places and circumstances, to act up to the wise and tolerant spirit of our political institutions. I have therefore been careful to treat every Christian, and especially every Christian under my command, with exemplary justice and ungrudging liberality. Of this you have had clear proof, so far as my command of the "Vandalia" is concerned, from the lips of Lieutenants Lanier and Maffit.

I have to complain—more in sorrow than in anger do I say it—that in my official experience I have met with little to encourage, though with much to frustrate, these conciliatory efforts. At an early day, and especially from the time when it became known to the officers of my age and grade that I aspired to a lieutenancy, and still more after I had gained it, I was forced to encounter a large share of the prejudice and hostility by which, for so many ages, the Jew has been pursued. I need not speak to you of the incompatibility of these sentiments with the genius of Christianity or the precepts of its Author. You should know this far better than I, but I may ask you to unite with the wisest and best men of our own country and of Europe in denouncing them, not only as injurious to the peace and welfare of the community, but as repugnant to every dictate of reason, humanity, and justice.

THE OFFICERS' CONSPIRACY

In February, 1818, I was transferred by Commodore Stewart from his ship, the "Franklin," seventy-four, to the frigate "United States," under the command of Captain [W. N.] Crane. Under the influence of the double prejudice to which I have alluded, a conspiracy was formed among certain officers of the frigate "United States" to prevent my reception in her. Commodore [Thomas ap Catesby] Jones, in answer to the eighth interrogatory on my part, gives a full account of this conspiracy. He says:

Lieutenant Levy, for several months, was fourth and first lieutenant of the frigate "United States," where he discharged his duty satisfactorily to the captain as well as to the first lieutenant, notwithstanding his advent into our ship was attended with such novel and discouraging circumstances as, in justice to Captain Levy, renders it necessary here to record them.

On the arrival of the "Franklin," of seventy-four guns, at Syracuse [Sicily], in 1818, bearing the broad pendant of Commodore Charles Stewart, to relieve Commodore [Isaac] Chauncey, then in command of the Mediterranean Squadron, it was understood that Lieutenant Levy, a supernumerary on board the "Franklin," was to be ordered to the frigate "United States," then short of her complement of lieutenants. Whereupon, the wardroom mess, without consulting me, determined to remonstrate against Levy's coming aboard.

I was called on by a member of the mess to communicate these wishes to Captain Crane and ask his interference. Astonished at such a proposition, I inquired as to the cause, when I was answered that he was a Jew and not an agreeable person, and they did not want to be brought in contact with him in our then very pleasant and harmonious mess of some eight or nine persons. And moreover, that he was an interloper, having entered the navy as master, to the prejudice of the older midshipmen, etc., etc. Such was the reply, in substance, to my inquiry.

I then asked the relator if he or any member of our mess knew anything, of his own knowledge, derogatory to Lieutenant Levy as an officer or as a gentleman. The answer was No, but they heard thus and so, etc., etc. I endeavored to point out the difficulties that might result from a procedure so much at variance with military subordination and the justice due to a brother officer, against whom they had nothing but vague and ill-defined rumors, but my counsel then did not prevail. The remonstrance was made directly to Captain Crane, and by Captain Crane to Commodore Stewart.

Levy soon after reported on board the frigate "United States" for duty. When Lieutenant Levy came on board, he asked a private interview with me, wishing my advice as to the proper course he ought to pursue under such embarassing circumstances. I gave it freely and simply . . . viz.: Do your duty as an officer and a gentleman; be civil to all, however reserved you may choose to be to any, and the first man who observes a different course toward you, call him to a strict and prompt account.

Our messmates were gentlemen, and having perceived their error, before Lieut. Levy got on board, had, in accordance with my previous advice, determined to receive Lieutenant Levy as a gentleman and a brother officer, and to respect and treat him as such, till by his conduct he should prove himself unworthy. I continued a few months longer on board the frigate "United States" as her first lieutenant, during the whole of which time Lieutenant Levy's conduct and deportment was altogether unexceptionable, and I know that perhaps with a single exception, those who opposed his joining our mess not only relented but deeply regretted the false step they had incautiously taken.

During the few months that Commodore Jones remained in the ship, his wise and just counsels had the effect he describes. After he left her, I am sorry to be obliged to say, the old prejudice revived in too many of my associates. . . .

PROMOTION AND RECOGNITION

I remained in the frigate "United States" until June, 1820, when she returned to the United States. My next service was in the brig "Spark," Captain [John H.] Elton [commanding], as first lieutenant, in which vessel and capacity I remained several months, leaving her in October, 1822. Shortly afterwards I took the command of the "Revenge," gunboat No. 158. In 1823 I visited Europe on leave of absence, and in compliance with the orders of the [Navy]

Department, joined the frigate "Cyane" in the Mediterranean, the flagship of Commodore [J. O.] Creighton. (I defer to a subsequent stage of this defense, some incidents connected with my service in that vessel.)

In 1824, I went in the "North Carolina," by order of the Department, to the Mediterranean to rejoin the "Cyane," Commodore Creighton [in command]. In the "Cyane" I remained from June, 1825, to June, 1827. During the first four months she was commanded by Commodore Creighton, for the rest of the time by the distinguished Commodore Jesse D. Elliot[t].

In 1837, I was promoted to the grade of commander, and in 1838-9 I was for one year in command of the corvette "Vandalia." In October, 1838, when I took command of her, she was the flagship of Commodore [A. J.] Dallas, and so continued until I sailed in her on a cruise by his orders. Subsequently, Commodore [W. B.] Shubrick succeeded him as commander of the West India Squadron, and a second cruise was made by me in the "Vandalia," under his orders. In 1844, the President [John Tyler] nominated me to the Senate for promotion as captain. This nomination was confirmed on the [thirty-first] of May, 1844, my appointment to take rank from the 29th March, 1844.

The circumstances attending this appointment were of peculiar interest to me, and it is most important that they should be fully understood by the court. Attempts were made outside the Senate, by certain officers of the navy, to induce that body to reject my nomination. The Naval Committee of the Senate, to whom the nomination had been referred, were approached by officers hostile to, or prejudiced against, me, and such objections were made to my appointment that the committee felt it proper to call on the Secretary of the Navy for all papers on file relating to my official conduct. The archives of the Department were ransacked; charges preferred against me during my service as sailing master, lieutenant, and commander, growing (with a single exception) out of those personal altercations and quarrels unfortunately too common in our profession, were raked up; and the records of all the courts-martial before which, in the course of thirty years, I had been brought, were laid before the committee. These documents having been thoroughly examined by them, they reported in favor of the nomination, and on their reports it was unanimously confirmed.

Several witnesses refer with more or less particularity to these facts. Mr. Watkins, who had charge of the records of courts-martial in the Navy Department in 1844, testifies that in March or April of that year, the records of the several courts-martial by which I was tried from the time of my appointment as sailing master to that of commander, both inclusive, were taken out of his possession for the purpose, as he understood at the time, of being sent to the Senate. They remained out of his possession a considerable time. He presumed they were taken to the Senate on the pendency of my nomination for promotion, as that was the only reason why they should have been sent there. Captain James McIntosh, in answer to the third cross interrogatory, refers to the opposition made by those prejudiced against me to the approval of my nomination, and Commodore Thomas ap Catesby Jones, in his answer to the same cross interrogatory, speaks of the clique which then opposed and still opposes me, and of the thorough examination of the charges by the committee of the Senate.

In my memorial to the Senate and House of Representatives in Congress assembled, and to the Senate in its executive capacity, complaining of the action of the Board of Naval Officers, read in the Senate in December, 1855, all the facts connected with my nomination as captain and its confirmation by the Senate, after thorough investigation of the records of the department, as above mentioned, were particularly stated, and so far as I know or have heard, were never disputed in the Senate or elsewhere. Indeed, they were matters of public notoriety.

FRUSTRATION

Having thus reached the highest grade of service in the navy, I had an anxious desire to be actively employed in it at sea. For this purpose I made, from year to year, frequent and earnest applications to the heads of the Navy Department. Many of these applications were made by me personally, many also in writing. . . .

Having failed in my efforts to obtain war service, and Ireland being then wasted by famine, I sought employment with a view to the relief of her people, and addressed Secretary [of the Navy, John Young] Mason, as follows:

New York, Feb'y 26, 1847.

Sir:

Understanding that a vessel of war may be detailed for the conveyance of grain to the distressed people of Ireland, I beg permission, should the government select a vessel for that purpose, to tender my services to take command of her, having already intimated to the committee not only my willingness to render my services, but at the same time to devote all my pay during the performance of this duty in aid of the benevolent object in view.

I have the honor to be,

Your ob'd't serv't,

U. P. Levy,

Captain, U. S. N.

Hon. J. Y. Mason,
Secretary U. S. Navy.

A ship of war was sent with provisions to Ireland, but I did not receive the command of her. . . .

After waiting in anxious suspense . . . without any further communication from the secretary [James C. Dobbin], I addressed him, in March, 1855, as follows:

Washington City, March 12, 1855.

Sir:

I have had the honor repeatedly and respectfully to solicit from the department some active service in common with officers of my rank. These applications have been accompanied with the earnest testimonials of distinguished statesmen and friends who believe and know me to be, in every way, worthy of the confidence of my government. Notwithstanding the strong and influential appeals that have, from time to time, been made in my behalf, I have had the frequent mortification to see my juniors in rank and inferiors in experience preferred in the distribution of commands and other service. I have been unemployed ever since the President and Senate, with great unanimity, did me the honor to promote me to a captaincy.

Such disregard of my just rights as an officer of the navy I can only impute to some unseen influence that seeks to heap unmerited prejudice upon me, and which, I fear, has operated to my injury with the department. I have been the subject of religious persecution for years, notwithstanding the proudest boast of our republic is that it secures to all civil and religious liberty, and I have only been enabled to sustain myself by my firmness in maintaining my honor untarnished.

I respectfully request that you will do me the justice to remove all implied imputations upon my competency and honor as an officer by assigning me to an appropriate command in the service, in the glories and perils of which I have shared.

I have the honor to be,

> Your ob'd't serv't,
> U. P. Levy,
> Captain.

Hon. J.[ames] C Dobbin,
  Secretary of the Navy.

Receiving no reply to this letter, I addressed the secretary as follows:

> St. Marks Place, New York, June 4, 1855.

Sir:

I have the honor to call the attention of the department to my communication of March 13th [12th?], which, I regret to say, still remains unanswered. It is a courtesy which, I think has not been neglected heretofore to officers of my rank. Consequently I feel the omission more acutely, and I am only sustained from deeper mortification under the belief that my letter has been mislaid during your illness, as it was sent to your private residence.

I therefore respectfully enclose a copy and solicit that it will meet with your earliest attention, and that justice to an oppressed officer will be no longer deferred by the department.

He who seeks it is the last wardroom officer of the celebrated brig "Argus," which, in the War of 1812, destroyed twenty-one sail in the British Channel, valued at $5,000,000, and raised the insurance from two and a half to twenty-five percent.

May I request that the enclosed letters may be put on the files of the department after you have read them, one from President [Zachary] Taylor, the other from Hon. Philo White [our minister to Ecuador]? The accompanying note will show when, and how it came to your very ob'd't serv't,

> U. P. Levy,
> Captain.

Hon. J. C. Dobbin,
  Secretary of the Navy.

This letter produced the following reply:

> Navy Department, June 5, 1855.

Sir:

Your letter of the fourth inst. with its enclosures has been received.

In reply I have to inform you that in omitting to reply to your former communication, the department was very far from any intention of treating you with disrespect. It would not only be inconvenient, but physically impossible, to reply to all applications of officers for orders. The applications are placed on file for reference when occasion requires.

The papers enclosed will be placed on file as requested.

> I am respectfully,
> Your ob'd't serv't,
> J. C. Dobbin.

Captain U. P. Levy,
  U. S. Navy,
    New York.

In the full belief that I yet stood in official relations to the head of the Navy Department, I addressed to him, on the twenty-fifth of August, the following letter:

> St. Marks Place, New York, August 25, 1855.

Sir:

The command of the squadron on the coast of Brazil, and the Navy Yard here, will be vacant by limitation this fall. I am the next captain in rank on the register entitled to the command of a squadron or a station, and being capable of performing promptly and efficiently all my duties, both on sea and on shore, I therefore respectfully solicit that as an act of justice long deferred, you will confer the appointment of either of the commands on your ob'd't humble serv't,

> U. P. Levy,
> Captain.

Hon. J. C. Dobbin,
  Secretary U. S. Navy,
    Washington.

At the date of this letter, the decree for my destruction, though unknown to, and unsuspected by, me, had already gone forth, the Board of Fifteen, as was afterwards disclosed, having completed their labors on the twentieth of July.

I received no reply to this letter, but on the 14th September I received from the secretary a communication superceding the necessity of such a reply, for he informed that in consequence of the action of the board my name had been stricken from the rolls. This communication was in the following words:

Navy Department, Sept. 13, 1855.

Sir:

The Board of Naval Officers, assembled under the "Act to Promote the Efficiency of the Navy," approved February 28, 1855, having reported you as one of the two officers who should, in their judgment, be stricken from the rolls of the navy, and the finding of the board having been approved by the President [Franklin Pierce], it becomes my duty to inform you that accordingly your name is stricken from the rolls of the navy.

Respectfully,
Your obedient servant,
J. C. Dobbin.

Mr. Uriah P. Levy,
Late Captain, U. S. Navy, New York. . . .

THE TAR-AND-FEATHERS CASE

The evidence produced on the part of the government [in this Court of Inquiry, 1857,] is of two kinds: matters of record and the testimony of witnesses examined in the present investigation. Under the first head, the judge advocate has introduced the charges, specifications, findings, and sentences against me, of sundry courts-martial held in the years 1816, 1818, and 1819, 1821, 1827, and 1842, the last, however, founded on my conduct in 1839. . . .

The sixth and last of the courts-martial was held at Baltimore, in 1842, for the purpose of trying me upon charges and specifications preferred by the Secretary of the Navy [Abel P. Upshur] on the information of Lieut. George Mason Hooe. I think it needful to give the charges and specifications at length. [Only the first charge and specification are given here.]

Charge 1st—Scandalous and cruel conduct unbecoming an officer and a gentleman.

Specification—In this, that the said Commander Uriah P. Levy, being then in command of the United States ship "Vandalia," did, on or about the seventh day of July, eighteen hundred and thirty-nine, cause John Thompson, a boy serving on said ship "Vandalia," to be seized to a gun, his trowsers to be let down, and a quantity of tar to be applied to his naked skin, such punishment being highly scandalous and unbecoming the dignity of an officer to inflict, and in violation of the third and thirtieth articles of the first section of the act of Congress entitled "An act for the better government of the Navy of the United States," approved 23rd April, 1800. . . .

I now propose, Mr. President and gentlemen of the court, to examine the evidence in relation to the treatment of the boy Thompson. . . .

It may be necessary to premise, may it please the court, that this boy Thompson did not only mimic an officer in giving his orders, as was shewn by the testimony of several witnesses, but he was actually in the habit of doing so whenever an occasion presented. No one will deny that such practices are calculated to bring an officer into ridicule and contempt, and thus very materially impair that subordination and good government which ought to exist on board a ship of war, and also to abridge the personal respect which is due to every individual in authority, and yet this mimicry may be classed among the non-enumerated offenses for which the law has provided no specific punishment. It was a new and novel case, calculated, it is true, to lead to unpleasant consequences, but still it was considered by me as a trick, a folly, a boyish misdemeanour. In such light I viewed it, and in such light I noticed it.

I was unwilling to call all hands to punishment and flog the boy on his naked back with a cat[-o'nine-tails], for what might possibly be termed a trivial offense; but as a *commutation* of punishment, I deemed it right, by exposing *him* to ridicule, to satisfy him of the impropriety of ridiculing others. Accordingly, I called the boys together to witness the example to be made of juvenile offenders of this class, had his trowsers taken down, a little tar, on a piece of oakum, dabbed on his bottom, and a few colored feathers from a dead parrot stuck on him to ridicule his mocking propensities, and the whole affair ended in a few minutes. And yet this light and trivial circumstance, originating in jest, not in anger, more as a caution hereafter than punishment for the present, of which nothing was thought of then, nor since, excepting in the humane imagination of the complainant, is magnified into a grave offence, and I am charged with scandalous and cruel conduct and brought before this court to answer such charge.

Now, may it please the court, is such an isolated, trifling case, in which no harm is done or intended to be done, no injury to the service, a mere admonition for better conduct in future, to be tortured into a grave charge that a citizen was tarred and feathered, and I made amenable to the imputation of cruel and scandalous conduct in inflicting upon a boy a mere boy's punishment? But I repeat, I did not intend this as a punishment, but even if it should be deemed punishment, will any member of this court say that it was cruel as specified in the charge? Unusual, I admit, but cruel it certainly was not.

The testimony of every witness goes to prove that there was no cruelty and no design of cruel punishment at all in the whole affair. Lieut. [A. E.] Downes, the executive officer of the ship, testifies that "a small quantity of tar was put on his skin by the boys, after which some very few feathers—a half dozen." These are his words. Acting Lieutenant Maffit confirms the testimony of Lieut. Downes. Midshipman [Israel C.] Wait says: "A small quantity of tar and a few feathers" applied to his posteriors with a brush, as he thinks. Is there anything, therefore, that would give to the application of a little tar to the posteriors of a boy the character of cruelty here sought to be fixed upon me? Is there anything so alarming in the use or application of a little tar? Why, sailors live in the midst of it, their whole body is smeared with it, their hands are continually begrimed in it. It has no terrors, no shame to them, and they would scout the idea of complaining because a little tar was dabbed on a piece of oakum and applied to a boy's skin, and a few colored feathers stuck on the tar for some five minutes for disgrace. It is thus, may it please the court, that mountains are sought to be made out of molehills, and a spirit of revenge attempts to give to an unusual act the colour and character of crime and ferocity.

The statement of this affair, however, by several witnesses is made to bear another complexion. Something must be tortured out of it. Of itself, the complainant knew it amounted to nothing; some direful consequences must be made to grow out of this tar and parrot's feathers; a mutiny or rebellion must be shown in embryo; the honest tars, indignant at this tarring process, were about to mutiny. Acting Mid[shipma]n Wait says they appeared to be very indignant and murmured, and a man was punished for it. Lt. Moffitt [Maffit] says the same. Lieut. Downes, however, the first lieutenant of the ship, and the officer in a position best calculated to know what *did* happen on board the "Vandalia," testifies that he heard no murmuring. A man named Van Ness, he says, was reported to Capt. Levy for making improper remarks, and he was punished. There can be no mutiny or rebellion manufactured by the complainant out of this affair. No such thing occurred. The men were not called together;

they were employed on various duties throughout the ship. Some
eight or ten boys were present; the whole affair did not occupy five
minutes, and the men, those who saw it, cared nothing about it, and
as to murmuring or mutiny, it did not belong to my crew.

If I had not the good fortune to enlist the regard and attachment
of all my officers, I was always secure in the confidence, devotion,
and attachment of my men. They were always anxious to remain
with me. They were always devoted to me on sea or land. They
knew me as the sailor's friend, and their hearts and hands were ever
at my disposal and command. *Their* comfort, *their* character, *their*
rights, were ever uppermost in my thoughts, and I could have carried my crew at all times in the hottest and most dangerous position
of the fight, and I say this without vanity or ostentation, for it is
true, and therefore I deny that on this occasion there were any
manifestations of mutiny or rebellion in my crew.

The complainant in this case has been exceedingly anxious to
impart to this trifling affair the most offensive character. If he could
only have it said that a man, a white man, was tarred and feathered
on board my ship and by my orders, he could create a prejudice
and awaken an indignation against me strong enough everywhere to
cover me with odium. If he could only blow this *spark* into *flame*,
why, he would "feed fat the ancient grudge he bore me." But, may
it please the court, it is beyond his power, his ingenuity, to torture
this contemptible affair into such an issue; he has a thinking, a dis-
cerning, and a sensible court and community to deal with, capable
of discriminating and arriving at fair, reasonable, and equitable
results in this matter.

Stripping a citizen naked and covering him with tar and feathers,
which is understood to be the meaning of the words tarring and
feathering, is an odious as well as an illegal punishment, and never
is inflicted in this country, unless it is for the highest crimes and
misdemeanours, which for want of proper testimony could not be
legally reached. The traitor, the coward, the seducer of innocence,
and the common cheat have suffered such odious and unwarrantable punishment, but can any citizen for a moment believe that *I*
even contemplated such a ruffian-like attack, and on a boy, between
fifteen and seventeen years of age, a boy under my command, on
board my ship, and consequently under my protection and likewise
for a trivial offense? Why, may it please the court, the prosecutor
or complainant himself, with all the phials of his mouth filled to
overflowing against me, would smile at the idea of calling this affair
tarring and feathering a citizen in the odious sense in which it is

understood. I scout it with indignation; the world, and I hope this court, will do the same.

If the spies placed around me to detail any little flaw in my discipline, and then, after a lapse of three years and upwards, to originate charges against me and transmit notes and memoranda to the complainant had done their duty, they would have apprised him also that I had a habit of spanking the boys instead of lashing their backs with a cat or a colt [a rope whip], and he could have reported me for cruelty or unusual punishment on this count of the indictment.

I launched my bark on the stormy ocean of life as a cabin boy. I had no powerful interests to urge my promotion, no hereditary rank and power to build up claims, or friends at court to enroll my name on the list of favorites to be provided for. I did not jump from the drawing room, with ruffled shorts, perfumed locks, and white kid gloves, into the wardroom, but in the constant labor and hardship of a seaman's life, studied, and I hope well and practically, a seaman's duty and a seaman's character.

Mr. President and gentlemen of the court, in all the charges against me on this trial, the affair of the boy Thompson is the only one to which the slightest importance can be attached, and I now proceed to shew that my conduct in that affair was entirely *legal* and comes within the purview of the regulations governing the navy. I read, sir, from the circular issued from the Navy Department, September 26, 1831:

> Flogging is recommended to be discontinued when practicable by courts as well as officers, and some *badge of disgrace*, fine, etc., substituted where discretion exists.

As this was a case of discretion, I exercised it humanely, as I conceived, by a *badge of disgrace*, such as the instruction just read seems to indicate. The act therefore was legal, and also humane.

In the course of this examination questions have been asked in relation to my system of discipline, and my rules and regulations on board the ship under my command. These questions may have grown out of a collateral question, which I put to a witness, which opened the door to a new issue, and a general scrutiny of my administration on board ship was the result. It may all have been proper, for if my system is illegal and contrary to usage, if it is cruel, scandalous, or injurious to the service, the proper corrective should be applied. It has been my misfortune to differ with abler and older officers than myself, for whose judgment I had great respect, in relation to the discipline necessary for the government of the navy. With the law always for my guide, I differed in the manner of its enforcement, and the rigid construction applied to it by severe disciplinarians.

Commencing, as I have before said, as a cabin boy, I made the character, temper, and habits of seamen a close and particular study, and in the forecastle and yardarm had ample opportunities of ascertaining the peculiar characteristics of the sailor, and years of practical illustration had served to convince me that strict discipline, obedience to orders, sobriety, and a sense of duty can be secured without the constant, unwavering, and unflinching application of the lash for almost every offence. No one will deny, who are familiar with seamen, that an occasional use of the cat to the refractory cannot be dispensed with, but my own experience has led me to place a high estimate on the value of a mild and moral system, which sinks deep into the heart, without the necessity of lacerating the body, of using light punishments for subordinate offences, of efforts to create shame and regret by proper examples and salutary reproofs.

It appeared in evidence on this trial that to punish a drunkard I did not put him in irons and allow him to beat his head and body on deck until he was bruised to a jelly and unfit for duty when he became sober, but placed him in a safe place, and when his senses were restored, I hung a wooden bottle around his neck on which "Drunkard" was inscribed. This may have been unusual, but it is not cruel, and the result satisfied me that shame will do more to correct intemperance than stripes. The incorrigible pilferer I punished by placing a wooden collar round his neck. It was also proved on this trial that I had what was called a blackguards' mess. I had such a mess, determined that men who used indecent, vulgar, or profane language from habit should mess by themselves and not contaminate the more orderly and decent portion of the crew. But I am happy to say, in order to relieve the apprehensions of the gentlemen who testified to this fact, that I had no blackguards in the mess.

Mid[shipma]n [James A.] Doyle testifies that two men, Maxem and Marr, one a deserter and thief, the other he did not know for what, were chained together by a long, linked chain. He could not say how they were chained, whether by the head, the waist, or the heels, but thinks they were chained at the wrists. After the lapse of some time, he is permitted to correct his testimony, which he does by saying that he cannot be at all certain whether they were chained by the feet or hands. I have no recollection of ever ordering these men to be chained or whether they were chained at all. The law

authorizes the commander of a ship to put a man in irons if necessary, either by the hands or heels. I may have substituted a long,
light chain, so as to have enabled the parties to take exercise, but
have no recollection that it was ever done. It was also proved that I
employed a wooden horse and punished men for certain offences
by making them ride upon it. As this is not a novelty in our service,
no defence is necessary.

Lieut. Downes testified before this court that he saw less punishment on board my ship than in any other, save one, that he had ever
sailed in. I admit my aversion to the free and constant use of the
cat, much less lacerating the backs of boys of tender age, covering
them with stripes and blood, and punishing them as hardened felons,
and, therefore, governed by the discretion which the law allows the
commander of a ship of war, I have studied and practiced all the
reforms, which mildness could suggest, as substitutes for corporeal
punishment, and it was under the same sense of duty that the light
punishment inflicted on the boy Thompson was adopted, instead of
the lash.

What, then, are the results of my system? No ship in the navy had
a better or more orderly set of men, none obeyed orders more cheerfully, in no ship was there less severe punishment, and in none less
manifestations of mutiny and disaffection. If I am to be censured for
this course, for this departure from higher examples, I may regret it
as unmerited, but it does not shake my faith in the system, nor my
conviction that finally it will be the universal and successful one for
the government of the navy.

Mr. President and gentlemen of the court, I feel mortified in being
called upon to defend myself from charges of cruelty and scandalous
conduct unbecoming an officer and a gentleman, founded upon allegations such as the prosecutor in this case has thought proper to
prefer. I entered the navy thirty years ago, without the advantage,
as I have said, of powerful friends or influence, with limited education and still more limited means, amidst hard and severe duty. I
have been gradually advanced to the station I now hold, without having been charged with intemperance, neglect, or ignorance of my
duty, cruelty, insubordination, or vice of any kind, nor can I admit
that any of the allegations contained in the present charges, trivial
as they are, have been sustained by the evidence.

I have had in my long career of public service many painful conflicts with my brother officers, growing out of mere questions of duty
and matters of trivial importance, and yet I have never allowed myself to cherish vindictive feelings toward anyone, but have been ever

ready to extend to them my hand, my friendship, my purse, my services, free from malice or ill will. My errors (and who are free from them?) have never been of heart. . . . I feel humiliated in being charged with scandalous conduct and cruelty, when my whole life has been passed in efforts to avoid whatever may be deemed dishonorable, discreditable, harsh, and injurious, and [to] adopt what is mild, upright, and beneficial to the service of the country. . . .

The court found "that the specifications of the first charge is proven, that of the first charge the accused is guilty." . . . And then the following sentence was decreed: "The court, having passed upon the charges and specifications, proceeded to take into consideration what sentence should be adjudged, and after mature deliberation, the court does adjudge and sentence that Commander Uriah P. Levy be and is hereby dismissed [from] the Navy of the United States."

Secretary Upshur recommended to the President [John Tyler], whose approval was indispensable to the validity of the sentence, that it should be approved, but the President disapproved the same and directed the court to reconsider it, by his communication in writing addressed to the Secretary of the Navy, and attached to the record as produced in this investigation, in the words following:

Washington, April 28, 1842.

Sir:

Upon a mature consideration of the record of the court-martial, I have come to the conclusion, without designing any disrespect to the court, that the punishment denounced against Captain Levy by the sentence of the court is exceedingly severe and disproportionate to the offence charged. The punishment, in order to be just, must be proportionate to the crime. In arriving at this conclusion, I have not permitted myself to look beyond the charge and its specification.

Whether the officer be good or bad, whether his deportment in the general be correct or otherwise, ought not to enter into the enquiry.

My respect for the court, sustained as it is by your opinion, would lead me to desire to carry out its sentence, but for the fact that in so doing I should establish a precedent which would bind me in all other cases and adopt as a rule for future action that which might involve in a similar fate any other officer who had departed in any respect from the rigid rules of the service.

I desire, therefore, that you will submit the sentence to the court for its reconsideration, with directions that their judgment shall

be confined to the single point of the treatment to Thompson, and
that on this point any new testimony, either in illustration of the
motive or the fact, may be admitted on the part of the prosecution
or the accused.

Be assured of my great regard.

John Tyler.

To the Secretary of the Navy.

The court having reassembled in pursuance of the President's decision and [having] heard some additional testimony, they say in
respect to it that it furnished no ground for a change in their opinion
as to the extent of my offence. They then proceeded to consider the
question whether the punishment awarded by its sentence was dis-
proportioned to the offence charged. They state as a first principle
the following proposition:

> The court is a military and not a civil tribunal; the act which
> they are called upon to try is a military and not a civil offence;
> the laws which govern their judgment are those which regulate the
> naval service of the United States, and the court, as judges, are
> bound to consider what these laws require for the honor and wel-
> fare of that service.

In this view of the subject, they proceed to consider my offence,
"first, with reference to the boy Thompson; secondly, with reference
to its effect upon the service; thirdly, with reference to Commander
Levy himself." The court then enter into an extended argument on
these points, and, in reference to the last, they use the following
language:

> As to Commander Levy himself, he was bound to know the law,
> and yet he openly violated it. He was bound to set an example of
> decency and propriety in his own personal conduct, and yet he has
> disregarded both. He was bound to preserve the discipline of his
> ship, and yet he pursued a course calculated more than any other
> to destroy it and to produce disobedience and excite a mutinous
> spirit in the service, and to bring it into odium and contempt.

They close their argument by reiterating their former sentence, as
follows:

> We, therefore, upon full and impartial reconsideration of our
> sentence, submit these as our reasons for adhering to it, and do
> adjudge and sentence Commander Levy to be dismissed from the
> naval service of the United States.

This second sentence was also disapproved by the President, by his decision in writing, and the punishment decreed by the court mitigated as follows:

CASE OF CAPTAIN LEVY

I have read the argument of the court in this case with great pleasure and have examined the record with care, and if my convictions force me to differ in opinion with the court, it arises from no disrespect to it, or indisposition to sustain its authority. The law imposes on the President the necessity of revising the judgment of the court, and as a faithful public agent he must pronounce such opinion as his best judgment shall dictate.

The argument of the court may be conclusive to shew that Captain Levy should undergo some punishment, but I cannot but differ from it as to the extent of the punishment.

The fourth rule under the head "Court-Martials," prescribed for the government of the navy in the code of rules and recommendations issued by Mr. [Levi] Woodbury, when Secretary of the Navy, and which was in full force at the time Captain Levy was in command of the "Vandalia," and may not yet have been abrogated, is in the following words: "Flogging is recommended to be discontinued when practicable *by courts, as well as officers, and some badge of disgrace,* fine, etc., substituted when discretion exists."

The recommendation of the secretary was fully observed by Captain Levy. Corporal punishment was almost entirely abolished on board his ship. Around the neck of a drunkard he suspended a wooden bottle with "Drunkard" on it. Other badges were adopted; on a boy whose age is variously stated as from sixteen to eighteen, and who was a mimick, and was reported for mimicking an officer, a small quantity of tar, not extending over a space represented by some of the witnesses as of the size of a dollar, by others of the size of a man's hand, was daubed on the back of the boy, and a half a dozen parrot's feathers put on it, was substituted in place of twelve stripes with the cats, and it is for this that Captain Levy is sentenced to be dismissed [from] the service.

Now, under the rule of the Department, a discretion was left to the officer in command as to the substitution of punishment; for the soundness or unsoundness of that discretionary judgment he is certainly answerable. If under *the pretence* of substituting a milder punishment, he resorted to one which malice alone could suggest, he would deserve the severest condemnation. But no such motive or feeling is ascribed to Captain Levy.

He meant to affix temporarily to the boy a *badge of disgrace* in order to correct a bad habit, to teach him and others that the habit of mimicking was the quality of the parrot whose feathers he wore. The badge was worn only for a few minutes. No harm was done the person. No blood made to flow, as from the application of the cats, and no cruelty was exercised, unless the reasoning of the court be just, that this badge of disgrace was more cruel than corporal punishment.

True, many men would prefer death to either receiving twelve lashes with the cats, or wearing for a single moment such a badge of disgrace, but no officer would recommend the abolition of all punishment because of this. Captain Levy erred by resorting to an extremely disgraceful punishment, I admit, and in order to protect the service from its repetition in future, he should be punished.

While, therefore, in the absence of *any bad motive* on his part, I cannot concur with the court in approving the extreme sentence *of expulsion* from the navy, yet a modified sentence under the law is what is properly due to the service.

I therefore mitigate the sentence of Captain Levy from dismissal from the service, to the punishment of suspension without pay for the period of twelve months.

John Tyler,

June 8, 1842. . . .

PREJUDICE IN HIGH QUARTERS

I now propose to consider the several facts stated by the government witnesses [at this Court of Inquiry, in 1857].

Commodore [Matthew C.] Perry, first of the number, states no one fact of any consequence whatever—I speak of facts as contradistinguished from rumors and opinions—unless it be the fact of my not having been employed by the government in my present grade. The importance he gives to this fact makes it proper that I should give to it a thorough examination.

When, in 1855, I complained to Secretary Dobbin of "some unseen influence," seeking "through unmerited prejudice to injure me with the Department" and to prevent it from according to me my just rights, I stated what I then fully believed and what I had long before suspected to be the fact. I was driven to this conclusion by the persistent refusal of the several secretaries [of the Navy] to employ me, in the face of all the proofs of my fitness in the records of the department, and of the recommendations and support of so many distinguished men in support of my applications. I could draw from the circumstances no other inference, nor do I think that any other can be drawn by you. But the fact is not now left to inference merely. You have before you, in the deposition of the Hon. George Bancroft, late Secretary of the Navy, direct evidence of the fact.

In answer to the ninth interrogatory on my part, he says:

When Secretary of the Navy, I never had cause to doubt, and never doubted, Captain Levy's competence to serve the United States in the grade of captain. I did not find myself able to give him a command for three reasons: first, the excessive number of officers of his grade made it impossible to employ all of them who were fit; second, the good of the service, moreover, seemed to require bringing forward officers less advanced in years than most of the captains, and the law sanctioned that course; third, I perceived a strong prejudice in the service against Captain Levy, which seemed to me, in a considerable part, attributable to his being of the Jewish persuasion, and while I, as an executive officer, had the same liberal views which guided the President and Senate in commissioning him as a captain, I always endeavored, in fitting out ships, to have some reference to that harmonious co-operation which is essential to the highest effectiveness.

To the first of these reasons no exception can be taken. The second is founded on a favorite theory of Mr. Bancroft while secretary, to which, were it impartially carried out, I should be as little disposed to object as any other officer of my rank and age.

The *third* reason assigned by Mr. Bancroft, though last in order, is not least in importance. The fact that it is assigned by him as one of the reasons for not giving me a command justifies the inference that the first two reasons would not have been sufficient to produce that result without the addition of the third.

From what sources or in what manner Mr. Bancroft "perceived" the "strong prejudice in the service" against me of which he speaks, he does not state. But it is easy to trace it to its origin. He had never been officially connected with the navy until he came to Washington, in 1845, as head of the department. He was then brought into intercourse with such officers of the navy as were enabled by their rank, their connexion with the bureaux, or their social position, to cultivate the acquaintance and get the ear of a secretary.

It was only by means of such intercourse that it was possible for him to become acquainted with the prejudice which existed in the service against any of its members. It was only in this way that he could learn that any such prejudice existed against me. Among the officers of the navy to whom the secretary was thus peculiarly accessible, there were some who were friendly to me, but there were others who were not only unfriendly but also active and bitter in their hostility against me. How else than through intercourse with those who have the motive and took the pains to force it upon him was it possible for Mr. Bancroft to know that any prejudice existed against me in the navy, and how could he form any estimate as to its strength except from the frequency and rancor with which it was obtruded upon his notice?

From the same source which informed him of the prejudice, he learned its nature and grounds, the chief, if not the sole, ground being my peculiar religious faith, my "being of the Jewish persuasion." Doubtless those who could make such a fact the pretext for a prejudice against a brother officer so inveterate and unyielding as to compel the head of a department reluctantly to recognize and admit it as an element of his official action, would not scruple to disparage and traduce in other respects the object of their aversion.

But even their efforts failed to awaken for a moment in the mind of the secretary a solitary doubt as to my *competence*. This he tells us in the most emphatic terms. In the satisfaction which this avowal gives me, in the gratitude I owe to one who, in spite of such efforts, retained towards me an opinion so favorable, I could almost pass over, without remark, the injury done me, most unwittingly I am sure, but not the less real, by his allowing to such an objection any weight whatever, and by his omitting to communicate it to me while importuning him for employment.

Had it then come to my knowledge, I could have shewn him, just as I have now shewn to you, from the records of the department, that during my year's command of the "Vandalia," my religious faith never impaired the efficiency of my ship, that I never permitted it to interfere with the rights or to wound the feelings of my Christian officers and men, and that I did what I could, and all that they desired, to respect and satisfy those rights and feelings.

I might also have shewn to him, as I have shewn to you, by the evidence of the many officers who, in this investigation, have testified in my behalf, that the prejudice to which he was constrained to give such fatal effect against me was far from being so general or so strong as he was led to believe; that officers more in number than my traducers, and far better qualified to judge, were untainted by it, treated it with contempt, and denounced it as inconsistent with the spirit of our institutions, unworthy of the present age, and degrading to the honor of the naval service. And I might thus, perhaps, have afforded him the opportunity, which I doubt not he would gladly have seized not only from a sense of justice to myself, but in accordance with his own liberal and enlightened convictions, of setting "his face like a flint" against the hydra of religious intolerance and driving it forever from the councils of his country. The benefit of such an act to myself would have been insignificant in comparison with the vindication it would have furnished of the dignity of our government, and its faithful conservation of the most sacred of our public and private rights. . . .

A Damned Jew

By Commodore Isaac Mayo I proved an attempt (already briefly alluded to) to prevent my reception on board the United States ship "North Carolina." He gives the following account of this transaction:

I am acquainted with Captain U. P. Levy. I have known him ever since the last war; I don't recollect the precise period. We were associated together in 1824 or 1825, in service on board the "North Carolina." I should think we were together more or less than a month. I was flag lieut. to Commodore Rodgers. Lieut. Levy was a lieut. and had been ordered to take passage in the ship to the Mediterranean.

I had returned from my recruiting (I had been absent six or eight months), and upon my rejoining the ship, circumstances occurred which I will mention. Some of the junior officers of the ward mess asked me if I knew that Levy had been ordered to take passage in the ship, which at the time I was not aware of, and the object of some of them was to keep him out of the wardroom mess. I asked them if there was anything particular against Levy, any particular reason why he should not be admitted in the mess. They said he was a damned Jew, and they wouldn't mess with him, to which I answered that if that was all they had against him, I should vote for him to come into the mess. And as he was ordered there by the Secretary of the Navy, we had no right to exclude him, and I heard no more of it.

Being cross-examined by the judge advocate, he said:

Two of the officers who used the language about Lieut. Levy were marine officers, [L. N.] Carter and Randolph, and they were violently opposed to him. Another was the junior lieutenant (Lieut. [Allen] Griffin). There were one or two masters. It was the junior officers of the mess; I think it was the marine officer Carter who used the language referred to, and they all assented to it. . . .

A Patriot Abroad

Moral fitness in an officer of the navy, as indicated by his commission and by the articles for the government of the navy, includes first and chiefest of all, *patriotism, valour,* and *fidelity.* In all my official career I have endeavoured to cultivate and exhibit this moral fitness. I refer to the following incidents in my life as tending to show that I have not been altogether unsuccessful in this effort:

First.   In 1809, in my seventeenth year, when I was impressed on board the "Nermyea," British sloop of war, I was repeatedly promised, by Captain Scobel, commander of that vessel, a midshipman's appointment if I would sign the articles and enter the British service. I refused the offer, and the moment I obtained my release returned to my country and to my master, Mr. Coulter.

Second. My selection of the navy as my profession on the breaking out of the War of 1812 and my volunteer services in the "Argus" give, as I hope, some proof of my patriotism.

Third. In 1827, while serving as lieutenant in the "Cyane," an incident occurred which belongs to this topic, and which is thus related by Lieutenant Peter Turner, one of the witnesses on my part:

When the "Cyane" was at Rio [de] Janeiro [Brazil], some time early in the afternoon there was a report that one of our officers, Midshipman [John W.] Moores, who had charge of one of the gangs, had been knocked down, and that Mr. Levy, in rescuing him, had got himself into trouble. I called out to my gang to seize hold of anything they could get hold of and follow me, and I believe the other officers did the same, and we all started off together.

We had got just barely under way when Mr. Levy was seen coming down towards us, waving us back, and ordered us to keep the men back and together under the shed where they could come to his call. Directly, we saw Mr. Levy come down with Mr. Moores

and an American seaman who had been pressed and was the cause
of the trouble. They were followed by a crowd. The man had been
impressed by the Brazilians and had thrown himself upon Mr.
Moores for protection. Mr. Moores refused to deliver him up, and
the Brazilian admiral pushed Mr. Moores and called him some
opprobrious names. Mr. Moores knocked the admiral down; he
floored him.

When Mr. Levy approached, as I observed that his hand was in
a sling or held in the other rolled up in a handkerchief or glove,
I asked him what was the matter. He told us that in warding off
a blow of a sabre aimed by an officer at Mr. Moores, who had
been knocked down, his, Mr. Levy's, little finger had been dis-
located. He received the blow intended for Mr. Moores. Mr. Moores
stated that he thought that in warding off the blow Mr. Levy had
saved his life; at the same time he spoke of a thrust in his side
from a bayonet. It bruised him very much. That is what he told
me.

Dom Pedro, first emperor of Brazil, was in the habit of visiting
the Navy Yard very often, and I think every day while we were
at work fishing the mast and, as we understood, to expedite the
fitting out of a squadron which was going to St. Catharine's [in
South Brazil] to suppress an insurrection. Previous to the affair
of Mr. Moores, the Emperor took notice of our party and con-
versed with Mr. Levy in French, and on the subject of the work,
I presume, because he pointed at it and seemed to be observing
it while talking; I did not understand the language.

The Emperor visited the yard on the next morning after the
affair and, immediately after receiving the salutes of his officers,
came up and commenced conversation with Mr. Levy. I was not
more than a couple of yards from them. Lieut. Levy's hand was
then in a sling. Their conversation was in French and continued
probably between fifteen and twenty minutes. The Emperor's manner was polite, pleasant, and Mr. Levy's manner indicated pleasure,
satisfaction, gratification.

There was a Capt. Haddaman, a foreigner, who was present at
that conversation. He was our professor of mathematics and languages; he had been a captain in one of the Austrian regiments.
He stood two or three feet off me, and perhaps two or three yards
from the Emperor.

Capt. Haddaman interpreted for me, the moment the Emperor's
back was turned, what he had said to Mr. Levy. The substance of
his interpretation was that the Emperor complimented Lieut. Levy

for the prompt and handsome manner in which he had rushed in
and rescued his brother officer and fellow seaman, a common
man, and wished he had as zealous officers in his own service, and
concluded by offering or inviting him to take command of a new
sixty-gun frigate which had been just brought out by Lieut. (now
Capt.) Franklin Buchanan. This was in 1827.

I do not recollect that Capt. Haddaman translated to me Mr.
Levy's reply. I recollect the reply made by him to the emperor or
the Brazilian Admiral Taylor on a repetition of the offer made
to him a short time subsequent. Mr. Levy's answer expressed gratitude for the honor, but [he] declined it; [he said] that he loved
his own service so well that he would rather serve as a cabin boy
in his own service than as a captain in any other service in the
world.

Fourth. On the Fourth of July, 1833, I was present in Paris
[France], at a banquet given by the American residents of that city,
in honor of the day. The Hon. George W. Ewing, formerly U. S.
minister to Spain, presided, and Gen'l LaFayette, Gen'l Barnard,
and others were present as invited guests.

Among the regular toasts was one in honor of [George] Washington, then followed: "Andrew Jackson, President of the United States,
like Washington firm and patriotic, like Washington, happy in the
union of men and principles." I proposed nine cheers; will it be
believed, this toast in an assemblage of Americans in a foreign land,
instead of being cheered, was received with groans and hisses! And
though repeated attempts were made to drink this national toast, in
the modified form, "Andrew Jackson, President of the United States,
nine cheers," the major part of the company persistently refused
to drink it with cheers, although the French national toast, "The
King of the French," was drunk with three times three and one more.

Regarding the Chief Magistrate [President] of the Union as the
representative of my country's sovereignty, I promptly resented this
insult to her and to him, and on its first outbreak threw to one of
the most prominent in the outrage, a glove merchant, my glove, with
an invitation to the Champs Élysées the next morning, an invitation
not accepted. A similar proposal to another drew from him, the next
day, a written apology to me, which I have yet in my possession.

Charles F. Pond, Esq., of Hartford, Connecticut, was present on
the occasion; he was summoned to this court, as a witness on my
part, but being prevented from attending, my senior counsel [Ben-
jamin F. Butler] sent him a statement of the occurrence, drawn out

in more detail than the above, and inquired as to his recollection of the circumstances. The following is Mr. Pond's reply:

Hartford, December 12, 1857.

Benjamin F. Butler, Esq.

Dear Sir:

I am unable after so long an interval to confirm all the particulars mentioned in the statement of Captain Levy.

I think he has given the facts in the main, as they occurred. The essential point is this: when the name of Andrew Jackson (then President of the U. S.) was proposed, the insulting manner in which it was received was too apparent, and Captain Levy resented the indignity in a most spirited and gallant manner. He was an honor to his country on that occasion, and conspicuous above all others he denounced the insult to his government in the terms it deserved.

Yours truly,
C. F. Pond.

[Fifth.] I refer to an incident which occurred in 1839, and of which Lieut. Maffit gives the following account:

In going into the harbor of Sacrificios [near Vera Cruz], in passing a French sloop of war, we carried away her flying jibboom, and with that her fore royal mast. The first lieut. of the ship "Vandalia" was sent on board to make an apology, which was not courteously received. At the time of the accident, the commander of the French sloop of war, from the forecastle of his ship, made use of the most insulting and provoking language, most of which was personal to the commander of the "Vandalia." Upon my taking charge of the deck, after the anchorage of the vessel, I reported to Commander Levy the language and the manner of this French captain while on the poop. I was corroborated by Surgeon Smith and Midshipmen [Alphonse] Barbot and Wait; these gentlemen were conversant with the French language.

When Commander Levy became convinced that the Frenchman had been officially as well as personally insulting to him, he ordered his boat to be manned and directed that Midshipmen Barbot and Wait, in consequence of their understanding French, should accompany him on board the French sloop of war. He was absent about half an hour; on his return he ordered the midshipmen who had accompanied him to inform me, as officer of the deck, of the result of his demand of the French captain for an apology, both official and personal. The midshipmen informed me officially that the French commander, upon Captain Levy's peremptory demand for a prompt and unequivocal apology, made it upon his quarter-deck.

Sixth. But the moral fitness of an officer of the navy, though as between him and his government fully met if he be truly patriotic, valorous, and faithful, embraces also his relations to his fellow-men and require[s] him to give succor and relief to his brother in distress, without stopping to inquire whether he be Jew or Gentile, black or white, bound or free. It is a crowning glory of American marine, commercial as well as naval, that its officers and men are prompt and chivalrous in the discharge of this duty.

To show that I have not been insensible to its claims, I refer to the newspaper statements . . . published in 1822, by which it appears that on the twenty-seventh day of September, 1822, being then at North Inlet, on Duboardiuns [Yahany] Island, South Carolina, during a violent tornado which desolated the coast of that state and by which many dwelling houses and other buildings were prostrated and their inmates swept into the ocean and very many lives lost, I made great personal efforts to save from destruction the family of Mr. Solomon Cohen, residing on that island, and also that at the hazard of my own life I succeeded in rescuing from death by drowning Mr. R. F. Withers and his two servants.

Had I recited, ever so modestly, the story of my efforts at the North Inlet, as given in the South Carolina newspapers and republished in other parts of our country, or the incidents at Rio de Janeiro proved by Lieutenant Turner, [the] apology of the captain of the French ship (with the [attendant] circumstances) to the ward-room mess of a frigate in the Mediterranean, and had Messrs. String-ham and their associates [my enemies] been among the listeners, they would doubtless have deemed the narrative incredible, and when my back was turned and I was out of hearing, they might possibly have given utterance to this scepticism. [Lieut., later Commodore Silas H. Stringham once said that Levy "had not been on board long before we found that he had money enough to buy us all."]

How many of my calumniators have saved the lives of their fellows, by imperilling their own? How often have they done it? Which of them, when a junior lieutenant, has ever had the chance of accepting an offer like that made to me? Is there one among them, who, circumstanced like me, pursued in the service of my own country by narrow-minded prejudice, surrounded by enemies, and with no strong ties to bind me to any particular spot—is there one of them who would not have jumped at the opportunity of so brilliant a transfer to the service of a foreign state?

If there be one who would have declined the offer, is there one who would have made to it the decided reply it elicited from me? Would the devotees of rank and caste, the sticklers for etiquette, the dons and hidalgoes [snobs] of the Circumlocution [red tape] Offices, whose frowns I have incurred, would these, think you, have ventured to whisper in the ears of royalty the thoroughly American words in which I made known to the Emperor of Brazil the love I bore to the land of my birth, and my preference for the humblest lot in her service, rather than the proudest position in that of any other country? . . .

THE WEIGHT OF EVIDENCE

I have now completed the examination so far as the limits of this defence have permitted, or the necessity of my case has required of the mass of testimony, oral and documentary, which has been laid before you on the part of the government and on my part. I have shown you my ten years' experience and instruction in the merchant marine. I have shown you my sea service in the navy, as sailing master, acting lieutenant, lieutenant, and commander, embracing the greater part of the twenty-seven years for which I held those commissions, under circumstances always of responsibility, often of peculiar difficulty and danger. I have shown you that no one of my commanders or superiors ever made a charge against me for disobeying his commands or neglecting my duties. I have shown you that from my service in the "Argus," in 1813, to my command of the "Vandalia," in 1839, my particular duties were performed to the satisfaction of my commanders.

I have shown you that in every station I have filled I have given myself with wholehearted alacrity and vigor to the duties of my profession, shrinking from no toil or peril or self-denial; meeting, as they arose, the claims of each day with cheerfulness and zeal, not limiting my labors to the mere requisitions of my post or the interests of the navy, though these were always uppermost in my heart, but habitually doing what I could to promote the extension and safety of commerce, the welfare of my fellow-citizens, and the honor of my country, and, in every stage of my career, striving to merit the commissions she had granted me by giving to her, as they required, the whole measure of my abilities, and by showing myself earnest, eager, and unwavering in patriotism, valor, and fidelity.

These proofs I have brought down so far as it was possible to this very hour. I have shown you by my presence before you, from day to day, during this long investigation, my physical capacity for all the duties of my grade, ashore and afloat, and, so far as they have been called into exercise in your presence, I have also demonstrated my mental fitness for those duties. By the evidence of fifty-seven witnesses from the navy and from the various departments of civil life, many of them eminent by their official rank, their public services, or their high social positions, some of them acquainted with me from my early years, and all of them respectable and trustworthy, I have proved my abundant fitness for the naval service (in the active list of the grade from which I was dropped) in all the particulars demanded by the law, physically, mentally, professionally, and morally, and that I ought to be promptly and honorably restored to it.

Against this array of proofs, what is there on the other side? First, the records of six courts-martial, by which, between 1816 and 1842, I had been found guilty of certain military offenses, two of which judgments were disapproved and the sentences thereon nullified by the superior authorities, and the other four of which judgments were fully carried into effect, immediately after their rendition, by the execution of the sentences decreed. Of the four judgments thus approved and executed, all but one were for offenses so trivial or so qualified by the provocation which led to them that I was only sentenced to be reprimanded; in the other case, the punishment finally decreed extended to suspension from duty for twelve months, without pay and emoluments, and this, too, has been completely carried into effect.

There is next the report of the Court of Inquiry, made in 1823, in relation to the gunboat "Revenge," No. 158, which contains nothing bearing on the present investigation. [While in command of the gunboat, Levy had trouble with a Spanish man-of-war. Later his gunboat was wrecked. The Court of Inquiry, although dissatisfied with certain acts and decisions of Levy, did not recommend that any action [should] be taken against him.]

There are next the unfavorable opinions, prejudices they should rather be called, of half a dozen naval officers, only one of whom has served with me at any time within the last thirty years, and he only in the same squadron (not in the same ship) some eighteen years ago. All the others, so far as they speak from personal knowl-

JOSEPH JONAS
First Jew in Cincinnati, 1817
(see page 205)

CINCINNATI IN THE LATE 1820's

edge, speak of me as I was known to them from thirty-two to forty years ago.

It were an insult to the understandings of sensible men to argue, in this case, as to the weight of evidence. The evidence is all on one side. It speaks in one concurrent and harmonious voice; it tends to one and the same end; above and beyond dispute or cavil, it establishes one and the same conclusion: my pre-eminent "fitness, physically, mentally, professionally, and morally, for the naval service."

This is the first question on which you are to pass. It is a question of fact, and it is by the evidence, and the evidence only, that you are to determine it. Such is the plain and explicit injunction of the oath you have taken. It requires you "well and truly to examine and inquire, according to the evidence, into the matter now before you.". . .

THE APPEAL TO THE COURT

Mr. President and Gentlemen of the Court, my defense, so far as it depends on the examination of the evidence you have received, is before you. I have shown what I promised in my opening remarks: first, my nautical experience and education as a seaman prior to my entering the navy; secondly, the history and character of my connexion with the naval service; thirdly, the gross injustice of the ex parte sentence by means of which I was dismissed from that service; fourthly, the provisions made by Congress, in the act under which this court is organized, for the reviewing of that sentence; and lastly, that it is the solemn duty of this court, under the laws by which it is governed and upon the evidence before it, to report to the President, as the result of this investigation, my "physical, mental, professional, and moral fitness for the naval service," and that I ought to be restored to the active list of the grade from which I was dropped.

Here, perhaps, I ought to stop, but the peculiarities of my case, the importance and far-reaching interest of the principles it involves, require, what I hope you will allow me, a few additional remarks.

That the case alleged against me by the government was wholly unsupported by any sufficient evidence; that the little it contained to my prejudice has been perfectly repelled by me; and that I have made out a complete defence against the attempt to justify my dismissal and an affirmative title to my restoration, by the proofs on my part. These I regard as undeniable propositions.

And yet there are those connected with the navy, who, notwithstanding the proofs I have produced, are still hostile to my restoration. This it would be in vain to deny to others or to attempt to conceal from myself. If any of these should dare to obtrude upon you the opinion or the wish that I should not be restored, or being restored, should not be placed upon the active list, you have but to refer him to the oath that you have taken to silence and rebuke him.

Permit me, not that I suppose that you can have forgotten its terms but because of their peculiar pertinency to my case, to quote all the words of this oath. It not only requires you, as before remarked, "well and truly to examine and inquire, according to the evidence, into the matter now before you," but to do this "without *partiality* or *prejudice.*" This oath, though exceedingly brief, is exceedingly comprehensive and precise. The lawmakers who framed it well knew the special dangers to which courts of inquiry are exposed. Partiality towards influential prosecutors and accusers, prejudice against the accused: against these the oath solemnly warns you, and if ever there was a case in which such an admonition was right and reasonable, this is that case.

The government, with its vast power and influence, is, in name at least, my prosecutor. Men in high places, who have once done me grievous wrong, are interested to prevent the remedying of that wrong. There are others, not without their influence, who by their activity in support of the wrong and in opposition to the remedy, have a common interest with my prosecutors, whoever they may be.

Never, on the other hand, was there a man in the ranks of our profession against whom, in the breasts of certain members of that profession, prejudices so unjust and yet so strong have so long and so incessantly rankled. Such, too, are the origin and character of these prejudices, as to make them, of all others, the most inveterate and unyielding. The prejudice felt by men of little minds, who think themselves, by the accidental circumstances of wealth or ancestry, better than the less favored of their fellows; the prejudice of *caste* which looks down on the man who by honest toil is the maker of his own fortunes—this prejudice is stubborn as well as bitter, and of this I have had, as you have seen by the proofs, my full share. But this is placable and transient compared with that generated and nourished by religious intolerance and bigotry.

The first article of the amendments to the Constitution of the United States explicitly declares that "Congress shall make no law respecting an establishment of religion, or prohibiting the free exercise thereof," showing by its place, no less than by its language, how highly freedom of conscience was valued by the founders of our republic. In the constitutions of the several states, now in force, the like provision is contained. In this respect, we have been honored by the friends of liberty and of human rights as "the sole exception in Christendom."

An eminent British writer, about forty years ago, in the ablest of their reviews, used in reference to this point the following language:

'They [the Americans] have fairly and completely, and probably forever, extinguished that spirit of religious persecution which has been the employment and the curse of mankind for four or five centuries—not only that persecution which imprisons and scourges for religious opinions, but the tyranny of incapacitation, which by disqualifying from civil offices and cutting a man off from the lawful objects of ambition, endeavors to strangle religious freedom in silence and to enjoy all the advantages, without the blood, and noise, and fire of persecution. . . . In this particular, the Americans are at the head of all the nations of the world.

Little did the author of this generous tribute to our country dream that, within a period so short, it should come to be a question in America whether a Jew should be tolerated in the navy. Still less could he have dreamt that at the very moment when in Great Britain, according to advices just received, a representative of the illustrious house of Russell [Lord John Russell], eminent by his services in the cause of freedom, of education, and of justice, is giving himself, with the full assent of his government, to the work of Jewish emancipation, the spectacle should be presented, in this land of equal rights and equal laws, of an officer whose services, Israelite though he was, were gladly accepted by his government in the hour of national peril, of an officer long tried in his country's service, who had given to that service the freshness of his youth and the vigor of his manhood, one (proved by half a century [hundred] of witnesses) still pre-eminently qualified therefor by his patriotism, his valor, his fidelity, and his abilities; of such an officer, struggling to regain the privilege, wrongfully wrested from him, of serving his country while he lives and of dying in her defense; that to his success in this struggle there should be one and but one serious impediment, and that this should be found in the fact of his religion.

And yet this is the case before you. My case is the case of every Israelite in the Union. I need not speak to you of their number, but I may speak of the fact that they are unsurpassed by any other portion of our people in loyalty to the Constitution and to the Union, by their quiet support of our laws and Constitution, by the cheerfulness with which they contribute their share of the public burthens, and by the liberal donations many of them have made to promote the general interests of education and of charity, and in some instances along with these, of which the name of Judah Touro will remind you, of charities controuled by Christians and, sometimes, exclusively devoted to the benefit of Christians. Again, how rarely does one of my brethren, either of foreign birth or American descent, become a charge on your state or municipal treasuries! How largely do they all contribute to the activities of trade, to the interests of commerce, to the stock of public wealth!

Are all these to be placed under the ban of incapacitation? And is this to be done while we retain in our Constitution the language I have quoted? Is that language to be spoken to the ear, but broken to the hope of my race? Are the thousand[s] of Israel and the ten thousands of Judah, in their dispersion throughout the earth, who look to America as a land bright with promise, are they now to learn, to their sorrow and dismay, that we too have sunk into the mire of religious intolerance and bigotry? And are American Christians now to begin the persecution of the Jews, of the Jew who stands among them the representatives of the patriarch and prophets to whom were committed the oracles of God; the Jew from whom they received these oracles, and who is the living witness of their truth; the Jew, of whom came the founders of their religion; the Jew, to whom Christians themselves believe there yet pertain "exceeding great and precious promises" [II Peter 1:4], in whose fulfillment are bound up the hopes not merely of the remnant of Israel, but of all the races of men?

And think not, if you once enter on this career, that it can be limited to the Jew. What is my case today, if you yield to this injustice, may tomorrow be that of the Roman Catholic or the Unitarian, the Presbyterian or the Methodist, the Episcopalian or the Baptist. There is but one safeguard: that is to be found in an honest, wholehearted, inflexible support of the wise, the just, the impartial guarantee of the Constitution. I have the fullest confidence that you will faithfully adhere to this guarantee, and therefore, with like confidence I leave my destiny in your hands.

Mordecai Manuel Noah

Ebullient Politician

Mordecai Manuel Noah, the politician, was the best-known Jewish layman in the country in the decades before the Civil War, although he was neither the greatest Jew nor the most distinguished of his clan. Like his relatives Uriah P. Levy and Raphael J. Moses, he came from old Spanish-Portuguese American stock. His father was said to have been a veteran of the Revolution, and his grandfather, Jonas Phillips, had served for some time as a militiaman during the War for Independence.

Our hero was born in Philadelphia in 1785 and died in New York City in 1851. In his early teens he was apprenticed to a carver and gilder, but soon went to work as a clerk in a government office in Philadelphia, and, still under twenty, became a reporter at the Pennsylvania Legislature in Harrisburg. Journalism then became his life's work, first in Charleston, South Carolina, and afterwards in New York. In the latter city he edited a series of newspapers, and because of his power with the spoken word, as well as with the pen, he acquired considerable influence in politics. He was a Tammany Democrat—ultimately Grand Sachem—a Jacksonian, and even a Whig. Power brought him office, and he consecutively became sheriff, surveyor of the port of New York, and a judge. Noah was also a lawyer, but no one ever accused him of being learned in the law.

He always wrote well. At the age of twenty-three he had published a play, and later Noah wrote and published several other dramas. An ardent patriot, he frequently chose national themes and dwelt with pride on the American love of freedom and liberty.

His first political plum—it turned out to be a very sour one— was his appointment as consul to Tunis during the War of 1812, when the United States had its hands full with the British. It was Noah's duty to placate the marauding Tunisians and to attempt surreptitiously to free American sailors who had been imprisoned by the Algerians.

Noah arranged for the liberation of some Americans in Algeria (1813-14), but the State Department, headed by James Monroe, believed that he had freed the wrong men and had spent too much

117

money. It refused to honor his drafts and faced him with the prospect of imprisonment for debt in a Tunisian jail. Gross insult was added to injury when, in 1815, Commodore Stephen Decatur appeared off the coast of Tunisia, carrying sealed orders from the State Department for Noah: the consul was recalled because of his religion and of confusion in his accounts.

His situation was truly desperate, but Noah pulled himself out of a bad hole by quick thinking and even quicker action. Utilizing the presence of Decatur's flotilla, the consul compelled the Bey of Tunis to pay an indemnity for his improper surrender of American prize ships. Thereupon Noah used the indemnity to settle his official obligations and returned to Washington. He was eager to explain his accounts and determined to demand an explanation for the statement that his Jewish religion was a bar to consular service in North Africa. Because he got no satisfaction from President James Madison or Secretary Monroe, he brought his case before the bar of public opinion in a vigorous, forthright statement: Correspondence and Documents Relative to the Attempt to Negotiate for the Release of the American Captives at Algiers; including Remarks on our Relations with that Regency *(Washington City, 1816).*

The following year the government settled its fiscal difficulties with him, but nothing was said about the delicate matter of religious prejudice. In a very friendly letter which Madison sent Noah in 1818, the great Virginian spoke of the freedom which every sect enjoyed in this country, expressed his pleasure that Noah's accounts had been closed in a manner favorable to the late consul, and assured him that his religious profession was not a motive in his recall. It is not improbable that Madison was not party to that action and that the real culprit, as Noah suspected, was the ill-fated Colonel Tobias Lear.

The prejudice which Noah had experienced probably helped to make of him a "good Jew." As a consul in Tunis, he had blandly avoided his Barbary coreligionists, but on his return he became very active and something of a leader in the Jewish community. In 1825 Noah blossomed forth with an apparently harebrained scheme to settle the unhappy, disfranchised Jews of Europe on Grand Island, near Buffalo. Such land settlements, utopian schemes, were not uncommon in those days. That new city of refuge was to be called Ararat, but no land was sold to Jewish immigrants and no colonists came. Some two decades later, in 1844, Noah came forward with a proto-Zionist appeal to the Christian world to help the Jews regain their ancient homeland.

The following "memoirs" are a composite of several sources. The *autobiographical account of his career as a dramatist is in the form of a letter sent by Noah to William Dunlap, and was incorporated by the latter in his* History of the American Theatre *(New York, 1832), pp. 380-84. The material on the Tunisian* affaire *is taken in the following order from* Correspondence and Documents, *pp. 3-10, 78-80;* Travels in England, France, Spain, and the Barbary States, in the Years 1813-14 and 15 *(New York, 1819), pp. 376-81, XXIV;* Correspondence and Documents, *pp. 125-28;* Travels, *pp. 381-85, 414-16.*

NOAH THE PLAYWRIGHT

New York, July 11th, 1832.

William Dunlap, Esq.,

Dear Sir:

I am happy to hear that your work on the American drama is in press, and trust that you may realize from it that harvest of fame and money to which your untiring industry and diversified labours give you an eminent claim. You desire me to furnish you a list of my dramatic productions. It will, my dear sir, constitute a sorry link in the chain of American writers. My plays have all been *ad captandum* ["to capture" the fancy of the mob]; a kind of amateur performance, with no claim to the character of a settled, regular, or domiciliated writer for the greenroom, a sort of volunteer supernumerary, a dramatic writer by "particular desire, and for this night only," as they say in the bills of the play.

My "line," as you well know, has been in the more rugged paths of politics, a line in which there is more fact than poetry, more feeling than fiction, in which, to be sure, there are "exits and entrances," where the prompter's whistle is constantly heard in the voice of the people, but which, in our popular government, almost disqualifies us for the more soft and agreeable translation to the lofty conceptions of tragedy, the pure diction of genteel comedy, or the wit, gayety, and humour of broad farce.

I had an early hankering for the national drama, a kind of juvenile patriotism, which burst forth, for the first time, in a few sorry doggrels in the form of a prologue to a play, which a Thespian company, of which I was a member, produced in the South Street Theatre, the old American Theatre in Philadelphia. The idea was probably suggested by the sign of the Federal Convention at the tavern opposite the theatre. You, no doubt, remember the picture and the motto: an excellent piece of painting of the kind, representing a group of venerable personages engaged in public discussions, with the following distich:

These thirty-eight great men have signed a powerful deed,
That better times, to us, shall very soon succeed.

The sign must have been painted soon after the adoption of the federal constitution, and I remember to have stood "many a time and oft," gazing, when a boy, at the assembled patriots, particularly the venerable head and spectacles of Dr. [Benjamin] Franklin, always in conspicuous relief. In our Thespian corps, the honour of cutting the plays, substituting new passages, casting parts, and writing couplets at the exits, was divided between myself and a fellow of infinite wit and humour by the name of [George] Helmbold, who subsequently became the editor of a scandalous little paper called the *Tickler*. He was a rare rascal, perpetrated all kind[s] of calumnies, was constantly mulcted in fines, sometimes imprisoned, was full of faults which were forgotten in his conversational qualities and dry sallies of genuine wit, particularly his Dutch stories. After years of singular vicissitudes, Helmbold joined the army as a common soldier, fought bravely during the late war [of 1812], obtained a commission [as a lieutenant in the Thirteenth Infantry], and died.

Our little company soon dwindled away. The expenses were too heavy for our pockets. Our writings and performances were sufficiently wretched, but as the audience was admitted without cost, they were too polite to express any disapprobation. We recorded all our doings in a little weekly paper, published, I believe, by Jemmy Riddle, at the corner of Chestnut and Third Street, opposite the tavern kept by that sturdy old democrat, Israel Israel. [Israel was a Quaker; his father had been a Jew.]

From a boy, I was a regular attendant at the Chestnut Street Theatre, during the management of Wignell and Reinagle, and made great efforts to compass the purchase of a season ticket, which I obtained generally of the treasurer, George Davis, for $18. Our habits through life are frequently governed and directed by our early steps. I seldom missed a night, and always retired to bed after witnessing a good play, gratified and improved, and thus, probably, escaped the haunts of taverns and the pursuits of depraved pleasures, which too frequently allure and destroy our young men. Hence I was always the firm friend of the drama, and had an undoubted right to oppose my example through life to the horror and hostility expressed by sectarians to plays and playhouses generally.

Independent of several of your plays which had obtained possession of the stage, and were duly incorporated in the legitimate drama, the first call to support the productions of a fellow-townsman was, I think, [James Nelson] Barker's opera of the *Indian Princess*. [Barker's first play, produced in Philadelphia in 1807, was *Tears and Smiles*.] Charles Ingersoll had previously written a tragedy, a

very able production for a very young man, which was supported
by all the good society. But Barker, who was one of us, an amiable
and intelligent young fellow, who owed nothing to hereditary rank,
though his father was a Whig and a soldier of the Revolution, was
in reality a fine-spirited poet, a patriotic ode writer, and, finally, a
gallant soldier of the late war. The managers gave Barker an excellent chance with all his plays, and he had merit and popularity to
give them in return full houses.

About this time [1808], I ventured to attempt a little melodrama,
under the title of the *Fortress of Sorrento*, which, not having money
enough to pay for printing, nor sufficient influence to have acted,
I thrust the manuscript in my pocket, and having occasion to visit
New York, I called in at David Longworth's Dramatic Repository
one day, spoke of the little piece, and struck a bargain with him by
giving him the manuscript in return for a copy of every play he had
published, which at once furnished me with a tolerably large dramatic collection. I believe the play never was performed, and I was
almost ashamed to own it, but it was my first regular attempt at
dramatic composition.

In the year 1812, while in Charleston, S. C., Mr. [Charles] Young
requested me to write a piece for his wife's benefit. You remember
her, no doubt, remarkable as she was for her personal beauty and
amiable deportment. It would have been very ungallant to have refused, particularly as he requested that it should be a "breeches
part," to use a greenroom term, though she was equally attractive in
every character. Poor Mrs. Young! She died last year in Philadelphia. When she first arrived in New York from London, it was
difficult to conceive a more perfect beauty. Her complexion was of
dazzling whiteness, her golden hair and ruddy complexion, figure
somewhat *embonpoint*, and graceful carriage, made her a great favorite.

I soon produced the little piece, which was called *Paul and Alexis,
or the Orphans of the Rhine*. I was, at that period, a very active
politician, and my political opponents did me the honour to go to
the theatre the night it was performed for the purpose of hissing it,
which was not attempted until the curtain fell and the piece was
successful. After three years' absence in Europe and Africa, I saw
the same piece performed at the Park [Theatre] under the title of
the *Wandering Boys*, which even now holds possession of the stage.
It seems Mr. Young sent the manuscript to London, where the title
was changed, and the bantling [the new work] cut up, altered, and
considerably improved.

About this time, John Miller, the American bookseller in London, paid us a visit. Among the passengers in the same ship was a fine English girl of great talent and promise, Miss Leesugg [Catherine Lee Sugg], afterwards Mrs. [James Henry] Hackett. She was engaged at the Park as a singer, and [my Uncle Aaron] Phillips, who was here about the same period fulfilling a most successful engagement, was decided and unqualified in his admiration of her talent. Everyone took an interest in her success. She was gay, kind-hearted, and popular, always in excellent spirits, and always perfect. Anxious for her success, I ventured to write a play for her benefit, and, in three days [June, 1819], finished the patriotic piece of *She Would Be a Soldier, or the Battle [Plains] of Chippewa*, which, I was happy to find, produced her an excellent house. Mrs. Hackett retired from the stage after her marriage, and lost six or seven years of profitable and unrivalled engagement.

After this play, I became in a manner domiciliated in the green-room. My friends, [Stephen] Price and [Edmund Shaw] Simpson, who had always been exceedingly kind and liberal, allowed me to stray about the premises like one of the family, and, always anxious for their success, I ventured upon another attempt for a holiday occasion, and produced *Marion, or the Hero of Lake George*. It was played on the twenty-fifth of November [1821], Evacuation Day, [the anniversary of the British departure from New York City], and I bustled about among my military friends to raise a party in support of a military play, and what with generals, staff officers, rank and file, the Park Theatre was so crammed that not a word of the play was heard, which was a very fortunate affair for the author. The managers presented me with a pair of handsome silver pitchers, which I still retain as a memento of their good will and friendly consideration. You must bear in mind that while I was thus employed in occasional attempts at playwriting, I was engaged in editing a daily journal, and in all the fierce contests of political strife. I had, therefore, but little time to devote to all that study and reflection so essential to the success of dramatic composition.

My next piece, I believe, was written for the benefit of a relative and friend [Uncle Aaron Phillips], who wanted something to bring a house, and as the struggle for liberty in Greece was at that period the prevailing excitement, I finished the melodrama of *The Grecian Captive* [1822], which was brought out with all the advantages of good scenery and music. As a good house was of more consequence to the actor than fame to the author, it was resolved that the hero of the piece should make his appearance on an elephant, and the heroine on a camel, which were procured from a neighbouring menagerie, and the *tout ensemble* was sufficiently imposing. Only it happened that the huge elephant, in shaking his skin, so rocked the castle on his back, that the Grecian general nearly lost his balance and was in imminent danger of coming down from his high estate, to the infinite merriment of the audience.

On this occasion, to use another significant phrase, a "gag" was hit upon of a new character altogether. The play was printed, and each auditor was presented with a copy gratis, as he entered the house. Figure to yourself a thousand people in a theatre, each with a book of the play in hand. Imagine the turning over a thousand leaves simultaneously, the buzz and fluttering it produced, and you will readily believe that the actors entirely forgot their parts, and even the equanimity of the elephant and camel were essentially disturbed.

My last appearance as a dramatic writer was in another national piece called *The Siege of Tripoli* [actually in 1820], which the managers persuaded me to bring out for my own benefit, being my first attempt to derive any profit from dramatic efforts. The piece was elegantly got up, the house crowded with beauty and fashion, everything went off in the happiest manner, when, a short time after the audience had retired, the Park Theatre was discovered to be on fire [May 24, 1820], and in a short time was a heap of ruins. This conflagration burnt out all my dramatic fire and energy, since which I have been, as you well know, peaceably employed in settling the affairs of the nation, and mildly engaged in the political differences and disagreements which are so fruitful in our great state.

I still, however, retain a warm interest for the success of the drama, and [in] all who are entitled to success engaged in sustaining it, and to none greater than to yourself, who has done more, in actual labour and successful efforts, than any man in America. That you may realize all you have promised yourself, and all that you are richly entitled to, is the sincere wish of, dear sir,

Your friend and servant,
M. M. Noah.

THE NORTH AFRICA PROBLEM

The relations existing between the United States and the Barbary Powers have, of late [1815-16], assumed a more lively interest, not only from our operations in the Mediterranean, but from the continuance of a naval force in those waters, to protect our commerce and check the increasing hostility of those states. The situation of the regencies [the North African powers], their unchangeable policy, and their connexion with the Christian powers, are, at this day, vaguely known and imperfectly described.

The people of the United States know little of them, their maritime resources, or their military positions, except it was either in relation to the captivity of our countrymen, or the tributes which we have been compelled to pay. Both of these subjects, however, have been deeply interesting to us. Humanity for our captive citizens and regard for the just rights of the nation have induced the government to use their efforts for the liberation of the one and security of the other.

To redeem our captives from an ignominious bondage and remove every check to the operation of our arms, the government of the United States, in addition to my official duties, charged me with the attempt to negotiate for the release of the crew of the brig "Edwin" captured [August, 1812] by the Algerines. From the partial success of this mission, the administration have been induced, in some measure, to disavow the authority under which I acted, by refusing payment of my drafts, and by an insinuation of exceeding my orders, so as to render it an indispensable duty [for me] to explain the nature of the transaction and lay all the correspondence before the people of the United States. However injurious this step will prove to our credit and character abroad, it is nevertheless unavoidable. A system must at once be adopted which will place our foreign relations on a different footing, extend our national character, strengthen and increase our friends, maintain our faith, and give stability, protection, and character to the representatives and consuls of the nation.

Several months prior to my appointment as consul for Tunis, the conduct of the Algerines towards the American agent and the subsequent capture of the brig "Edwin" of Salem [Massachusetts], left no doubt on the minds of the people of the United States of the hostile disposition of that power [Algeria]. The distressing appeals to the government from the American captives, and their repeated importunities for the interference of their country, not only created a general sympathy among the people, but produced a sincere disposition, on the part of the [Madison] administration, to seize upon the first favorable occasion to procure them their liberty. This benevolent disposition, which should be evidenced on every occasion when the freedom of any of our citizens are implicated, was strengthened by the sufferings and privations of these unfortunate people.

The war [of 1812], existing at that period with England, had closed the Mediterranean to American vessels. It was, therefore, reasonable to believe that no additional capture had been made by the Algerines, and the government was disposed to interfere [infer?], from the well-grounded belief that the number of captives being comparatively trifleing, [they] could, without difficulty, be purchased and, from the same cause, the disbursements for their ransom would be deemed inconsiderable. The tribute annually paid to Algiers, the biennial presents, and the vast sums of money expended in our relations with that regency for the last ten years were justly considered oppressive, and were deemed by the people as discreditable to their character as an independent nation, and would be found hereafter injurious to their commercial interest.

In this light, also, it was viewed by the government, but the pressure of other events, more important in their operation and effects, prevented any alteration of our measures towards that power, until their rapacity, which had construed our extraordinary liberality into motives of fear, led them to promote an open rupture by dismissing the consul and capturing our vessels, calculating, at the same time, on the ready disposition of the American government to arrange this [diplomatic] difference by the payment of a considerable sum of money.

To afford a school for the practice and improvement of our officers and seamen, to open a road for the development of genius and character, to set an example to the European world, to cause our rights and country to be hereafter respected and feared, and to renew our relations on our own terms with Algiers, it was the determination of government, so far from approving their views and expectations, to seize upon the first moments after peace with England to employ all our naval force in chastising the arrogance and punishing the depredations of that power. Independent, therefore, of motives of benevolence, it was an object of policy in the government to use every effort to redeem our captive seamen, calculating that no addition would be made to the number, desirous of removing every check to our operations, and causing those operations to be unrestrained and vigorous.

The entire confidence reposed in me by my political friends throughout the United States, and their representations in my behalf, gave me every reason to believe that the government was no less favorably impressed towards me, and deemed it a proper opportunity to avail themselves of my services by authorising me to purchase the release of those seamen at Algiers. Accordingly, in the instructions forwarded to me from the Secretary of State, the following paragraph refers to that object:

On your way to Tunis, perhaps at Malaga [Spain] or Marseilles [France], you may probably devise means for the liberation of our unfortunate countrymen at Algiers, whose situation has excited the warmest sympathy of their friends, and indeed of the people generally of this country. Should you find a suitable channel through which you can negotiate their immediate release, you are authorised to go as far as $3,000 a man, but a less sum may probably effect the object. Whatever may be the result of the attempt, you will, for obvious reasons, not let it be understood to proceed from this government, but rather from the friends of the parties themselves. As yet we have information only of eleven persons, the crew of the brig "Edwin," of Salem, being confined at Algiers, and it is to be hoped that no addition has been made to that number. If success should attend your efforts, you will draw upon this department for the necessary funds for paying their ransom, and providing for their comfortable return to their country and friends.

It appears to me that these instructions are clear and not to be misunderstood. Lest, however, I may have misconstrued those orders and gone beyond the views and wishes of government, I will be allowed the privilege of examining more closely the paragraph relating to those captives: "On your way to Tunis, perhaps at Malaga or Marseilles, you may *probably* devise means for the liberation of our unfortunate countrymen at Algiers."

If it is said that the release of the seamen was intended to be left to chance, and that the government, though willing to redeem them, was not anxious to make an attempt to purchase their release, the consuls at Malaga, Marseilles, or Cadiz [Spain] could have been notified that if the Dey of Algiers would dispose of his American captives, they were authorised to purchase, but no steps of this nature was taken. Their release was desirable—the sympathy of their country was excited—attempts and efforts were to be made, and the government kept out of view, and the disbursements were to be drawn for on the Department of State.

All this goes to prove that, so far from being an object of indifference, it was, in fact, a delicate and confidential mission. The government can only reason on *probable* grounds. With the most serious intentions, the government could not say that means *must* be devised, but that means may *probably* be devised to release those persons, and, as an inducement to provide means for their liberation, I am distinctly told that "their situation has excited the warmest sympathy of their friends, and *indeed* of the *people generally* of this country." It was, therefore, the people, who, through the government, were anxious that I should devise means to restore these seamen to their friends and country.

"Should you find a suitable channel, therefore, through which you can *negotiate* their immediate release, you are *authorised* to go as far as $3,000 a man." This clause is clear and definite. I am only to inquire what is meant by a "suitable channel." It could not be expected that I could personally negotiate for the release of those seamen, or charge an American citizen with that mission. Either would have been imprudent, personally dangerous, and, in the event of accident, expensive and embarrassing to the nation, without promising any essential benefit.

Neither did I deem it the interest of the United States to authorise any of the consuls in Algiers to make an offer for the release of those captives, for, however desirous they might be, from benevolent motives, to serve these unfortunate persons, I was not ignorant of the divisions and dissentions always existing among the foreign agents of that regency, together with the espionage, suspicion, and distrust of the Algerines, which would defeat the object by attributing the offer as emanating from the American government direct. It therefore only remained for me to select an agent on whom perfect reliance could be had, and authorise such a person to conduct the negotiation.

The instructions proceed as follows: "Whatever may be the result of the attempt, you will, for obvious reasons, not let it be understood to proceed from this government, but rather from the friends of the parties themselves." Here it is clearly intimated that an *attempt* is to be made. The situation of these men excite the commisseration of government; their release is anxiously called for. It is not left to chance, but the consul, newly appointed to Tunis, as it should seem, with the confidence of his government, is specially ordered to make an attempt to ransom his captive countrymen. "As yet," says the honorable Secretary of State [James Monroe], "we have information only of eleven persons being confined at Algiers, the crew of the brig 'Edwin' of Salem, and it is to be hoped that no addition has since been made to that number. If success should attend your efforts" (and here again efforts are to be made), "you will *draw on this department* for the necessary funds for paying their ransom, and providing for their comfortable return to their country and friends."

Impressed with the belief that these instructions were not of a vague and indefinite character, commisserating, likewise, the situation of these unfortunate persons, and possessing the most anxious desire to be instrumental in restoring them to liberty, I could not but seize on a favorable occasion to select an agent of character and talents, to whom I gave the necessary powers to treat for their ransom. . . .

CONSUL IN TUNIS

[Taking advantage of the fact that the United States was at war with Great Britain, the Algerians, as we have read, enslaved an American crew. Noah was commissioned by the State Department to effect their ransom. To accomplish this purpose, the consul employed Richard R. Keene of Cadiz, Spain, a native of Maryland, who had become a naturalized Spaniard. Noah, as an American consular officer, could not afford to admit that his government was interested in ransoming the captives, for the Dey of Algiers would have jacked up the price. Keene was only partially successful in his mission. He secured the release of two of the crew of the "Edwin" and of four others, reputedly Louisianians. When Noah, through an agent, drew on his government for the ransom of those men, the draft was not honored. The State Department was of the opinion that the consul had exceeded his instructions.]

Having thus acquitted myself of the duty imposed upon me to examine and explain the measures I deemed proper to pursue, in reference to the ransom of those seamen, and viewing these measures with the most impartial eye, I cannot accuse myself of going beyond the views and expectations of government or wilfully expending one dollar of the public money, beyond the pressing and absolute occasion which caused these disbursements. Neither will it be said that the expenditures were unwarranted or unexpected. Admitting, however, without knowing what are the objections of the government, that errors have been committed, no officer can possibly be exempt from error in the discharge of his public duty, and when it is evident that there was no violation of orders, no desire to extend authority, no disposition to impose upon the United States, and that the expenditures incurred was in pursuance of instructions and with a view of benefitting the interests of government, the obligations incurred by that officer, in their name, should be strictly fulfilled.

The consuls in the Barbary States require from their government a stronger protection, more liberal construction of authority, and a facility of obtaining funds for the public service, beyond what would appear necessary for an agent in a civilized part of the world. In Barbary, a consul is only tolerated from fear and not from favor, and the people who govern seize upon every occasion and improve every opportunity to humiliate him, and to deprive him, if possible, of the respect and consideration to which he is entitled.

He is called upon by his country to maintain the honor of the flag assigned to his protection, at every hazard, and he is compelled to defend his rights against every species of outrage and despotism, as well as to guard, with vigilant attention, the interest of the citizens trading to his consulate.

To discharge his duty faithfully to his country, and with satisfaction to himself, his government must afford him their countenance and protection. Care must be taken that his rights are supported and his credit unimpaired. If the situation accorded to him is of distinguished importance, it would appear that the confidence reposed in him should be full and implicit. *When the obligations of a consul in Barbary are once impaired by his government, he can no longer remain at his post with credit to himself or honor to his country!* . . .

The Commission Revoked

[That crisis in the status of the consul, facing imprisonment for debt because of the protested bill of exchange, was exacerbated by troubles with the Tunisian authorities. Two prizes, brought into Tunis by an American privateer, had been retaken in Tunisian waters by the British while the war between them and the Americans was still in progress. Quite correctly, Noah turned to the Bey of Tunis and demanded compensation in the amount of $46,000 for the loss of the prizes.

This was the situation in July, 1815, when Commodore Stephen Decatur appeared off the coast of Tunisia with his squadron. The war with England was over, and Algiers had been compelled by Decatur, on June 30th, to make peace with the Americans and to release her captives. Now the guns of the avenging American flotilla were trained on the Tunisians.]

The squadron lay off Cape Carthage [near Tunis], arranged in handsome order; the "Guerriere," bearing the broad penant of the commodore [Decatur], was in the centre, and the whole exhibiting a very agreeable and commanding sight. In less than an hour, I was alongside of the flagship and ascended on the quarter-deck. The marines were under arms and received the consul of the United States with the usual honours. Commodore Decatur and Capt. Downs [Master Commandant John Downes], both in uniform, were at the gangway, and most of the officers and crew pressed forward to view their fellow-citizen. After the customary salutations and a few inquiries, Commodore Decatur invited me into the cabin, where, after being seated, he went to his *escrutoire* [*escritoire*, "desk"], and from among a package of letters he handed me one, saying that it was a despatch from the Secretary of State, and requested me to use no ceremony, but to read it. It had the seal of the United States, which I broke, and, to my great surprise, read as follows:

Department of State, April 25, 1815.

Sir:

At the time of your appointment as consul at Tunis, it was not known that the religion which you profess would form any obstacle to the exercise of your consular functions. Recent information, however, on which entire reliance may be placed, proves that it would produce a very unfavourable effect. In consequence of which, the President has deemed it expedient to revoke your commission. On the receipt of this letter, therefore, you will consider yourself no longer in the public service. There are some circumstances, too, connected with your accounts, which require a more particular explanation, which, with that already given, are not approved by the President.

I am, very respectfully, sir,
Your obedient servant,
(Signed) James Monroe.

Mordecai M. Noah, Esquire, etc., etc.

The receipt of this letter shocked me inexpressibly. At this moment, at such a time, and in such a place, to receive a letter which at once stripped me of office, of rights, of honour, and credit, was sufficient to astonish and dismay a person of stronger nerves. What was to be done? I had not a moment to determine. I cast my eye hastily on Commodore Decatur; I was satisfied at a glance that he knew not the contents of the letter. It was necessary that he should not, for had he been made acquainted with the determination of the government, it would have been his duty, and he would have exercised it promptly, to have sent an officer on shore, taken possession of the seals and archives of the consulate, and I should have returned to Tunis, stripped of power, an outcast, degraded, and disgraced, a heavy debt against me. And from my consulate, from the possession of power, respected and feared, I should in all probability have gone into a dungeon, where I might have perished, neglected and unpitied, and for what? For carrying into effect the express orders of the government!

I had no time to curse such perfidy. I folded up the letter with apparent indifference and put it in my pocket, and then proceeded to relate to Commodore Decatur the nature of our dispute with Tunis, which was corroborated by the documents I had prepared and brought with me. I suggested the propriety of his writing a letter to the minister and demanding payment for the prizes without delay, and the better to give effect to this demand, it would be well for the commodore to remain on board his ship until it was complied with. This course I urged with a zeal corresponding with the stake I had at issue and with my peculiar situation. The commodore could not account for this great anxiety to recover the money. My object was to pay the protested bills, redeem the credit of the country, and thus enable me to return home with honour. He must have imagined that other motives dictated this extraordinary warmth and arguments upon arguments, all of which I enforced with vehemence.

"You may probably," said he, "imagine that I am under your orders; if you do, it is proper to undeceive you." I saw a storm gathering which would destroy all my plans, and I tranquilly assured the commodore that I requested nothing more than his cooperation to maintain our treaty inviolate, and by such measures as his prudence dictated. We were only there to serve our country in the best manner. Thus satisfied, the commodore, who originally was pleased at the prompt manner pointed out of terminating this difference, consented to write the letter, which was done forthwith. Night came on, and I betook myself to rest on the cabin floor, and in a state of mind better imagined than described.

RELIGIOUS PREJUDICE

At daybreak the next morning, the lively drum and fife played the reveille. The officer on duty furnished me with a boat and hands, which landed Abdallah [my interpreter] and myself under Cape Carthage. I had ordered horses to be on that spot at an early hour, and we ascended to the rugged summit to look for their approach. I seated myself on the extreme height of the cape. The sun was just rising, and the beautiful amphitheatre by which I was surrounded was tinged with gold. Not a soul was stirring. Below me were the diminished masts of our squadron, which was tranquilly at anchor; at a distance, the smooth surface of the Mediterranean, without a solitary bark to break the prospect. The birds were singing cheerfully; everything appeared at ease, except myself.

I once more read the letter of Mr. Monroe. I paused to reflect on its contents. I was at a loss to account for its strange and unprecedented tenor: my religion an object of hostility? I thought I was a citizen of the United States, protected by the constitution in my religious, as well as in my civil, rights. My religion was known to the government at the time of my appointment, and it constituted one of the prominent causes why I was sent to Barbary. If, then, any "unfavourable" events had been created by my religion, they should have been first ascertained, and not acting upon a supposition, upon imaginary consequences, have thus violated one of the most sacred and delicate rights of a citizen. Admitting, then, that my religion had produced an unfavourable effect, no *official* notice should have been taken of it. I could have been recalled without placing on file a letter thus hostile to the spirit and character of our institutions. But my religion was not known in Barbary; from the moment of my landing, I had been in the full possession of my consular functions, respected and feared by the government, and enjoying the esteem and good will of every resident.

What injury could my religion create? I lived like other consuls; the flag of the United States was displayed on Sundays and Christian holidays. The Catholic priest, who came into my house to sprinkle holy water and pray, was received with deference and freely allowed to perform his pious purpose. The barefooted Franciscan, who came to beg, received alms in the name of Jesus Christ. The Greek bishop, who sent to me a decorated branch of palm on Palm Sunday, received, in return, a customary donation. The poor Christian slaves, when they wanted a favour, came to me. The Jews alone asked nothing from me. Why then am I to be persecuted for

my religion? Although no religious principles are known to the
constitution, no peculiar worship connected with the government,
yet I did not forget that I was representing a Christian nation.
What was the opinion of Joel Barlow [U. S. consul to Algiers,
1795], when writing a treaty for [Tripoli, 1797] one of the Barbary
States? Let the following article, *confirmed by the Senate of the
United States,* answer:

> *Article 11th*—As the government of the United States of Amer-
> ica *is not, in any sense, founded on the Christian religion*—as it
> has, in itself, no character of enmity against the laws, religion,
> or tranquillity of Mussulmen [Mohammedans]; and as the said
> States never have entered into any war, or act of hostility against
> any Mahometan nation, it is declared by the parties, that no pre-
> text *arising from religious opinions,* shall *ever* produce an inter-
> ruption of the harmony existing between the two countries.
> [Actually, the Arabic of Article 11 says nothing about Chris-
> tianity. It does, however, ask for reciprocally good treatment for
> Americans and Tripolitans in the respective two lands.]

If President Madison was unacquainted with this article in the
treaty, which in effect is equally binding in all the States of Barbary,
he should have remembered that the religion of a citizen is not a
legitimate object of official notice from the government. And even
admitting that my religion was an obstacle, and there is no doubt
that it was not, are we prepared to yield up the admirable and just
institutions of our country at the shrine of foreign bigotry and
superstition? Are we prepared to disfranchise one of our own citizens to gratify the intolerant views of the Bey of Tunis? Has it
come to this, that the noble character of the most illustrious republic
on earth, celebrated for its justice and the sacred character of its
institutions, is to be sacrificed at the shrine of a Barbary pirate?
Have we then fallen so low? What would have been the consequence,
had the Bey known and objected to my religion? He would have
learnt from me, in language too plain to be misunderstood, that
whoever the United States commissions as their representative, he
must receive and respect, if his conduct be proper. On that subject I could not have permitted a word to be said.

If such a principle is attempted to be established, it will lay the
foundation for the most unhappy and most dangerous disputes. Foreign nations will dictate to us the religion which our officers at
their courts should profess. With all the reflection, and the most

painful anxiety, I could not account for this most extraordinary and novel procedure. Some base intrigue, probably one who was ambitious of holding this wretched office, had been at some pains to represent to the government that my religion would produce injurious effects, and the President, instead of closing the door on such interdicted subjects, had listened and concurred. And after having braved the perils of the ocean, residing in a barbarous country, without family or relatives, supporting the rights of the nation, and hazarding my life from poison or the stiletto, I find my own government, the only protector I can have, sacrificing my credit, violating my rights, and insulting my feelings, and the religious feelings of a whole nation [the Jews]. O! shame, shame!

The course which men of refined or delicate feelings should have pursued, had there been grounds for such a suspicion, was an obvious one. The President should have instructed the Secretary of State to have recalled me, and to have said that the causes should be made known to me on my return. Such a letter as I received should never have been written, and, above all, should never have been put on file. But it is not true that my religion either had, or would have produced injurious effects. The Dey of Algiers had appointed Abraham Busnah his minister at the court of France; Nathan Bacri is Algerine consul at Marseilles; his brother holds the same office at Leghorn. [All are Jews.] The treasurer, interpreter, and commercial agent of the Grand Seigneur at Constantinople are Jews.

In the year 1811, the British government sent Aaron Cordoza [Cardozo], Esq., of Gibraltar, a most intelligent and respectable Jew, with a sloop of war to Algiers, to negotiate some important point connected with commerce. He was received with deference, and succeeded. The first minister from Portugal to Morocco was Abraham Sasportas, a Jew, who formed a treaty, and was received with open arms. Ali Bey of Tunis sent Moses Massias [as] ambassador to London, the father of Major Abraham A. Massias [a Jew], who was at present serving in the army of the United States. Innumerable instances could be adduced, where the Mussulmen have preferred employing the Israelites on foreign missions, and had any important dispute arose, requiring power and influence to adjust, my religion should have been known, and my success would have been certain. But I had sufficient power and respect, more than have ever been enjoyed by any consul before me, and none who succeeds me will ever possess a greater share.

It was not necessary for a citizen of the United States to have his faith stamped on his forehead. The name of freeman is a sufficient passport, and my government should have supported me, had it been necessary to have defended my rights, and not to have themselves assailed them. There was also something insufferably little, in adding the weight of the American government, in violation of the wishes and institutions of the people, to crush a nation [the Jews], many of which had fought and bled for American Independence, and many had assisted to elevate those very men who had thus treated their rights with indelicate oppression. Unfortunate people, whose faith and constancy alone have been the cause of so much tyranny and oppression, who have given moral laws to the world, and who receive for reward opprobrium and insult! After this, what nation may not oppress them?

That the subject of religion should ever have commanded the *official* notice of the government of the United States cannot fail to create the greatest surprise when a reference is had to the Constitution of the United States, and equally so to the enlightened state of the times. In the War for Independence the Jews were unanimous in their zealous co-operation, and we find them holding a high rank in the army and fighting for liberty with a gallantry worthy of the descendants of Joshua, David, and Maccabee[u]s. After the adoption of the constitution, we see them on the bench as judges, in the legislatures as members, and assisting the government, in gloomy periods, to regulate and strengthen the financial system. In all the relations of life as fathers, husbands, and citizens, I persuade myself that they yield to no sect, and they have ever been distinguished for their liberal sentiments towards every denomination of Christians. . . .

Surely it is not too much to expect that under all these circumstances, the officers of government will conform to the wishes of the people and treat them with a delicacy becoming freemen. It is not, however, to satisfy the Israelites in this country that I notice this subject. They are capable of defending their own rights, but it is done to prove to the Jews in Europe, who have great commercial connexions with the United States and are capable of serving or injuring us, that this act of intolerance, of which I have had so much reason to complain, is not the act of the people, is not warranted or approved by them, but it is the simple mandate of the Executive Officer [the President] or the Secretary of State, acting either under an imaginary right, or gratifying a prejudice which I reluctantly believe has had some small influence in dictating the measure. . . .

I will defend my rights and measures at every hazard, and will not permit the government to treat them lightly without a full and clear explanation. I have no reason to believe, neither would I wish to insinuate, that either the President or Secretary of State are desirous, by any official act, to disqualify a citizen, [and, to paraphrase George Washington in a letter to the Jews, to] "give a sanction to bigotry," or awaken the most unhappy and unfortunate prejudices that can possibly exist, those of religion. It would be very inconsistent with their character, but the experiment is too dangerous to countenance.

My dismissal from office, in consequence of religion, has become a document on file in the Department of State. This may hereafter produce the most injuries [injurious] effects, establishing a principle which will go to annihilate the most sacred rights of the citizen. And if men of such enlightened and liberal minds, as Mr. Madison and Mr. Monroe, the very fathers of our institutions, and selected as their guardians, can, in the decline of their well-spent life and services, treat with so much indifference the most solemn and delicate among them, what security can the people of the United States have from any succeeding administration? An event of this nature will be promptly seized upon by our enemies abroad, to show the little confidence that can be reposed in our faith and institutions. Emigration may be checked, and the regard of a numerous and useful people be alienated from us.

The citizens of the United States who profess the Hebrew religion have merited, by their exemplary conduct, the rights which they enjoy. They have been the constant, unwavering friends of the Union. They took an active part in the War of the Revolution, which secured, and ought to secure to them, an equality of privileges in common with the rest of their fellow-citizens. Forty years of freedom have strengthened and secured their attachment and devotion to a country which had broken down the barriers of superstition in proclaiming and perpetuating civil and religious liberty. Their children [are] born among Christians, accustomed to associate [with Christians] from infancy, and to admire each other's virtues. Prejudice and illiberality were banished from their thoughts; the enlightened mind found no room for intolerance and bigotry. They presented a picture worthy of the imitation of the world: a nation forgetting religious distinctions, shunning the horrors of religious intolerance, and uniting as one family in harmony and affection, rewarding merit, and stimulating each other to honorable acts of ambition.

The late War [of 1812] found every Israelite, the descendants of a powerful, though unfortunate race, in arms, actively co-operating in the defense and support of the just rights of the nation—not with apathy or indifference—but with a warmth and spirit worthy of the cause. At New Orleans and in Canada, in the south, the east, and the west they were seen in the ranks, faithfully performing their duty. Their blood, shed in the defence of their country, commingled with that of their Christian brethren, cemented their union by the most solemn ties, while it forcibly displayed the vanity of all earthly distinctions. These are a people who should not be treated with disrespect or indelicacy.

If we once establish distinctions of religion in the appointment of our officers abroad, we shall not dare to send a Catholic to England, a Protestant to France, or a Jew to Spain. Instead of shameing, by our liberality, and by the force of our noble institutions, these unworthy and destructive prejudices, we shall nourish them by the example unworthy [of] freemen and shall, in time, forget that distinction in religion, rank, rights, opinions, and privileges, are all absorbed in the honorable name of American. *That* should be the only passport which he should bear about him, who serves his country on a foreign mission. His conscience should be shielded from the dark scrutiny of bigoted power, and considered as a private affair, between his God and himself.

The institutions of the United States are the property of the nation. The faith of the people is pledged for their existence. The most distinguished feature in our compact, the brightest link in our chain of union, is religious liberty, is the emancipation of the soul from temporal authority. We cease to be free when we cease to be liberal. From the height of fame and honor we shall fall like "a bright constellation in the evening, and be seen no more!". . .

These reflections I could not avoid making; they were inseparable from my situation and from the unexpected motives of my recall. Abdallah, my honest drogaman ["interpreter"], had taken the pipe from his girdle, filled it, and was seated on some ruins, calmly smoking, occasionally casting on me an eye of anxious solicitude. There was something in this letter which I had not yet examined. Mr. Monroe informs me that there were some circumstances, too, connected with my accounts, which require a more particular explanation, and which the President had not approved of. This was an additional cause of complaint; yet no officer should be recalled for want of mere *explanations* in his accounts. Probably my bills were received and not my despatches. Yet, had I assumed a power not specially delegated, had I gone beyond orders, squandered or embezzled the public money, this would have been a good and sufficient cause to have recalled me. This would have been the *proper* ground to have placed the dismissal upon, and not my religion. But the government knew better; they were satisfied that I had kept within the purview of my orders and was able to give a correct account of my disbursements. On this subject I was perfectly easy; they could not venture to predicate the removal on such objections.

MISSION COMPLETED

The morning, by this time, had far advanced and I saw no horses. . . . [I] left the ruins of Carthage and walked to Marsa, where I met my friend, the Danish consul, to whom I recapitulated the measures we were about pursuing with the Bey [Mahmoud]. He fully concurred in the promptness and expediency of our steps, and we went to Tunis together.

In a short time the Minister of Marine sent for me. He had received the letter from Commodore Decatur and was in no very pleasant humour. "This is not," said he, "a proper and respectful manner of doing business. Why does not your admiral make his complaints to the Bey in person? Why does he demand the payment of us for prizes which the British have illegally carried away, and demand an answer forthwith? We are not accustomed to be treated in this manner. There was a time when you waited our pleasure to establish a treaty, and paid us for it, and gave us presents whenever we demanded them, and all within my recollection."

I calmly assured the minister that these measures were indispensable to the preservation of our rights; that he must have anticipated them, and should, as I recommended, have terminated the affair before the arrival of the squadron; that it was now too late; Commodore Decatur had determined not to land without a favourable answer. The minister finally assured me that the money would not be paid, and I left him.

There was some bustle and confusion at Bardo [the Bey's palace]. The Bey sent for Mr. Nyssen, the Dutch consul, and consulted with him. Nyssen advised him to resist the demand, and stated that we had no authority to declare war, and would not dare to commence hostilities. This was told to me by the Christian slaves. I sent a mild and friendly message to Nyssen, urging him not to interfere in our business, that he would lose his head in twenty-four hours after hostilities had commenced for giving improper advice to the Bey.

The minister sent for me three or four times. He appeared to be troubled, yet always assumed that grave and imposing demeanour which they know so well how to put on. "What is the reason, consul," said he, "that you are so tranquil? Before your fleet was here, you were loud and positive. Now that you are backed by a force, you have suddenly become very quiet and indifferent." I stated to him that remonstrance was no longer necessary and that war was inevitable, except redress was obtained for the infraction of our treaty, that having made peace with Algiers on our own terms, the squadron was prepared for new contests, and that it was rather desirable than otherwise, for it was better to have no treaty than to have one that was not respected. The minister, finding me so serious, left Tunis for Bardo. A report reached the palace that Commodore Decatur, disguised as a common sailor, was seen with four hands in a small boat taking soundings of the bay to ascertain how near the ships could be brought to the fortress of the Goletta. I knew not if this was true; it may have been so, but it served to create a great alarm.

In the afternoon, several officers came up to Tunis by land; among them was Captains [Charles] Gordon and [Master Commandant Jesse D.] Elliott, with a number of midshipmen. They rushed through the gates of the town with perfect indifference and appeared to be much at home. The Turks regarded them with astonishment, and on their arrival at the consulate, they expressed a desire to go to a Turkish bath immediately, and I sent Kaleel, the young drogaman, to the principal one to have it ready. These baths are considered very wholesome. The person is carried into rooms of considerable heat raised by steam, which, in a short time, produces a copious perspiration. They are then rubbed down with woollen cloths, their joints cracked and, thus relaxed, they are rinsed with several pails of tepid water, and wrapped up in a sheet to cool gradually. After the ceremony of bathing had been concluded, I went to the bath to see the officers. They were laying on mats arranged round the room like the wards of an hospital, and thus infolded with linen, and in a languishing lassitude. They were employed in smoking long pipes of sweet tobacco, and some were sipping coffee. They appeared to be delighted with the operation and effect, and some the next day repeated the visit.

Captains Gordon and Elliott were instructed by Commodore Decatur to accompany me to the palace to learn the ultimatum of

the Bey. We were at Bardo at an early hour. Anxiety and curiosity
had brought a number of persons about the walls. The hall of
audience was crowded and Hassan and Mustapha, the two sons
[of the Bey], were present and were extremely active and insolent.
A commanding appearance has great influence with the Turks. Accustomed to measure everything by the eye, they course over the
exterior, and make few allowances for mind or character. Captain
Gordon, who is now dead, had not an impressive figure, nor did
he carry in his face or person any token of that firmness of character and generous and just sentiments for which he was distinguished. The Bey looked at him with the utmost indifference; he
[Gordon] was a short man, wore down by illness.

"Who are you?" said he. "I am second in command of that
squadron, sir," said Capt. Gordon, "and I am here to know whether
you are ready to do us justice." "Why does not your admiral come
on shore then?" said the Bey. "Why am I treated with so much
disrespect by him?" "He will not land, sir, until you decide to
pay the value of these vessels which you permitted the British to
take from us." Mustapha Bey then interfered, and, in a tone of
uncommon insolence and violence, was about to contend the matter,
when Capt. Elliott observed: "We did not come here to be insulted;
this interview must be cut short. Will you, or will you not, pay for
these vessels? Answer nothing but that." "Well, then," said Mustapha, thus pressed and with a furious look, "we will pay for them,
but have a care; our turn comes next." "Tell your admiral to come
on shore," said the Bey. "I'll send the money to the consul. I am
a rich prince, and don't value it—go."

Thus ended the interview, and thus were the rights of the United
States, as guaranteed by treaty, faithfully supported and rigidly
enforced. Opposition is invariably made by these people to any
demand affecting their interest, but when they are compelled to
yield, it is like destiny and is met with resignation; they think no
more about it. The Bey ordered a letter to be written to Commodore
Decatur and doubtless felt a respect for that nation which would
not abandon a point of honour.

On the following day the commodore landed, and while the consuls called to pay him a complimentary visit, Rais Hassuna [a
Tunisian naval captain] entered with a slave, carrying the money.
Seeing the British consul in conversation with the commodore, he
lost all patience, and throwing down the bags, exclaimed: "See
there, sir, what we have to pay for your insolence and the shameful
conduct of your vessels. It is thus, sir, you violate the rights of

others and leave us to answer for it." "If any wrong has been done you, Hassuna," said Mr. Oglander, with great mildness, "address your complaints to the British government and you will have justice."

The amount paid was $46,000, and a promise on the part of the Jew merchants to repay 44,000 piasters for the merchandise [in the prize ships seized by the British]. They, however, had time allowed them, and, after the squadron had departed, I could not obtain more than one-fourth that sum from them. The money paid was in the base coin of the country. Commodore Decatur probably expected to have carried that sum to the United States, and was rather pointed in his inquiries as to my right to receive and retain it. I satisfied him on this head, but could not inform him of the protested bills of exchange, which remained unpaid, and the nature of the despatch that he had delivered to me. He probably thought that I was to remain in Tunis, when I expected to be in the United States before him and, from the want of explanation, probably arose some unfavourable impressions on his part which, however, I could not distinctly learn had existed. . . .

EPILOGUE

[On his return to the United States, Noah went to Washington to see James Monroe, the Secretary of State, in order to straighten out his affairs.]

Mr. Monroe, declining to see me, instructed Mr. Graham [his chief clerk] to inquire *what I wanted*. I had expressed but one desire, from which I never varied. It was to do me justice, settle my accounts, and if there is a dollar due me, let me know it officially. That was the first step in my situation, and after mortifying, perplexing, and expensive delays, after twelve months had elapsed, after three special journeys to Washington, the *Attorney General* was instructed to *adjust my claims*, and at length I received the following letter:

Department of State, January 14, 1817.

Sir:

Your account as consul of the United States at Tunis has been adjusted at this department, in conformity with the opinion of the Attorney General of the 30th of December last, of which you have a copy; and a balance of $5,216.57, reported to be due you, will be paid to your order, at any time after Congress shall have made the necessary appropriations. A sum of $1,664, besides a charge of thirty-five percent loss on the disbursement of your agent at Algiers, is suspended, for reasons mentioned in the account of which you have been apprised. I am, sir, respectfully,

Your obedient servant,

(Signed) S. Pleasonton.

Mordecai M. Noah, Esq.

Thus ended my connexion with the government, and thus fell to the ground the charge "of going beyond orders." Nothing then remained of the official charge but my religion, a subject which, I had reason to believe, the President would have reconciled in a suitable manner, but which, after three years' delay, has not commanded his attention.

If I have occupied too much space in this work with recapitulating my official concerns, the reader will bear in mind that this is the first attempt, since the adoption of the constitution of the United States, to make the religion of a citizen an objection to the possession of office, a principle so foreign to the constitution, so much at war with the genius and disposition of the people, and so dangerous to the liberties of the country, that citizens cannot be insensible to the new and dreadful features which it exposes. None can hear with indifference this measure of the government, and none will turn a deaf ear to the representations of an individual who has sustained an injury.

Governments have a natural propensity to encroach upon the rights of citizens, and if those rights are worthy of being preserved, the utmost caution should be used to guard them with a vigilance that never slumbers. If a letter such as I received in Barbary had been written by order of a sovereign, presuming that a king could do such a wrong, I should have submitted to it without a murmur, knowing the tenure by which I held my office, but [for] my fellow-citizen, the President, to disfranchise me from holding the office of consul at Tunis, when I am eligible to the station which he holds, cannot but be viewed as an assumption of power neither known nor tolerated. Nothing is easier than to establish a principle in governments, and nothing is more difficult than to destroy this principle when it is found to be dangerous. My letter of recall has become a document on file at the Department of State, which hereafter may, without the present explanations, go to disfranchise a whole nation [the Jews].

I felt it to be my duty to clear up this affair, and as I caused my country to be respected abroad, it was not anticipating too much when I claimed a reciprocal respect and protection from the government. I had heard it rumoured that Col. [Tobias] Lear was the prominent cause of that letter having been written to me. He is now dead, and I have only to express my astonishment at the extraordinary and mysterious influence which he exercised over the administration. I, however, subsequently gave Mr. Monroe an opportunity of doing that justice, which I flattered myself he was disposed to do, by requesting that I might be restored to an appointment of equal rank, but no notice was taken of my application. I had no objections to make. The conferring of appointments is a power correctly vested in the Executive. If he thinks proper to exercise that right in accordance with his own feelings, in advancement with his own views, in support of his own attachments or prejudices, it may be lamented for the sake of the public service, but cannot be prevented. The check in the Senate is all that the constitution provides. Still, it is expected that the Executive, chosen for a transitory period by the people, will, in all cases, consult what is most acceptable to the people and creditable to the country.

It is not necessary for me to say that Mr. Monroe is emphatically an honest man. I measure men by the aggregate of their virtues and vices. All are liable to error. Many pertinaciously adhere to their measures, though they may be manifestly erroneous, and such is the imperfection of our natures, that when a wrong is done intentionally or accidentally, a second wrong is frequently added in confirmation of the first, if complaint is made or clamour heard. Still, with these errors, the balance is greatly in favour of the President for past services, sincere attachment to country, and strict integrity. He has his weak points like other men. When these do not affect the public service or go to establish dangerous doctrines, they are not necessary objects of inquiry. But recurring to the first principles of our government, there is nothing which will tend more securely to preserve our liberties than freedom of speech and the press, a scrutiny into public measures, and a firm but respectful tone to men in power.

Mr. Monroe regretted the steps which he had pursued towards me; there was an idea floating on his mind that I had not been well-treated, but he only regretted it, as it affected him. He had no consideration for my feelings, for my rights or character. He would have been pleased to have arranged the affair in a manner mutually agreeable, but I had not presented myself to him with that submissive tone, with that "bondsmen key and bated breath," that he

Pencil sketch by Kates of portrait by Thomas Sully

MAJOR ALFRED MORDECAI

(see page 218)

Engraving by W. J. Bennett after a painting by George Cooke

probably expected. He said I threatened to appeal to Congress. He should have been proud to have seen a citizen thus anxious to support his rights and character, and he should have aided, not opposed me, nor bent the power of government to crush an individual.

I have said thus much in proof to political opponents, that I am under no obligation to Mr. Monroe, that my support of the administration is grounded on principle, on nobler motives than personal favour, and as long as he is in the administration and his measures are calculated to promote the honour and prosperity of our country, so long will I support him. I have no favours to ask or prejudices to indulge. I have considered it my duty not to labour under suspicions or insinuations and have thus endeavoured to explain them.

> The evil which men do lives after them,
> The good is oft interred with their bones.

Raphael Jacob Moses

A Southern Romantic

Raphael J. Moses of Columbus, Georgia, was still living when Isaac Markens, in his book, The Hebrews in America *(1888), wrote of him: "The esteem in which he is held by the great men of Georgia attests his right to the place he occupies as the foremost Hebrew at the bar and in the politics of the Southern States" (pp. 181-82).*

This Georgia orator, politician, and lawyer, born in Charleston, South Carolina, in 1812, and a descendant of the Machados of New York and the Nunezes of Georgia, was a fifth-generation American. As we shall see, he left school at an early age and became a merchant, first in Charleston, and then, in the late 1830's, in the new town of St. Joseph, Florida.

Early in the next decade, Moses, then a married man, turned to law in the nearby town of Apalachicola. When that early Florida boom town collapsed, he went up the Apalachicola River and its tributary, the Chattahoochee, to Columbus, Georgia. Favored by steamboat access to the Gulf of Mexico, Columbus even then shipped about 80,000 bales of cotton a year. It was a good place for a first-class commercial lawyer, such as Moses was. He soon became a leader of the Columbus bar, acquired wealth, and built up the beautiful Esquiline plantation. At one time he had 20,000 fruit trees on his estate and was among the first, if not the first, to ship peaches, by stage, railroad, and steamer, to the New York market.

It was only natural that a man like Moses, endowed with unusual ability as a persuasive public speaker, should turn to politics. Back in 1847, during his stay in Florida, he was a delegate to the Democratic convention which nominated Lewis Cass for the Presidency. In the following decade, he was active in Georgia politics. When the Civil War began, Moses, although overage, went in, followed by three of his sons. By virtue of his training in business, he was assigned to do commissary work. For a time, he headed that service in General James Longstreet's corps; later he served his own state of Georgia in a similar capacity.

During the Reconstruction period, Moses sat in the state legislature and became the recognized leader of the House. In his attempt to secure a nomination for Congress, however, he was unsuccessful. His own colleagues failed to back him; they feared that he could not be controlled: Moses was too independent.

Anti-Semitic prejudice also held Moses back. He was a loyal Jew, devoted to his "race," and was eager to go to Congress to fight prejudice against his group; "race feeling," he called it. One of the most interesting letters in American Jewish literature, written with dignity and pride, was sent by Moses to W. O. Tuggle of La Grange, Georgia, a politician who had taunted the Columbus attorney with being a Jew. "I wanted to go to Congress as a Jew, and because I was a Jew, and believed that I might elevate our people by my public course," Moses wrote.

After his retirement from the practice of law, Moses lived on his plantation in somewhat reduced circumstances. At the request of his youngest child, Marie (Mrs. James Whyte, of New York), he wrote his memoirs in the form of letters to her. Begun in 1890, when he was seventy-eight, they were finished in 1893, several months before his death in Brussels, Belgium. A number of versions of these autobiographies are extant. The following excerpts are taken from a copy in the American Jewish Archives.

Raphael Moses was a cultured Southern gentleman: romantic, sentimental, and a local patriot. In 1832 or 1833, during the controversy over the Nullification of the Tariff Acts of 1828 and 1832, he enlisted in the militia to fight for his native state of South Carolina. In 1850, when most Southern leaders still opposed secession, he was an ardent fire-eater. The South may have been reconstructed after the War; Moses never was. When he visited his daughter in Europe in 1893, his calling card still read: "Major Raphael J. Moses, C.S.A."

INTRODUCTION TO AN ANTE-MORTEM DIARY

D<small>EAR</small> M<small>ARIE</small>:

You want me to write my autobiography. You have sent me a book to write it in and a pen to write it with, so that I am fully equipped with everything but a subject of interest, while [since] I have always considered myself "a pious fraud" in impressing the public with a reputation for talents which I did not possess.

I think I have always had one element of wisdom which is said to be uncommon; I have always *known myself*. My conception was quick, my language good, my business education a great advantage in my profession as a lawyer, and because I understood bookkeeping and business methods, and could always understand a merchant's case, and because I evinced a familiarity with their business pursuits, I soon earned the reputation of being a first-class "commercial lawyer," irrespective of how much or little I might know of the commercial law contained in the books. While I had (not altogether undeserved) considerable reputation as an orator, there was one thing that I could never do: make something out of nothing, and that is what I am required to do now. My temperament was sympathetic, and I had language and manner enough to make others feel what I felt, but unless I feel the subject myself, I could never have made others feel. So that, boiled down, my legal reputation could be largely attributed to my business education and my oratorical standing [which] spring[s] chiefly from my strong, sympathetic nature. My knowledge was more the result of observation than reading; my taste for books was limited, my memory was never good, and getting ideas from books was with me like pouring water through a sieve; the fluid passed quickly away but the sediment remained. And so with my reading: the language passed away, but some of the ideas remained, and, particularly in law, the principles remained, but the book, page, case, etc., soon passed out of my mind.

As I said before, my perception was always quick and my judgment good. I seldom had a case presented to me that I did not at once form an opinion upon it, what lawyers call "first impression," and afterwards, in searching the books, I usually found authority

148

to sustain my views. I was never a technical lawyer, nor what is familiarly known in the profession as "case lawyer." The two preceding pages ought to compose the begin[n]ing and end of my autobiography, but what you want, I suppose, is an anti[e]-mortem diary, a sort of retrospective glance at my life from the cradle to the grave, or sufficiently near the latter to leave it an easy matter for you or anyone else to fill out the few blank pages that may remain.

CHILDHOOD AND SCHOOLING

Well, then, to begin, I was born on the night of January 20th, 1812, in Beaufain St., Charleston, South Carolina. Like most babies, I suppose I entered upon life with a cry. I was born an ugly baby, remained an ugly boy, and lived an ugly man. My mother had two other children, both handsome, but they died in infancy. Death loves a shining mark; they shone, I didn't, and so I was left to become the pet of my mother and the pest of everybody else, "a spoled child," and I went through an extraordinary share of spoiling, and nothing saved me from utter ruin except good luck or some undeveloped, innate virtue.

At two years old, I have heard, I knew my letters, and my dear mother thought she saw the germs of a concealed genius which has remained invisible ever since. She kept a school, and I was one of her scholars, cutting a figure in her classes when I should have been cutting my teeth!

My boyhood may be condensed into one word: I was the impersonation of mischief; my pranks were without limit and much to the annoyance of a maiden cousin, Bell Cohen, who had charge of me in the occasional visits paid by my parents to Philadelphia and New York. At school I never took a very high stand as I was much more given to play than to study. I had the reputation at school of having excellent capacity, but lacking industry in my classes. I was seldom "head," and if I got there by accident, I seldom remained there more than a day or two at a time. When the examinations came on annually, I crammed for them, and as I could acquire very rapidly, I generally took a stand with the boys that were up with their lessons all the year round.

The first school that I have any recollection of after leaving my mother's school was kept by a Mr. Southworth. He was an excellent teacher and a severe disciplinarian. I improved very much under him, but one day one of the boys who shall be nameless, but who belonged to the South Carolina aristocracy and was the bully of the school, undertook to whip a little boy, and I interfered. And though I have never been much of a fighter, being neither active or particularly strong, I found my adversary like many other bullies, not much of a hero when put to the test; and it was my good fortune to come off victor in the fight. But alas! as we fought in the schoolyard, which was against the rules, Mr. Southworth was even more victorious than I was, for he whipped us both. I, of course, complained to father, and he went with me to the teacher, justified my course, denounced his inflexible rules, and withdrew me from school. I was then between ten and eleven.

From there I went to Bishop England, a celebrated Catholic divine! He had a very large school. All the teachers were priests; the bishop did not teach, but visited the school about once a week. There was no discipline at all; the boys "ruled the roost" and ruled it with a high hand. I remember on one occasion I loitered by the way, having become much more interested in a game of marbles than in heathen mythology, which was the lesson for the afternoon. Arriving late, Mr. Monk, the priest and teacher, gave my companions and myself a sharp lecture on our being tardy!

At that time, the fashion prevailing were Wellington boots and Wellington coats; in fact, everything was Wellington, and when the priest asked me how some heathen god's feet were covered, for want of a more historical answer I replied: "In Wellington boots!" Monk, already outraged at our late arrival, lifted his rattan, a kind of cane, and was about to come down on me, when I presented a pistol minus a cock, which deficiency being unknown to the priest, his rattan remained suspended in mid-air. And instead of the whipping, I was ordered to leave the class and informed that I would be reported to the bishop, which being done, on the bishop's next visit, I was summoned to his room for a confessional, not to be absolved by payment of Peter's pence.

I trembled in my shoes for the consequences and wilted before the bishop's steel-grey eyes; they were the greyest eyes I ever saw in any human head. I was, of course, very penitent, and I think the cockless pistol which I exhibited to show how utterly harmless it was and that there was therefore no malice prepense, that the action was the result of a sudden impulse and, as the darkies say, done "unthoughtedly," for all of which I was very sorry. The bishop let me off with a well-deserved lecture on the impropriety of my conduct and require that I should express my regrets to Mr. Monk before the class, which I did, resolved in my own mind henceforth and forever, or as long as boyhood lasted, to be a model boy.

I don't think, however, it was many moons before some of the boys, one of which was your little reformer, ripped up the flooring of the schoolrooms. Why or how we did it, I do not remember. The big boys were the masterminds in this escapade, and the perpetrators of the diabolical act were never discovered.

The next thing on the tapis was the examination. I remember it well; it was in the cathedral. At one end of it there was extemporized a platform about five feet high, all around which there were benches, and the priests seated thereon, their legs encased in knee breeches and black silk stockings. The bishop occupied a seat in the center of the platform. The cathedral was crowded. The recitations were made on the platform. I recited with éclat "Aurora Fair Daughter of the Dawn," [from Pope's *Odyssey*] but in the intervals we boys, who were not "tickling" the public for the time being, stationed ourselves around the platform and tickled with pins the underpinning, not of the platform, but the priests, and when the signal was given, "stick a pin there," priests' legs were rubbed and lifted as if mosquitoes were gathering a harvest, and none of us boys ever knew whether a Catholic priest knew the difference between the point of a pin lightly inserted or the bill of a mosquito perseveringly presented.

I remained at the bishop's school about a year, and not being entirely without conscience, nor unlike [Cowper's] *John Gilpin*, who although on pleasure bent yet had a frugal mind, I actually acknowledged to my parents that I was not learning anything but mischief at the bishop's, in which, by the way, you will see I was pretty well graduated, and requested them to send me to another school! Alas, for the change!

They sent me to Isaac Harby [the founder of the Reformed Society of Israelites], father of Octavia Moses, a splendid teacher who believed as "the twig is bent the tree's inclined" and "spare the rod and spoil the child." He bent the twig but never spared the rod. I remember a mulberry tree that grew in the yard. I remember it denuded of many limbs. I remember further the uses they were put to, and the further fact that the boys, with whose backs they were to be made familiar, were, with a quizzical look (I think I can see it now), ordered to go and cut a bunch and be sure to get good ones, too. . . .

I continued with Mr. Harby untill I was twelve and a half years of age. I was studying Latin and just about to commence Greek when it suddenly occurred to me that I had absorbed through the skin as much knowledge as I cared to acquire in that way, and I proposed to my overindulgent parents to consider my education finished, and they so considered it. I then left school and entered on the business of life, of which more anon.

I ought not to omit from my boyhood memories as illustrative of my father's character the mortal dread I always had of a butcher boy named Coagley. He was a sort of John L. Sullivan among the boys. He looked to me as tough as a lightwood knot and was certainly as pugnacious as a bulldog. I have, many a time, gone a square out of my way to avoid meeting Coagley; I had a mortal dread of him, and my father, one day seeing me trying to shirk him, came out with a coachwhip, which in his hands was as formidable a weapon to me (he weighing over 300 pounds) as was Sampson's [Samson's] historical jawbone to the Philistines.

He said: "I see you are afraid of that boy. Now you have either got to whip him or I will whip you." The choice of two evils in this instance was full of difficulties, but when I looked at little Coagley and my big father with his threatening whip and flashing eye, supplemented by an oath or two indicating his determined purpose, I think if Goliath had stood before me, I would have sailed in, by no means regardless of consequences, but wisely considering the blows of the butcher boy the lesser evil of the two. And with the consequences of the defeat present to my mind, I came out victorious, but so battered and bruised that it would have taken a very short argument to satisfy me that "ten such victories would be equal to a defeat." The boy never troubled me again, but I always thought his peaceful bearing was attributable more to his vision of the father of the boy who conquered him than to any apprehension he would have felt for your humble servant if he had had no daddy. But the lesson was a good one, for it taught me, like the Irishman, that the best way "to avoid danger was to meet it plump in the face." So much for this digression.

I also forgot to say that I can't remember the day when I didn't have a pony. He was an Indian pony or marsh tackey [nag], and his name was Cherokee. He had a mind of his own, and when he said stop, stop it was. Many a time I started to go to Tivoli Garden or the Four-Mile-House, but if Cherokee took a notion, when I was half way, to go thus far and no farther, Cherokee had his way, especially after, on one occasion, when I was imprudent enough to get down to cut a switch and force him onward. I found myself, with my first returning consciousness, emerging from a ditch, bespattered with mud from head to heel, and saw Cherokee looking on as totally unconcerned as if he had not done it, and did not know who did. From that day forward he had pretty much his own way, and whenever he indicated that he had gone far enough, I invariably yielded to his better judgment.

Another peculiarity of my youthful career was that I never put on a new suit of clothes that I did not get a whipping before the day was over, generally because I had not worn them with due care and circumspection. My good mother always had excuses for me, but unfortunately my father in spite of them stuck by his maxim not to "spare the rod and spoil the child," but I was spoiled nevertheless.

EDUCATION FOR LIFE

Soon after I quit school I went to Philadelphia with my parents and stayed with my aunt, Mrs. [Michael] Esther Hart, the grandmother of Louisa Lyons, née Hart, who is the mother of Rachel Huestes. They left me in Philadelphia.

I nominally stayed in Bacon & [Cousin] Hart's music store [on South Fourth Street] in the daytime and attended law lectures at night, given by Judge [Joseph] Hopkins[on], and I was very much interested in them. They were altogether on commercial law, but my mind was too much on pleasure bent. I was not much more than thirteen. My companions were generally several years older than myself. I had the very free use of money and used it. I always thought my father was wealthy. He was then in the auction business, kept horses, and lived up to his means, if not beyond them, as I discovered in later years, and being an only child whose wishes were law, I was not very particular about what might or might not be his bank balances so that my purse was not empty.

It would fill a volume to detail all my indiscretions, they were [to quote Milton] thick as leaves of Valambrosia [Vallombrosa], but I had no vices and no fixed habits, good or bad, but my pursuit of fun was so indefatigable that I enjoyed it, careless of what older heads thought about it. My impulses governed me, and fortunately they were not bad but only mischievous.

I had an old-maid cousin, Anna Hart, who late in life married Mr. Bacon, on the firm of Bacon & Hart. [Allyn Bacon was a Gentile.] She was a typical old maid and a model housekeeper, always kept the rooms darkened to keep the sun and flies out, and I always opened them [the windows] to let the sun and air in, irrespective of how many flies might come with me. Of course, I was her horror. Then I had another cousin, Louisa [B. Hart], a very cultivated and charitable woman, and as ugly and outré ["bizarre"] in her style of dressing as she was intelligent and benevolent. And she found out that I had said, or somebody had said that I had said, [that] I would not walk with her on Chestnut Street because of her ill-favored face and want of taste in dressing. And, of course, with her my fat was in the fire and sizz[l]ed as bad as if I really had said it, which, by the way, at this late date I am not prepared to deny.

I soon quit attending law lectures at night, much preferring the theater, for which I had a passion. The next year, when father went north, as he did every summer, I returned with him [to Charleston] and went to stay with Abraham Tobias, an auctioneer and particular friend of D. C. Levy's [the merchant and banker]. I received small compensation, but after being with him a few months, he raised my salary and paid me at the increased rate from the beginning.

I think I stayed with him about a year, and then another auctioneer, Calvin Baker, offered me better pay, and I left Tobias and went to Baker. He was a very clever man, but he had a son, Calvin Baker, [Jr.], who was as tyrannical and overbearing as he could be. There was another boy [who] stayed there with me. I forget his name, but we got into a way of not being able to repress our immoderate laughter on very trifling occasions, and one day a man came in and asked if we had any "boiled cider." Neither of us had ever heard of boiled cider, and the idea excited our risibility. We tried not to laugh, and the more we tried not to laugh, like two fools as we were, the louder we laughed. The customer looked on in amazement. About this time Calvin Baker, Jr., came in, and I went behind the desk. He got into a passion and abused us for everything he could lay his tongue to, for we *couldn't* stop laughing, until he became so abusive that the pendulum swung to the other extreme, and I whirled first a ruler and then an inkstand at him and broke for the door to return no more.

I went from there to father's auction store. These experiences make me say to young men always—"STICK." If I had stuck to law when I attended Judge Hopkinson's lectures, I would probably have entered life in the profession which I finally adopted. If I had stayed with Mr. Tobias instead of going to Baker's for an increase of salary, I might very likely in time have become a partner in the business, for he was very much pleased with me. Certainly I made nothing by the changes then made or afterwards, so that my motto now is, "Stick."

Again I went to Philadelphia with father; I suppose I was about fifteen. We dined with Mr. [Abraham Cohen?] Peixotto, a West Indian. He had been quite wealthy, but was less so because of the emancipation of his slaves, but he was still well off. [Actually, the Jamaica slaves were not emancipated for several years, in 1833.]

[He] had no children, but had adopted two nephews and two nieces and a very sweet girl, Betsy Shaw. The latter was a Christian, and although he was a very Orthodox Jew, he was scrupulously exact in her attendance of church. He was a very arbitrary man. His wife, who we all called "Gam," an abbreviation for grandma, was as kind as she could be.

Much to my surprise and satisfaction—anything to stay North— father arranged with Mr. P.[eixotto] for me to stay in his office and to be an inmate of his house. He did a large business in Kingston, Jamaica, and had a copy of his daybook sent by vessel to Philadelphia. There the entries were journalized and posted, so that he always had before him the daily transaction of his West India business. The books were kept in £, s. d. [pounds, shillings, pence], and it was with him that I learned practical bookkeeping.

I think I must have stayed with him about two years. It was to me a very happy home. I was really one of the family and very fond of Betsy Shaw, but never thought of engaging myself to her, for I knew that Mr. Peixotto would never consent to her intermarriage. Besides, we were both too young for serious love. Gam was like a mother to me; she was a warmhearted West Indian. Mr. Peixotto, as I have already indicated, was a very benevolent man but very dictatorial. I was then, as much as it may contrast with my present habits, very fond of dress and fashion. Chestnut Street was the fashionable street. I generally walked that way home, wore gloves, and twirled a rattan. One day about dinnertime he [Mr. Peixotto] came into the office and said: "Ralph, I have bought a pair of turkeys; they are on Front Street, and I must take them home. You come with me, and I will take one, and you will take the other."

I was amazed. Our path home would be right down Chestnut Street. I respectfully declined the "hazardous adventure." Mr. Peixotto insisted; I resisted. At last he said: "When I hire a boy, he must do what I tell him." I replied: "You employ me to keep your books; I am no *hired* boy." "Well, sir," said he, "hired or employed, you will carry that turkey or quit." "Then, sir, it is quit, for I shan't carry it," and quit I did. We always remained friendly, but with him it was absolute obedience; with me it was anything but toteing a gobler and we split on the turkey. . . .

From Mr. Peixotto I went back to my aunt's. And soon after, as I was very much troubled with dispepsia, I got from Simeon Dreyfous (who boarded there and was an importer of Swiss watches) an assortment of Swiss watches and a traveler's trunk, made to carry samples, and started for Easton, Pennsylvania, where my mother had lived in her early life. I went by stagecoach and stopped at Redding [Reading], Allentown, and other small places between Philadelphia and Easton, exhibiting my watches at the different small towns, and made more than enough to pay all my travelling expenses.

Between Philadelphia and Allentown there was a very pleasant fellow traveler, a Dr. Myrick, who hailed from the neighborhood of Easton. We got to be as thick as two thieves; he stopped over with me at Allentown and we took a walk together. In the course of our rambles, he casually mentioned having lost his pocketbook and gave that as his reason for stopping over, as he would have to write to Bucks County for money and await its receipt. He did not ask me to lend him what he wanted; it was only a small sum, about $10 or $15 (I think). He accepted the loan with apparent reluctance, and we travelled together as far as Easton. Pottsville was then just being started; coal had just been discovered there, and iron in close proximity. There was a perfect craze for town lots, and I remember there were so many people going to Pottsville that we had, with many others, to sleep on the floor of the hotel at Easton.

The next morning Dr. Myrick bid me an affectionate farewell, expressed his great obligation and promised to send the money as soon as he got home, but I suppose he forgot to do it. I never heard of him any more until I returned to Philadelphia, and then I found that my interesting friend had just been discharged from the penitentiary, where he had been imprisoned for some time for forgery. He was of good family and did live in Bucks County, near Easton. The lesson I then learned was not to get too intimate with traveling acquaintances, and I have given travellers a wide berth ever since.

I stayed in Easton some time and then went on the Mauch Chunk R. R. to the mines and went into the mines and saw the miners at work. The R. R. was propelled to the mines by horse power, hauling the cars upgrade empty, and then they came back loaded, down a gradual incline, by their own momentum. Contrast that mule team with the great Pennsylvania R. R. I went to the Delaware Gap and other places of interest, was charmed with the beautiful scenery, and returned to Philadelphia sound in health and purse.

I then clerked for Dreyfous and boarded at Mrs. Reynolds' on Chestnut Street, and the way I happened to go to Mrs. Reynolds was this: I saw a very pretty girl on Chestnut Street and followed her home. She went into a house just opposite the Mint. I took another opportunity to look at the doorplate and found Mrs. Reynolds. Then ascertained that she kept a boardinghouse and, to make the story short, I left my aunt's and went there to board. [I] made the acquaintance of pretty Kate, for such was her name, attended her wedding soon after, and there became acquainted with a lot of good fellows, all seven or eight years older than myself, and all in business and able to spend freely. . . .

It was while I was living at Mrs. Reynolds' that I walked, one night, down Chestnut Street with Hetty Pisoa [Pesoa] and her cousin, Henry M. Phillips [later a congressman]. When we were between Second and Third Streets, near an alley, someone from an upstairs window cried out: "The house [is] on fire!" I ran round the alley, got over the back fence and into the back door. The front room, on fire, was a cigar store. I rushed up the stairs and at the second story called aloud to the inmates, but received no reply.

By this time the fire was spreading rapidly, the stairs were burning. I came as far down as I could without going through the flames. I jumped the balance of the way over the banister into the back room behind the store; it was filled with smoke. I remember distinctly keeping my head near the floor to breathe, and the singular thought that passed through my mind was this: I had written an article for the paper; I don't remember the subject, and I thought: "When mother reads it, I'll be dead." I remember getting up and feeling around the room for a place of egress, and I came to what I supposed to be a window and tried to dash it through with my hand, when to my despair it proved to be a looking glass. I have not the least idea of how I escaped, but when I woke up I was lying in the yard, bleeding. Someone came to my assistance and I asked to be carried to my aunt's. I was taken there and had something like pneumonia.

I remained in a sick chamber several weeks, was severely cupped; my wrist was badly cut (I have the mark yet), and just missed severing the artery. The doctor determined that my only safety was to return south, and once more I was home again. There were two or three persons killed at the fire, inmates of the house, by attempting to jump from the third story onto a kitchen roof in the rear.

I remember another time I was nearly drowned in the Delaware River. The boat that I rowed got under the bow of a steamer, and I was caught up by one of the sailors; she [the steamer] was just coming into the wharf.

These two escapes confirmed my detractors that the old adage was true, and a man or boy born to be hung could only die by the rope, but I have disappointed them in this, for I am nearly seventy-nine and am still unhung.

My trips to and from the North were so frequent that I am a little confused in dates, but think this is a trip that I made by stage, via Washington and Richmond. At the latter place [Uncle] Abraham Cohen lived. He was quite a talented man and was rabbi (then called hazan) for a number of years. His father [Jacob Raphael Cohen], my grandfather, for whom I was named, was minister for about thirty years in Philadelphia [1784-1811], and my mother inherited all of their Orthodox ideas, so that all the influence of birth and education were with me on the religious side, but I never became indoctrinated with their views.

I always doubted the interviews which the Bible asserts were so frequently held by the Lord with his chosen people, *but I never doubted that a Supreme intelligence controlled the world, and I have always felt* (long before the advent of the Fox sisters [spiritualists] and the rappings [which they heard]) *that there was no death, and that the dissolution of the body was but the transition of the soul or mind, or whatever you may choose to term the element that lifts man above the beasts of the field (and which predominates so unequally in different men), continued to exist after we ceased to occupy this mortal casement, and I have always felt, further, that those who loved us and guarded us on earth continued to love and care for us after they have passed away.*

So fixed has this impression always been in my mind that I can truly say that I have never undertaken an important matter or become involved in serious trouble, that I did not involuntarily seek or pray for the interposition of the spirit of my mother for direction in the beginning, or extrication, when difficulties surrounded me, and I have generally felt that my appeals were heard and answered. This, by some, will be called superstition; by some it will be called sentiment; and by the majority of persons it will be called weakness, but call it what you please, though it may have no foundation in facts, it has been my strength and support in many a trying hour.

I did not intend this digression, but I am writing down now whatever impressions occur to me at the moment, assured as I am that my children, at whose request I have somewhat reluctantly consented to write this sketch of myself, will not criticise my style so long as they have a reflex of myself in which my faults, as they will see, are not extenuated, nor my virtues ostentatiously exaggerated. The former will mark the causes of my failures, by them to be avoided and not imitated; and the latter may serve to animate them to improve upon my feeble efforts to retrieve the errors, resulting in a great measure from overindulgence.

My escape from utter and hopeless ruin may be attributed to the fact that I inherited no vices from either parent. Had I done so, it is easy to foresee what would have been the end of an impulsive boy under no earthly restraint from the time he was twelve years old, with a mother to find excuses for all his faults, having the free use of money, living most of his time in Philadelphia and New York away from parental influence, and respecting no authority that relatives might vainly have attempted to exercise. The extent of my overindulgence cannot be better emphasized than in the fact that I was an only child. My parents were, of course, devoted to me; they would have asked for no greater happiness than my companionship at home. And yet, with no view of any advantages that offered, but merely to gratify my pleasure, I was allowed to spend most of my youth away, the parental heart accepting the sacrifice of domestic desolation, that their idol might seek pleasure at more congenial shrines.

I tremble when I look back at the temptations that surrounded me, while I revolt at the selfishness that could reconcile me to the unnecessary separation. It certainly was not from want of filial affection, for I loved both my parents, and my feeling for my mother was one of devotion, but they showed me the gates of youthful pleasure and gave me the silver key to turn them on their hinges, that I might tread the labyrinth of what seemed to youth more gorgeous than Tallmadge's golden streets and pearly gates of heaven. [Thomas De Witt Talmage was a sensational preacher.] There were but few of pleasure's paths over which I did not ramble, but as I had the good fortune to escape the evils of excessive indulgence, I found safety in surfeit, and after a few more lessons which I will go on to recite, I began life in earnest at an age when many men first embrace its follies.

What changes have taken place since the time of which I write! Not only in myself, from youth to age—old age—but in this world of ours. No telegraphs, no railroads, no steam; no electricity, unless it was Benjamin Franklin's experiment with his kite and the lightning; not even a match to catch a lightwood knot, no gas, no kerosene, no *Heralds* or *Worlds* or *Tribunes* with thirty-page Sunday editions, no Wall Street with its robbers, and last, but not least, no millionaires. I might almost say, no New York; certainly none compared with the present. When I remember it, Canal Street was high uptown, and Harry Kostar [Henry A. Coster II], who kept Bachelors' Hall on Canal Street, was a very [veritable] Croesus, his wealth being estimated at $150,000 to $200,000.

I will not take time to state the changes; you, who will read this,
know them all. But I state a proposition, the truth of which you may
doubt, but it is true nevertheless. People were happier then with
their tallow candels run through a mould than you are now with
your electric lights. There was not the same unrest, the same envy of
those whose heart burnings are concealed beneath the diamonds that
we hopelessly covet; all were not at the top of the ladder but its
topmost pinnacle seemed to be a possibility to the humblest. . . .

UNCLE ABRAHAM'S WIFE

I suppose I might as well state here that my uncle, Abraham
Cohen, fell in love with a Christian girl [a Miss Picken]. She went
through the usual probation of converts, so as to ascertain whether
she was influenced by any other motive than a conviction of the
truth of Judaism. She passed through the ordeal without the smell of
fire upon her garments, became a Jewess [1806], was married to my
uncle, and I remember visiting her at her house in New York in my
boyhood when she was scrupulously particular in adhering to all
Jewish forms, dieting and others, and she so remained until sometime after her elder daughter, Rebecca, married a cousin of the
distinguished Rabbi Isaac Le[e]ser and was herself the mother of
a child. Mrs. Cohen, who had always lived happily with her husband, who was then minister of the Richmond congregation, lost
her youngest son and afterwards became herself seriously ill. During
her sickness, in a nervous condition, she imagined (this, I suppose,
was the effect of [her] early Christianity) that her son appeared to
her and urged her reconversion to Christianity, which she then re-
embraced, and joined the Episcopal Church [about 1831], which
was the church of her childhood. She then had three single daughters, Ellen, Henrietta, and Esther. My uncle, then a minister, separated from her, but they lived in the same place, Richmond, and he
continued to support her. . . .

I mention this incident in my uncle's life to show the strong impression made upon the human mind by early religious education.
Mrs. Cohen was a strict Jewess for forty or fifty years [?] and died
a believing Christian in about her eightieth year. She lived a Christian
until her marriage, when she was about seventeen, so that about half
of her life she was a devotee to Christianity, and about half equally
devoted to Judaism.

The Pranks and Escapades of Youth

I think it took about eight days, night and day, to travel [from Philadelphia] to reach Charleston [South Carolina] by way of Washington, Richmond, Columbia [South Carolina], etc. The travel was, of course, slow and rough, but it was much more sociable and pleasant than the R. R. travel of today. In less than twenty-four hours everybody tried to contribute to the amusement of everyone in the stage. Those who could sing, sang; those who could tell good stories told them. The audience was appreciative, and as I was a good mimic and a good racounteur, if good for nothing else, this made me good company, and while I told all the jokes that I knew, and they were many, it was in stagecoaches that I learned some of my best, with which I would afterwards set the table in a roar. These experiences made me "a jolly good fellow," but did little to improve my business education or fit me for the great battle of life which sooner or later all men are compelled to fight, and often discover, when too late, that it is only earnest work that makes success possible.

When I reached home, I went to my father's auction store. I think Mr. Isaiah Moses had some interest in the business. At all events, L. I. [J.?] Moses, the father of Moses Bros., of Montgomery, was bookkeeper, and in imitating his signature I obtained my present sign man[ua]l [signature]. In order to equip me better for business (I suppose), my father purchased for me a horse and gig, a two-wheeled concern; four-wheeled buggies were then unknown. My mother gave me a library. I did not use the library *much*, but I never failed to use the horse if the weather was fine. An afternoon drive to Tivoli Garden or the Four-Mile-House, where young men congregated to roll tenpins, play billiards, and drink brandy smashes, mint juleps, and other inspiring drinks, was my regular routine. In the mornings I staid in the store, in the evenings I drove out, *and at night I helped to regulate the town.*

I have outlived all my friends, for I was by many years the junior of all my companions. I will only mention one, who then must have been at least thirty-five. He was a leader among the young men in everything. He was aide to the governor, a high officer in the Jockey Club (and then Charleston was famous for its fine horses), he was a fine boxer, an exceptionally good horseman, an incomparable mimic, the terror of all men who had the misfortune to have a peculiarity that would make them ridiculous if closely imitated. He labored as teller in a bank and found the chief pleasure of life in being a practical joker. His name was Abraham Miller, and no man was more popular or better known in Charleston than was this un-conquerable joker in his day and generation. I could fill this book recounting his pranks but I will only mention one or two, when I was an eyewitness and participated in the sport.

There was an Italian trumpeter in Charleston, named Salvo, whose wife was a famous fortuneteller. The Fourth of July was a great day for military parade, and Salvo's trumpet was in great demand, of course. The weather was always hot, and as a consequence Salvo perspired freely. Being very careful of his uniform, he was accustomed to hanging it out of his window, as my wife does my clothes after a hard day's work. Miller knew this to be his habit, so in the small hours of the night, when sound sleep was endeavoring to restore Salvo's tired nature, Miller would happen to pass by and with raps loud and long and strong enough to raise the dead, he would bang away on Salvo's door, and when he would at last be raised from his slumber, open the window and exclaim: "What for you breaky down my house?" "Excuse me, sir, but I was passing and saw your coat hanging out of the window, and I thought I would let you know as you had no doubt forgotten it." "No, sir, I not forget. I hang him out to *dry!*" "I am sorry that I disturbed you, good night."

In about half an hour, when Salvo would be again asleep, Miller would return and with a broad Irish brogue repeat the same conversation and again Salvo would say: "I hang him out to *dry!*" He returned after a while with as genuine a Dutch accent as if he had just arrived from the fatherland, and [would] go through the same uncalled for information, when Salvo exclaimed in broken English: " 'Merican, Irish, Dutch, are all d——d fools. I parade today, I sweat much, my coat he is wet, I hang him out to *dhry*, but I will take him in. He will have to stay wet or I have no rest, and tomorrow me have to work all day."

Another of his victims was Dr. Faber, a highly respectable citizen and a member of the German Friendly Society. So was Miller, being of German descent. The society had a night meeting to celebrate one of their anniversaries. Miller slipped off and went to Faber's house. Now Faber was celebrated for his fancy poultry, of which he had all the new varieties of fowl, ducks, geese, and turkeys. Miller knocked at the door and called out, imitating Faber: "I hurried from the society to let you know I am going to bring several members home to supper, and I want you to have everything nice."

"My heavens, Dr. Faber, how can I prepare a supper this time of the night?" "Why not? You have plenty of servants and plenty of

poultry." "But Dr. Faber, your poultry is all expensive." "Never
mind the expense, kill anything, light up the diningroom, and be
ready. I must go back to the society; I just slipped out to give you
time to prepare."

When he [Dr. Faber] did come home, he was amazed to see preparations for a feast. "Mine Got, Elizabeth! Vot is all this?" "Why,
Mr. Faber, you came here and told me to prepare for company. You
were going to bring some friends to supper from the society, and
when I told you it was impossible, you ordered me to kill your fine
poultry or anything, not minding the expense but to be sure to have
everything nice, and I woke up the servants and have worried myself
nearly to death to do as you wanted." The D[octo]r assured her he
had not been near the house, and as he had on several occasions been
the victim of Miller's mimicry, a light flashed upon him and he exclaimed: "Betsey, it is not me, but that rascal of Abraham Miller
has been at his tricks again." . . .

Such companionship, while it gratified my appetite for fun, did
not materially improve my business habits. I always had a night key,
came home late or early (generally late), as best suited my pleasure,
and was never catechised as to how or where I spent my time. While
I staid with father, I made my first money (outside of my allowance) for services by buying sample cotton, and realized a profit of
$30, which $30 I invested in a lottery ticket and had visions of un-
told wealth. But, unfortunately, my tickets drew blanks and my $30
and fortune vanished into thin air.

I ran this schedule about nine months when, one day, father sent
me to the post office and I, for some reason, demurred about going.
He was very quick-tempered, and I was not very amiable, and we
had some altercation about my going to the post office, when he took
up a twenty-five-pound weight and threw it at me, I suppose with no
idea of hitting me, but rather to frighten me into obedience, but it
did not frighten me worth a cent. I went to the office, but as I was
going, I called back to him that I wouldn't stay with him any longer,
that I would go back to the North. I remember his reply: "You may
go to hell if you want to after you go to the post office."

I went to the office and then home, and told mother I couldn't stay
with father, and that I would sell my horse and gig, and that I was
going to New York and from there out West, and that I would not
come back until I made a fortune. She tried to persuade me not to
go, but finally contributed to my going by buying my library. This,
with the sale of my horse and gig, gave me between $200 and $300,
and I started for the Far West via New York.

I must then have been about nineteen, and still believed my father to be rich when, in fact, he was comparatively poor, but he always lived easily and looked rich. He was of a very bright, cheerful temperament, never fretted about anything, was remarkably handsome, weighed then about 300 lbs. (and before he died weighed 387 lbs.), was fond of jewelry and fine clothes, always kept horses, and was typical of what a youth would suppose a rich man would look like, when, in fact, a lean and hungry Cassius would better represent the unrest, care, and anxiety with which avarice paints a genuine "Gold Bug."

My preparations being made, I started for New York with my mother's blessing. In the sailing ship "President," Capt. Halsey [commanding], we had a splendid run to New York bar, and were expecting to take a pilot when we were blown off [shore] in a dreadful storm that lasted three or four days. During the height of the gale the bowsprit was blown away, and the sailors were ordered to take in the debris. One of the men was slow, and if I live to be 790 years instead of 79, I shall never forget this oath that Halsey hurled at him: "You d——d wishy-washy Molly-put-the-kettle-on! You need never be afraid of going to hell, for you haven't soul enough to be d——d." This seemed to me to embrace all the epithets known to the vocabulary of oaths.

We weathered the gale and arrived safely in New York. I went to a hotel somewhere near Wall Street on Broadway (I forget the name of it), but in a day or two several of my friends found me out and we had a royal time. I was about as far west as I ever got. New York was good enough for me. I paid about $75 for a circular, cloth cloak lined with velvet facings. They were called Spanish cloaks. One end was drawn over the chest and thrown over the left shoulder, hidalgo fashion. I gave a champagne supper and broke a looking glass. This absorbed about $60 more. After a few days, with $120 left, I went to Philadelphia and boarded at a tailor boardinghouse (not being on terms with my aunt's family) at $2 a week, swapped my Spanish cloak off in cold December for a season ticket to the theater, and soon got to where I could count my dollars on the fingers of either hand. Then I again got a place with Simeon Dreyfous, the watch importer. I stayed with him until about the year 1832, when South Carolina proposed to nullify the tariff law.

I then returned to Charleston, joined the heavy artillery, of which John Lyde Wilson (the famous duelist and author of the *Code* [of *Honor*]) was captain and my father was lieutenant. At one of the meetings I made some statement about tactics, which I had read, and Wilson said, as I thought, that what I said was not true. I gave him the lie and he challenged me. E. W. Moise [later attorney general of Louisiana] acted as my second. I accepted the challenge, but much to my satisfaction the matter was referred to a board of honor. When it turned out that Wilson had said what I *read* was not true, and as that impugned the veracity of the author of the tactics and left mine untouched, of course I retracted, and the matter was peac[e]ably settled to the honor of all parties, no one being more gratified than the writer of this. Wilson's moderation, I afterwards understood, was in deference to my father's conduct, who allowed things to take their course without any interference on his part.

This third escape made it still more probable that my way out of the world was predestined to be hempen, but some men disappoint all reasonable expectations and I seem to be one of that class. I think I went once more to the North, but I am not sure. But I do know that about this time I realized that my father was a poor man. My mother owned the house we lived in, which was also in Beaufain Street, next to the one that I was born in. She bought it with money earned from her school, and I inherited it when she died.

CONTRACTS NUPTIAL AND COMMERCIAL

As soon as I realized that my father was poor and that I had been a drain upon him, I determined to go to work in earnest. With no capital, but about $600 indebtedness, principally for tailors' bills in Philadelphia . . . I stepped down from my platform of fun and fashion to the earnest work of life by opening a very small "Cheap Cash Store," retail, of course. Father helped me some, and M. C. Mordecai [a wealthy merchant and civic figure] helped me some, but it was not much help I required. The auction stores seldom credit, making weekly collections on account, and I sold only for cash, and soon began to drive a right smart trade. I quit folly and went into calico, and as I knew most of the auctioneers from having been employed on what was then called vendue range [auctioneers' row], I soon found myself on my feet and my visions expanded until it embraced purchases in New York. But how to make them was the question. I resolved to try.

I went to New York without money and without letters of credit. I walked through Pearl Street and Maiden Lane and William Street. These were then the principle jobbing streets. Wherever I could see boxes marked for any of the Charleston retail merchants, I would stop in and price the goods, and when I was ready to buy, I would tell a plain story, that I had no capital and no expenses, except business expenses, that I lived with my parents, had done a small cash business and succeeded very well, that I did not expect to buy much or keep a large stock, and I do not remember ever to have been refused a moderate credit. The jobbers would, of course, inquire of the retailers with whom they dealt, and they would confirm my statements, for I told only the truth.

I had, too, become well-acquainted with several of the principal retail men, and had occasionally bought small bills from them, and being a genial and pleasant companion, I soon became popular with those with whom I was in contact. But to cut the story short, I did not want to buy much, and I found no difficulty in buying what I wanted to buy, and having made a beginning and met my payments, it was not long before I had to be circumspect in my purchases least [lest] I should overload myself. At that time, it was the practice to go North in the spring and fall to purchase, when the principal stock had to be laid in and the credits were four and six months. The present facilities for replenishing did not exist then. . . .

My business increased, and my credit with it. I soon did a leading business in retail dry goods. About this time, the Bank of Charleston was established, and there was a severe contest for the presidency and consequent buying up of the shares by the candidates and their friends. My mother sent me downtown to collect $500 for a negro girl she had sold. At that time $10 per share was paid in on the stock, and it commenced rising. I invested, without consulting her, the $500. The stock kept going up, and I kept buying, using my original purchase as a margin. I operated for about two days, and then, having a profit of about $2,000 in the stock, and hearing that one of the candidates had secured a majority, I directed my broker to close me out that evening at whatever the market might be, and he did so. The next morning the demand flagged and the stock declined, but I had made for mother about $2,000 on $500, and she had no complaints to make.

The next bank started was the Bank of Camden, and the charter required all subscribers to the extent of five shares to be supplied before any larger subscriptions could be filled, and a premium was offered on the stock before the books were opened. I saw the opportunity, and paid $1 each for names to subscribe for and proxies constituting me the agent to subscribe. The next thing was to get the money to pay up the first payment. I enlisted my landlord, John C. Ker, who was a rich man, and Dr. Della Motta, whose endorsement of my note would insure its discount in the bank. [Dr. Jacob

De La Motta was one of the leaders of the Jewish community.] For this I was to allow them one half of the profits. I think I gathered up about 300 names. The subscriptions in fives was so large, for I was not the only agent who had names, that, as well as I remember, the subscriptions for five shares only got a pro rata of two shares to each name, but these shares were immediately worth a premium of $5 to $6 per share, so that my profits in this transaction were over $1,500, and, besides, I made the reputation for knowing how to turn a penny.

Then I got on the right side of as mean a miser as the Lord ever made, one Jacob Barrett [a Jewish merchant and banker], who, by degrees, endorsed for me to the extent of $5,000, and his endorsement was [as] good for that amount as Vanderbilt's would be for $50,000. He would never charge me any commission, because he always wanted to be a preferred creditor (as he was) in case of accident. But he never endorsed a note for me in his life that he didn't buy enough out of the store to amount to a five percent commission, and he always forgot to pay for anything that he bought and, as I understood his tactics, of course I made no charges against him. . . .

About this time another piece of good luck befell me, perhaps the best luck that had ever befallen me in all my life before, or in all my life since. I met your mother, not having seen her before since we were about thirteen years old, she being one of the girls that attended my Bermitzma [Bar Mitzvah: "confirmation"] party. She was very ill with country fever when I returned to Charleston, and the probabilities of her death were a constant subject of discussion among our friends when I returned from the North. My sympathies became enlisted for this Miss Eliza Moses, whose life was hanging on a thread, and when I first met her, a fresh, blooming, pretty, modest girl, my heart went out to her and I am happy to say the feeling was reciprocated.

We were soon engaged, with the understanding that I was not to marry for two years. I tried courting for six months and found it very pleasant, but began to think marriage would be more to my mind and so proposed to her father [Isaac Clifton Moses, a former justice of the peace,] to have the marriage consummated. To this he was opposed, and I well remember his coming to the house to convince father of the propriety of waiting two years, and I equally remember my father's reply. It was this: "I don't know whether it would be prudent for Raphael to marry or not just now, but if you knew my son as well as I know him, you would know that he never stuck to anything two years in his life, and if you expect him to marry Eliza, you had better let him marry her now. That is all I have to say about it."

The argument, I suppose, was unanswerable, for on the twenty-second day of January thereafter [1834], about six months from the time of our engagement, we were married, and although we have lived together fifty-six years, we have never had occasion to regret our early wedding. . . .

Marie suggests . . . that I should be sure to tell all about my courtship. Now, I have said very little about it, as there was very little to say, and have omitted to declare that I made a big fool of myself, as most young men do, and Eliza seemed, like most young women similarly situated, to be very well-pleased with the folly. I make this declaration and say that all these facts existed.

There was nothing peculiar about my courtship. Very shortly after meeting Eliza at Mr. Nathan Hart's, where I was dining (at which time I fell in love with her), I commenced paying her marked attention. She went with her sister, Caroline (Mrs. A. Moise), to spend a part of the summer on Sullivan's Island. I used to go down to see her and walk on the beach. One evening, after having walked with her the evening before, I called to see her at Mrs. Moise's. While there, her son, Charles, a boy about two years old, came in the room and said to me: "I saw you kiss Aunt Eliza on the beach." No such thing had happened; Eliza caught the unfortunate child in her arms and rushed out of the room with him. They say she put him to bed and never woke him for twenty-four hours.

There has always rested a suspicion on Eliza for having given the child an overdose of catnip tea or some strong narcotic. How the child ever got the idea in his head no one ever knew. It was surmised that, on Eliza's part, "the wish was father to the thought." Charles slept with her, and it is supposed she kissed the boy in his dream and called him Raphael, and he was awakened by it, got the thing mixed in his mind, and when he saw me he had a confused notion that he saw me kiss his aunt on the beach, but certainly there was no truth in the statement.

While I was paying court to Eliza, it was reported that the parents on both sides were trying to make up a match between her and a cousin of hers, Marx Cohen, who afterwards married Armida Harby, the mother of Lee C. Harby, now of New York. [Cohen was later a planter and a magistrate.] It was further reported that the young people took kindly to the arrangement.

This was, to me, a source of considerable anxiety, and one Sunday evening at Mr. Lopez', E. M. [W.?] Moise and Theodore, his brother, who were my very intimate friends and confidents in this love affair, and I had a conference on the chances of my success. The result of the caucus was that they thought there might be some understanding between Eliza and her cousin, and advised me not to precipitate things. They thought that if I would give myself a year, whatever E's present feelings might be, I would succeed in my suit. After due deliberation and consideration of all the surrounding circumstances, it was unanimously resolved that I should wade in and keep wading for a year and then try my chances, sink or swim, and they thought that I would swim with their assistance. That night a proposition was made that we, with the Misses Lopez, would go over to Mr. Moses and then all go to walk on the Battery.

Have you ever been on the Battery? 'Tis a beautiful promenade, with the sea washing its base, and on a moonlight night, bright as it was that night, its surroundings are all provocatives of love. Well, it so happened that Eliza and I were paired and in watching the billows and the moon we somehow got separated or fell behind the rest of the party. I made myself as agreeable as I could, sounded her to the very depths on the Marx Cohen sensation, and found her "fancy free," but [I] resolved that, if I could help it, she would not long remain so, and about the time we were nearing her home I *proposed*. She wept (whether for sorrow or joy I never knew, but guessed). She neither then or since has given me any answer, but she did not object, only criticised a little more, when I told her that I should ask her father's consent. I suppose I did and he must have given his consent, for it was soon reported that we were engaged, and the unanimous opinion of our friends was that Eliza Moses was a brave girl to risk her happiness with Raphael Moses, but she was in for taking risks and she took them.

While we were engaged, she went to Edishio [Edisto] Island [South Carolina], to visit her brother, Charles. The steamer plied between Charleston and Edisto weekly. I kept a kind of diary which I used to send her by the steamer. Sometimes it contained thirty pages; what was in them I don't remember, but I am happy to say they were all burnt in one of the fires that pursued me and they can no longer be brought up in judgment against me.

When Eliza was in Charleston, I went to see her every night, and I staid until some sign was given that they were about to lock up the house. Along in January it began to be disagreeable, going out of a warm room into the wintry night, and I proposed to stop that foolishness, that we might begin the voyage of life together. We started out as I have said, January 22nd, 1834, and we have had an exceptionally happy life. . . .

I read the foregoing to Eliza and she says it is not true that which I relate with reference to Marx Cohen; that there was no understanding, etc. I never stated that there was an understanding; I only said that there was a *report* to that effect which gave me some uneasiness, and I still say that there was such a report, and that it did give me some uneasiness, but as she wished the truth of history to be recorded and is unwilling that this statement should be handed down to posterity, I now say to posterity that the report was without foundation. . . .

DECLINE IN BUSINESS AND DEATH IN THE FAMILY

My business grew with my happiness. I carried a large stock and did a large business, and it occurred to me one day (very fortunately), that if there was ever a large fire on King's Street, the chances were that the Charleston [insurance] offices would fail and be unable to pay their policies, and even if this did not happen, it was safer to insure in foreign offices. And carrying out those views, I placed most of my insurance in Augusta [Georgia] offices and kept them there.

In a year or two the most disastrous fire that had ever been known in Charleston broke out on King's Street, and the losses were so heavy that every insurance office in Charleston had to compound [make a settlement] with the assured. My policies being principally in Augusta, my policies were good. I bought a pair of horses and a dray the night of the fire and saved about $1,500 or $2,000 of my stock after moving it two or three times.

I made an assignment to M. C. Mordecai and had no trouble in getting a discharge. I had a customer, a Dutchman, to whom I was in the habit of jobbing goods, which he sold in Tallahassee and other points in Florida, and he persuaded me to buy the remnant of goods saved at the assignee sale and take them to Tallahassee. I arranged with Mr. Mordecai to do so, and my recollection is that I had to ship the goods by wagon from Augusta to Tallahassee. When I got them there, a Mr. Maynu was selling out a retail stock of goods, and I volunteered to help him sell out (without salary), so that I could learn the prices and know what to ask for my goods. In this way I familiarized myself with Florida values and got rid of my goods at fair prices and paid for them after I sold them in Florida.

While at Tallahassee, the new town of St. Joseph [Florida] had been started and lots had sold for immense prices. It was started in opposition to Apalachicola, which was owned by the Apalachicola Land Co., which held the lots in Apalachicola at exorbitant prices. St. Joseph had a fine climate and a bay said to be as beautiful as the Bay of Naples. Its approach was easy, while Apalachicola had a very expensive lighterage [place of loading], and was not regarded as healthy. A syndicate from Columbus [Georgia] bought up the land on St. Joseph's Bay and connected it with the [Apalachicola] River by railroad.

I went over to St. Joseph with a party of gentlemen, having no idea of locating there, but when I got there the town was "on a boom." Lots 80 x 100 were worth $5,000. It was but a few months old and shipped 30,000 bales of cotton. Butran, the secretary of the railroad, died while I was on a visit there; and strange as it may sound, I got the situation of secretary to the Lake Winneo & St. Joseph Railroad at a salary of $2,000 a year. So much for being a pleasant fellow and knowing how to tell a good story and telling them on all occasions, and, with all, being a good bookkeeper, the very thing the railroad company wanted. I think that was along in 1838.

I tried to hire a house and offered $600 a year for one that I couldn't get. I then hired a temporary place and had a house put together in Charleston by David Lopez [the builder] at a cost of about $600 and shipped to St. Joseph, but carpenters' wages were so high that this house, in the course of three or four years, with improvements and additions, cost me over $4,000. I soon got to know everybody in St. Joseph, and everybody knew me. I made friends that lasted all my life. . . .

I spent about five as happy years in St. Joseph as I ever spent anywhere. It was a delightful climate, a lovely situation, and has as generous and whole-souled a population as is to be found anywhere. But about the year 1843 the yellow fever broke out in St. Joseph and was very fatal. I myself had a very narrow escape from death; so did my wife.

I forgot to say that after I had been in St. Joseph about a year, Dr. Price, the agent of the Union Bank of Florida, wanted to go to Kentucky to spend the summer and, to my surprise, asked me, a comparative stranger, to take charge of the bank during his absence. As this added to my income and no bond was required of me, I accepted and attended to the bank and the R. R. books. When the cash was turned over to me in packages, I took the precaution to re-

ceipt for the loose bills and so many sealed packages, not opened or
counted.

After a while my deposits began to fall short, and I found I would
have to open the packages or have money sent to me from Tallahassee. I therefore wrote to Col. Parkhill of the Union Bank at Tallahassee either to send me over money or to come over and see the
packages opened, as I would not break the seals except in the presence of some officer of the bank. He came over. We opened the
packages, and one package was $13,000 short and had Price's memo-
randum in it for that [the full] amount, which accounted for his
willingness to trust me with the bank, for nothing would have suited
him better than to have me turn out dishonest, run away with the
funds, including his memorandum, and then cover his default, but
the course pursued by me uncovered his default, caused his removal
and the appointment of Parkhill's relative, a Mr. Hixon, as agent.
Price moved to Texas.

During my residence at St. Joseph, my father and mother followed
their wayward son, built a house next to mine. My mother died there
[1848], and my father died about six months after in Apalachicola
[1849]. He never recovered from the blow caused by my mother's
death, had her body buried in the yard near the house, and used to
pray at her grave daily, though he was never before religiously inclined.

My mother was a very religious woman, a strict conformist to all
Jewish customs, and the day before, though in apparent health, she
seemed to have a premonition of her death. I tried to rouse her and
made her go to walk with me. On the way we met an old Irishwoman
on whom she had been accustomed to bestow charity. She took her
aside and talked with her, and the Irishwoman told me that she gave
her $1 and told her to take that and remember her. The next day
was [my daughter] Nina's birthday and she promised me, if she was
well, she would throw off her depression and give her a party. But
she felt that a calamity was impending over us. We parted that night,
and she told Eliza to be sure to take care of father. This I did not
then know.

The next morning I went over as usual to see her, but she had not
been out of her room, and father said he supposed she was washing.
I knocked at the door and, receiving no answer, made our boy
[Negro servant], Joe, go in at the window, and alas, mother was on
the bed—dead. Her shrouds were on the bureau, and on a slip of
paper was written, "Where the tree falls, let it lay," intimating, I

suppose, that she did not wish her remains to be carried to Charleston to be laid in the Jewish cemetary.

She had her best linen sheets on the bed and every indication that she expected her room to be visited by strangers. Knowing how scrupulous she was about Jewish rights [rites], Eliza, with her usual self-sacrifice, performed all the duties of preparing her for burial, and thus, at seventy-two, passed from earth as pure a spirit as ever dwelt in human form. God bless her memory. I know that she has gone to her reward, and feel that she still lives and loves us.

CALLED TO THE BAR

I must now go back a little to my own life. The town went down, the R. R. Co. failed, and I bought for $37.50 the house and lot that I had a few years before offered $600 a year rental for.

With the failure of the R. R. and the town, I was in a bad way. No money and no business. The only thing that I could do which required no other capital than self-reliance, of which I had a goodly share, was law. I decided to study law. I studied six weeks and knew just as much law as I did when I started. Examinations were private then, and I managed to get my friend Hawkens and others appointed on the committee. They reported me qualified, and I appeared thereafter not a briefless lawyer, for I had already won my spurs by what was considered a very shrewd trick in humbugging a court of three magistrates, of which trick I was as innocent as the babe unborn, but I had sense enough to keep the world in ignorance of my simplicity. . . .

It happened thus: a young man from St. Andrew's Bay, about thirty miles from St. Joseph's, came in with about ten head of cattle for sale. They were purchased by a butcher, name[d] Scuyler [Schuyler?]. The cattle, no doubt, had been stolen from a farm on St. Andrew's Bay and belonged to a very respectable citizen, name[d] Blackwell. He demanded the cattle; the young man and the butcher refused to give them up. Blackwell, by the advice of his son-in-law, Chandler Younge, a lawyer of some eminence, sued [swore] out a warrant against the young man and had him arrested for larceny. Some of the neighboring circuit courts were about being held, and Younge and all the attorneys were obliged to be absent on the day set for the trial, but Younge very properly told Blackwell all he had to do was to prove the cattle his property by the marks and brands, and then it would devolve on the accused to show

how he came honestly in possession, and failing to do this, he would be bound over to the Supreme Court for larceny.

All the lawyers being absent, Scuyler gave me a conditional fee of $20 to defend the young man. He [the young man] said the cattle were his father's, and I really believed him—really believed him. The court met; three justices, one, I well remember, presided in his shirt sleeves.

Blackwell took the stand, was sworn, and would have proved property in the cattle, but I objected on the ground of his interest and made a conscientious argument on this line, that the young man was a stranger in this community, and if Blackwell was allowed to testify, the result of his evidence would be to transfer this man's property to himself, and, what was vastly more important, its effects would be to brand as a thief a poor youth, whose good character was his only capital. I pressed this as a man would press it who believed it true. The accused mouth was closed, he was away from home, and without witnesses, and I appealed very feelingly to the court not to be instrumental in the commission of such an act of injustice. Consequence: Blackwell had to come down and remain as dumb as an oyster; my client was discharged, and I received my first fee of $20.

When the lawyers returned, they twitted me with having humbugged the court, and my character for shrewdness was established. They little knew that I was for the first time learning that I had humbugged the court, when I really thought that I had made a fair law argument, but I made no sign, and it was a long time before I let the "cat out of the bag." . . .

I then commenced practicing in Apalachicola, twenty-four miles from St. Joseph. I used to get up early enough to ride twenty-four miles before breakfast. My family remained in St. Joseph. I came home every Friday and returned to Apalachicola on Monday.

I remember the first case I tried in Apalachicola was before Judge Carmack on a question of where administration attached on a particular statute. I took a great deal of pains with my brief. Brockenborough, a very talented lawyer, was on the other side. When I commenced my argument, he was reading a newspaper; he continued reading it all through my argument. When I concluded he merely read a few lines from the code. The judge sustained him in his objection to the state's having any jurisdiction over the administration, and when I was nonsuited, my client said if he hadn't had a jacklegged lawyer for his case, he would have won it. I was terribly crestfallen and mortified at the idea that, when I supposed I had an impregnable brief, it was not even considered worth an argument in reply. I went to my office and took up the code, read the statute that Brockenborough had read, wept over my obtuseness, pitched my book away, and resolved to quit a profession that I was evidently unfit for.

That night I dropped in at Brockenborough's office. I was intimate with him and told him that I was going to quit law. He asked me why. I told him very frankly that I had studied the question very closely, made my argument, that he read the newspaper all the time, and that my argument did not even elicit a reply. He laughed and said: "Moses, the only reason that I didn't reply to your argument was because it was unanswerable. Unless the statute controlled the question, there was no getting over your argument," and he advised me to stick to law.

This made me feel much better, and I thought that I would go and see Judge Carmack. Maybe he might say something about the brief. I hadn't been in the room long before he said: "Moses, I have been thinking about my decision today, and I believe I was wrong. If you will move to reinstate the case, I will make an order reinstating it." I told him what Ned Wood, my client, had said about a jack-legged lawyer, and that I would have nothing more to do with the case, and that I had pretty nearly made up my mind to quit practicing. Judge Carmack said: "Quit practicing! Why, it won't be long before the best man at this bar won't be more than your equal." When I left Carmack's room I was on stilts, but I never moved in that case again, and I told Wood why I didn't move. . . .

I distinctly recollect that my office was in the third story of a brick building, the lower story of which was a ship chandle[r]y, and the second was a carpenter shop, and many a time, when I thought I heard the step of a client on the stairs, it would stop at the carpenter shop—either one of these mechanics or someone having more use for a carpenter than for a tyro at the bar. And I further remember that I slept on a cot without a mattress, made my own coffee, and lived on crackers and cheese and cold ham. . . .

I got on rapidly in Apalachicola and was soon employed in all the principal cases; I made a very large fee—I think it was $2,500— foreclosing a mortgage on the St. Joseph R. R., a mortgage made by the new company in favor of John D. & William Gray. They bought the road at the sale, took up the iron, carried it to Georgia to complete a contract they had for building the Monroe R. R.

St. Joseph went all to pieces—the very brick chimneys were taken down during the war [the Civil War] to make salt vats for evaporating the salt water. The graveyard is the only landmark left of the former city; it is again as it was before St. Joseph was founded—a wilderness of pines where the bear and deer roam unmolested. It is so utterly deserted, except by the beasts of the forest, that after the war I had what was left of my mother and father and uncle exhumed, and they now lie in the graveyard of the Esquiline [my plantation in Georgia].

I remained in Apalachicola until 1849; my family moved over after a while, but [it was] not until I was burned out once in an office that I moved too. We moved into a house I had won in a litigation; we lived in there in the winter and in the summer at St. Joseph, next to where my mother and father lived until she died, and then my father moved over and lived with us a short time, when he died at the age of sixty-two from a surgical operation. He continued sinking after mother's death—a blow from which he never recovered.

One summer, while we were at St. Joseph, a carpenter walked over from Apalachicola to inform me that my house was burned down from a fire originating in the neighborhood, and he wanted to secure a contract to rebuild. I didn't rebuild, but collected my insurance (about $900); it was a small house.

About the time I had settled in Apalachicola, there was a great deal of litigation growing out of the mortgages of the Union Bank. The Union Bank was founded somewhat on the subtreasury plan. It was a kind of farmers' scheme, but instead of advancing on cotton, it advanced three-fourths of the value of negroes and land. These advances caused money to be abundant, and as negroes and land were favored with securities, they rose rapidly in value. This left a margin between the original three-fourths and the three-fourths caused by inflated value. For this excess the farmers would make a second mortgage. When I first went to Tallahassee, the Union Bank was in full blast; the planters all had money and the bank had mortgages on all the property. Times were flush. Four-in-hands [carriages drawn by four horses] were as common as pairs are now; parties were given in the most expensive style; and Tallahassee was one round of fashion, fun, and frolic, but alas, what a change came over the people!

About the time I commenced to practice law in Apalachicola, the mortgages began to mature, the interest was in default, foreclosures were being pressed, negroes had legs, and the debtors began to run them off (principally to Texas). Apalachicola was a good shipping point then. The debtors came with their negroes in the

NATCHEZ, MISSISSIPPI, IN 1840

(see page 270)

BOSTON IN 1840

night, and the bank following up with the mortgages, attachments, and foreclosures. This made a legal harvest and I gathered in the fees.

Some of these mortgages had been transferred by the bank. I remember one was assigned to a Frenchman. I was employed in the defense. He came to see me and I said: "Monsieur (I forget his name), it is a very plain case. My client's rights are so and so." I went into a long explanation. The Frenchman kept getting more and more excited, pacing up and down the room, shrugging his shoulders at every half turn. At last he turned around to me and said: "Monsieur Moïse, you call zis a *plain* case, eh? I like you to show me one vich is complicate." . . .

My business prospered so much that I was, after a while, able to refuse a fee of $1,000 from one A. I. Bennett, who was robbing, with a high hand, Farish Carter of Georgia. He [Carter] held mortgages on negroes that were being run off, and followed them to Apalachicola. Bennett bought them with knowledge of the facts and attempted to defy Carter, his attorney, and the sheriff with shotguns and a lot of toughs. It was therefore that I refused to be employed, but I lost nothing by it, for when Brockenborough (Carter's lawyer) died about a year after, Carter employed me. The litigation lasted for some time after I went to Columbus [Georgia]. I argued and gained one branch of it before the Supreme Court in Tallahassee, and another branch at Jacksonville before the United States Court. Jacksonville was then a village without sidewalks, with the sand ankle-deep, and it is now a fashionable resort with magnificent hotels. I suppose, first and last, I made several thousand dollars out of the Carter-Bennet[t] case. It not only involved $30,000 or $40,000, but an intense amount of feeling.

Home Life

About the year 1844, my wife and children went to Charleston, where my son Albert was born. That summer we went north, Eliza; Isabell, her sister; Isaac, Hannah, Major [Israel], Albert, and a white nurse. I had about $2,500. The money went so fast in New York that I could hardly realize it, and we all started for Stamford, Connecticut (where my wife's father, soon after our marriage, was killed by being thrown from a buggy, and his wife was so much injured that she died about six months after, in Charleston).

We went to visit the grave of her father, Mr. Isaac C. Moses, and staid with the Beach family, at whose house he died. It was on this trip that I insisted I was made cross-eyed by watching the children and the baggage in different directions at the same time.

I had some business in Portland, Maine, and left the family at Beach's about ten days or two weeks. They were a plain Connecticut family, lived very comfortably, had an apple orchard (the delight of the children), and it was on this farm that I caught Isaac turning the handle and Major literally with his nose to a grindstone, where it has been metaphorically ever since. He was then proposing to have his nose rounded off so as to be as nearly like mine as possible. Eliza made a nice lot of preserves, with the assistance of Mrs. Beach and her granddaughter. They kept no servants, and the children milked the cows and cleaned the shoes, and everything was neat and clean.

When I asked for my bill, Mrs. Beach hesitatingly inquired if I thought $10 would be too much. I emphasized my opinion by handing her $20 and considered that I got off cheap. They lived on a farm about a mile from Stamford, which was a village of half a dozen houses. Now it is quite a city, penetrated by railroads and fine hotels from $2.50 to $3.00 per day. Everything is so changed that in 1887 or 1888, when we were in New York, my wife wished to visit her father's grave, but the oldest inhabitant remembered nothing of the incident, and the sextons of the graveyard, none of them had any record of his burial, so that in less than a half of a century from the time his body was turned to dust from whence it sprung, all trace of him was lost, except to our immediate families. Such is the fate of man. And even in our families, after two or three generations our descendants have a very confused idea of who their ancestors might have been. . . .

LAST DAYS IN FLORIDA

I remained in Apalachicola untill 1849. During my stay there its business had dwindled from 130,000 bales to about half that amount. The railroads were carrying cotton direct from Columbus [Georgia] and other points to New York. I saw the end was coming and determined to seek a new location. I went to Texas at the suggestion of Judge Duval, stayed in Galveston about a week, found a strong bar there, and, further, that there was more land than cash in fees. I finally determined to settle at Columbus, where I had a good business acquaintance, as many of my clients that I had in Apalachicola were residents of Columbus.

When I went from Apalachicola, the citizens gave me a very

handsome farewell banquet, and I left there with many friends and
not an enemy that I knew of—Bennett and Caro had moved to New
Orleans.

I have already stated who Bennett was and will now develop
Caro. He was a Spaniard who kept a store in Apalachicola, and I
had some suits against him. He had prepared for his failures, and
I had nothing I could levy my judgments on, but on looking into
his affairs I found that a steamboat stood in his name which really
belonged to his brother-in-law, who was then running her as captain
on the Apalachicola River. His brother-in-law became embarrassed
a year or two before, and Caro then being good credit, the steamer
was then registered in Caro's name, and I suppose they forgot to
change the register when Caro failed. I levied my judgment on the
steamboat. This made Caro furious.

The morning after the levy, as I was going to my office with my
mail in my hand, he overtook me in the side street and commenced
to have an altercation with me. He finally called me a liar, and I
drew back to strike him, and Spaniard like he had a knife concealed
up his sleeve and in an instant I was cut across the throat. Being
unarmed, I stopped to pick up a brick, but he ran off, and it was all
that I could do, from loss of blood, to get back to Bay Street and sit
down until Dr. Gorrie could be sent for. All that saved my life was
my whiskers, which I wore very heavy on my throat; he cut me
right over the carotid artery. Dr. Gorrie sewed it up, and I went
home with my head in bandages. Your mother had a fright, of
course; the knife was so sharp and the cut so smooth, that it healed
by the first intention, as the D[octo]rs say, and I suffered very little
pain. I was confined to the house for some time, and never saw Caro
any more. He considered New Orleans a safer place than Apalachicola and went there. This was the only serious trouble that I had
while I was there.

I lived in Apalachicola five or six years; it was then a gay place;
it had a fine set of merchants and its principal business was cotton,
and as the cotton buyers either made a great deal or the reclama-
tions for losses are so large that they can't begin to pay them, economy in their expenditures had no place in their programme; water
was scarcer than champagne and jolly good fellows were as plentiful
as blackberries.

Apalachicola, like St. Joseph, went down, down, down, until it
ceased to ship a single bail [bale] of cotton. Of late years it has
done considerable trade in lumber, sponges, and oysters, but before

I was forty, two flourishing cities were in ruins, "all of which I saw, part of which I was." . . .

I find that I have made no mention of the fact of a painful chapter in my life's history. I had to perform the burial service for my mother, father, and uncle. They died in Florida, where we were about the only Jews, and again I performed the burial services over Percy Levy, brother of my son-in-law, to whom I became much attached. This was done at his request.

I also omitted to mention that I was, in 1847, a delegate from Florida in the [Democratic] presidential nominating convention at Baltimore, when [Lewis] Cass was nominated. It was a very stormy convention. The slavery issue was even then the bone of contention. [The secessionist, William L.] Yanc[e]y, of Alabama, and myself tried by correspondence to commit Cass to the right of Southerners to carry slaves into the Northwest Territory. Failing to commit him, we endeavored to incorporate in the Democratic platform a recognition of that right and, failing there, Wm. L. Yanc[e]y for Alabama and I for Florida addressed the convention, protested against the platform, refused to endorse the nomination, and with our delegations withdrew from the convention.

I wrote the manifesto to the people of Florida, advising them to be neutral in the election, and received a very handsome letter from John C. Calhoun of South Carolina (to whom I sent a newspaper copy), commending my course. No man who has not been through such a scene can realize the embittered feeling and wild excitement of a convention of political partisans against delegates with nerve enough to refuse to endorse a nomination and withdraw from the convention. Of course, our states voted for Cass, and my co-delegates themselves voted for him "under protest." I could never exactly tell what that meant or who but themselves they protested against. . . .

The Rise of a Georgia Lawyer

In 1849, I came to Columbus to meet the strongest bar in Georgia, but I had, among my Florida clientage living in Columbus, Daniel McDougald, the brainiest merchant I have ever been intimate with; John G. Winter, then president of St. Mary's Bank and an acknowledged power in Columbus; Hamp Smith, a kind of cotton king. I knew all the Howards from having been associated with Thacker B. Howard as president of the St. Joseph R. R. Co., I being the secretary. I knew Seaborn Jones intimately, he having been interested in

St. Joseph, where he made frequent visits; it was the same [with] Benj. Fontaine, another leading merchant.

So, I did not come to Columbus a stranger, and the fact of my having done business satisfactorily with all these men while practicing law in Florida was the main reason why I selected it as my future home. Still, the bar was formidable, and it took a man with large development of hope to confront it and hope to meet with success. . . .

I had about $4,000 when I came to Columbus. I bought a house for $1,000 and spent about $500 improving it. I bought a carriage or landau and a fine pair of horses, believing that the best way to procure business was to seem independent of it. I determined to place myself in a position that when a client came to me, I would know that he came because it was his interest to come, and that he did not come to help me or to get cheap work because of my necessities.

I had been in Columbus a very short time when John G. Winter, for whom I had done business in Florida, employed me as counsel for the St. Mary's Bank, of which he was president. He gave me an office in the bank building and $200 for a year. The salary was small, but Winter had the leading business in Columbus and, of course, threw into my hands all the business that he controlled, and as, at that time, collections were an important branch of the business, this situation paid me incidentally more than my salary and, besides, it was a good send-off for a man who was new in a place.

The very fact that Winter was a power in Columbus and had confidence enough in me to give me his general business was in itself a very valuable indorsement. At the end of the year I resigned my position. . . .

My practice grew steadily until finally I had the most lucrative practice of any member of the bar. . . .

My family consisted of Isaac, [Israel, called Major], Nina, Albert, Lea [Raphael: last three letters spelled backward!], and Hannah. The latter was quite delicate and could not stand the summers in Columbus. On account of her health, I had to go to Warm and Chalybeate Springs in summer. My son Isaac was also very delicate, and I sent him with a friend to the Hot Springs in Arkansas. When he reached there the physician said he had rheumatism of the heart, and it should be fatal to him to use the waters and that I must meet him in New Orleans at his Aunt Septimer's [Septima's], Mrs.

Solomon Levy. I went there for him and was shocked to find him terribly swollen with dropsy.

I brought him home; he lingered a few months and died. This was the second death among my children. The first was my daughter Sarah, whose apron was drawn into a grate when she was standing near it and burned her, chiefly around the neck, down to the carotid artery. The *burning* was a sad misfortune to us; she was our first child. But I never wished for her recovery after I learned from the doctor that, if she recovered, her neck would always be drawn down to one side from the contraction of the muscles, and it would have been pure selfishness to wish a girl to live, deformed, and a constant source of mortification to herself.

Life *may* be worth living to a boy despite of deformity, but I doubt it, for my opinion is that life is only worth living under the very best conditions. Isabel was born a few months before Isaac died.

In the fall of 1850, on account of Hannah's health and my love of suburban life, I purchased from John G. Winter my present home, then called by Winter "Bunker Hill," but when I purchased it my friend John Forsyth [the famous Democratic editor], then editing the Columbus *Times*, compared me (jocularly) to Ma[e]cenas [Roman patron of literature, and statesman], who delighted in his leisure in horticulture on the Esquiline (one of the seven hills of Rome), hence the name by which it has ever since been known, one that I much prefer to any New England production.

POLITICS AND PEACHES

After moving to Columbus I took an active part in politics and was decidedly in favor of seceding when [in 1850] the admission of California destroyed the balance of power as provided in the Constitution. It was the entering wedge of sectionalism.

I soon made a reputation as a political speaker and could have gone to the legislature long before necessity carried me there, but I had no desire for public position. The issues in 1850 were very exciting. In fact, they were the same that culminated in the war of 1861! But individuals changed their positions: [Robert A.] Toombs, who was at the head of the revolution in 1861, was a prominent Unionist in 1850. [Alexander] Stephens and [Howell] Cobb were also for the Union; [Charles J.] McDonald, Colquit [Walter T. Colquitt], and others were for secession.

McDonald and Cobb opposed each other for governor [of Georgia in 1851] on these issues. Excitement ran very high. It was in one of Toombs's Union speeches at Columbus that he said he "had carried the first white shirt in the Democratic party that ever entered it, and now these fellows, with [John Caldwell] Calhoun at their head, talk about overturning the government. Why," said he, "they have not strength enough to overthrow a smokehouse, eight by ten!" He was very abusive of Calhoun and South Carolina. There we made our acquaintance. I pressed my way up to the front of the stage and, pointing my finger at him . . . hissed him and announced that I would reply to him at the same place that night, which I did. I invited Toombs to be present, but he didn't come.

The meeting was the stormiest political meeting that I ever spoke to. I don't remember exactly when Toombs and I met again, but I think it was long after in a consultation on the bank cases, when all the counsels for the various defendants (of whom Toombs was one and I another) met for conference. After a time we became excellent friends, and when the issue was made in 1861, we were both on the same side and became very close friends.

Shortly after we moved to the Esquiline, Hannah married Mr. Isaac I. Moses. We had a very large wedding, I think 300 or 400 guests, and about thirty slept here that night. Hannah had two children, a boy, Isaiah, who died in infancy and is buried in our cemetery, and a daughter, Rebecca Hannah. Her mother [i.e., my daughter Hannah] was attending to a Miss Jonas [later Mrs. Abraham I. Moses] in Montgomery, warming some water for her, when her clothes accidentally caught fire and burnt her dreadfully. She suffered terribly, lingered some months and died [1860]. Just across the river, she is buried in our cemetery. Her daughter Hannah survived her, married Jacob I. Moses, has two children (boys) and lives in New York. This was our second child burned to death. . . .

I don't think of any other incident that happened worth recording before the war unless it may be that the Esquiline had a fine orchard and that I shipped, as an experiment, the first peaches, etc. sent from the South. This was in 1851 before there was any through connection by R. R. The two champagne baskets, one of peaches and one of plums, went by stage to Macon, then by R. R. to Savannah, and then by steamer to New York.

I received $30 per basket.

I then extended my orchard and, when the R. R. commenced, shipped largely to New York, getting very remunerative prices. I started a fruit and flower nursery with a Mr. John Lee, an Irishman, as superintendant. This failed—Mr. Lee and my son, Major, had a quarrel about a cow getting into the nursery.

I was out riding and when I came home Mr. Lee had left and the nursery went "where the woodbine twineth."

I continued extending my orchard and the year the war broke out my sales had reached $7,500 per annum. I then had 100 acres in fruit, 20,000 trees, young and old, a vineyard of 18 acres under the management of a Frenchman, Joseph Dantell [Dautel?], who drew none of his salary during the four years; [he] made enough outside to pay his current expenses.

When I returned from the war, to my amazement his salary was $2,400, which was all due him, and he demanded it in gold. I refused to pay it. He moved to Tennessee, sued me in the U. S. Court, and I finally had to pay about $3,200 after the vineyards were ploughed up, they being Catawba grapes, which rotted badly.

I started a canning factory, which was also a failure, as the war broke out about the time I was ready to operate it.

I built a fruit-drying house, and this burned up with all the fruit in it, owing to a defective flue.

My time was wholly taken with a large law practice, and I could give these matters but little personal supervision.

Moral—undertake nothing that you can't give sufficient personal supervision to, to reasonably insure its success.

When the war broke out I had forty-seven slaves, and when it ended I had forty-seven freedmen—all left me except one, old London, who staid with me until he died.

Wartime Commissary

The war broke out in April, 1861. That put an end to northern shipments, and so I went to Virginia and had my fruit shipped there, and I was generally known as the peach man. I sold several thousand dollars' worth of fruit. The currency was good then, and I invested the net proceeds in negroes, whose value turned out to be four years' service during the war, involving an annual loss.

I was overage but, while in Virginia, I sought a place on Toombs's staff (he was a general of a brigade). He offered me the position of commissary, which I refused. I did not want the place of a noncombatant, but Howell Cobb persuaded me to accept it as a matter of public duty. He said it was a place hard to fill with a competent man, and he was sure I could do more good in that position than any other. I accepted and went into service without returning home, thinking that I could get a furlough (after entering the army) without any trouble, but in this I was mistaken. Furloughs were not lay-

ing about loose, and it was very hard to obtain one. My son Albert
went off with the City Light Guards, and Major remained at home
for a time to attend to farm matters.

In about eighteen months or two years I got a furlough and came
home. Major went into the army. I was promoted from commissary
of Toombs's to commissary of D. R. Jones's division, of which
Toombs's brigade formed a part. I was again promoted to chief commissary of [General James] Longstreet's corps. I kept the army
supplied in Tennessee six weeks after Longstreet thought he would
be obliged to retreat for want of supplies.

I did it by ascertaining that the wheat was threshed on toll [on
a percentage basis] by machines, and I got the books of the wheat
threshers and so knew exactly who had wheat and how much. When
they hid the bacon so effectually that it could not be found for
seizure, I went after the sheep that wandered upon a thousand hills.
Now at that time in the fall, mutton was not fit to eat, but they
wanted wool (the Tennesseeans) for winter clothing.

I seized the sheep in flocks and gave receipts for them as commissary. Then I offered two pounds of sheep for one pound of bacon,
and this unlocked the secret places where the bacon was hid, and
the sheep proving a good currency, I got nearly all the bacon necessary for rationing the corps. Now and then I would have to give the
brigade "sheep meat," which was, in its thin condition, very distaste-
ful to the soldiers and, as a mark of their displeasure, a soldier in
[Henry L.] Benning's brigade one night cleaned his poor sheep,
took the entrails out, then took a cross stick to hold his legs apart,
set a candle where the bowels were wont to be and went about the
camp, Diogenes-like, seeking to find "an honest commissary."

I remained in this position, chief commissary of Longstreet's
corps, until just before the Battle of the Wilderness [May 5-6, 1864],
when the difficulty of supplying the army became almost insurmountable.

Georgia was the chief source of supply, and the speculations of
the men who were buying food for the army in Georgia became so
intolerable that the farmers refused to sell. It occurred to me that
if I could go to Georgia and speak to the people who had sons,
brothers, relatives, and friends who were suffering for [lack of]
supplies, I could get supplies; that one coming from the army, and
having no motive to deceive them, would enlist their sympathy, and
command their attention, and unlock their granaries and pigstys.

I suggested to General Longstreet to give me a furlough for this
purpose. He consented at once, but it required the approval of Gen.

[Robert E.] Lee. I carried my furlough, signed by General Longstreet, to General Lee's headquarters which were nearby. There was
never any difficulty about approaching General Lee; he had very
little red-tape routine. He was writing in his tent when I entered.
He looked up with a friendly smile and said: "Major, what will you
have?" I handed him my furlough; he read it and said: "Major, I
would approve of it, but I really can't spare you." I then explained
to him my plans. He hesitated a minute or two and then said: "Well,
Major, if you think you can do anything for my poor boys, go,
and may God crown your efforts with success." He approved my furlough and I started for Georgia.

The first meeting I called was at Columbus, in Temperance Hall.
There were about thirty persons present. I thanked them for their
presence and stated when I last spoke in this hall it was to urge the
people to send their sons and brothers to confront the hazards of
war and to redress their country's wrongs, the house was full from
pit to gallery with patriotic citizens ready for the sacrifices asked.
Now I come from those near and dear to the people here, to appeal
to them for bread for the starving army, and I am confronted with
empty benches. I must try more fruitful fields; an appeal to the few
who are here could promise no good results. I thanked those present
for their attendance and closed the meeting.

I went from there to s.[outh] w.[est] Georgia and was met with
a very different spirit and had a very successful trip. While on this
trip, Major Locke, the Confederate commissary for the state of
Georgia, died, and without any soliciting from me or any such
expectation on my part, the commissary general, Col. Northrope
[L. B. Northrup], telegraphed me from Richmond [Virginia], assigning me to duty as Confederate commissary of the state of
Georgia, in which position I remained until the War closed. . . .

Previously [September, 1862] . . . I went on a foraging excursion
through the Valley of Virginia with a train of wagons, buying bacon
and flour, and seizing cattle. While riding along, I spied some cattle
in a pasture and sent a detail down to drive them along with our
herd, and they were accordingly brought. When we had proceeded a
half mile or so, an old woman came up to me in great distress and
said: "That is my 'pet heifer' you have driven away, and would
you kill it?" She seemed almost heartbroken at the loss and probable fate of her heart's darling, and my sympathies got the better
of me when I said: "Certainly not. Take her back."

I shall never forget the joy that illumined the old woman's face,
and when she went back with her pet heifer it occurred to me that

if she had a prodigal son who had strayed away, that if on his return she killed for him a fatted calf, it would surely not be her "pet heifer." This is a small matter to note down, but it impressed itself very much on me at the time, and it is one of my good deeds that comes back to memory and cheers my waning years.

My trip was a very fatiguing one. It lasted about two weeks, but as I returned to camp with a train well-loaded with stores, for which the troups were in great need, I felt fully compensated for my labor and fatigue. I arrived in camp on the morning preceding the Battle of Sharpsburg [Antietam, September 17, 1862], and that night we had to hurriedly retreat and leave the stores and supplies.

I let the soldiers take what they could on their bayonets and in their knapsacks, the adornment of a flitch of bacon being in no case objected to, and except what was thus saved and the cattle that we could drive, my two weeks' labor were lost. So much for the uncertainties of a boardinghouse-keeper in the midst of war, and as I had, including teamsters and noncombatants, a family of nearly 54,000 to provide for, this depletion of the larder was very serious.

Just here an incident occurs to me in strategy which, as it surprised me, I suppose I might as well relate. Lee had ordered [General Thomas J. ("Stonewall")] Jackson's troops to join him. We were greatly outnumbered and it was very important, as the fate of the day turned against us, that an impression should be made on the enemy that reinforcements had arrived. And General Lee effected this by having a considerable amount of brush cut and dragged by horses along the roads, so as to cause an immense dust to arise and make it appear to the enemy that fresh troops had arrived. I presume it had the desired effect, as we were not pursued, and pursuit would have been very disastrous. . . .

MEN AND INCIDENTS OF THE WAR

Before entering into any of my duties here I will go back a little to army life, as my children seem to wish it. . . .

Among others on Gen. Longstreet's staff were . . . Col. Fairfax, of the old Virginia Fairfaxes, fond of his bottle, his Bible, and baths—always in front when danger pressed, very much given to show, a fine-looking fellow, and nothing pleased him better, when the army arrived at a new place, than to be mistaken for General Longstreet, and this happened more than once. He carried, all through the campaign, a bathtub in the shape of a tin hat, and a chest supplied with an assortment of liquors. He took a bath and five or six nips (drinks) before breakfast, always had hanging in his tent a linen housewife, or sack with two pockets; in one he kept his bottle and in the other his Bible. Sunday was his maudlin day and he would lay down with his bottle and his Bible beside him.

One Sunday, when, Tam O'Shanta [Tam O'shanter-] like, he was "o'er the ills of life victorious" [Burns], I wrote on two sheets of paper; on one, "This in a moment brings me to an end," and on another, "While this informs me I shall never die." I fixed the first to the bottle and put the second between the scriptural leaves. When Fairfax awoke and read them he said: "Moses, by the Lord."

On another occasion, in East Tennessee, we stopped at Greenville, and I had my headquarters in the law library of Andrew Johnson, afterwards President of the United States, within sight of his office, which, by the way, was in one of the side rooms of the tavern. We were in sight of the little shop, still standing, where Andy, as the Tennesseeans called him, had his tailor shop.

After leaving Greenville, we went to Morristown, about fifteen miles, and while there I happened to mention a heavy box in Johnson's library which was nailed up. Fairfax immediately "snuffed not tyranny, but whiskey in the tainted air" and exclaimed: "By George, Moses, why didn't you tell me before we left? Old Andy was very fond of his nibs, and I will bet that box was full of good old rye whiskey and I mean to have it." He immediately got a detail of soldiers and a wagon and had the box brought to camp. When it arrived Fairfax's eyes glistened with anxious expectation, soon followed by despondency, as on opening the box, it contained, instead of old liquor, nothing but Andy Johnson's letters and private papers.

The question was, "What shall we do with it?" It was too heavy and cumbersome to carry on the campaign with our limited transportation. Fairfax and the rest of the staff said: "Burn the cussed thing." I said: "Oh, no, not until I look over the contents."

We staid several days at Morristown, and I amused myself looking over the papers, selected what I wanted, and destroyed the rest. Among the papers I selected were several giving details of a patent for cutting out clothes. [Johnson was a tailor once.] Some were for laboring men, as illiterate as Johnson then was (it is said that he learned to read and write after his maturity).

Some of these letters, written without lines, would commence at the top left hand corner of the sheet and cross at almost right angles, terminating near the middle. On the back of one of them was written by Johnson thus: "The time will come, the time will come, the time will come, the time will come," only, of course, not so well as the above. He was evidently practicing to write and anticipating the time when he would be more important than he was then.

I took some letters written to a Mr. Wm. Lowry, who I knew in Tennessee, and who after the war became a banker in Atlanta. Some [had been] written, as he advanced in life, to James K. Polk of Tennessee, afterwards President of the United States, and some to his wife from the Congress of the United States, about the year 1860, when the crisis was about to mature which resulted in the revolution [Civil War]. By the way, it was said in Tennessee that Mrs. Lincoln was afflicted with kleptomania, and when she would appropriate goods clandestinely, commonly called stealing, Abe Lincoln requested the storekeeper to send the bills to him, which he always paid without a murmur and thus earned the soubriquet of "Honest Abe." This has no connection with Andy Johnson, but I got the two mixed up in my mind as they both began at the bottom of the ladder and ended as President of the United States.

After the war I met Lowry in Atlanta. Johnson was then President. I knew they were intimate, and I also knew that Johnson would very much prize the letters which I had selected. There were probably forty or fifty, commencing when he was a poor, illiterate tailor and tracing him from time to time as he rose in public estimation and became a power in the land!

I told Lowry that I had some papers of Johnson's which I knew he would prize very much, and I would give them to him for Johnson if he would promise not to let Johnson know where he got them. He so promised me, and I delivered him the package of papers, which I suppose he gave to Johnson, who was then President of the United States, being Vice President when Lincoln was assassinated. And as we had no law which protected a Southerner then, I was a little afraid to let Johnson know that I had been among his papers.

Among the papers was a blank Tennessee State bond. I filled it out for $1,000, filled in all the coupons, and signed Johnson's name to the bond and the [name of the] secretary of state to the coupons, making a pretty good imitation of them both; of course, I had not the seal of state to put on, but that escaped notice.

I went into Fairfax's tent and said: "Oho! you didn't get any whiskey and would have burnt the papers, but I looked them over and found this thousand-dollar Tennessee bond, good for me. . . ."

"No, sir," said Fairfax, "I am chief of staff, and I sent for the box, and the bond is mine." I let Bob Wooley of Kentucky, a very talented fellow, and D. T. Cullen of Barksdale [Virginia], on Longstreet's staff, into the secret, and we had a long powwow over it, and they decided that the bond was mine. Fairfax was not satisfied and proposed to refer the matter to General Longstreet.

We went over to his room. He was sitting by the fire; the case was stated, and while Longstreet had on his thinking cap I said: "Well, I'll settle this matter," and before you could say "presto," the bond was in the fire blasing away. Longstreet and Fairfax were both amazed at my reckless destruction of a valuable bond and only understood it when I explained that it was a blank filled up by me and that I was only playing a joke on Fairfax. Fairfax didn't know whether to laugh or get mad, but concluded that the former was the wiser course and so the matter ended.

In my army intercourse I saw General Lee almost daily while in Virginia, for his headquarters were very near General Longstreet's always. I think he relied very much on General Longstreet, who was a great soldier and a very determined and fearless fighter. He (Longstreet) had a very high opinion of Toombs. I heard him say that if Toombs had been educated at West Point, he would have learned self-control; he would have been as distinguished a soldier as he was a civilian, but his insubordination ruined him as an officer.

Longstreet once ordered Toombs, after a hard day's march, to send a detail of several men to guard a bridge. Toombs replied that his men were tired and worn out and that he could guard the bridge with an old woman and a broomstick. He didn't send the guard, and Longstreet arrested him and kept him under arrest for six weeks. They were always friendly afterwards, and Toombs knew better than to disobey Longstreet after that.

It is an axiom that no man is as great to his valet; in other words, that as you get near to a great man, his stature diminishes, and he proves to be very much like other men. It was not so with Toombs; the more you were with him, the more you became impressed with his extraordinary mental power.

I have often known him to predict a disaster from army movements taking place in Virginia and on the Mississippi campaign. He was seldom wrong, and his predictions were before, not after, the events had happened. His knowledge seemed to be almost universal. I remember hearing him converse with Harvey Hall, of Columbus, who was on a visit to the army and wanted to start a rifle factory in Columbus. Toombs told him that it wouldn't do, and why it wouldn't do, and exhibited as much familiarity with the manufacture of rifles as if he had been apprenticed to a gunmaker. I think he satisfied Mr. Hall that it would not succeed.

I was so surprised at his knowledge of the manufacture of guns that, when we were alone, I asked him of the source of his knowledge, and he replied that on one of his trips to Europe he had gone through a factory and was quite interested in its works. He seemed to think that a very sufficient answer, but, "thinks I to myself thinks I," I might have lived in a factory for six months and not carried off half so much information. I heard Howell Cobb say once (and he was himself one of Georgia's most gifted sons) that "Toombs had altogether the best mind of any statesman in the United States, but that he lacked balance." His impulses were generous and noble, his faults were bluster and a vivid imagination that was not always hampered by facts! He was decidedly given to boasting.

I remember on the Peninsula at Virginia, at the battle of Dam No. 1 [April 16, 1862], I was riding home with Charles Cleghorn (I had just bought a fish, which hung on my saddle), having no idea of a battle. On our way the shells began to sing, and Cleghorn proposed that we should ride up to the line and see the fight. I consented, and we went up. It was getting pretty hot; when we got there, the line opened for Toombs to go nearer to the front.

He was a very poor horseman. A shell whistled near him and Alice Gray, his mare, pranced about a good deal more than Toombs bargained for, but after a little she went on and our men made a most successful fight; it was afterwards favorably commented on. A Texas commissary got his head shot off, and the army said it served him right; what the devil right had he, the commissary, to be in the battle? He should have been with the wagons, looking after his stores. On this hint I didn't speak, but I thought: "If this is the way they talk about commissaries with their heads shot off, I'll so conduct myself hereafter as to avoid similar comments." But let me go back to General Toombs.

The next day we went over to General Cobb's headquarters. Cobb weighed about 200, and when he laughed every particle of his avoirdupois shook like a jelly bag. Toombs commenced talking about the fight at Dam No. 1, his prowess, how his men fought, how he passed to the front, etc., and then, in describing the opening of the line for him to pass through, he gave a glowing account of Alice Gray's antics: "Never saw a mare as frightened in his [my] life. By God, Cobb, she trembled like an aspen leaf and seemed to think that all the shells were aimed at her! Moses, did you ever see a mare as scared in your life, now say?"

I replied that she was very much scared, but it reminded me of a story told on a French barber in New Orleans. I imitated the Frenchman when I told it; that I can't do here, and the story loses much thereby.

A French barber bought a cheval ["horse"], saddle, bridle, and spurs, and started out on the shell road. He was ambling along very contentedly when his horse shied. This caused the Frenchman's spur to stick the horse in the side. He cavorted and threw the Frenchman right across a snake that lay in the road.

The Frenchman came back to New Orleans and was relating the story to some of his friends and wound up by saying: "Be Gar, gentleshmen, if you ever see one snake scared, it was zat snake." The audience concluded that they might reasonably have both been slightly alarmed, and the unsettled question was, which was the most scared, the Frenchman or the snake? I left them to make the application to Toombs, his mare Alice Gray, and the shells which were flying at Dam No. 1. Did Cobb laugh? Didn't he, and all of his staff, and Toombs, too!

I remember one night Longstreet came to headquarters at about 11 o'clock P.M. He had been riding all day through Paris Gap and reconnoitering other passes of the Blue Ridge. I remarked that he must be very tired. He replied: "No, I have never felt fatigue in my life." He was afterwards wounded at the Battle of the Wilderness. I received a letter from him a few days ago. In it he says: "My arm is paralyzed, my voice that could once be heard all along the lines is gone, I can scarcely speak above a whisper, my hearing is very much impaired and I sometimes feel as if I wish the end would come, but I have some misrepresentations of my battles that I wish to correct so as to have my record correct before I die." What a change! I suppose Longstreet is sixty-nine or seventy and I am nearly seventy-nine. In comparison, how much I have to be grateful for, and I certainly am filled with gratitude.

My position at headquarters threw me in contact with all the principal officers of the army: Hood, [Cadmus M.] Wilcox, Pickett, Stewart [Stuart], Walker, etc. I never saw much of [Pierre G. T. de] Beauregard. He was always hedged in by guards, red tape, etc. I remember one time he sent an order to General [W. H. T.] Walker at Fairfax Courthouse to reconnoiter the enemy and make "an ostentatious display." Walker, who was very profane, after a volley of oaths, said: "Ostentatious display! I suppose he wants me to wear a red felt, stand on my head in the saddle and open my legs like an inverted compress. Wouldn't that be an ostentatious display?" Walker was a Georgian, killed near Atlanta, and proverbial for his reckless bravery.

[General George E.] Pickett was a very dashing officer and led the celebrated and fatal charge at Gettysburg; he was very foppish in his dress and wore his hair in long ringlets. He was what may be called a dapper little fellow, but brave as they ever make men.

[General John B.] Hood, as brigadier of the Texas brigade, won a great deal of distinction. He was one of the best brigadiers and poorest commanders in the army.

Jeb Stewart [General James E. B. Stuart] was a splendid cavalry officer, but O! how frivolous! He carried a banjo player with him whereever he went, and his favorite pasttime, when not dancing with the girls, was to have his banjo player thrum and sing, "Come jine the cavalry." He entered Winchester once with his staff and the band playing, "See the Conquering Hero Comes." He was as vain and frivolous as he was brave and dashing, a splendid horseman and a jolly good fellow.

Robert E. Lee Was Kind to Animals

How different he was to [from] General Lee! The latter was [a] plain, splendid-looking, courteous gentleman, with such wonderful self-control that no one ever knew when he was overwhelmed with anxiety; in victory and defeat the same, unruffled exterior, kind to his men, and kind to animals. I remember once at Cromptons Gap in Virginia, a young cavalryman came dashing up to where General Lee was sitting surrounded by several officers. When he reached the spot, he saluted the general, jerked his horse back on his haunches and delivered what he considered an important piece of news, and it was rather important, but this young cavalryman was out of his line of duty, or would never have known it.

After he had delivered himself and expected to be overwhelmed with thanks, General Lee said very quietly: "Young man, don't champ that bit so; you are worrying your horse. What command do you belong to?" The young man answered. General Lee said: "You had better join your command." After the young man retired, General Lee acted on his information, but the young man was improperly away from his command, and Lee's judgment was not to encourage him to be off the line of duty.

Near Richmond, when I was commissary for Toombs's brigade, [U. S. General George B.] McClellan made a demonstration against Richmond. Toombs was at the front. I had charge of the headquarters—you may say that I kept house in Toombs's absence. The situation of our headquarters was deemed by General Lee the best location for him during the sudden changes that he had to make in the quick movements of the entire army. He sent his cot down by a wagon, and some other things, and soon after followed them with his staff.

When he arrived he had on a brown, linen summer suit (sack coat), brown thread gloves; his appearance was one of perfect repose. Soon after he arrived, couriers came dashing in; generals and other officers were riding up, ever and anon, for more minute instructions. It was an important time. We were on the eve of a great battle. Corps, brigades, and divisions had to change positions, and be placed so as to meet the contemplated attack. If Toombs had been in Lee's position, the vocabulary of oaths would have been exhausted. No one about the headquarters would have known whether he was on his head or his heels, or how long it might be before the heels would have to be put in requisition to save his head.

But how different it was with General Lee! He was as calm as a summer cloud, gave his orders with precision and courtesy, and anyone seeing him surrounded by a bevy of officers, and not knowing the cause of their concentration, might just as well have supposed that they were specially invited to partake of hospitality, of which he was the splendid and courteous host, as to believe that they were suddenly called to meet some important change in the grim visage of war.

This lasted the best part of two or three days, I don't remember which. But I do remember that one day, when we were seated at dinner, I at one end of the table and General Lee at the other, with members of his staff on either side, an officer came to the door, saluted the general and said: "I am ordered by General Longstreet to inform you that General McClellan has retired." General Lee bowed to the officer and then said: "Well, major, you see what trouble that young man [McClellan] has given me!" Only this and nothing more. We finished dinner, and after dinner General Lee ordered his traps packed up and returned to his own headquarters. I think it was soon after this that he made his great move in the Valley of Virginia, and fought the second Battle of Manassas [August, 1862], etc.

MISTAKES AT GETTYSBURG

When we entered Chambersburg, Pa., [June, 1863] we had two spies: Harrison and Schrieber. They used to travel as regularly between Washington and our headquarters as a mail. They were so successful and regular in their trips that General Lee began to apprehend that they were in the pay of the Union Army and, unfortunately, he lost confidence in them. General Stewart [Stuart], who was scouting around the Union lines, had not been heard from in about two weeks. One of these spies brought in an account of the exact position of the Union Army, and if General Lee had trusted implicitly in the report, we could have been between Gettysburg and Baltimore, our objective point, before the Union Army reached Gettysburg, but he doubted their fidelity and we moved from Chambersburg to a place near Cashtown.

I think this was on Monday, at or near Cashtown, which was about nine miles from Chambersburg and about eight miles from Gettysburg. We encamped our army and remained there the rest of the day, and until the next [Tuesday], until about three o'clock, waiting for [General Richard S.] Ewell's wagon train which, with his command, was at York [Pennsylvania]. Lee sent for them. Tuesday afternoon we started for Gettysburg, and on the way a courier came up with the information that [General Ambrose] Hill's corps had engaged the enemy. We marched on and reached the neighborhood of Gettysburg that night.

These delays I have never heard alluded to. The report of the information of the spies was current at headquarters. The truth of this I did not know of my own personal knowledge, but I do know that we could have marched easily from Chambersburg to Gettysburg in the day and been there before the Union troops, but for the delay caused by encamping near Cashtown to await the arrival of Ewell's trains. Col. Freemantle, an Englishman, in the Cold Stream Guards, was with us; he shared my tent. I remember him well because, when he arrived at our headquarters, his boots were so wet that he couldn't get them off, and afterwards was afraid that if he got them off, he could never get them on again, and for two weeks that he shared my tent but not my bed (I am happy to say), he remained booted, though not spurred, the entire time.

General Longstreet did not wish to fight the Battle of Gettysburg [July 1-4, 1863]. He wanted to go around the hill, but General Lee objected on account of our long wagon trains and artillery.

I remember in a conversation between Longstreet and Fre[e]mantle, the former said, after expatiating at some length on the advantages of position that the Confederates had at Fredericksburg [Virginia] over the Union forces which were very great, he remarked that the Union Army would have greater advantages at Gettysburg, but he was not hopeless of our success. . . .

At the Battle of Gettysburg I saw Freemantle up a tree watching the fight, and I was not far from General Lee. I had a splendid view of the grand and disastrous battle. The thunder of the artillery was terrifically grand. The charge of Pickett's [division] driven right up a long hill in the face of the Federal cannon was not exceeded in valor by the charge of the Six Hundred [in Tennyson's *Charge of the Light Brigade*]. But we lost the battle, and then came the retreat. The rain poured down in floods that night! I laid down in a fence corner, and nearby on the bare earth, in an India rubber, lay General Lee, biding the pelting storm. The Shenendoah, I think that was the name of the river, was very much swollen the next day, but the army crossed safely into Virginia with little loss of cannon or baggage. . . .

My Sons in the Armed Forces

That my son, Lea [Raphael], was a prisoner I knew, but I could not remember how he became a prisoner and how he got back into the ranks as a private soldier, and as he was expected here on a visit, I left this space blank until I could see him, which I have done. And now [I] learn from him that when in the navy he was stationed on the James River, and went with a squad to the other side to get some green corn out of a field. And after loading and dispatching the boat, he waited its return, not seeing a number of the enemy in a ravine between him and our lines; but they were there, and surrounded him and made him a prisoner. He was sent to the old Capitol Prison at Washington and Fort Delaware, and exchanged about the March before the surrender. He entered as a private soldier, surrendered with Lee at Appomat[t]ox [April 9, 1865], and after the surrender was paroled with the army and walked home.

Albert [another son of mine] had an old friend in the North Carolina troops who had gone to college with him at Chapel Hill, named Nat Gregory. At his instance he [Albert] accepted a lieutenancy in a North Carolina company and was killed at the Battle of Seven Pines near Richmond in 1862. I was near the battlefield, and after the battle tried to learn his fate. I saw several members of his company. They all knew him, of course, and the best information that I could get was that he was slightly wounded in the leg. This information I followed up and visited the different hospitals to find out where he was, without success. As I passed the treasury office in Richmond, Col. Clayton called out to me that a young man by my name had been carried by in an ambulance, and that he was shot in the head. I never for a moment thought of its being Albert, as his [adopted] name was Luria, and as my wife's brother, Perry

Moses, had a son in the same battle, I naturally supposed that it was his son, and I thought that I knew that Albert's wound was a slight one in the leg. But as I was interested in the fate of my nephew, I went to the hospital where Col. Clayton informed me the ambulance had carried young Moses, and inquired for the ward in which the wounded had been carried that day. The ward was pointed out to me and I passed among the wounded. I saw some ladies standing by a cot and heard one of them say: "What a handsome young man!" I crossed over to the cot, and my shock was beyond my power of expression when I saw my son Albert lying unconscious with a wound in his head. I removed him in an ambulance to Perry's house, where he remained unconscious, never recognizing me. He died that night from loss of blood when the surgeon tried to relieve the pressure of the brain, and it was in this manner passed away a bright, promising youth of nineteen.

PETTY GRAFT AND CONFEDERATE BULLION

I think I have said enough about the war to satisfy my children and will return to my services as commissary of the Confederate States, in charge of Georgia. But before I do so, I will explain why I have not referred to General Jackson. I never knew him personally. I have seen him at a distance and only knew of him what history records. He was an untiring and successful general, and a religious fanatic. I doubt whether he ever went into battle without a prayer to God "that we might kill more of them than they did of us." He was beloved by his men and recognized by his generals as a genius, if not the genius, of the war.

When I was appointed commissary of the state of Georgia, I found a perfect robbery being carried on by some of the district commissaries. One of them ran a distillery in Macon. He would seize corn in the name of the government, give credit to the government for a part, and distill the greater part into whiskey for his individual profit. He would seize wheat, flour, and tobacco, and pay the government schedule of prices, ship to Mobile and Montgomery the larger part and realize about ten prices paid for his own benefit. He controlled the railroads, which were obliged to give the government the preference, and used the railroads for his private emolument.

I determined to stop this plunder and stationed men at the railroad depots through which his freight would have to pass as government freight, and on their arrival in transition would have them seized and stored in behalf of the Confederate States, because my receipt was sufficient voucher, but if he was only using the name of the Confederacy for his individual profit, it blocked his game and stopped his profits.

I further ordered that no transportation should be controlled on any of the railroads in Georgia except by my authority, and I adhered to this policy despite of all his protests and appeals in the behalf of all the suffering soldiers at Mobile and other points, simply replying that I would take care of the soldiers. In about six weeks after I took charge, . . . this commissary (he was a Tennessean and his speculations were well-known, but I don't care to name him here) tendered his resignation, as it would not pay him to remain at a salary of about $162.50 a month in that depreciated currency.

He went to New York after the war, loaded down with gold, the fruits of his spoilations [spoliations] upon the people, and I am happy to say that in less than two years Wall Street unloaded him. I had to but wink at his practices and participate in his unholy profits, and if I had done so I could have been among the men who laid the foundation of colossal fortunes while the war lasted. But I sacrificed my business and my comfort to patriotic impulses, and I am prouder in my poverty and happier in my limited means than I could have been had I a world of wealth tainted with dishonor!

I never made a cent out of my position, which was full of temptations, nor profited a dollar by speculation, except in Augusta, where I made about $2,000 in Confederate money, very much depreciated, by purchasing a small amount of gold, which, of course, appreciated as Confederate money depreciated. This speculation I was obliged to make, for the government ordered me to Augusta when board was about $50 per day, and my salary, I think, was $162.50 per month and rations (a major's pay). After I had been in Augusta about a week, my old friend, Dr. Steiner, who I knew in the army as a surgeon on Toombs's staff, invited me to stay at his house, which I readily consented to do, the choice being between paying $50 per day for indifferent board or living for nothing with a congenial and refined family!

Shortly after [Confederate General Joseph E.] Johnston's surrender [April 26, 1865], I was ordered to Washington, Wilkes County [Georgia], soon after [Confederate President Jefferson] Davis and his cabinet arrived there. Mrs. Davis met her husband in Washington. A train containing gold and silver bullion accompanied his cabinet; it was brought from the Richmond banks. I was staying with General Toombs. [J. H.] Reagan [the acting Confederate Secretary of the Treasury] (now of Texas) also stopped with Toombs! We slept together during his short stay in Washington. Breckenbridge [John C. Breckinridge], his Secretary of War, was with Davis. An order was passed paying a cavalry company, with its soldiers and officers, $20 each in specie. I remember General [Braxton] Bragg waiting under a tree to get his $20.

I received an order from General J. E. Johnston to provide 250,000 rations at Augusta for the returning soldiers. I had, a few days previous to Johnston's surrender, about one million rations between Augusta and various points along the Georgia Railroad, but as soon as the news of the surrender of Johnston was received, the warehouses were depleted by the citizens in wagons and every means of conveyance that could be improvised. I sent a copy of the order to the Secretary of War, asking for gold with which to buy rations, based upon an order I had previously drawn and had signed by [General I. M.] St. John (I think that was his name), who succeeded Northrop as commissary general, and who was also staying with Toombs, directing me to draw the gold, carry it to Augusta, and there arrange as best I could with General Mollyneux [E. L. Molineux], who then occupied Augusta with Federal troops, to protect me in furnishing the troops as they passed through Augusta, and to provide for the sick and wounded in the hospital there.

I could not get the gold [from the Secretary of War], and I told General Toombs that unless I got it, I would publish Johnston's order and state that I had made an unsuccessful effort to get an order from the Secretary of War on the Secretary of the Treasury (Reagan, I think) for the means to supply the returning soldiers, and in that way relieve myself from responsibility. He interceded with the Secretary of War, and I received the last order of the Confederacy for $40,000 [$10,000?] in gold. . . .

Ten thousand dollars was paid under the order to R. R. Wood, major and Q. M. [Quartermaster] for General A. R. Lawton, Q. M. General. I got this [the balance, $30,000] at night on the road out of Washington in front of where General [Lafayette] McLaws' family were then staying. It was all bullion in boxes. I returned with it to Washington that night, and then the question was: "What shall I do with it?" The town was full of stragglers, cavalrymen who had just been paid $20 each. They had arms but no consciences, and the little taste they had of specie provoked their appetites and, like Oliver Twist, they wanted more.

Toombs gave me the names of ten of the Washington Artillery, all gentlemen well known to him. I agreed to pay them $10 each in gold to guard it that night and go with me to Augusta. I then took a squad of them and destroyed all the liquor I could find in the shops. I then got part of a keg of powder and put it in a wooden building that was unoccupied and put the boxes of bullion in the same room, placed my guard outside and around the building, and gave out that I had laid a train from the powder to the outside and, if the guard was forced, the train should be fired.

I remained up and about all night, and the next morning had the boxes put on a freight car bound for Barnett [Georgia], a station twenty miles off, where this Washington City Railroad connected with the Georgia Railroad running from Atlanta to Augusta. The train was made up of a number of open cars filled with about two hundred returning soldiers, and about twenty-nine cavalry soldiers, who said they were going to Barnett to get salt. Of course, I realized the danger. My specie, guard, and myself occupied a boxcar with the door shut.

When we got within a mile or two of Barnett, the conductor, a nice, old fellow, came to our door and said: "Major, from the talk, I reckon the boys are going to 'charge' your car when we get to Barnett." "Charge" meant to attack it and divide out the specie among themselves. I asked him if he could not switch us off on some sidetrack and run by Barnett. He said no, that might cause a collision on the Georgia R. R.

When we got near Barnett, there was an embankment for the R. R., about five feet high, and I thought it would be better for our car to stop there than to go up to the platform, which was on a level with the car and could, therefore, be more easily forced, and I held a counsel of war with my guard. I told them if they would stand by me, keep cool, fire and reload through an opening we would make in the doors, I thought we could successfully defend the car, but if they were not ready to do this, we would be overcome! They consulted together, and I was afraid they would conclude to "jine the cavalry," but they finally said: "We'll stand by you as long as there is a chance to save the specie."

I then got out of the car through as small an opening as I could squeeze through, went among the men, who were as thick as black-birds, talked quietly to them, read my orders, told them I had no interest in the world in protecting the bullion except to fulfill my orders, that every dollar of it would be devoted to feeding their fellow-soldiers and caring for the wounded in the hospital at Augusta, that I should do my best to carry out these orders, that they might kill me and my guard, but they would be killing men in discharge of a duty in behalf of their comrades! That if they killed us it would be murder, while if we killed any of them in defending the bullion, which we certainly should do, we should be justified, because the killing would be in self-defense and in the discharge of a sacred duty.

Then Shephard, a brother of E. T. Shephard of Columbus (I think his name was Andrew), spoke out and said: "Men, I have got to go as far as any of you, my home is in Texas. I know Major Moses, and I am sure he would not touch a dollar of the money, except to carry out his orders."

Then Col. Sanford of Montgomery spoke up on pretty much the same line that Shephard had spoken, and the crowd began to disperse, and those that were appeased by the appeals of Shephard and Sanford moved up towards the platform, but a number remained around the car.

I went back into the car and said to the conductor: "You had better take us up to the platform. All who are satisfied are there, and here I am in the midst of unfriendly organizers." We moved up to the platform, and if we could have gone immediately on to Augusta, we would have had no further trouble. But, unfortunately, we had to wait as the Atlanta train was an hour late, and we had to wait at Barnett more than an hour, and as the billows of one sea rise and fall when disturbed by the winds, this restless crowd at the depot would surge and press up against the doors of my box[car], trying to get in, and I would have to threaten and appeal. At last the storm seemed to be subsiding, when a commissary who I knew in Bristol, Tennessee, said to me: "Major, you think the trouble is over, but it ain't by a d——d sight. They have just had a talk about charging the car, and some officers are in it. You see that young man walking up and down the platform, him with the court plaster on his cheek? Well, he is leading the men on." He was a Tennessean.

I thought a minute and then concluded that my only chance of safety was to take the bull by the horns. I walked up to the young man and said: "You appear to be a gentleman and bear an honorable wound." I then read my orders to him, explained my position and how trying it was to be forced to take life and lose my own in the performance of a duty that I could not voluntarily avoid. I told him that I had a guard and some friends in the crowd, but we would be outnumbered unless I could enlist a man like himself in my behalf. He seemed embarrassed, but said: "I don't think you will have any further trouble," and I did not. We went to Augusta; the most of the soldiers went the other way, but the young Tennessean went to Augusta.

When we reached Augusta, the banks were afraid to take charge of the bullion. I applied unsuccessfully at Metcalf's bank. I then went to General Mollyneux [Molineux], explained to him my position, got a guard from him, and had the bullion carried to the commissaries' office in Augusta.

The next day I met the Tennessean and told him I was glad he was in Augusta as it would enable me to show him that I had no interest in the specie except for the benefit of the soldiers as required in my order. He went with me to Gov. Cummings (formerly gov. of Utah). We met General Mollyneux at his office. He agreed to receive the silver and gold, ration the troops as they passed through; appropriate $2,000 to the hospitals, and at his request I wrote the correspondence on both sides. He signed one in duplicate, and I the other, and he faithfully fulfilled his contract. I never knew whether the U. S. government got the bullion or not. I delivered it to a Mass. provost marshall by Mollyneux['s] order. I tried afterwards to trace it into the Treasury and left all the papers with Jerry Black of Penn. [sylvania]. He was, I think, Johnson's [Buchanan's] attorney general. [Black was also one of Johnson's lawyers at the impeachment trial.] James Waddel [the Confederate naval officer] was with me when I delivered the papers, but I have never heard anything more about the bullion. . . .

Joseph Jonas

The Jews Come to Ohio

The first known Jew in Ohio was quite a curiosity. When the twenty-five-year-old settler arrived, an old Quakeress came to see him. She asked: "Art thou a Jew? Thou art one of God's chosen people. Wilt thou let me examine thee?" She turned him around and finally said, probably with a tinge of disappointment in her voice: "Well, thou art no different to other people."

That Jew was Joseph Jonas, a native of Exeter, England, who had come to Cincinnati in 1817. Though warned by coreligionists in Philadelphia to avoid the frontier, he came west because of the glowing accounts he had read of the Ohio Valley.

Jonas was completely devoted to his Jewish faith. Even though he was the only known Jew in the city—in all Ohio, for that matter— he was determined to remain a Jew, and, if possible, to create, some day, a center of religious life in his town. After a few years he succeeded: he held services, organized a congregation, and built a synagogue. Most of the worshipers came from England; a number were kinsmen; one of them was his brother Abraham Jonas, the friend of Abraham Lincoln.

Though Jonas was a "mechanic," a watchmaker, and silversmith, he had political and literary ambitions. In 1860-61 he served in the Ohio State Legislature, as a Democrat. His literary aspirations voiced themselves in addresses to the congregation, in studies on Biblical themes, and in contributions to the Jewish press. He was an observant Orthodox Jew of the Isaac Leeser school, mildly progressive, interested in furthering systematic religious instruction for Jewish youth.

In December, 1843, writing in the third person, he sat down and recalled his early days in Cincinnati. His communication was published in the form of a letter in Leeser's Occident, *I (1843-44), 547-50; II (1844-45), 29-31, 143-47, 244-47.*

He died in Spring Hill, near Mobile, Alabama, on May 5, 1869, at the home of a daughter.

The career of Jonas is of historic significance because he built the first Jewish community west of the Alleghenies, a community that became increasingly important with the industrial development of Cincinnati and with the coming of Rabbi Isaac Mayer Wise, the organizer of American Reform Jewish institutions.

THE FIRST CINCINNATI JEW

It was in the month of October, 1816, that a young man arrived in New York from the shores of Great Britain, to seek a home and a residence in the New World. This individual's name was Joseph Jonas, from Plymouth, in England. He had read considerably concerning America, and was strongly impressed with the descriptions given of the Ohio River, and had therefore determined to settle himself on its banks, at Cincinnati. This he was encouraged in by a relative he met with in New York.

On arriving at Philadelphia, he was persuaded to settle in that city, and took up his residence for a short time with the amiable family of the late Mr. Samuel Joseph (peace be unto him). He here became acquainted with the venerable Mr. Levi Philips, who took a great interest in him, using many persuasive arguments not to proceed to Ohio. One of them was frequently brought to his recollection: "In the wilds of America, and entirely amongst Gentiles, you will forget your religion and your God."

But the fiat had gone forth, that a new resting place for the scattered sons of Israel should be commenced, and that a sanctuary should be erected in the Great West, dedicated to the Lord of Hosts, to resound with praises to the ever-living God. The individual solemnly promised the venerable gentleman never to forget his religion nor forsake his God. He received his blessing and, taking leave of the kind friends with whom he had resided, departed for Pittsburg on the second of January, 1817.

On his arrival, he found the navigation of the Ohio stopped by being frozen over. He procured profitable employment during the winter, being a mechanic, and, at the breaking up of the ice, was wafted on the bosom of this noble river to the then rising city of Cincinnati, where he arrived on the eighth day of March, 1817. The city then contained about 6,000 inhabitants, but the only Israelite was himself. With the assistance of the God of his ancestors, he soon became established in a lucrative and respectable business, and his constant prayer was that he might be a nucleus around whom this first congregation might be formed, to worship the God of Israel in

205

the great western territory. Solitary and alone he remained for more than two years, and at the solemn festivals of our holy religion, in solitude was he obliged to commune with his Maker.

Some time in December, 1818, his heart was delighted with the arrival of his lamented and ever-valued friend, David Israel Johnson (from Portsmouth, England), with his wife and infant child. But they were bound for Brookville, Indiana, and again for a while solitude was his portion. In the month of June following, three members of our nation arrived, viz., Lewin Cohen, of London, Barnet Levi, of Liverpool, and Jonas Levy of Exeter, England. And the following *yamim tobim* ["holydays"] were duly solemnized in Cincinnati, and probably in the western country, for the first time, my friend, D. I. Johnson, being summoned from Brookville, and joined us on the occasion.

A few days afterwards the solitary sojourner was joyfully recompensed by the arrival of his brother, Abraham Jonas, his sister and her husband, Morris and Sarah Moses; there also came with them Philip Symonds, his wife and child, all from Portsmouth, England. We began from this time to form a community of Israelites. In 1820 arrived Solomon Buckingham, Moses Nathan, and Solomon Mi[e]nken, all from Germany, and the *yamim tobim* of 1820 were solemnized in due form with the legal number and a Sepher Torah [Scroll of the Law]. In 1821 arrived Solomon Moses, from Portsmouth, England. In 1822 arrived Phineas Moses and Samuel Jonas, another brother of the solitary; and now were our hearts rejoiced, for the prospects of a permanent congregation were near at hand. During the ensuing year, 1823, arrived Simeon Moses, from Barbadoes, and Morris and Joseph Symonds, from Portsmouth, England.

We are now arrived on "terra firma," and have official records for reference. On the fourth of January, 1824, a majority of the Israelites in Cincinnati assembled at the residence of Morris Moses, who was called to the chair, and Joseph Jonas appointed secretary, when the following proceedings took place, and the subjoined preamble was adopted:

WHEREAS, It is the duty of every member of the Jewish persuasion, when separated from a congregation, to conform as near as possible to the worship and ceremonies of our holy religion, and as soon as a sufficient number can be assembled, to form ourselves into a congregation for the purpose of glorifying our God, and observing the fundamental principles of our faith, as developed in the laws of Moses:—with these impressions, the undernamed persons convened at the residence of Morris Moses, in the city of Cincinnati, state of Ohio, on the fourth day of January, 1824, corresponding to the fourth of Shebat, 5584.

Present, Morris Moses, Joseph Jonas, David I. Johnson, Jonas Levy, Solomon Moses, Simeon Moses, Phineas Moses, Samuel Jonas, Solomon Buckingham, and Morris Symonds.

Sundry preparatory resolutions were adopted, a committee on constitution and bylaws appointed, and the chairman authorized to summon every member of the Jewish persuasion. We then find the following proceedings officially recorded:

In accordance with a resolution of a convention which met at the residence of Morris Moses, in the city of Cincinnati, state of Ohio, on the fourth of January, 1824, corresponding with the fourth of Shebat, 5584, a full convention of every male of the Jewish persuasion or nation was convened at the house of the aforesaid Morris Moses, in the said city and state, on the eighteenth of January, 1824, corresponding with the eighteenth day of Shebat, 5584.

Present, Joseph Jonas, Morris Moses, David I. Johnson, Philip Symonds, Abraham Jonas, Jonas Levy, Solomon Buckingham, Solomon Mi[e]nken, Solomon Moses, Phineas Moses, Samuel Jonas, Simeon Moses, Morris Symonds, Joseph Symonds. Morris Moses being in the chair, and Joseph Jonas secretary, a constitution and bylaws were adopted, and the following officers duly elected: Joseph Jonas, parnass; Phineas Moses and Jonas Levy, vestrymen. Resolutions were then passed to procure a room, and to fit it up as a temporary place of worship.

JEWISH WORSHIP IN CINCINNATI

Before proceeding further, permit me to make a few remarks. From the period of the arrival of the first Israelite in Cincinnati, to this date, the Israelites have been much esteemed and highly respected by their fellow citizens, and a general interchange of civilities and friendships has taken place between them. Many persons of the Nazarene faith residing from 50 to 100 miles from the city, hearing there were Jews living in Cincinnati, came into town for the special purpose of viewing and conversing with some of "the children of Israel, the holy people of God," as they termed us.

From the experience which we have derived by being the first settlers of our nation and religion in a new country, we arrive at the conclusion that the Almighty will give his people favour in the eyes of all nations, if they only conduct themselves as good citizens in a moral and religious point of view, for it is already conceded to us by our neighbours that we have the fewest drunkards, vagrants, or individuals amenable to the laws, of any community, according to our numbers in this city or district of [or] country. And we also appreciate the respect and esteem those individuals are held in, who duly conform to the principles of our religion, especially by a strict conformity to our holy Sabbath and festivals.

The original founders of our congregation were principally from Great Britain, and consequently their mode of worship [like many British Jews] was after the manner of the Polish and German Jews. But being all young people they were not so prejudiced in favour of old customs as more elderly people might have been, and especially as several of their wives had been brought up in Portuguese congregations. We therefore introduced considerable chorus singing into our worship, in which we were joined by the sweet voices of the fair daughters of Zion, and our Friday evening service was as well attended for many years as the Sabbath morning.

At length, however, large emigrations of our German brethren settled amongst us. Again our old customs have conquered, and the sweet voices of our ladies are seldom heard. But we have so far prevailed as to continue to this day the following beautiful melodies, the Twenty-ninth Psalm, *mizmor le-david* ["a psalm of David"], which is chaunted as the procession slowly proceeds to deposit the Sepher Torah (Book of the Law) in the ark; also the *en ke-lohenu* [song: "There is none like our God"], and after the service is concluded none attempt to quit their seats until the beautiful hymn *adon olam* ("Universal Lord! who the sceptre swayed") is finished, being sung by all the congregation in full chorus.

For several years we had no hazan (reader), and the service was read and chaunted in rotation by Messrs. David I. Johnson, Morris Moses, and Joseph Jonas. We had purchased a burial ground about three years previous to our organization, and at that time Jonas Levy was our *shohet* [ritual slaughterer of cattle]. Messrs. Morris Moses and David I. Johnson were elected parnass and gabah ["treasurer"] for the year 5586 [1826], about which time Nicholas Longworth, Esq., gave the congregation a piece of land adjoining our burial ground. During this year, a committee of correspondence was appointed to correspond with several congregations for the purpose

PITTSBURGH IN 1849

(see page 308)

LOUIS STIX
(see page 311)

of procuring aid from our brethren to build a synagogue. Applications at this time were responded to from Charleston, S. C., and a remittance forwarded to us of $100, also $50, from Benjamin Elkin, Esq., of Barbadoes, W. I. The names of all the donors were duly recorded. Twenty dollars were also received from Joseph Andrews, Esq., of Philadelphia. Some time in the year 5588 [1828], the corresponding building committee reported £16.2 equal to $71.55 cents, received from the congregation of Portsmouth in England; the name of each donor was also recorded.

About this time we lost a worthy member of our congregation, Samuel Joseph, Esq., late of Philadelphia, but originally from Plymouth, England. He lived respected and esteemed, and died regretted by everyone (peace be unto him). Also during the years 1826 and 1827, the God of our fathers thought proper to take to himself two amiable young women, sisters, and daughters of the late Rev. Gershom M. Seixas, of New York; lovely in their lives, both mental and personal, it may easily be supposed how deeply they were lamented by their bereaved husbands, Abraham and Joseph Jonas.

THE FIRST CINCINNATI SYNAGOGUE

During the year 5589 [1829], Messrs. Morris Moses and David I. Johnson were appointed a special committee to procure subscriptions, towards building a synagogue, from our brethren at New Orleans, and they reported $280 collected. Each individual's name was entered on record. About the same time Augustus Emden, Esq., gave us a donation of $10.

During the month of July this year, the congregation purchased a suitable lot of ground on the east side of Broadway below Sixth Street, on which our present synagogue is erected; thus far had the Lord prospered our way. . . .

Nothing of interest took place, except a gradual increase of the congregation, until 1834, when Messrs. Joseph Jonas, Elias Mayer, and Phineas Moses were appointed a committee for building a synagogue, with full powers to raise funds, collect materials, make contracts, etc.; and it is with considerable gratification we have to record the liberal donations given through the influence of the committee. Fifty-two gentlemen of the Christian faith, our fellow citizens, gave us towards the building $25 *each*.

With very inefficient [insufficient] funds we commenced the good work; but during its progress, with the blessing of God, we were enabled to procure additional subscriptions. With these, and loans from the city banks, we were enabled to bring the holy work to its completion. On the fourteenth day of Sivan, 5595, corresponding to the eleventh of June, 1835, the foundation stone was laid, with suitable enclosures and inscriptions; and with all due form and ceremony, attended with prayers to the supreme Eternal, it was solemnly deposited, in the presence of the building committee and many of the members, by the Rev. Joseph Samuels, our venerable pastor (now no more).

During this year we received the following donations from our brethren abroad: $100 from the late Harman Hendricks, Esq., of New York; $470 from a number of our brethren in Philadelphia and Baltimore, whose names we have duly recorded. . . . Five large brass chandeliers were received from the Holy Congregation Shearith Israel, New York, with the condition attached, "that in case the congregation in Cincinnati at any future period should decline to use them, then to return them to the trustees of this congregation." They were originally used in the old synagogue at New York, and were received by us with much pleasure. The original donor could have little dreamed at the time that his munificent gift would adorn and enlighten a temple erected to the service of the ever-living God in the far west. . . .

During the months of May, June, and July [1836], we sold seats in our new synagogue to the amount of $4,500, which enabled us to finish the interior of the building in a much superior style than we originally intended. The edifice is erected with a handsome Doric front, a flight of stone steps over the basement, with a portico supported by pillars. The building is eighty feet in length by thirty-three in breadth, including a vestibule of twelve feet. It has a very handsome dome in the centre, ornamented with panels and carved mouldings in stucco.

On entering the building from the vestibule, the beholder is attracted by the chaste and beautiful appearance of the Ark, situated at the east end. It is eighteen feet in front, surrounded by a neat low white balustrade, ornamented by four large brass candlesticks; it is ascended by a flight of steps handsomely carpeted. The entablature and frieze are composed of stucco work, supported by four large fluted pillars of the Corinthian order. The doors are in the flat, sliding into the sides; when opened, the interior appears richly decorated with crimson damask; the curtain is handsomely festooned in front of the doors. Between the pillars on each side are two marble painted slabs containing the Decalogue in gold letters. The entablature and frieze contain suitable inscriptions. The whole is surmounted by a large vase in imitation of the pot of incense.

Near the west end is the *taybah* ["reading platform"]; it is a square surrounded on three sides by steps imitating marble, with seats enclosed for the parnassim in front. It is handsomely painted, as well as all the seats, in imitation of maple; the balustrade of the *taybah* is surmounted on the four corners by four large brass candlesticks. On the platform is the reader's desk, neatly covered, and supported by two small columns. The gallery, with a neat white front, is over the vestibule, supported by pillars, with six rows of seats. The seats in the area are placed four in a row, fronting the Ark, on each side of the *taybah*. The ceiling is handsomely finished, with five circles of stucco work, from which are suspended five large brass chandeliers.

The edifice, when finished, was much admired, and the building committee received a vote of thanks from the congregation for their unremitted attentions in procuring the necessary funds and materials, and for the time and trouble bestowed by them in superintending the erection of the building. The ninth of September, 1836, corresponding to the twenty-seventh of Elul, 5596, was appointed for the consecration.

The day having arrived, the crowd of our Christian friends was so great that we could not admit them all. We therefore selected the clergy and the families of those gentlemen who so liberally had given donations towards the building. The members of the congregation assembled in the basement rooms, a procession was formed, with the sepharim ["scrolls"] in front (under a handsome canopy), carried by Messrs. Joseph Jonas, parnass; Elias Mayer, G. Z. [Gabah Zedakah, "charity treasurer"], and Phineas Moses, treasurer (these gentlemen being also the building committee). Mr. David I. Johnson officiated on the occasion and chaunted the consecration service. He also led the choir of singers, supported by a band of music. The choir consisted of about twenty of the ladies and gentlemen of the congregation.

Who did not enjoy supreme delight and heavenly pleasure, when the sweet voices of the daughters of Zion ascended on high in joyful praises to the great Architect of the universe on the glorious occasion of dedicating a temple to his worship and adoration? And what must have been the exciting feelings of the *founder* [Joseph Jonas] of this congregation, at the consecration of this first temple west of the Alleghany mountains, when, on knocking thrice outside the inner door, he was addressed by the reader within: "It is the voice of my beloved that knocketh," and when he responded: "Open to me the gates of righteousness, I will go into them, and I will praise the Lord!" (The consecration hymns and service were composed and selected by the Rev. Henry Harris.)

The ceremonies and service being concluded, an appropriate address was delivered by the parnass, Mr. Joseph Jonas. The Sabbath evening service was then solemnly chaunted by Mr. David I. Johnson, in which he was again harmoniously supported by the vocal abilities of the ladies and gentlemen of the choir. The Sabbath of the Lord having commenced, the labours of man ceased, and the instrumental music was heard no more. The whole was concluded by one of the ladies leading in the splendid solo and chorus of *Yigdal* [a Hebrew hymn], after which the numerous assemblage dispersed highly gratified.

THE CINCINNATI JEWISH COMMUNITY

Having passed this great epoch in our history, and established our congregation on a firm basis, and having returned thanks to the Giver of all good for the protection afforded us, and for the prosperity, with His assistance, to which we have arrived at this period, let us now rest awhile, and view the Jewish horizon around us. Alas, it is a bleak and dreary view. In the whole Mississippi Valley, from the Alleghany Mountains to the city of New Orleans included, excepting Cincinnati, not a single community of Israelites is to be descried. Numerous families and individuals were located in all directions; but not another attempt at union, and the worship of our God appeared to be dead in their hearts.

This with many might be considered a stopping place to conclude our history; but not so, we are but in our infancy, only numbering at this time 62 members, and about 400 individuals of all ages. During the following year, 5597 [1837], Mr. Morris Moses being parnass, we bought the adjoining lot of ground and added it to our cemetery, with a *metaher* house [a chapel in which the dead are prepared for burial]. A Hebrew school was established in the basement room of the synagogue; Mr. David Goldsmith was appointed the first rabbi or teacher. I perceive on the records, Sept. 6, 1838, among the officers elected for the year 5599, Mr. David Mayer, parnass; Rev. Hertz Judah, hazan [cantor] and rabbi; and Mr. David Goldsmith, shohet and shamas [beadle].

Having received from the congregation at Charleston, S. C., the intelligence of the destruction of their synagogue, we could not resist the appeal, and immediately $119.50 were subscribed by the members, and remitted with our sympathies to our Charleston brethren. It must be recollected that at this period we were still indebted for the erection of our own building.

During 1838, The Hebrew Beneficent Society of Cincinnati was incorporated. They have a burial ground attached to their institution. Their contributions are $3 per annum. At present they consist of near 140 members. If any of them are prevented from attending to their several avocations, through sickness or accidents, they are entitled to demand $4 per week. At their annual meeting in Tishri [September-October], the following gentlemen were elected officers for the current year: Morris Moses and Philip Symonds, gabahim [presiding officers]; Simon Crouse, treasurer; Henry Hart, secretary.

About the same period two other societies were instituted by the Jewish ladies, viz.: The Hebrew Ladies' Benevolent Society and The German Hebrew Ladies' Benevolent Society. They are both in a prosperous condition, and were instituted for the purpose of assisting distressed widows and orphans. Their contributions are $3 per annum.

The congregation K. K. B. I. [*Kehillah Kedoshah B'nai Israel,* "Holy Congregation of the Sons of Israel"] rapidly increasing, it was found necessary, in 1841, to erect additional seats, and to enlarge the ladies' gallery. Mr. Moritz E. Moehring being parnas. When completed, a number of the seats were sold for a sum much more considerable than the expense of the alterations. Also several additional sepharim [scrolls] were procured and deposited in the Ark, with the usual prayers and ceremonies. During this year the Congregation Benai Jeshurun was founded, and at the ensuing session of the legislature was incorporated. They are in a very flourishing condition, occupying a large room fitted up as a synagogue, and consist of about eighty members.

Some time near this period the first settlement of Jews and the formation of a congregation commenced at Cleveland, Cuyahoga County, Ohio, situated on the shores of Lake Erie. This is likely to be a very thriving settlement, and is in a very wealthy portion of the state. The congregation was formed by considerable emigrations of our German brethren. Being at a great distance from them, and having very little correspondence, we are not able to give their numbers. Travellers inform us they are very numerous.

With the additional seats to our synagogue we are now enabled to accommodate 250 gentlemen and 100 ladies. Mr. Elias Mayer was elected parnass for the year 5602 [1842]; the Hebrew school was reorganized, and Mr. David Barnard appointed teacher.

In the month of January, this year [1842], we have to record the death of Mr. David I. Johnson, lamented by every one that knew him; truly may we say, "a good man has fallen in Israel." Peace be unto him. He was the second individual of our nation that arrived in Cincinnati; morally and religiously he laboured in the formation of our congregation.

On the twenty-fourth of April, 1842, a number of ladies of the congregation met at the vestry room, and commenced the establishment of a Sunday school, nominating Mrs. Louisa Symonds their first superintendent. Some time after, finding it interfered with other duties, she resigned her office, when, by a unanimous vote of the teachers, Mr. Joseph Jonas was requested to superintend the school, which since then has been under his direction. There were forty-six children in attendance, and still every appearance of increasing; the field is large, and the harvest has every appearance of being abundant. Considerable proficiency has been made by the children; but a blight appears to be moving over our prospects, from a source little to be expected—the *rabbonim!* [rabbis], who ought to be the promoters, not the disturbers of a plan to forward the principles of our Holy Religion in the minds of youth. But perceiving that good might be done without their interference, the *craft* was in danger! and the school must be put down. It was consequently anathematized by them for being held on *Sundays* [the Christian Sabbath]! In consequence, the school is not increasing, and through their influence most of the German, and some English children, are prevented attending. The leader amongst these bigoted mischief-makers is Rabbi ———— ————, a *talmid,* or scholar, of the Rev. Mr. R[ice] of B[altimore].

I am well-convinced that righteousness and true religion must prevail, and that the evil spirit of bigotry will be overwhelmed. We have endeavoured to reason and compromise with them, but to no purpose. Still, whilst there are ten children in attendance, their teachers will not weary in superintending, knowing the benefits already done. We feel warm in the cause of the rising generation, and hope that this publication, sanctioned by some remarks in your useful periodical, may have some influence on their future conduct.

In the month of Heshvan, 5603 [October, 1842], the Hebrew Benevolent Society of Cincinnati was instituted. Its first president was Mr. Phineas Moses, under whom it flourished exceedingly. It now consists of seventy members, with every prospect of being much more numerous. Their anniversary dinner was well attended, and the voluntary contributions remarkably liberal. Mr. Joseph Jonas was elected parnass for 5604 [1844].

The congregations in this city are continually increasing, their character stands high for morality, honesty, and sobriety. Sorry am I to say that I cannot state the same of many of them in a religious point of view. If only a *few* of the most able and respectable would commence *sincerely* keeping their Sabbaths and festivals, it would have considerable influence on the minds of their erring brethren. But the "Solitary" [I, Joseph Jonas] is still thankful to the God of Israel that he has been made the humble instrument in collecting near 2,000 of his brethren of Israel, to worship the Lord of Hosts in this beautiful metropolis of the Great West.

Alfred Mordecai

Brilliant West Point Cadet

Alfred Mordecai, born at Warrenton, N. C., in 1804, was appointed a West Point cadet at the age of fifteen.

Well-educated at home by his family, he distinguished himself in his studies at the military academy, where he graduated at the top of his class in 1823. The army detailed him to remain at the Point and teach. It was not until 1825 that he left the school and began his brilliant career as an army engineer and ordnance expert. Without question he was one of the great authorities on ordnance in the United States Army in ante-bellum days. He was in charge of various great arsenals, wrote learned reports on the subject of guns and gunpowder, and served as a member of the military commission that was sent to the Crimea in 1855. He was then a major.

Had he remained in the service in 1861, he would undoubtedly have become a general—his son Alfred, Jr., became a lieutenant colonel during the War, at the age of twenty-five. But Major Alfred Mordecai, on the threshold of a great career, resigned his commission rather than make munitions to destroy his own kin and the South which had given him birth. Nor would he fight against the North.

His resignation entailed great personal sacrifices, for as a man of fifty-seven he had to seek a new career. At first he taught mathematics in Philadelphia; two years later he took a position as a railroad engineer in Mexico. After the War he returned to the States and became an executive of the Pennsylvania Canal Company.

In 1879, then a man of seventy-five, the major sat down and wrote a memoir—personal memoranda, he called it—for his children. Later he continued the story, although briefly, to June, 1886. A year later he died.

The following extracts, taken from the Mordecai Papers in the Library of Congress, deal with his early life in Warrenton, his cadet days at the academy, and his special assignment as assistant professor at the Point. (Copies of the manuscript memoirs are on deposit at the American Jewish Archives; a printed transcription was pub-

lished in The North Carolina Historical Review, *XXII* [1945], *64 ff.)*

Major Mordecai's father, Jacob (1762-1838), was a very observant Jew, something of a Hebraist, and a writer of apologetic theological material touching on Judaism in its relation to Christianity. Jacob's son, Alfred, seems to have had little, if any, interest in the faith of his fathers. Without doubt, his marriage to Sarah Hays, which brought him into the circle of the more observant Hayses and Gratzes, kept him well within the Jewish fold. Rebecca Gratz mentioned him often in her letters.

His memoirs and, even better, his life and career afford many insights into the process of assimilation to the common American cultural pattern, a process to which men in public life were constantly exposed.

AT THE time of my birth, my father was a country "merchant" (as the term was) in my native village, Warrenton, No. Carolina. His "store," which I remember well after it had passed from his hands, was in the centre of the village, and my father's dwelling was on a lot adjoining the store. My earliest recollections are of playing as a child in the shady yard of the dwelling, and of mounting by an outside stair to a room, once the store, where I began to learn to read when I was about four years old.

In 1808 my father, who had discontinued his mercantile business, determined to open, with the assistance of some of his older children who had all been well educated, an academy for young ladies. With the view of enlarging the school, he purchased a large lot of ground at the northern end of the village and erected on it a house capable of containing a large boarding school, which was soon filled. I remember the general arrangement of the building, but my recollections of it are concentrated in the memory of the terrible calamity which occurred before the workmen had quite completed their labors.

In the night of April 27th, 1811, the house took fire, in consequence of the unpardonable heedlessness of one of the scholars reading in bed by the light of a candle without a candlestick, and, there being no sufficient supply of water, the building was burnt to the ground. I slept, with one of my brothers, on a pallet bed laid down in the schoolroom. We were roused by a servant and were wrapped up and taken over to the boys' academy, which was quite near. The female scholars were distributed among the neighbors, and you may imagine the anxiety with which the roll was called the next morning at the several houses, and the happy fact ascertained that no one had perished in the flames.

With wonderful confidence and perseverance, my father immediately procured another lot, at the opposite end of the village, with a large house on it, and The Warrenton Female Academy, having more than a hundred scholars, soon became well known in No. Carolina, Virginia, So. Carolina, and Georgia; in all of which states, and in others of the West and South West, there still remain elderly women who retain grateful recollection of the benefit derived from the moral and intellectual instruction imparted to them at this academy.

My oldest brother, Moses, was at this time established as a successful lawyer in Raleigh, and my second brother, Samuel, as a merchant in Richmond. The principal instructors in this large school were my [half] brother Solomon and oldest [half] sister Rachel, and to them nearly all the children of *my* mother are indebted for their scholastic education. My mother's health was not very strong, and the two younger daughters by my father's first wife relieved my mother in a great measure from the care of the large household of pupils, and assisted her in supplying the physical wants of us younger children.

I may say here that the great success attending the establishment of this school, although due in part to the manifest want, in that region, of such an institution, is very remarkable when it is considered that my father was, by birth, education, and conviction, an observer of the Jewish faith, and that his family was the only one of that religion to be found within a large circuit of his home; whilst, with slight exceptions, his pupils were members of Christian families. I believe that no serious embarrassment ever ensued, in social or other relations, from this difference of religion, in our retired village.

From the time of the fire and the removal consequent on it, my recollection of all occurrences around me is very vivid, but few of them are worth recording here. I remember distinctly the great comet of 1811, which extended from the zenith nearly to the horizon, and was regarded as the precursor of the war [of 1812] with Great Britain, declared next year. In the same year, in a violent thunderstorm, one of the chimneys of our house was either struck by lightning or blown down, and that was the last time I can remember being afraid of lightning and thunder.

The association with my young companions, many of the female scholars, and a few boys who were allowed to attend as day scholars; the Greek and Latin lessons I used to say to my brother whilst he was shaving, before breakfast, to economize his time; the tree under which I first read *The Lady of the Lake* (the very copy, I believe, which I have now) and learned a great part of it by heart— these and a thousand other little things of the same kind crowd on my memory when I look back to the pleasant days of my childhood, almost unclouded by a sad recollection. I cannot remember the time when I was not devoted to books and to study.

Often in those young days have I risen before daylight to pursue my lessons by the light of the fire with which old Jenny was baking her bread at the great oven in the yard, or by that of the fire which I myself kindled in the chimney with wood which I had collected in play time, the evening before. I remember, particularly, preparing myself in this way for my examination in Blair's *Rhetoric*, and to this day I can repeat from memory many of the quotations conned at that time as illustrations of the author's critical remarks. Although I was a healthy and sufficiently active boy, it was often with great reluctance that I laid down *Miss Edg[e]worth's Tales*, or *The Arabian Nights*, etc., to join my young companions in playing at marbles, hop-scotch, and mumble-the-peg, or to shoot robins and other small birds with arrows fired from the mulberry bows which Old Cy (Cyrus) used to make for us in the intervals of his occupation of running a country mill.

One of the great rewards of application and good conduct was given by my good sister Rachel, in coming to the side of our trundle bed on Saturday evenings and entertaining us with pleasant stories until sleep "steeped our senses in forgetfulness." In later days it was a great privilege to be allowed to sit in a low chair, or lie on the hearth rug in winter evenings, whilst my father or some other member of the family circle read aloud the charming *Waverly Novels*, as they came out.

Among the earliest public events that impressed themselves on my memory were the occurrences of the War of 1812: Perry's victory on Lake Erie and the invasion of Maryland and the District of Columbia, with threats of hostile operations in Virginia. The last caused the temporary abandonment of Norfolk and Richmond by some of the inhabitants, and our relatives, the Marx and Myers families of Richmond, took refuge for a short time in our retired village. The family of Mrs. [Beverley] Kennon of Norfolk took up their residence also in Warrenton, and an intimate friendship between them and our family, commenced then, has been continued without interruption. The news of the Battle of New Orleans was soon followed by the illuminations for the celebration of peace, and I was then interested in following on the map, by the aid of newspaper reports, the operations of Napoleon and the allied armies which terminated in the battle of Waterloo and the march on Paris.

I was not twelve years of age at this time, but I have no doubt that my intellectual development, as regards knowledge acquired under the assiduous instruction of my indefatigable teachers, was a good deal in advance of my years. *My* brothers and sisters and myself had no instructors, except in French, out of [except in] our own family. Yet, when I ceased to receive it at the age of fifteen, I was well-versed in the English language and literature, in geography and history and arithmetic, knew something of geometry and trigonometry, and had completed a great part of the collegiate course of Latin and Greek, having read in the latter language the whole of the *Iliad*. I could read French fluently and write it pretty well. Our instructor in that language was a refugee planter from San Domingo, Mr. [Achilles] Plunkett, who afterwards married my sister Caroline. Another gentleman of the same class, Mr. La Taste, gave us lessons in dancing. Mr. Plunkett and one of his sons also taught music to the young ladies in my father's school. . . .

In 1817, when I was thirteen years of age, I accompanied my father on a stage journey to Richmond, Va., my first absence of more than a day from home. There was nothing memorable about the journey, unless it was what may now be thought the rather primitive nature of the "stage" wagon, open in front, with our baggage secured to a rack behind with leather straps. As the journey was made partly at night, we had a small cord tied to our trunk and passed into our hands, that we might know if the trunk was cut off. The post office laws or contracts required that the mail should not be carried by a negro; so our skilful black driver was accompanied by a mail guard, in the shape of a white boy eight or ten years old, who sat beside him, to save the law. This boy's name, I think, was Mice, and I believe that was really the family name. We returned home, after a pleasant visit and cordial reception from our relatives in Rich[mon]d.

In 1818, my father, thinking that the harrassing labors of himself and his older children had secured a sufficient provision for the future support of the family, determined to retire from the occupation of teaching, and he therefore sold the property and good will of the academy. The purchasers were Joseph Andrews and his son-in-law, Thomas Jones (two of Fielding's novels!), of Philadelphia, who took possession of it in 1818. Our family moved to a smaller house, preparatory to a further removal to Virginia, where my father proposed to purchase a farm.

WEST POINT CADET

At this time the reform of the Military Academy at West Point had begun, under the able government of John C. Calhoun, Secretary of War, and [an] admirable organization [was] instituted by Major [Sylvanus] Thayer. Consequently, the academy was becoming generally known, and it occured to my father to try to procure me an appointment of cadet. These appointments were not yet in great demand, and mine was easily obtained through the kind and influential interposition of Mr. Nathaniel Macon, then late speaker of the House of Representatives in Congress, and then United States Senator from our state, and a resident of Warren County (where, by the bye, he was generally known as Nat. Mekins).

It turned out, unfortunately, that the hard-earned savings of years had not been well-invested, and my father's means of support were much smaller than he had expected. Carrying out, however, his plan, he purchased a property, called Spring Farm, about six miles north of Richmond, Va., to which the family removed in the spring of 1819, and which was their home for about eight years.

In June of that year, when I was a little more than fifteen years old, I took leave of them and went on board a little coasting schooner, to get my first experience of seasickness in a voyage to New York. My brother Sam. had furnished me with some claret wine which I tried to drink, and the experiment gave me such a disgust to that beverage that it was many years afterwards before I could taste it again. After putting into Lewes, Del., on account of a storm, our little vessel reached Sandy Hook, and, for what reason I know not, went through The Kills, and at last landed me in the lower part of New York, where almost the first person I met was (oddly enough) Arthur Gloster, of my native village, who had also received an appointment to Mil[itar]y Acad'y, where, however, he did not remain many months.

I soon found out my mother's brother, Mr. Benj'n Myers, who was in business in N. York, and I think it was then that I staid a day or two with him and saw something of the city, which at that time extended little, if at all, above Canal Street. I remember that the Sailors' Snug Harbor (now on Staten Island) stood on an eminence in the vicinity of that Street and Broadway; Niblo's Garden (the Metropolitan Hotel) was enclosed by a fence and quite out of town. The fashionable residences were on the Battery and Bowling Green and in the lower part of Broadway. My uncle took his meals at Bunker's Hotel, near the Bowling Green. His modest rooms were in the lower part of Pine Street, and I well remember the fireplace there, faced with blue Dutch tiles, containing a Scripture story, which would now, I supposed, be almost worth their weight—in *silver*, at least—if not more at the appointed time, June 14th, 1819.

I went up the Hudson in a steamboat, of which there were not more than two or three, perhaps, then running, and was put on shore at West Point from a rowboat attached to the steamer by a line, as was then the customary manner of making all but the principal landings. Having reported myself to Major Thayer, I was soon quartered with several of my classmates in a room in the old North Barracks and set to work at the preliminary drill. I can recollect the stiffness caused in my left arm by carrying for two hours a day the unaccustomed weight of the heavy old-line musket, eleven lbs., which was the only one then, and for some years after, in use. Prepared as I was by the faithful and kind instruction which I had received at home, my examination for admission presented no difficulty. I can remember that when the French teacher, Mr. [Claudius] Berard, was examining us in grammar, he gave the boy next to me an example of a reflective verb and asked him to name the class to which it belonged, which he could not do. The question was passed to me, and I answered it, but I added that I knew it from the French and did not think that the designation was recognized in English grammar. This was pretty cool for a boy of fifteen, under the circumstances.

The next day Mr. Berard sent for me to go to his house and questioned me about my studies, which seemed to surprise him, for he said: "Why did you leave them, to come here?" I hope he was satisfied with the answer which he received in four years. In consequence of my father's removal to Virginia, about the time of my leaving home, my name was entered as from that state and so printed in the first register after my admission. My friend, Mr. Macon, determined, as he said, that Virginia should not steal "all the clever men from No. Carolina," took a good deal of trouble to obtain an order from the War Office to have the error corrected, much to the amusement of Major [William Jenkins] Worth and some of the other officers.

We had not been long in our first encampment, under Capt. John R. Bell, then Commandant of Cadets, when the order came for us to make a march into the country; so we crossed the river to Cold Spring and marched to Poughkeepsie and Hudson. We stopped at Livingston Manor to pay our respects to the widow of Gen'l

[Richard] Montgomery, who fell at Quebec. From Hudson we returned to West Point by water, whether on a steamboat or a sloop, I forget, and the next morning in barracks was the only time that I ever missed reveille roll call, having overslepped myself. In that encampment the last of the Cadet Commandants [Commandants], Ed. G. W. Butler, used to drill the batallion, and the capt. of my company was Andrew Donelson, the nephew of Gen'l [Andrew] Jackson and his private secretary, when President.

Habits of study and regular conduct made my academic duties easy and pleasant to me. French, of course, gave me no trouble. The professor of mathematics, Mr. Andrew Ellicott, was then at a very advanced age and although he sometimes visited the section rooms, as our places of recitation were called, he took no active part in the instruction. I and some others used to humor his fancy of having examples in arithmetic and algebra worked on our slates in very small characters and presented to him.

There were few graduates of the academy then capable and willing to act as instructors, and the want had to be supplied by cadets of the higher classes. Thus the teacher of even our highest section was a cadet, Wm. H. Bell, of No. Carolina, whom your mother and some of you knew as the ordnance officer who relieved me in command of Washington Arsenal, in 1855.

At the general examination in June, 1820, I was second in my class, and in the encampment which followed I was made a corporal, which made my military duties easier when we marched that summer to Philadelphia. Major Worth had then relieved Capt. Bell in the command of the "corps," and just before our departure he called for my equipment, to see what weight we boys had to carry. I do not remember exactly the weight, but with our heavy muskets, our knapsack filled with linen clothing, and our blanket and a stiff leather cap, we could not have been charged with much less than forty pounds, carried by the Roman soldier of old.

We went down to New York on a sloop, the prevailing river craft, and crossed over to Staten Island, where we encamped some days. We then marched through Brunswick, Princeton, and Trenton, to Bristol, by water to Bridesburgh, and over to Mantua, where we encamped for some time, nearly on the ground now occupied by the mansion of Powelton. The site was then open fields or woods extending to the Schuylkill [River]. The yellow fever prevailing in the city prevented our visiting it, and we saw the inhabitants only in our camp. My good brother and instructor, Solomon, was then pursuing his medical studies in Philadelphia, and we had the pleasure of meeting. I saw some members of your mother's family [the Hayses], but not herself, as I happened to be out of camp when she visited it. She has an account of the march to Phil'a which was prepared by one of the cadets and printed, and which you can consult if you have any curiosity on the subject.

On the opening of the next academic year, I resumed my studies with increased interest, as they became more advanced, and at the close I maintained my former standing. The leader of our class was Wm. T. Washington, of the District of Columbia, who had brilliant mathematical abilities and talents, but was in a fair way to be spoiled by the favor shown to him and by the flattery of his superiors. His health was not robust, and at the end of our second year he was permitted to go, on furlough, to Europe. He did not rejoin the class before the end of their term, but he received a commission in the army which he resigned after a short time. His subsequent brief career may be passed over in silence; he died in Greece, during the revolution.

In the summer of 1821, my furlough year, I paid a visit to my parents and relatives at Richmond. My sister Rachel had been married a few months before and had taken my younger sister Eliza with her to Wilmington, No. Carolina, where the latter remained, under the excellent care and instruction of our sister, until she was grown up. Whilst I was at home, Major Thayer, with kind consideration for the gratification of my friends, sent me notice, "officially," of my appointment as acting assistant professor of mathematics. This appointment, carrying with it increased pay, exemption from military duties (drills, etc.), and from inspectors' visits to my room, rendered my situation at the academy even easier than before, and as pleasant as it was possible to be. I was permitted to join the special mess of twelve cadets who were boarded by the Widow Thompson, in a house that stood on part of the ground now occupied by the ordnance buildings. The walk over the plain in winter, in the face of the northern blasts and snowstorms, was sometimes rather trying, but the temporary inconvenience was more than compensated by the comfort of a quiet room and neat table, to say nothing of female society; *you* can remember the three Misses Thompson in advanced age.

In the absence of Washington I kept without difficulty, and perhaps with diminished application, the place at the head of my class, during our third year. Regarded with favor by the officers of the academy, and well-received in my visits to their families on Saturday evenings, and having pleasant associates among my companions, the time passed rapidly away. We had a set who called ourselves "the cold-water club"; not that our potations were confined to that simple beverage, but if we committed any infraction of the regulations, they were either unknown to the authorities, or winked at, on account of the good character of the members of our club, of whom I believe only Stephen Lee and George Greene, Jno. K. Findlay, and Saml. McCoskry have borne me company, so far as the present day, in the journey of life. We never played at cards, or other forbidden games, but at our social, buckwheat cake suppers, in a small house just below Fort Clinton, segars were used, and I adopted, perforce as it were, the habit of smoking them in moderation, which, however, I discontinued in the course of a few years.

Cards were never seen in my father's house, and when I left there, I did not know one card from another. My first lessons were taken from some young ladies, Misses Kingsley, who lived with their widowed mother in a cottage still standing on the river bank, just above Corzen's Hotel. Their brother, a graduate of the Mil'y Acad'y, was then one of the tactical officers, and a proverbially rigid enforcer of the regulations. He was the father of Mr. K. who lives just below West Point. As an evidence of the good will of the officers towards me, and one which I always remembered with surprise, I will mention that at one time Lieut. Dimmick [Justin Dimick], a tactical officer, who occupied two communicating rooms in the South Barracks, invited me to share them with him. Our friendships continued to his last days, when I assisted, a few years ago, in paying the funeral honors to his remains, in Philadelphia.

My position as ass't prof'r exempted me from camp duty, so that in 1822 I paid another visit home, stopping, on my way, in Philadelphia, where my brother Solomon, having received his diploma of M.D., was an attending physician at the Alms House, between Tenth and Eleventh Streets below Spruce. It was then that I first became acquainted with your mother, at her father's house in an out-of-the-way part of the city, Chestnut St. above Twelfth! My journey this year was extended to Wilmington [N. C.], with stops at my sister Caroline's (Mrs. Plunkett) in Warrenton, and my brother Moses' in Raleigh. My sister Rachel had been my regular correspondent ever since I first left home, and we continued to exchange the most confidential letters up to the time of her lamented death. Besides the unceasing affection manifested for me in her letters, I had frequent occasion to observe and admire the wisdom, foresight, and sagacity by which they were marked and made serviceable to me as guides for conduct in life. Her agreeable and admirable style of writing appears in her interesting letters to Miss [Maria] Edgeworth, which you have read.

My last year's course of studies at the academy was pursued by me with renewed ardor and industry, on account of the nature of the subjects and the interest imparted to them by the lessons of the instructor, Professor [Claude] Crozet. Our class having entered the academy soon after the reformation of the course of instruction, under Major (now, 1823, Lieut. Col.) Thayer, it naturally fell to our lot to lead the way in many of the new studies, inaugurated by him, with the assistance of Prof'r Crozet, a graduate of the Polytechnic School in Paris. Thus in mathematics we were the first to study the differential and integral calculus. A feeble beginning was made by us in chemistry in our third year, and civil engineering and the principles of machines were first taught to us by Prof'r. Crozet. In all these studies, except chemistry, we had to use French textbooks, Lacroix, Sganzin, and Hachette, for want of any in English.

COMMISSIONED OFFICER AT WEST POINT

At the final examination of our class, in 1823, I stood at the head, and soon after received the commission of second lieutenant in the Corps of Engineers. Having been notified of being detailed as ass't professor of philosophy at the academy, I spent the intervening two months again at home. On my journey I was accompanied by my friend Dallas Bache, who was on furlough that year, and I passed a few pleasant days at his home in Philadelphia. His father was postmaster of that city, and he lived over the post office, on Chestnut Street below Fourth. The acquaintance then commenced with his excellent and charming mother laid the foundation of a friendship which continued to the end of her life and has descended, as you know, to succeeding generations in our respective families. I returned to New York by a steamer from Richmond. The yellow fever then prevailed in New York, and the whole of the lower part of the city was cut off by a fence across it at the City Hall Park. As our steamer passed up the West Side, and we looked at the deserted wharfs and streets, the appearance of desolation was complete and malancholy indeed.

On returning to West Point, I found that I had contracted the ague and fever (probably on the James River), from which I suffered great inconvenience for two years. The physician tried Peruvian bark in substance, but my stomach would not retain enough of it to stop the chills. Quinine was just becoming known,

but it was not on the list of supplies of the Army Medical Department, and arsenic was at length used to check the disease in my
case. During part of my illness, Prof'r [David Bates] Douglass,
who had succeeded his father-in-law Prof'r Ellicott in the mathematical department, and, on the resignation of Professor Crozet, had
been transferred to the chair of engineering, took me to his house,
where I was kindly taken care of by Mrs. D. for some weeks.

At the next academic vacation, I determined to make an excursion
to the western part of New York and see the Falls of Niagara. I
stopped first at Caatskill [sic], where the Mountain House had been
just opened. I went up to it in a gig and had to take shelter, at
the foot of the mountain, from a heavy storm. When I reached the
top, the whole landscape was hidden by a sea of white vapor, but
as the sun declined, a strong wind scooped out openings in the
cloud through which portions of the country could be seen, until
at last the setting sun lit up the whole of the extensive scene, making altogether a beautifully varied picture. Arrived at Albany, I
found my troublesome disease returning in a worse form, and I
went over to Saratoga for some days, until I thought myself able
to resume my journey. Congress Hall was then almost the only
hotel at the little village, which had just superceded Ballston as a
watering place.

At Troy I had to send again for a physician, who gave me a
dose which made me sleep about twenty-four hours. From there,
or from Schenectady, I adopted, for greater ease of locomotion,
the conveyance of a canal packet on the Erie Canal. I liked very
well this mode of travelling, which I used on several subsequent
occasions, when not pressed for time. The monotony of the easy
motion is relieved by an occasional walk whilst the boat is passing
through locks, and, with a pleasable companion or two and an
amusing book, the time passes pleasantly enough. I can hardly class
among the amusing books some six volumes of an *incomplete* copy
of [Richardson's] *Sir Charles Grandison*, which I found, on a rainy
day, in the cabin of my boat in the Mohawk Valley, but it is the
only time I ever read any of it, and it served to while away the
hours that I could not give to fine scenery and pretty cultivation
of that fertile valley.

I continued my canal journey through the long level of seventy
miles, I think, without a lock, at the end of which I took the stage
route through the pretty towns and among the picturesque lakes
of western New York, turning aside to make a visit, by means of a
farmer's wagon, to the little villages of Syracuse and Salina and

their new salt works, and stopping at Lockport, which consisted chiefly of a collection of shanties (chantier?) to shelter the workmen, who were making the deep cut through the rock, and building Neptune's Staircase, the series of locks by which the canal was to reach the higher level of Lake Erie. In Rochester the aqueduct was built, but the stumps of forest trees were still standing in the hotel yard and in some of the streets. From near Lockport, a short trip on the canal again took me to the village of Black Rock, a little below the mouth of Buffalo Creek on the Niagara River. My friend Lieut. Sam. Smith, the principal assistant prof'r of philosophy at the Mil'y Acad'y, had fortunately given me a letter to Mrs. Porter, the wife of Gen'l Peter B. Porter, a prominent officer in the "late war" (as that of 1812 was called then), who resided at Black Rock, and whose family had large possessions there and at Niagara Falls.

On the very day of my arrival, I think it was, after dining at Gen'l Porter's hospitable house, I was seized with a violent attack of dysentery, which confined me for some weeks to my room at the hotel. There was a young medical man in the village, who was very attentive to me, and the assistance of a more experienced physician was called in from the neighboring village of Buffalo. To them and the kind nursing of Mrs. Porter I was indebted for a release from a very serious illness. Mrs. P. was a Breckenridge and the widow of Grayson, before she married Gen'l P.; was an elegant and accomplished woman, and, better, a woman of kindly disposition and warm heart. She continued always my good friend and occasional correspondent.

When I was at Black Rock, Gen'l Porter was deeply engaged in forming a harbor there, hoping to make that point the terminus of the Erie Canal, instead of its rival Buffalo, but the latter soon took the precedence and maintained it, as you know. When able to travel, I crossed the Niagara and went down on the Canada side to Forsyth's tavern, just above the falls, which was almost the only place of accommodation on either side of the river for visitors (not very numerous) to that wonder of nature. I saw it as well as my still feeble condition would allow, and then proceeded, on the American side, to Lewistown, and by the Lake Shore Road, through Rochester, to Utica.

After an excursion to Trenton Falls, in company with Mr. Alston [Robert F. W. Allston] of So. Carolina, a retired graduate of the Mil'y Acad'y, I made my way, not without some trouble from my malady, to Albany and back to West Point, where I remained another year, as instructor in the department of engineering, under Prof'r Douglass. In 1824 the visit of Gen'l Lafayette to this country, on the invitation of Congress, took place, and it was in New York, where I had gone to attend a grand fête given to him at Castle Garden, that I heard, from my Uncle Ben., the sad news of the death of my oldest brother, Moses, at the Virginia W. S. [White Sulphur] Springs. Although he had not attained the age of forty, he had stood high among the most eminent lawyers in North Carolina, and was regarded as one of the most prominent and useful citizens of the state. He had acquired a handsome fortune, in the practice of his profession, but the attendance on the county courts in the lower and less healthy parts of the state brought on a malarial disease which caused his premature death. His loss was deeply felt by us, for we had always looked up to him, with a sort of affectionate *reverence,* as a kind and wise counsellor, and, in looking back, it was always hard for us to realize that he had died at so early an age.

There was then no hotel at West Point, and the few rooms at the disposal of the steward, in one end of the Mess Hall building, could not accommodate many visitors. Consequently, we saw few strangers, even in summer, and hardly any in winter. But we had a pleasant bachelor mess of officers, supplied with a good table by the prince of caterers of that day, Wm. B. Cozzens, and afternoon rambles, for exercise, over the hills, followed by social evenings at one another's rooms, passed away the time not given to academic duties or to study.

It is curious to recollect the shout, almost of derision, which greeted, at even our *military* mess, the first announcement of Gen'l [Andrew] Jackson as a candidate for the presidency. Dr. [Josiah] Everett, the oldest member of the mess, was almost the only one to predict that it would succeed with the people. One of the stories of the day was that, when it was mentioned to the general himself, he exclaimed: "A hell of a President *I* should make." Perhaps many persons afterwards thought that his anticipations were realized. Very different was the reception of the news of the death of [the poet, Lord] *Byron;* many of us felt it as the loss of a personal friend.

At this time [there] began my participation in those delightful Saturday dinners and evenings at Mr. [Gouverneur] Kemble's hospitable cottage at Cold Spring, which I enjoyed, with various intervals, for fifty years, the last time being a few months before Mr. Kemble's death, after a useful and honorable life of ninety years.

Perhaps you may expect me to say something on the subject of religious differences among so many associates. I have often thought, with some surprise, of the fact that by some sort of silent consent, in our meetings, when we were cadets, that subject was never broached, and the same reticence was observed among our companions as officers, unless it may have entered indirectly in the free talks I sometimes held with Capt. (afterwards General) [Ethan Allen] Hitchcock, on *philosophical* themes, to the study of which he was much addicted.

The regulations of the academy required regular attendance at services in the chapel on Sunday, to which we were marched as to any other duty. Neither I nor anyone else objected, in my time, to sitting there whilst good Mr. [Thomas] Picton, the chaplain, uttered his Presbyterian prayers and dull sermons, although there were no doubt many, besides myself, who did not concur with him. I confess that, especially after I had the opportunity, as ass't prof'r, to go alone to the chapel and choose a corner seat, I often indulged in a nap there, or read some book which I could smuggle in my pocket. Mr. Picton was an excellent man and very friendly to me, and I was glad to visit his house, especially after his pretty daughter Mary (Mrs. Edmund Stevens) was grown up, but he confined himself to his official duties as chaplain and professor of ethics, and I think that it was acknowledged that a great mistake was made when, in 1825, he was removed to make room for the more eloquent and ambitious Mr. (Bishop) [Charles Pettit] McIlvaine.

I am dwelling, you may think, a long time on the details of this part of my life, which was only a preparation for more active duties, and I am certainly loth to quit the recollections of the happy years I passed at West Point, up to the time when I had reached the age of manhood, for I was just turned of twenty-one when I was relieved from duty at the Military Academy.

Ellen Mordecai

Life on a Virginia Farm

One of the most interesting characters in early American Jewish history is the educator Jacob Mordecai, the grandfather of Ellen.

Born in Philadelphia in 1762, Mordecai early became a business-man, but an unsuccessful one. After moving about for some time, he took up residence in Warrenton, N. C., where, about 1809, he established a seminary for young ladies, which speedily became one of the finest institutions of its type in the South. Within a decade, he had acquired a competence and moved back to Rich-mond, where he had once lived. He settled down, a few miles from the city, on a place which he called Spring Farm. Much of his leisure time was doubtless spent on biblical and theological studies. Apparently, he had a good knowledge of the biblical Hebrew text, and certainly he was an avid student of Jewish lore. It was during this period that he met a young German clerk, Isaac Leeser, whom he set on the road toward his career as the first great Jewish religious leader in America. Mordecai remained on the farm dur-ing the 1820's but returned to the city around 1827. Eleven years later he passed away.

Jacob Mordecai married twice, in each case a daughter of the well-known silversmith and merchant, Myer Myers. Consequently, he had a large family, which gathered at Spring Farm during summers and on festive occasions.

Mordecai himself was an observant Jew who, in all probability, maintained a kosher kitchen even on his farm. Some of his chil-dren, however, including Moses, his first-born, married out of the faith. Moses, for instance, had two boys and two girls who were reared as Christians. After Moses' death in 1824, at least two of his orphaned children were sent to live, for a time, with their Jewish grandparents at the farm. One of the little ones was Ellen, who later married a cousin and thus retained her maiden name, becoming Mrs. Ellen Mordecai.

In 1907, Ellen, then eighty-seven, dictated a record of her early

*experiences at Spring Farm. Her story is an almost idyllic picture of
life in a Southern country home a generation before the War Between
the States. The following account, with minor omissions, is taken
from a copy in the American Jewish Archives. The original is in
the library of the Virginia Historical Society, Richmond.*

SPRING FARM

WHEN I was a little girl I paid two visits, one of nearly two years and the next of shorter duration, to my grandfather, who then lived at a farm five miles north of Richmond [Virginia]. It took its name of Spring Farm on account of a mineral spring on the place. The house was a small country house, a passage running through it, with grandma's and grandpa's room on one side, and the dining room on the other; the dining room opened into a large room, which my grandfather added as a parlor. There was a small entry between these two rooms and a piazza, the length of the house, in front. There were two bedrooms upstairs and a large room which had been added over the parlor, and between the bedroom and this new room was this same little entry, which was given to "Aunt" Laura and myself for our doll house, where we spent many happy hours with our dolls, Mr. and Mrs. Summers, and their children. There was a closet upstairs for linen, and near it, in a very narrow passage, was a box containing children's books, and this was a most delightful object to me, for though I could not read, Aunt Laura [Mordecai], who was only two years older, could, and many a happy hour have we passed, with her reading the stories which were in vogue then for children, such as *Mary and Her Cat, Ellen the Teacher, The World Turned Upside Down,* and last, and to crown all, *Mrs. Leicester's School,* which belonged to "Aunt" Emma (who was older than ourselves), and which was given to me, and I have it among my treasures now.

Downstairs, the passage which ran through the house terminated in a back porch, and near the steps of this back porch was a fine ash tree, and a little further on was the garden—but I won't go into the garden quite yet. I will say, first, that under this ash tree, Jack, the butler, gave to me and Aunt Laura our early tea, just before sunset. This yard was green and shady, and about the middle of it was grandma's dairy. Not far from the dairy was the kitchen, over which Aunt Sally Hicks and Aunt Judy, two black women, reigned as queens. Sally Hicks was noted for her fine cooking and her imperious character, though she never showed it to anyone higher

234

than her scullion. This was a little long-headed negro named Staf-
ford, and she (who had been acquainted with a Tidewater home)
used to call him "a little periagured [boat-shaped] limb of satan,"
alluding to the shape of his head being similar to a pirogue, a small
craft which she was used to. I have now a curious little jacket
which was given to old Sallie by her master for having cooked ex-
cellently some dish that he was fond of. It had figures on it as
large as an apple and red, and she always called it her "apple
jacket."

I have happy associations with the dairy, for sometimes, when
my grandfather had to stay in town all night, it was my privilege
to sleep with grandma. She would get up very early in the morning
to go to her dairy. She would not waken me, but I would soon miss
her, and I would slip out of bed and put on my clothes, and run
out and see her skim the milk and put it in the churn. Grandma
was the tenderest and most indulgent of grandmas.

On the front porch there was trained a sweetbrier, and in this
sweetbrier a song sparrow had her nest year after year. Under
grandma's bedroom window there was trained a woodbine, and in
that a robin had built its nest. My grandfather was very careful that
a bird should never be disturbed, and it was a high crime for a nest
to be robbed. My brother Henry was there at the same time I was,
and I remember his coming home with a nest that a little negro
boy had taken for him, and my grandfather was very angry with
the little negro, and he also represented to my brother the cruelty
of such as that, and he made them carry it back and put it where
they found it, and I hope the bird never discovered the danger her
nest had been in.

The yard in front of the house was very green, and there was a
walk running down to a little green gate not distant from the house,
and on each side of this walk there was a hedge of Scotch broom.
Outside of the gate, and nearly the width of the yard, was a lane.
Near the gate was the horse block, for the convenience of mounting
horses, and rings to tie them to, and on the other side was a large
farmyard with barns and stables. The long lane in front of the
house had a whitewashed plank fence on each side of it. The lane
had no turning, but came to a white gate, which opened on the
public road, and across that road there was a beautiful millpond,
which belonged to the Youngs, who lived across it and not far from
Spring Farm. This pond was very old and had all the beauty of
a natural lake. Below the dam were large rocks, over which the
water made mimic waterfalls, and the mill was a never-failing

source of interest to us, though we were not allowed to go into it unless someone was with us.

I remember grandpa taking Aunt Laura, brother Henry, and myself, and showing us the different wheels and explaining them to us, and we jumped happily from rock to rock, enjoying the scramble, and seeing the pretty water foaming between them.

The mineral spring was further down the road, and those of my aunts who were grown ladies used frequently to walk there, and Aunt Laura and myself would accompany them. One pretty morning, when I came downstairs, I heard that my aunts had gone to walk, and without consulting anyone I ran off to overtake them. I went through the big gate and down the road. I don't know how far I went, but it seemed to me it was a long way, and not meeting my aunts, I stopped at a little miniature rivulet, which I could step over, to play with some tiny frogs, and I also was delighted with my shadow; it looked to me like an old woman, and I got a little stick for a cane, and amused myself walking backwards and forwards across the little branch. I was so fascinated with the frogs that I felt as if I wanted to show my affection for them. I did this by jumping on one and mashing it to death, not from cruelty, but from excess of love. Here I was found by my kind Uncle Gus [Augustus Mordecai], who took me home. When we got home I found the family at the breakfast table, and I crept up to grandma and told her I had killed a little frog. I think grandma must have defined [understood] the feeling, for though she warned me against such as that, she did not scold me.

The garden, as I said before, was a large one, and many happy hours have Aunt Laura, brother Henry, and I played in that garden. Old Uncle Phil was the gardener, and though he was rather a cross old fellow, and though we stood in rather wholesome awe of him, he would always give us a little piece of ground for our garden, and would give us peppergrass and such as that to sow. This, to our delight, would come up freely, and we were satisfied with that, and never looked for further returns.

In the bottom of the garden there was a beautiful cherry tree, which made a natural arbor, and under that was a turf seat. Aunt Laura and I would lie on that seat, which was quite high, and the cherries hung so low that we could gather and eat as many as we wanted while we lay there. When I read Miss Mulock's [Dinah Maria Craik's] pretty story of the Brownie, in this my old age, I imagined that cherry tree looking like the one we played so happily under. Just outside of the garden fence there ran a little branch, and this Aunt Laura, who was only six years old, called "the Bristol Channel," as she was already studying geography. I had no idea what the Bristol Channel meant, but I had such faith in her knowledge that I accepted it without a scruple, and we used to sail our little pine bark boats on it, loading them with pebbles and grass. These little pine bark boats were made for us by Mr. [Samuel Hays] Myers, who was then courting Aunt Eliza, and who was afterwards the father of Edmund Myers and Caroline Cohen....

There were several apple trees in this large garden. One of them was a very big one, and we would get the apples and, according to the custom of the time, we would bury them in the ground to ripen, with what success I don't know, but we had faith, and that was enough.

When grandpa and grandma would go to town, they frequently took me with them to spend the day. The happiest part of the day would be when we would start back in the evening. Grandpa would frequently go by the baker's and fill the front seat with horsecakes [gingerbread fashioned in the shape of a horse] for the children. There would be room enough on that side for me, and I remember, after getting out of town, how I would enjoy the sweet air of the country and would sit there and sing my little tunes to myself, and enjoy the sweet odors, and I know now that one of those odors was grape blossoms, and I would feel so happy riding back with my kind grandparents and getting back home to Aunt Laura.

Aunt Laura and I slept upstairs in a little trundle bed, and grandma would come up every night after we were in bed to hear us [say] our prayers. Our prayer was a little hymn, I think, of Watts', beginning, "And now another day is gone; I sing my Maker's praise." In the morning we had to say our morning prayer, which began, "My God, who makes the sun to shine."

As I said, the garden was very large, and in an unused part of it there was a depression in the earth. I don't know what made it, but it was grassy, and on the side of it there was a large cedar tree. The roots of this tree showed above the surface, and soon after I got there I remember Aunt Laura saying:

> Come with me, and you shall see,
> All the roots of the cedar tree.

And I thought that was a beautiful verse.

At the breakfast table, where many assembled, for it was a large family, occasionally grandma would forget to give Aunt Laura her coffee. If no one remarked it, she would not mind, but if anyone said: "Poor little Laura hasn't any coffee," she would cry.

I never smell cedar now without thinking of the parlor. The hearth was always filled with cedar boughs in the summer, and the cool smell of a chimney on a damp day brings back that parlor to me.

Aunt Laura, though a little child, had to practice on the piano in there. She stood upon a little stool to practice, and I lay upon the sofa to listen to the music, which I thought nothing could excel, and I remember the tunes of the little exercises she used to play, and which I said was like a little child crying for his mother. . . .

My brother Henry, who was at grandpa's with me, used to draw me about the yard in a little wagon that Uncle Gus made for me, and was my loved playmate.

On rainy days, when Aunt Laura would be studying her lessons, and he [Henry] and I had nothing to do, we would go on the front porch, draw chairs around in a circle and cover them with an umbrella, and there we would pretend we were two old men, old Saum and old Taum, and there we would sing and think we composed new tunes. Brother Henry at that time had a great love of surgery, and I remember his being on the little back porch with me and catching a great "granddaddy longlegs" and saying: "Sister Ellen, I think he ought to be bled"; and I doubted it, but still had great confidence in his judgment, and he caught the spider and stuck a needle in it and turned it loose, and of course the victim to his skill made off as fast as he could, and he said: "See, sister Ellen, how fast he can run; how good it has been for him."

Brother Henry and I were as affectionate to the day of his death as we were as children, and I have missed him and mourned him now for over thirty years, and my younger brother Jacob, who was in every way as dear to me, he, too, has slept with those who had gone before him for nearly forty years. Sister Margaret and I still survive, old women, but loving each other, and loving the past, and loving the young ones who have grown up around us, and so I bring this reminiscence to an end.

Written by Mrs. Ellen Mordecai, when quite blind.

Dictated to her granddaughter, Annie Morel.

Raleigh, 1907.

Joseph Lyons

Random Thoughts of a Sick Soul

Joseph Lyons was a member of a family which arrived in Columbia, South Carolina, no later than the 1820's. His father, Isaac Lyons, was one of the founders of the Hebrew Benevolent Society, which was established there at that time.

Joseph, born in 1813, was graduated from South Carolina College at the age of nineteen. He turned to the study of law, reading Blackstone's Commentaries *in the office of a Savannah, Georgia, lawyer, and passed the bar examination in 1835. Two years later he died of consumption in Paris, France.*

Lyons was a diarist. One of his diaries, from which the following extracts are taken, covers the two-year period from April, 1833, to April, 1835. A copy may be found in the American Jewish Archives. At the time the diary opens, Lyons was already sick in body and, it would seem, in mind. His illness may account, in part at least, for his bitterness, his irascibility, and his black despair.

Lyons was constantly conscious of the fact that he was not only an American but, first of all, a South Carolinian. A supporter of the states' rights doctrine and a Nullificationist, he proudly sported a palmetto button when he traveled in the North. But the journal is important not so much for this reason, but because it contains the frank reflections of a well-educated young Jew who was completely assimilated to the contemporary cultural pattern. Lyons, a frequent visitor to Charleston, at that time the most cultured Jewish community in the United States, betrays the thought and feelings of an American Jew who had begun to question the verities of traditional Judaism. Lyons' opinions are revealing in the light of the Reformed Society of Israelites of Charleston, for although his attitudes on Jewish beliefs and practices were not typical of those of the Charleston Jews, it was in that city that the first Reform Jewish group in America was organized.

239

THE MAIMED MISANTHROPE

APRIL 29, 1833. Warm. I arrived in Savannah at 1:00 A.M. I never before knew what it is to be a stranger, nor would I be now conscious of the absence of "those I love now far away," could I read without pain; but a man in my situation [with a diseased eye], what can he do? Write, *c'est tout* ["that's all"]. And though I have never seen this book before, I feel as if restored to the conversation of a sincere friend, whilst imparting my feelings to the unconscious paper. I have not journalised for some months past, though I have witnessed more novelty during that [period than] any time . . . in all my preceding existence. I will give a retrospective review of all that when I am more in the humor.

Here I am in a new land and have an opportunity of being what I will. I have come to the conclusion that men are not to be admitted to your souls as companions, but the true road to success is to keep aloof; and when you mix with them, let it only be to command. Use them for your own purposes, and if you dance for them, let it be over their heads. All this is incompatible with sincerity, and I do therefore distrust the soundness of this view. However, at another time I will examine it. . . .

I took up a Blackstone this morning. *C'est le premier pas qui conte* ["It is the first step that counts"]. . . .

June 30th. Sunday. I recommence writing in my journal after an intermission of six [actually, two] months. I should have written before, but [for] frequent and irritating interruptions from a very annoying, though not painful, inflamation of the right eye. It is even now very dim, and I doubt its perfect restoration at any time. All maimed men are misanthropical and excusably so, for the constantly b[e]holding others as undeserving in the full enjoyment of their faculties begets something like envy and hatred of a vague nature which sours the mind. The only effectual remedy was purgative and cooling medicine and the strictest abstinence. Thus, at various times for a week together, I have lived on dry bread, tea, potatoes, and honey. Of course, the light, when too strong, must be avoided; but in my own case, I found a weak light more healing than darkness.

CINCINNATI IN 1848

(see page 319)

AUGUST PICARD

In his uniform as an officer in the Lafayette Guard

(see page 370)

From Harper's Weekly

JESSE SELIGMAN

(see page 345)

By reason of this interruption, I have made insignificant progress in law, having advanced but to the third chap., second vol. [of Blackstone]. . . .

I should find all studies disagreeable but that of mankind, and even that [is agreeable only when I am] in a very comfortable manner lolling on a sofa, and they passing in review before me. Of course, I have read but little of late. A book by [Edward] Bulwer [-Lytton] named *Asmodeus at Large,* a pleasant and very amusing thing and sublime in some parts. Everything that Bulwer writes is delicious to me without alloy. He is a nullifier in principle because a reformer. He admires Byron. His code of religion is the rational, so that he never offends me in his way of thinking. By the bye, [Robert James] Turnbull [the nullificationist] died on the 15th. I wrote an obituary for publication, but have not sent it yet.

I wish I had written all along in my journal. My opinions are so fleeting and various that I find myself eternally inconsistent. Besides, I have seen more of the world in the last six months than in all my life. Besides, I have been in new circles of people, made a sea voyage, been to Philadelphia, commenced a profession, fallen in love for two days together at least twenty times, and have done all that a man in his twentieth year, or nineteenth year, should do, except fight and whore.

So I must begin to write up my books [journals] and I will begin with my Charleston jaunt. I was graduated [from South Carolina College], I have forgotten the day, in December [1832], but at all events, it was early, just after my nineteenth birthday. I will not mention the few claims I had to a diploma, insignificant and contemptible as they were. Still fully on a par with at least one half of my class, which class, I must remark, was the youngest and meanest that has been graduated within the period of my experience. No emulation and but little talent, with two or three brilliant exceptions: Lescame [?] and Currell [?]. I passed through without being distinguished with even the paltry honor of an appointment on the Exhibition, which was a piece of injustice, which would not have amazed me but from the evidence of prejudice which it indicated against me. But dam all that! I do not complain of being unrewarded according to my deserts, but that others of equal pretensions should have superior honors. Thus I was graduated when I should have been a freshman; and when my mind was enlarged sufficiently to receive instruction, it was then I was deprived of it. So satisfied am I of the fact, that if I could support myself at a literary institution, I would, ere six months elapsed, be a soph[omore] in some college.

Indeed, the life of a student would not be a disagreeable anticipation, though it were to endure for ten years. I do not feel fitted to grapple yet with difficulties contingent to a public life. A little more exercise and maturity and I might be something.

This reminds me of an incident which took place whilst in Charleston. We had a very ingenious "fortuneteller." I went through the ceremony for obtaining an answer to the question, "What profession shall I adopt?" The reply was: "Make a bold push for the woolsack [high office]." I had just then lost all my cash by cards. I asked: "Shall I ever make my fortune by gambling?" The reply: "Can you put your hand in the pie and not burn it?" and I certainly am one of the most . . . unlucky rogues I have ever known. The same book promised me a wife, who should be amongst other women as the moon or sun amid the stars. *Nous verrons tout cela peutêtre* ["Perhaps we'll see all that"].

BANANAS, BOOKS, AND OYSTERS

July 12 [1833]. Friday. . . . I find an account of my journey to Charleston, etc., written on a sheet which I shall now proceed to copy.

On a sulky Sunday morning, viz., Dec. 31st, 1832, I set off from Columbia [S. C.] and arrived in Charleston, Jan. 2nd, 1833, where bananas, books, and oysters do abound. No farther accident happened to us than our horses becoming so fatigued as to compel us to proceed at a snail's pace for the last two days. It was irritating to see ourselves passed even by the dull wagons and old women transporting eggs, butter, game, and poultry to the city. We, at length, after a gloomy ride of some hours through mud and darkness, emerged into the city, which we were sensible of our approach to, no less by smell than sight. The coal smoke was very perceptible. The excitement of anticipation had been too far prolonged, and the reality of being at my journey's end found me dull. Somehow, too, I distrusted my arrival and felt that daylight would reveal the familiar scenery of Columbia. We rattled, however, over stoney King Street, and driving to the end of the town, I slept again in Charleston after three years' absence.

In the morning and before breakfast, I found Aunt's house and saw Cousin Leah for the first time. On the third or second night of my arrival, I was invited to a party at P. M. Cohen's. This was my debut, and I felt as a victim; and when at the very threshold, I had the greatest inclination to bolt off and leave the house; and I felt a hope, unfounded as it was, that they were not at home. My heart stopped actually as the door opened, and how foolishly angry I felt as I was ushered into the circle and introduced. I met one or two old ladies who, after enquiring after the health of the family, were mum. So was I, God knows. I felt as if I was doomed to be so forever. I felt horrid, silent as a post, and awkwardly dawdling [over] my coffee, which I could not swallow; for I felt my heart in my throat, face burning, shrinking and enraged, shrinking because feeling that I must be observed; and when I thought that absenting myself would have saved me from all this mortification, I was enraged.

Just then my host advanced and offered me a seat between two— ay, two young ladies. One of them was Rebecca Moise, who was my sweetheart twelve years ago, when I memorized "Yes, little birds, I hold you fast" from Webster's spelling book, and caught mudfish at the outlet of the city sewer with a bent pin for a hook and white thread for a line. I made some stupid, but not sentimental, remarks about school days to which she graciously responded, and as grateful for being remembered, etc., all in set phrase and good. We then somehow glided into discourse about love. Of course, I strove to be original and was so, I infer, from her surprise and attention. I recollect laying down as principles of my theory that all love is, or springs from, gratified vanity; and its semblance is preserved after its decay by the same motive, i.e., vanity. I began now to fail a little from weakness and adjourned with pleasure to the *vingt-et-un* [card] table, and was glad to be released from the task of conversation at the charge of fifty coppers. We retired, to my extacy, at eleven o'clock. . . .

I here [in Charleston] met Penina Moise [the poetess] who is somewhat famous, and deservedly so. Now at Otto's father's, of course, I saw her and said (very foolishly) one or two things which she will remember, though I have entirely forgotten them. In the interim of the two last [days], I attended the circumcision of twins, which was one of the national [Jewish] ceremonies novel to me. It did not seem attended with excessive pain, though possibly the extreme youth of the subjects forbade any very violent demonstrations of pain or suffering.

Again at Moise's. Oh, God, how dull and stupid I was! I neither talked, danced, nor played cards. How could it be otherwise? Such is the account of the coming out of Mr. Joseph Lyons, a youth of nineteen, and a graduate of the South Carolina College, Fellow of the Euphradian Society, etc., etc., etc., etc. Among all I met, not one whom I would have selected for a friend, none but whose company I should have felt disagreeable, had not the temptation to gratify vanity induce[d] an endeavor to display and to make a favorable impression. This always brings on an excitement which is delightful. About this time I had agreed to study law and was expecting Mr. D.[avid] Lyon. He came and the arrangements were entered into, and I was in a few days to set off for this place [Savannah]; but the Philadelphia campaign opened, which is the last of the Frolics and Fun! !

CHURCH BELLS, COCKROACHES, AND PHILADELPHIA

July 14 [1833]. Sunday. [Savannah] The church bells are now ringing, and if I do abhor anything or have an antipathy to aught besides cockroaches, and Bob Southey [the English writer and poet], it is to this sound. The worst of it is here that they ring every hour on Sunday, and full surfeit is given to the lovers of such music, which I have no difficulty in believing is very eficacious in the dispersion of demons, etc., for who that could escape would remain within hearing?

I must now commence the account of my sea voyage and visit to Philadelphia [in the spring of 1833]. . . .

I was now in the city [of Philadelphia]. I went to the fashionable Chestnut Street and to the Walnut Street Theatre. I here saw Fanny Kemble perform in *The Stranger* [by Kotzebue], [Otway's] *Venice Preserved,* and on another occasion. I have never seen her equal in grace. I also saw [Junius Brutus] Booth once, and he is the only actor according to my taste. I went out one evening to Fairmount, which is said to be beautiful in summer, and I can believe it, though the season was unfavorable to such displays. The houses in Philadelphia are all beautiful, materials and architecture. The bricks are superior to all others in color and polish. Many of them have the doors painted of pure white, and all the brass work on them silver-plated. The steps are of white marble, and the small, iron balustrades of blackened iron work. . . . The window panes [are] of a large plate glass, as it is called, which reflects, and thus answers the double purpose of screen and passage for the light, each admirably. The curtain [is] of an embossed damask or worked muslin, behind which, in beautiful contrast, is hung another scarlet curtain which seems as a border to the other.

The U. S. Bank is a noble building and is the only artificial structure which struck me as sublime. The Girard Bank seems prettier drawn on paper, its pillars being Corinthian. The carved capitals

have accumulated the dust, which makes them look, of course, dirty.
But the plain Doric columns in front of the U. S. Bank does not
render them liable to this defacement. The marble that is used here
is not purely white, nearly so, however. The Masonic Hall, on account of the singularity of its architecture, will strike everyone. It
is purely Gothic and very pretty. The Exchange was not finished,
but will no doubt be an ornament. It is, however, rather low, which
is the only fault with the U. S. B.[ank]. The Mint is in front, similar to that of the U. S. B., but smaller and having also wings on each
side; [it] has by no means such an effect as the unbroken façade of
the former.

I visited the largest ship in the world, which is unfinished, but I
can convey no idea of its size to others, for they have never seen
anything to which it can be compared. It is covered by a high house
of three stories, and you are compelled to ascend that number of
flights of stairs ere you reach the deck.

Whilst here, I saw the procession of all the fire companies, which
was the strangest sight I had ever seen. The riders of the horses
drawing the engines were some dressed as Turks, others as savages,
and one company represented the Quakers and the Indians present
at (the treaty of) the purchase of Pennsalvania, and with their drab
coats, broad brimed hats, and powder were no doubt as much alike
as possible. But all descriptions of buildings are uninteresting to
me, and I believe can be but the same to others, so *allons* ["let's
go"].

The women are not possessed of a tithe of the beauty usually attributed to them; as to gracefulness and symmetry, far inferior to
the Charleston ladies. . . . The men are much superior in appearance,
as are the horses, to those you would usually meet in Charleston.
What was constantly remarked by me was the indifference of the
citizens to the alarm of fire . . . which occurred very frequently.
None seemed to interest themselves but the fire company, who with
their engines, bell, and horn, and troops of boys screaming "fire"
made no small hubbub.

I was amused by the bakers, who carry with them narrow, flat
pieces of wood on which they notch the number of loaves taken. One
is also kept by the family which they serve. The coal carts with
their black masters was another strange thing. The negroes are so
numerous that one is never reminded, by their absence, of one's being
north of the Potomac. I was standing one day by the Catholic church.
Several boys stood near, and I heard them remarking amongst each
other on the singular sight of the palmetto button [symbol of South

Carolina] I wore. Among other explanations, one said he supposed that "I was a doctor and the button shewed it." One day, whilst standing on the Exchange steps, next to the Girard Bank, three little girls were passing bye. They, after walking slowly, looking up at my hat, passed, their heads still turned gazing at me. One at length turned back, and coming to the foot of the steps addressed me. "Mr., you have got a piece of brass in your hat." I said: "Yes, and I intend it shall stay there." [During the Nullification controversy South Carolina particularism was red-hot.] Indeed, though a common-sized waistcoat button, it attracted considerable attention. The confectionaires and cafes are all in beautiful style, and some of the other establishments beautiful. I bought one or two books, and I believe this is the sum of my seeing, sayings, and doings in the City of Brotherly Love [in the spring of 1833]. . . .

REFLECTIONS ON MAKING A LIVING

Aug. 29. [1833] Thursday, warm. Here is just the fourth return [month] of my day of arrival. [I landed in Savannah, April 29th.] Let us see what has been done in all this time. Read Blackstone once, the first volume. Only got a general and incomplete idea of law, yet I have partly a notion of applying for admission [to the bar] in the fall. I have read in English history through the reign of Henry the Second, and a very sufficient portion of periodical and other light matter. I have scribbled also more rhyme than usual, smoked not very many segars, and eat very little meat. Made no friends but one, and cared for the friendship of but that one. . . .

Penina Moise has published a *Fancy's Sketch Book,* a volume of poems. I have not yet seen it. She is a Jewess, and of universally acknowledged talent, unmarried, though not laboring under any charge of marriability. . . .

I do not love thee; for thy love I sue not. . . .

Sunday. Sept. 7. Poor girl! Poor Charlotte De La Motta! She died this morning about three o'clock. On the Saturday morning before the last, she was in good health. The Saturday following, and not before, she sickened and is now dead. Saturday week only and at her sister's party, she rattled away in the best spirits, and in a week from that hour she was sinking into the grave. She is dead and knows how much she now knows. What would I give for an hour's conversation with her! But perhaps she is no more. Perhaps—oh, these infernal doubts! If the truth we could but grasp and hold. However, what is the use of regretting my ignorance? I shall be informed at some time on all that my soul yearns to know of. It may be but a short week hence. A day. At all events, it will come. So will Sept. 20th. I am convinced that is my [fatal] day, though as to the year, I know not. Savannah is very sickly now [with yellow fever]. Twelve deaths last week and about fifteen or more this. I shall go to this poor girl's funeral this afternoon.

Sep. 22. Sunday, *en soir* ["in the evening"]. This is the day preceding the Day of Atonement, and everybody but myself and Mr. D. Lyon have gone to prayers at Dr. [Moses] Sheftall's. I have not gone, and why? Because there I should have to remain seated, listening to Hebrew chaunted by a voice very well adapted to the pronunciation of that gutteral, harsh, barbarous tongue. This conduct [on my part] is not very politic, for Jews, especially of the first American or the original European generation, do not look very kindly on those who are careless of their [religious?] forms. However, whenever there is a necessity for them to support [one of] two men, though he [be] a Jew but in name, they always rally around him. So, after all, there is no great harm.

I once was serious in the notion of becoming a reader [a "rabbi"]. I was told that the Charleston congregation would support any young man during the course of his studies in England. This, and no religious feeling, prompted my wish. The place, even now I think, would have suited me very well, as there would have been a house furnished me, and a salary of $1,000. Thus, I could with frugality have spent a life of ease, and ease literary is all that I am ambitious of just now. But still my support would have been precarious if I had depended only on this, for certainly a synagogue, as it exists under the present organisation, will not be found in the U. S. fifty years hence. However, my acquirements before that period would have preserved me from want. Indeed, I don't fear want as long as I have health, and who with such a material need fear difficulty in weaving competency from it? If I had not began law, I should almost be inclined to this course even now.

Speaking of schemes suggests another which I entertained for some time, namely, becoming a printer and working at the trade untill I had amassed enough for the purchase of a press, and then becoming editor; indeed, in the year '31, I took a dismission [formal permission to leave] from college with this view. Previous to that, I had an idea of studying mineralogy, etc., professionally. . . . But now, I suppose, I am [to become] a lawyer. That I like law and its technicalities is not the case, but the philosophical part is interesting and has an expanding effect on the mind. In reading Bacon's essays, I was struck with the applicability to myself of the following: "If he be not apt to heat over matters, and call upon one thing to illustrate another, let him study the lawyer's cases," for such is precisely the case with me. I am most unapt at heating over matters. . . .

GOD DAMN THE SKULLS

Well, *revenons aux* [*à*] *nos moutons* ["Let's get back to our subject"]. I was saying I had improved in industry. I can't record any previous week as well spent as the last. This was the routine of my occupations. Up by six, paid devoirs [did my duty] to Cloacina [the toilet], bathed my eyes for ten minutes in cold water, wrote or did nothing. Breakfast, played fiddle until ten, read to eleven, Blackstone until one, Cervantes until two. Dinner. Blackstone until five. Read papers. Supper. Nothing after that, for to use my eyes then is very improper. . . .

I have written more rhyme since my stay here than in all my life past. I have commenced a long flight. I have named it *Cigariad*. It is on the Don Juan model [of Byron], careless and digressive. I find no great difficulty in proceeding, having a plan, and the rhymes help me to more ideas than I would acknowledge to anybody, though it would seem written with but little attention to that particular. It is to treat principally of the pleasures of smoking. I begged [my friend] Currell to give me some hints about the happiness in chewing, and he says he will arrange them into the Juan stanza if I will "promise to insert them *verbatim literatim et punctuatim*" ["words and punctuation literally"]. I wrote this morning before breakfast seventeen stanzas, in part of which I have embodied what Currell calls "my philosophy of conduct," which he promises to discuss in some letter. I must detail my views some of these days in this book. Bless the book.

How easily I am gossipping now, and more pleasantly than if I had some troublesome biped to entertain. It is as improving, too, as the conversation of almost anyone I know in this place. This habit of journalising is one which gives pleasure, and also a disposition to egotism. We mark down everything about ourselves so minutely that at last these trifles are so constantly recalled, and thereby impressed, that we become rather too particular in our observations. It, however, also gives us a very useful habit of examining and analysing our motives and actions. For our confidence in this dumb friend is so great that we do not dread exposure when we spred out our thoughts, as on a dissecting table. I feel as much affection for

this book as I could for a dog, and I always greet it in its own style
—silently—when I look at it. Here I can joke and see no one sneer
at my nonsense, can dilate upon my feelings and thoughts and not
be chilled by apathy or inattention. I run no danger of being misunderstood and offend no one by going beyond their own circle of com-
prehension. . . .

I always had a taste for journalising. It is such a fireside winter-
evening enjoyment. I feel pretty good just now, but somehow I just
thought that I owed $43, and how I shall pay it, [only] Pluto knows.
I contracted it [the debt] in Philadelphia, and expected to pay it
from the proceeds of a speculation in phrenological casts. God dam
the skulls and mine, too. . . .

A Black Day

Sep. 23. Monday. Cool and cloudy. I have just finished a letter in
reply to one from mother, informing me of the engagement of Louisa
[E. Hart] and brother Jacob. I am glad, as I told mother, to the
very bottom (the Rabbins suppose the last and lowest joint of the
backbone the soul's house) of my soul, at the event. She is a fine
girl, and one whom I would wish to remember precisely in mind,
whoever may fall to my lot. She has that feminine delicacy so flattering and endearing to a man. She is so timid, too, and diffident
from a fear of giving offence. So, altogether, brother Jacob is a
lucky man, a very lucky man. This is about four o'clock in Kipur
[Day of Atonement] or Fast Day, which I undergo better than I ever
did before; but when I get hold of the mangeables . . . I will munch.
Nothing has passed down red lane [the throat], and the landlord
below is grumbling at the scarcity of boarders. Never mind. Be quiet,
and you shall be full to your content. . . .

October 16. Thursday. This is *un jour noir* ["a black day"]. I
yesterday felt as I expressed myself in the following lines, and I
will mark down the cause of this feeling. I passed a dog which was
laying before the door of a store in which some men were sitting. One
hawked and spit. I suppose I started a little as if the dog had barked.
I heard a laugh and my blood boiled. Now it is more probable
that the laugh had been occasioned by something else, but, etc.

> To be at the mercy of each careless fool and feel his power
> your heart to burst.
> This is the lot of the Children of Sense.
> This it is to be born to be curst.

To exalt your soul to a Godlike level,
As though it had been on ambrosia nursed,
Then to be fellowed with clods of the earth,
This it is to be born to be cursed.
To hate yourself and all you know,
And those you know best, hate worst,
To be unfriended and friendship disdain,
This it is to be born to be curst.
To search for Truth and have success,
And at its pure well, slake your thirst,
But to feel each draught your torment increasing,
This it is to be born to be curst.

YESTERDAY I COMMENCED CHEWING TOBACCO

Oct. 23. Thursday. Yesterday I comenced chewing tobacco. That morning I had been kept awake about two hours by the toothache, of which I have such horror, that I was engaged all the time in thinking of some method of relief. I recollected the virtues attributed to the weed, and so determined on chewing. So I have bought a paper of Masses Sweet-Scented Fine Cut Tobacco and behold me with a quid in my cheek. I never expected to use it in this manner, but *necessitatis* [sic] *non habet legem* ["Necessity knows no law"]. Old Dr. Sheftall says it is poison, and I almost believe him. I once thought and [that] I was fated to long life and a corporation. Now I look forwards to few days, and the leanes of a consumptive. . . . I took up Blackstone with renewed ardor. It likewise made me feel somewhat lighter of heart when I reflected that, though I had to contend with much, there were others who were compelled to [endure] more severe struggles. Now, this is bad enough that any part of my happiness should spring from contemplating the misfortunes of another.

I got this afternoon a letter from mother. She has had an attack of pleurisy, but is now recovered. When she dies, what will become of me? I shall feel truly desolate. Whenever I think of future prosperity, the pleasure of imparting the news of success to her is so constantly mixed up with my dream, that I expect if I were denied that gratification, I should cease all efforts because they would not lead to that end. Now this is all truth, yet the facts of which I am aware would not lead to such a conclusion. I have never exhibited that attention and kindness which a son should, and it has always been the case. For many years since, I recollect reading the confes-

sions of someone at his mother's tomb, and therein . . . all the faults
of which I was guilty were so feelingly enumerated, that it drew
tears of remorse from me. Indeed, so dreadful were my feelings that
I tore it up, that I might never experience them a second time. However, I was not suckled at her breast. Her ill health compelled her to
give me up to a black woman, and she nurished me. Who knows but
this may have affected me. I do not know it nor do I believe it.

From reading [David] Ramsay's account of the Jews [in his *Universal History Americanized*], I have got a notion that if I had time,
etc., I would write a work and call it *Monumentum Judaicum* ["The
Jewish Monument"]. It should embrace a complete history of the
Jews, a biographical account of their learned men, a critical account
of their writings, etc., etc. This would be the work of a lifetime and
would indeed be a work.

Mother writes me of the misery that Raphael [Moses, of Charles-
ton] has brought on his mother by . . . keeping his store open on
Saturdays. Now, this I would not have done and have . . . some idea
of remonstrating with him on the subject. I am superstitious thus
far as to believe that money made thus will [be] the fruits of disobedience [and] will never really profit a man. Moreover, I believe
that he who is unfilial in his conduct is destined to a sore retaliation.
I do not look on it as a judgement. . . . But I believe the man who
lacks the qualities to make a good son will be deficient in the requi-
sites for a good father. Yes, I will write to him, be the result what
it may. It is my duty as a friend to him and as a nephew. . . .

Oct. 28. Sunday. Cool, third frost this morning. I wrote the letter,
but have not sent it. Perhaps I may not. I have been employed in
this day in the following manner: rose about eight; before and after
breakfast read "Les Oreilles du Conte Chesterfield" in Voltaire's
Romans. It is like all of Voltaire's writing, playful, i.e. playful after
the manner of lightning blasting in its gambols as effectually as the
more ponderous efforts of another element. After that, took too large
a quid of tobacco, which made me as dull as be dam[n]ed and was
obliged to lie down. Read a few pages of [Joseph Marie] Degerand's
on *Self-Education*, and dosed [dozed] the rest of the morning. Got
up about one and commenced translating some verses very witty and
ingenious by Quevedo [y Villegas]. Finished it after dinner. Bad
tran[s]lation. Translated two other letrillas [short poems], one tolerably well. How a little perseverance does carry one on! *C'est le
premier pas qui conte* ["It's the first step that counts"]. Last year
this time I should have been occupied hours in writing what I now
accomplish in a little while. I design offering my *Cigariad*, when

finished, to the publisher of the *Cosmopolitan*, in Charleston. *Cacoethes imprimendi* ["This itch to print!"]. I once intended to send it to Cary and Hart [the Philadelphia publishers], and see what they would do for me; but now *soy menos ambicioso, como digamos en español* ["I am less ambitious, as we say in Spanish"]. . . .

CHRONIC INDECISION

I have lately resumed some thought of offering myself to the Charleston congregation to be educated at their expense for four years in Germany, in that time to qualify myself and . . . return and serve them as hazan [cantor], at a salary of [$]1,000 per annum. This would be a very desirable thing for the following reasons: I should firstly visit Europe; secondly, acquire an excellent education; thirdly, be permanently placed in a respectable office where I could enjoy all that I aspire to—literary ease. Besides what, [it] would be very gratifying to have the reputation of being selected for such an office by the most respectable congregation in America.

All that prevents me from making immediate application is that my principles are such that I should be guilty of actual hypocrisy if I accepted of such an office. How can I pray, who am almost an atheist? How comply with formalities which I despise? How assist and defend doctrines which I abhor? Such is my situation, and I must say that the sincere wish of my heart is that my opinions were the reverse of what they are. For I should not degrade myself by being one of the Orthodox; and if my creed should be erroneous, no evil consequences here or hereafter could result from the error.

It is certainly the safe side to believe in Scripture, etc. But yet, I cannot adopt it, for belief is not the creature of will. I will allow that in reading Ramsay I was struck with the similarity in the event and prediction contained in Deuteronomy, wherein Moses threatens the Jews with the fruit of their disobedience. But then, it is such an old book that I do not feel overdisposed to look on it as the great source of doubt and controversy. I am not happy in my opinions, far from it, and the only satisfaction I ever experience is in the "luxury of hate" and scorn at those who surrender reason and, therefore, are compelled to adopt the most extravagant fables and nonsensical mysteries because these qualities are certain marks of an origin other than human. But, I repeat, I have no calm satisfaction in my opinions, and yet I can[n]ot believe otherwise. However, I have never examined both sides, but shall do so ere long.

RANDOM THOUGHTS OF A DILETANTE

Nov. 24. Sunday. . . . In my last letter from home I am told that a fine school awaits me if I will accept it. I can see that father and mother wish me to take it, though they do not say so. I am not now qualified for it, but I could do so easily. I know I should have a troublesome and rebellious set to deal with, and I have not the years and strength to ensure obedience. I ought to take it, though, for I shall be then *independent*, and lay up something for my support before I can subsist on my practice. But I abhor schoolkeeping, and [my friend] Cole advises me never to engage in it unless compelled by necessity. I should be obliged to be in the country, and have access to but few books. However, I could study thoroughly what I had. But then, how am I to learn the practical part of the [legal] profession but in a lawyer's office, so that after keeping school, I should have to go to one again? All this would bring me to my twenty-sixth year. It is, indeed, a perplexing question, but it is wrong to remain undecided. I believe on the whole I will not; for a man in any profession who is industrious cannot starve. I think that Mr. D. L.[yon] had no other support than his profession, and surely good conduct will raise me up friends; if not, I can blow my brains out. Thank God, I have that resource, which I can fly to, unrestrained by my reason and conscience. . . .

Dec. 3. Tuesday. Very mild and pleasant. In four days' time, I shall be twenty, which I now reasonably consider one-half my life. I shall on that day bring up my accounts and give a full statement of my then situation, etc. I have seen a prospectus of a law school to be established at Augusta. Unless the expense forbids, I will propose to father to send me there. Unless the expense forbids it. How this dam[n]ed poverty stops me at every turn. Shall I ever be rich? Possibly, when wealth is useless, when business has so thrown its tram [m] els around me that, like the dog that turns the wheel, I can only live in the exercise of what makes life loathsome and a burden. Well, God knows what this dam[n]ed, ill-contrived world was made for. Just, I believe, as a purgatory for men, as the Roman amphitheatres were built in splendor and spaciousness to render them more fit for a scene of human torture. How exactly this simile fits! May we not suppose the world a huge amphitheatre, the seats filled by beings of a superior, happier order, who view wretches worried to death by the wild beasts, poverty, misfortune, etc? Wars are the gladiatorial shows, too, and diplomatic controversies ar[e] like them also. Ah, me! And how like, again, are we to those poor wretches whose grief was made more poignant by the sight of the happiness around them, and which, like us, in regard to this fair earth around us, [they] cannot enjoy!

I have been nervous all day from the dam[n]ed tobacco and, having just finished two segars, it [my nervousness] is increased; so, though it is but seven o'clock, I will go to bed, take a book with me, however, and put the candle near. It will hurt my eyes to read. Ah, well can I realise the misanthroping effect of any personal blemish on the mind.

Dec. 7. Saturday. I am twenty years old this day. Can I reckon up twenty happy days, even hours? I, from my soul, wish that no day in the 365 had ever been the epoch of my birth. More anon. . . .

April 4. [1834] Friday. . . . I read in Blackstone . . . since half past nine. I read a great deal too fast today, for I read 200 pages [of Blackstone], and what convinces me of what I was not before dubious, however, is that on going over it tonight, it seemed as if I had hardly ever looked at it. My mind wanders so much when I read that I despair entirely of ever being profound in anything. Everything hurries me off into such a vast and trivial chain of thought that when I recur to what is before me, I feel angry enough to cut my throat. I am now reading at the office in leisure time [Timothy] Pitkin's *Civil and Political History of U. S.* [*Political and Civil History of the United States*], and take notes on it for . . . some nullification essays which I have some idea of preparing. After writing at night, I read [David] Hoffman's *Legal Outlines*. It is a book rather unfit, perhaps, but I want something of the sort. My eyes hold out tolerably, and I have sent to Charleston for a student's lamp.

Miss Anne told me tonight that a gentleman who thought highly of me said I was the most irreligious young man, to which I rejoined in the following sensible manner: "Yes, I have no more Bible religion than that log of wood; and when I begin to grow religious, I shall think I have begun to grow foolish." This was all sincere, but, as the word of God runs, . . . the truth is not fit to be spoken at all times. So, the other day in my first conversation with a young man, I disavowed all belief in a hell or the immortality of the soul. This is all superfluous and useless, but to excite unpopularity, which is speedy poison to one of the profession I have adopted. So I must reform there, too. Ah, well, there are various kind[s] of extravagance in youth, and I daresay others will make allowances for mine; but that is no reason why I should spare myself. I sometimes think, when I do wrong, that other young men do the same, and then I think which of the young men who do so I should care to be classed with. . . .

May 16th. Quite cool. There are many things I would like to write down tonight, but I feel more in the humor of thinking. I feel badly. I am reading Sir W. Jones's [Orientalist and judge of the high court at Calcutta] letters. Oh, that I was such a man! Then my creation would have seemed a rational thing. Now I continually question God's design in making me. To read his letters and those of his noble and learned correspondents, to think of his attainments degrades me beneath the dust. At thirty-three, he determined to undertake no more rudiments. He was then in the expectation of a judgeship (and an English judgeship, too), had published histories, grammars, poems, philosophical and political works, and had acquired twelve languages. Great heavens! One half his learning could make me superior to the first men of the whole state. Ah, well, it is useless to continue this train of thought. I feel deep enough in "the slough of despond" already. What are my acquirements at twenty, as to languages? A superficial *notion* of Latin, Greek, French, and Spanish. A similar acquaintance with politics, metaphysics, and general literature, and a meagre proficiency on flute and violin. As to poetry, God wot [knows]—Ah, I am sick, sick of everything, and most of myself. . . .

Today I received a letter from [my friend] Donnelly. He blames my materialism, but I can overthrow, without arising from my chair, all his objections.

He is really a devout fellow and, though much application, little genius. I will in my next see if I can convert him, if he rests his belief only on such arguments as he has advanced. His understanding is very weak; but then he believes the Bible, and of course can make a final argument by saying: "It is so written." As to the Bible, that puerile, contemptible book, I must believe God, the Word of God giving the best mode of fornication, as Solomon's Song contains. Who can believe such things? *"Credat Judaeus Apella non ego."* ["Let the (credulous) Jew Apella believe it, not I."] By God, I should like to know what is to become of me. Let me see now what the Book of Fate says on the subject. It answers thus: "As the tall column is exalted above the petty ruins which surround its base, so shalt thou rise superior to thy present misfortunes." Well, I will go and consult my pillow farther. Sleep, sleep, grave of the soul. . . . Ah, well!

> Sleep! thou sepulchre of Soul,
> Whose cerements men escape
> But to curse thee: oblivious friend
> With specious Circe's shape.

Awful demon. It [sleep] consumes one half of life, and then offers itself as a relief from the regrets it has occasioned, which are acute, that oblivion is the most eligible resort. I wonder if she will visit me after all this hearty abuse. . . .

A FOOL WAS SORRY FOR ME

May 23, 1834. Friday. A fool told me today, she was sorry for me and I thought whatt I here write:

> *You* are sorry for me!!!
> Eternal God! am I then that *thing*
> As to excite pity!
> Give me deep scorn, without disguise,
> Most rancorous hate, abhorrence,
> Anything, but pity!
> By heaven, 'tis what you feel
> For the unresisting worm you've carelessly crushed
> And you pity it for its impotence,
> To escape or to retaliate.
> Am I so gifted—Am *I*, a poor,
> Crawling, weak, despicable reptile?
> If I am, *then* be *sorry* for me.
> But whilst I feel in my capacious soul
> A comprehensive power to enfold
> Passions that in their expansion
> Would shatter your pigmy soul
> Into indiscernible atoms,
> Dare not to reduce me
> To your petty, pitiful size
> And be sorry for me, as,
> You would for your fellows.

I DON'T LIKE BURR

May 25. Friday [Sunday]. It is possible we may spend the summer in the Sandhills, about twenty-four miles from town. I shall complete the *Cigariad* and endeavor to get Cary and Hart to print a whole volume. I will try to pay the $43 due Barney from its proceeds, but I will be satisfied to get that printed, and won't care a damn for the *compensatio in pecunia* ["monetary reward"]. It would be a bad reputation for a lawyer, but in New Orleans, who will know it, and as for a Savannah reputation—pugh!

May 26. Monday. Pleasant and showery. I was occupied for some hours this afternoon in skimming over Aaron Burr's trial [for treason in 1807]. Some men have lived before their time, as Galileo [the Copernican astronomer] and [the English philosopher] Bacon; but Aaron [Burr] was too late. A man of his ambition and craft should have been a Roman proconsul. In a year he had been [would have been] a Caesar. He should have lived when might was right, and where men directed their enterprizes by views of self-aggrandizement and plunder. What a scheme was his to revolutionize and conquer the vast and opulent empire of Mexico, or perhaps that of these United States! How could he possibly succeed? The only point which circumstances designated as the sole proper *appui* [base] of collection and organization of his army [these United States] was prohibited him irredeemably. How could he, without detection, levy and array forces in the U. S., and where else was it practicable? His lofty ambition overlooked all these inconveniences which were, nevertheless, insurmountable; and when he did fall, it was entangled by these toils which were spread on the very soil he stood and speculated so loftily on.

There was one striking incident in his trial which would be a good hint in a tragedy. One of the jurors was Hamilton Morisson. Burr questioned him. He said in return he had formed no opinion and could not imagine why he feared him unless because his name was *Hamilton*. Burr answered directly: "You are prejudiced." [William] Eaton stands in no very reputable light. By his own confession, he wormed himself into Burr's extended confidence, only in order to betray him. And then, when the whole plot is unfolded, his coward spirit does not urge him to public exposition; but he advises Jefferson to send him on a foreign embassage, as if it were feasible, when Burr had been his bitter opponent, and for many other obvious reasons, obvious even at this time. I could but sneer at Jefferson, the Democrat President, using the terms "we" and "our presence" in a letter to Chief Justice [John] Marshall, regarding a subpoena duces tecum, which Burr urged the court strenuously . . . to issue. This is a low trait in Burr. He had two petty motives: to make his trial more conspicuous by the presence of such a dignitary [Jefferson], and to have the pleasure of braving his antagonist before his face, as insolently as he had in his speeches and writings.

Altogether, I don't like Burr, to see him so perpetually carping at technicalities and playing his attorney tricks off at a solemn scene, where everything was so absorbing and grand. He should have done as Catiline [the Roman conspirator who was verbally attacked by Cicero in the Roman Senate], and listened with unbroken dignity to his accusation. If he was so anxious for life only, he acted contemptibly; and knowing the truth as he did, of the main facts alleged by Eaton, [Senator John] Smith, [General James] Wilkinson, and [Commodore Thomas] Truxton [Truxtun], he should have had the courage to abide the ruins of his bold schemes. So he was in some respects a contemptible dog, and how the chivalrous hearts must have shrunk from the homage they had plighted to such a man as chief. As for myself, had I been his dupe, I do think my mortification would have been excessive. Well, *bon soir* ["good evening"], Aaron Burr. You are now rich as to money, but, oh, how indigent in every other respect! I should like to know his early history. Millions to a cent his education was at first neglected. He was too inconsistent to have been always under the direction of reason, and such eminent reason as he owned. *Pour le second fois, bon, bon soir* ["For the second time, good, good evening"], Mons. Aaron Burr. . . .

This Day Makes Me a Man

June 24. . . . Since I wrote last in this journal I spent a week in the country, in which I did nothing. The week succeeding, I did nothing, and this week I have done less. The truth is my head, eyes, and belly are in bad plight; so if I continue to be as I am for two months longer, I think I may begin to consider an appendix to a *hic jacet* ["Here lies"].

Now it is I feel the fruits of having gone through college as superficially as I did. Did I but understand mathematics now, I could obtain a place in a school here which would yield me about [$]800 or [$]1,000 a year; but it is impossible. I don't know a cubic equation from a simple, and cosines and cotangents are almost cabala to me. But, Lord, I can write 100 trash rhymes very readily, and can play "Hail Columbia" on the fiddle, and can do a heap of things which are useful for all purposes, but that of earning bread, for making me independent. I am sick of myself. . . .

Nov. 7. Friday. Cold and clear. I don't [know] what [to] do, am miserably perplexed. Shall I be admitted to practice [of law] in

January, or wait till May? I learn nothing now. Shall not improve either here, so had as well end the pupilage at once. What a lawyer I shall make! [I] know nothing of theory, much less of practice; abominable, abominable. I wish I could go to Paris and study mining. Wish I had $3,000. Would become a farmer. Wish I had [$]50,000. Would turn literary. Can't have a single wish. Bah! What a miserable [life]! Suppose myself admitted [to the bar]. Where shall I go? To New Orleans.

Currell says I may die before I am known. He speaks a severe truth, but what can a man make of himself unless he is in the region of intelligence, i.e. in a city? A fellow must star[v]e where food is not to be had. . . .

December 7th, 1834. Sunday, cloudy. This day makes me a man. I am twenty-one.

Wednesday, Dec. 17th. . . . I have been in a state of great uneasiness of mind on account of a seriously entertained resolution to quit law. Every day more and more convinces [me] that my legal career will be a failure; yet circumstances, God confound them, prevent my relinquishing the profession. Deeply convinced as I am of the inutility of its pursuit, I do not disguise from myself that I am indolent, but I feel that one reason of it is that I have nothing to tempt me to energetic exertion. I believe if I had studied medicine, things would have worn another aspect. It is a study which is pleasing in all its features to me. All these considerations induced me to ask sister her opinion as to my contemplated step, and she dissuades by representing to me the fact that the news would have a serious effect on the feelings of father and mother. I knew it would, and so can't determine to wound them so deeply. I do wish to God that I had never been born. I seriously declare that I am unfit for the world in every possible way. What is to be my fate? God only knows.

Savannah. April [1835]. Friday. Good. Commenced boarding with Mrs. Davenport at the rate of $5 per week on Monday last past. What day of the month, I know not. Accuracy was never characteristic of me; indeed, no other practical thing is component of my microcosm. Alas, alas! What thoughts those two words do indicate!

Well, to put down the actual particulars of the few last months: After examination and admission [to the bar], two days, I set out for Charleston in the steamboat. Got to Ch[arlesto]n on Sunday A.M. Walked up the streets with as little feeling of novelty, desire, anxiety as if it had been all a daily scene, and stupid at that besides. Met father and sister, aunt, and Ralph. Remained for about ten days. Set out in company with father, sister, and Lenna. Got *home* about 4:00

A.M. Kissed mother, shook the dear captain's hand, greeted dear Theo, retired, and slept until breakfast. Well, the first thing was a discussion as to "location." God blast the . . . to hell! I, for reasons I must strive to forget, had chosen that emporium of wine, women, and segars, etc., etc., N.[ew] Orleans. Strenuously, and on good grounds, [I] opposed Savannah. Concluded on—dinner bell rings.

Clara L. Moses

War Days in Old Natchez

In 1929, Mrs. Clara Lowenburg Moses (1865-1951), a native of
Natchez, Mississippi, published a collection of memoirs and stories
for her nieces and nephews. She had no children of her own, and
after the death of her husband, Abram Moses, lived with relatives.
The children called her Aunt Sister, and the reminiscences which
she wrote and the stories she recounted were published as Aunt Sister's Book *(New York, 1929).* The following material is culled from
that work.

In Aunt Mellie's story *(pp. 1-14),* Clara Moses portrayed the fortunes of her grandparents, the John Mayers, as told to her by Aunt
Melanie Mayer Frank. Clara Moses' uncle by marriage, Sam Ullman,
recounted in a letter *(pp. 15-19)* his impressions of his mother-in-
law, Mrs. John (Jeanette Reis) Mayer.

Both these accounts give us an intimate, romantic picture of life
in a Mississippi River town during the Civil War period.

Aunt Mellie's Story of the War Between the States

In the beginning of the year 1800, one of your great-great-grand-parents, dear children, lived in Landau, France. His name was Simon Levy, and he and his wife, Jeanette Rachel Mayer, were comfortable and happy with their three sons and one daughter. But one of the boys was dissatisfied at home, and so ran away and settled in Paris, where he apprenticed himself to a shoemaker, and became a master of his trade. He was so afraid his father would find him and make him come home that he changed his name from Mayer Levy to Jacob Mayer. But his life in Paris during the 1820's was anything but pleasant, and he soon decided to embark for America.

One bright morning in October, 1833, a sailing vessel, hailing from Havre de Grace, landed at Nouvelle Orléans [New Orleans], after a most unpleasant voyage of ninety days, during which time the provisions and water became so scarce that each person aboard ship received only a small portion daily.

Among the passengers was Jeanette Reis, a beautiful French girl of fifteen years, who with her parents, sisters, and brother had come to the New World, believing that there Dame Fortune would be kinder to them than she had been in Obernai or Auperney, France. Jacob Mayer, now a young man of twenty-seven, was also one of the many passengers. During the voyage, he had often been attracted by the grace and beauty of the young French girl, and before the end of the journey had discovered that an affinity of souls existed be-tween them. It seemed to be a work of destiny in the lives of these two emigrants to a foreign land, for as each became a resident of Nouvelle Orléans their friendship became strengthened, and gradu-ally ripened into a love companionship for life. On the twenty-fifth of April, 1835, Jeanette Reis and Jacob Mayer were married, and they, dear children, are your great-grandparents.

During the first five years of a most happy union, while still living in Nouvelle Orléans, two sons and a daughter, Maurice, Emma, and Simon, were born to them.

Shortly after, in 1841, they moved to Natchez, Mississippi, and the other children who came to bless and enliven their home were

Caroline, Ophelia, your grandmother, Henry, Clementine, Melanie (myself), Adelaide, Theresa, John Jr., Benjamin, Eleanor Louisa, and Joseph Eggleston Johnston.

John, as he was now called, worked diligently at his trade, and eventually built up a fine business in which the elder sons were able to assist. The daughters, beautiful and lovely girls, attracted many friends, and life seemed only made for fun and gayety, music, dancing and songs.

In the years between 1860-65 stirring events changed their whole manner of living, for these were the years of the cruel War Between the States. Simon, the second son, Simon Lehman, and Oscar Levy, nephews, who had recently come to live with us from Landau, Germany, enlisted in the Confederate Army, and left Natchez in 1861. They were brave soldiers and at the close of the war returned covered with honors.

Brother Simon [Mayer] escaped being killed at the battle of Franklin, Tennessee, because he was of such low stature, being only four feet eight inches in height. He was galloping madly on his big horse through the lines, carrying a message to his general's headquarters, when a bullet aimed at him passed through his high campaign hat, but missed his head. He was reported as dead to his parents, but when mother and sister Emma were about to leave to bring his body home for burial a telegram came contradicting the sad report. His youthful appearance and small stature did not, however, keep brother Simon from being advanced to the rank of major and aide-de-camp on the staff of brave General Sharp.

One day General Sharp and his staff were invited, while in Tennessee, to a "fowl dinner." The dinner was a great occasion, as the poor Confederate soldiers had been living on very short rations. The table, decked with dainty linen, fine silver and cut glass, and laden with good things to eat, looked very beautiful to the smoke-begrimed eyes of the half-starved soldiers. As the officers filed in, General Sharp was assigned the seat of honor, and as the hostess took her seat, she said, motioning to brother Simon: "The seat next to you, General Sharp, is for your little boy."

"Madam," replied the general, "that little boy is my brave aide-de-camp, Major Simon Mayer."

Captains Steve Rumble and T. Otis Baker, Natchez comrades, have often told us stories of the bravery and kindness of the "Little Mississippi Major," as he was called in the army, and of how he often dismounted from his fine big horse to let some poor wounded soldier ride while he himself walked.

After the Yankees had taken New Orleans, before the fall of Vicksburg, the gunboats from Farragut's fleet passed up and down the river from time to time. Fearing that some of them would land at Natchez and take the town, all the older men who were left at home formed themselves into a company to resist such attempts; their weapon, rifles, against the cannon of the gunboats. The ringing of the courthouse bell was to be the signal for all to assemble at the courthouse yard prepared to fight.

On the second of September, 1862, the gunboat "Essex" was anchored in front of our wharf boat. Being a very hot day, some of the men came to shore to buy ice. The courthouse bell immediately rang out a wild alarm. Our family were at their noonday meal when the cries of "The Yankees have come ashore" were heard in the streets, and our father soon had his hat and gun and had rushed to join his comrades to protect his town and home. Soon the gallant little company, under the command of Douglas Walworth, marched in double-quick time down the hill leading to the river and fired a volley upon the imaginary intruders. But, alas, in quicker time they "marched up the hill again," for soon the bursting sound of shell was heard in all directions, and for two hours it seemed that our dear town and all its people were to be destroyed, all because our brave men, in the love of home and family, had been a little too precipitate in the zealous performance of duty.

Owing to the situation of our city on such a high bluff the shells fell against the hill and over the town. One of the shells was lodged in one of the pillars of the front porch of the Stanton house, thus saving that beautiful old home from destruction. I have in my possession an iron ball taken from a piece of bursted shell that was found several years after in the hill near my present home. Rosalie Beekman, aged seven years, was the only victim. She was struck by a piece of bursting shell while she and her family were seeking refuge from their home "under the Hill." She died during the night at our home on Main Street, where she had been brought for medical attention by her cousin, Miss Miriam Wexler.

Not content with the cruel punishment of shelling Natchez, the officers of the "Essex" sent word to the mayor that they would go further up the river, but would return in three days and burn the town. Imagine, dear children, the consternation of the terror-stricken people. Father bought a house in Washington, five miles from Natchez, a carriage and pair of horses, and mother, the younger children and sister Carrie were removed from the home in Main Street to our temporary home in Washington. Father, Henry, Emma,

and Ophelia remained in Natchez to pack all the household goods
and the merchandise in father's store, for he had, at that time, the
largest and most fashionable shoe store in town.

The gunboat did return on the third day and passed quietly down
the river. Our father resumed his business, Emma and Ophelia kept
house for him in town, while the rest of the family remained in
Washington. Mr. and Mrs. Tillman and their son Cassius were with
us in Washington also. Theresa, Cassius, and I came in town every
Monday and remained until Friday to attend school.

On the twenty-second of October, a fine little boy was born, and
mother named him Joseph Eggleston Johnston Mayer, after one of
the brave Confederate generals. Ella was eighteen months old, and
Mr. Tillman, who loved nicknames, called her, as did all of us,
"Confederate Ellell."

Our father, having more Confederate money than he wished to
keep, bought the big house on the hill on Monroe Street. Mother
and the children came in town when Joe was a month old and
occupied the new house, which you have learned to call the "old
home," and where we all grew to manhood and womanhood, were
married, and where many of the children of the third generation
were born.

After the fall of Vicksburg, in July, 1863, the Yankees took possession of Natchez. At this time Henry Frank, Isaac Lowenburg, and
John Hill came into our family life and helped to make its history.
They were in the commissary department of the Union Army. They
had visited our father at his store, the two former making themselves known as Jews, and father, the president of the Hebrew
[*Hebra*] *Kadusha* ["Holy Brotherhood"] Congregation, invited them
to attend the services during the Holy Days. We had no temple nor
weekly services, but during Roshashona and Yom Kippur ["New
Year" and "Day of Atonement"] some of the members officiated at
services held upstairs in the old engine house on North Union Street.

Father invited these new acquaintances to visit his family, and,
being cordially received, they became frequent visitors. Many were
the heated discussions between these Yankees and our rebel family,
until mother forbade political wrangling, but encouraged social
affinity, prompted by her usual tact and good sense, to say nothing
of her clever foresight, for two of these hated Yankees became loved
and loving sons to our dear parents.

Once during the war the soldier boys had written home that
they needed boots, shoes, socks, shirts, trousers, everything, it
seemed, but how could such contraband goods be sent to Confederate

soldiers? A fine scheme was planned. Our friend, Henry Frank, promised to get passes for mother, Emma, and Carrie to pass through the Union guards at the city limits, where friends living in the country would meet them and forward the clothes. Fortunately, the women in those days wore great hoop skirts, and under these, around their waists, mother, Emma, and Carrie hung all the needed articles. Thus laden, they were helped into the carriage, and were driven to the city limits, where the passes had to be examined. With fear and trembling, Emma handed the guard the papers. Imagine her delight when she noticed that he was trying to read them upside down! "Any contraband goods?" and all being fair in love and war, they answered "No." "Drive on then and have a nice day with your friends," was the pleasant rejoinder of the ignorant unsuspecting guard.

And now, dear children, I must tell you about a wedding which took place in our family toward the close of the war. On the twenty-seventh of January, 1864, the wedding of sister Carrie to Mr. Julius Weis was to be celebrated, and on the same evening Miss Babette Weis was to be married to Mr. Philip Wexler. We had no rabbi in our congregation, so the ceremony was performed by Judge Bullock of the Chancery Court. The parlor was beautifully decorated for the joyous occasion. A large number of guests had been invited and were assembled to witness the double ceremony. After the usual congratulations, all were invited to partake of the supper served on the back gallery, which had been canvased and appropriately decorated, and well lighted by gas, many candles, and lamps, for we had no electric lights in those days. The big gallery made a fine banquet hall, and all went as merrily as a marriage bell. Many toasts were drunk, with choice wines and champagne, to the two bridal couples. After lingering for some time at the table to the sound of music produced by a small band of colored musicians, many of the young folks were ready to dance in the long hall and through the rooms.

Suddenly there were sounds of the tramping of many feet on the front gallery, quickly followed by the beating of tin pans, tooting of tin horns, blowing of shrill whistles, with shouting and yelling of many voices, a regular charivari. This sort of serenade was always considered an insult instead of a compliment, but the Yankee soldiers only wanted to have some fun at a wedding in a rebel family, because none of them had been invited. Brother Jules could not see the funny side of the situation, and he became very angry, and wanted to rush out and pitch all of the soldiers over the hill. Had he gone out, most probably there would have been blood shed. How well I recall the picture of mother, brother Maurice, Henry Frank, and Isaac Lowenburg holding on to brother Jules' coat-tail to keep him from getting out the front door. After the excitement had somewhat subsided, brother Maurice went around the house and invited the soldiers to come around through the yard to the back gallery and have a drink. The wedding table was soon besieged by these rude men, and in a short time, all refreshments had disappeared as if by magic.

Now, they were really merry, for the wine and champagne had not been spared. They began to sing, and many of them jumped upon the table and began to dance, unmindful of the glassware. Brother Maurice felt that this was more than he should permit, and speaking to the captain, he advised him to take his soldiers away and immediately, or he would go at once and report him to headquarters. His threat had the desired effect, and the whole squad were soon heard tramping through the yard and down the long wooden steps as noisily as they had come. The gayety of the occasion had had a sudden ending. Most of the guests had left, and this wedding night has passed into the family history as one never to be forgotten—a sad souvenir of the cruel Civil War.

Shortly after the surrender at Vicksburg of Pemberton's Confederate Army to General Grant, General [T. E. G.] Ransom with his brigade was sent to take possession of Natchez. His headquarters were in the beautiful Wilson home overlooking the river. Natchez was under martial law. General Ransom was a gentleman, considerate of the humiliation of a conquered people, and soon won the favor and esteem of the citizens, but after several months he was ordered to take charge of some other post, and General [Mason] Brayman placed in his command at Natchez. Not content to occupy the same headquarters used by General Ransom, he chose the stately home of George Malen Davis, later occupied by Stanton College. General Brayman was a true type of the selfish conqueror: he had not the courage to be strong and firm yet kind to the subdued; he rejoiced in the distress which the cruel war brought to our fair Southland, and to its noble men and women. He resorted to the basest means to make them feel that they would eventually be overcome. Through the medium of well-paid spies, he learned that many of our young women were in constant correspondence with their soldier boy friends in the Confederate Army.

On one certain day one of his female spies, whose name I prefer not to give you, dear children, delivered a large batch of letters to him. Among them was one written by my sister Ophelia, your dear grandmother, in which she wrote of the removal of General Ransom and said: "In his place we have a miserable tyrant, Brayman, in command here." These words were thought very rebellious, and as each of the letters contained expressions of hatred and enmity against General Brayman, before sunset, Ophelia and twenty other women were arrested and placed in confinement in the City Hall, near the market, which building is still standing and in use for the meetings of the mayor and board of aldermen. Through the kind intervention of Henry Frank and Isaac Lowenburg, who knew Lieutenant Marble, the officer of that day, brother Henry was permitted to remain with her that night. Next day, being in a highly nervous condition with much fever, she was allowed to be taken home, through the kindness of Lieutenant Parker, the officer of that day, and a personal acquaintance of our good friends Henry Frank and Isaac Lowenburg.

Our home was surrounded by guards; no one was permitted to leave the house for three days. Father's store was closed, and all the merchandise, as well as the home with all its effects, would have been confiscated had not our good Yankee friends used their influence to the contrary. Ophelia's spirit was not subdued, but her health became much affected. Mr. Tillman, who nicknamed her "Old Kentuck," admired her for her spunk in writing the truth about the meanness of General Brayman. He once offered to buy her a French calico dress costing at that time $1.50 per yard if she would make and wear a blue cotton dress, such as the slaves wore, and walk down Main Street. She accepted the dare, and was soon on Main Street again dressed in her fine French calico.

She had many admirers, but none so ardent as Isaac Lowenburg. She had refused his attentions and his frequent proposals for her hand in marriage, for she believed him to be a Yankee and against the sentiment of the Southerners, since he came with the Federal Army. But when she learned to know him as a man of sterling worth, she realized that in him she would find congeniality of spirit for the rights to which she had been so loyal, a sincere protector and true defender. A final proposal was received and sanctioned by our parents, and on the fourth of January, 1865, they were married by Judge Thacher, a neighbor and close friend of our family, at the dear home, in the same room where one year before the double wedding ceremony had been solemnized. Our parents, profiting by experience, invited several of the officers of the Federal Army who had been kind to Ophelia and to the family during the trying ordeal of the days of the imprisonment.

Father [Jacob Mayer] lived to be seventy-five years of age, respected and honored for an upright, high-principled man, and mother lived only a year and a half longer. She died at the age of sixty-five, a woman of high ideals, who spared no pain or trouble in doing kindness to others. Intelligent, sympathetic, light-hearted and happy, she made her home, even in the darkest days, a haven of peace and pleasantness. She was a director in the Protestant Orphanage in Natchez and a friend to all the sorrowful. Her house was, as she often said every house should be, "as large as its mistress' heart," and there was always room for some homeless one. She was a fine nurse and during the terrible yellow fever epidemic organized a regular nursing corps, and joined the brave men and women who daily offered their lives in the cause of humanity. She was one of the women who began the planting of trees and the beautifying of the city cemetery in 1865. Her home was the center of all Jewish festivities, and at the long dining table (which had been bought from Judge Thacher and at which George Washington had once dined) there were often seated as many as thirty-five guests on Passover Eve, the feast of Seder, which was always celebrated with much pomp and ceremony.

Her stories were really wonderful, and many of them have never been forgotten; the children who heard them adored her, and she in her pureness of heart was like a little child with sympathy for their troubles and sorrows.

So to the end every one who knew her even casually felt the great influence of her noble soul. This is an ancestress of whom to be proud.

GRANDMOTHER MAYER

Birmingham, Alabama,
February 20, 1923

My Dear Clara:

I am about to attempt to give you some of my impressions of your sainted Grandmother Mayer. When I say sainted I mean all that this word implies, that is, a sainthood that is created in the hearts and minds of men. To do this, I conceive, I must go far afield to give you a perspective of what dear old Natchez was when I cast my lines within her borders.

At the outset I will have to ask you to throw the mantle of your charity in the use I make of the first (personal) pronoun. I am not attempting to write my biography, nor that of the sainted subject; I am not gifted to do her full justice.

I came to Natchez in July, 1865, almost a stranger. I was attracted there by the fact that there were two companies from Natchez in the Sixteenth Mississippi Regiment of which I was a humble member. I was further induced to make it my home, rather than Port Gibson (where I was raised), because of the larger field indicated.

The Jewish Community then was small, with little organization; what there was of it was extremely Orthodox and was known as the *Chevra Kadusha,* i.e., "Holy Society." At the nominal head was Mr. A. Beekman, with David Moses, Aaron Roos, M. D. Marks, Seligman and Mayer Shatz, Old Man Isaacs, Old Man Meyer (father of Victor and Adolph Meyer), and a few others, principally Polanders. What services they had were conducted in a fire engine house that stood then on Commerce Street near Benjamin's place. It was a very rare thing to see a woman present or a child. The situation to my mind was a tragedy.

I came in touch with your father, Isaac Lowenburg, Henry Frank, John Mayer, Charles Katz, Joseph Levy, Philip Wexler, and a few others, and found them in accord with my ideas of Reform, but they were more or less doubtful of attaining it. To do so meant to interest our women. A meeting was called and we met in the "Old Home on the Hill." The most interested person was your grandmother. She entered into the spirit of the idea with her heart and soul. She saw that the children were growing up like heathen. This pointed to the need of a Sunday school. I was asked to start one. My assistant, Emma Mayer, became my wife two years later. She made it a success.

It took but little time for me to discover that whatsoever reputation or character our people had was given to them by the Mayer family, the big spirit of which was your grandmother. To her fell the lot and duty to organize our women. Her spiritual, magnetic enthusiasm made them all willing workers. To her must be given the credit for the building of our temple, more so than any other. She was at the head of a number of fairs, which were handsomely rewarded because Mrs. Mayer and Mrs. Tillman were behind them. Of course there were others: your mother, Aunt Mellie, Mrs. P. Wexler, Mrs. S. Schatz, Bertha Katz, Emma Roos; Mrs. Roos, half-hearted, because of her husband's orthodoxy. The Beekmans, the Moseses, and a few of their followers gave little or no assistance and encouragement.

I was elected president of the congregation, the name of which had been changed to what it is today [B'nai Israel]. The congregation grew in every way, day by day; the Sunday school yielded fine results. The women, under the leadership of your grandmother, overcame the main obstacles in the way, and our temple was dedicated in 1871, and she was enshrined in the hearts of all people as a mother of Israel.

I am sure that in your memory is stored away those delightful visits to the old home nearly every Friday night and on holidays. It was like retouching the strings of the sacred harp. Cheer, fellowship, good will were the order of the evening. It was a family gathering where all drank deeply from the fountain of love, and life, as it were, was made over again, each one feeling the better fitted to meet the struggle of tomorrow.

You possibly recollect Bishop Elder. Along in the early seventies he was tendered a banquet reception by the Catholics of Natchez on his return from Rome. Your grandmother, and I think Mrs. Tillman, were the only non-Catholics invited. That was a measure of appreciation that worth alone invokes. You know that she was a director for many years of the Protestant Orphan Asylum, and if I mistake not, its president for a term or two. You may also recollect that she caused Dr. David Stern (along about the early eighties), who was our rabbi, to give a lecture, "Idealism vs. Materialism," for the benefit of the Protestant and Catholic orphan asylums. The lecture was a master's work. It brought Natchez together, dedicating them, as it were, to a recognition of the brotherhood of man.

The fields of charity, relieving distress, nursing the sick through the epidemics of yellow fever, regardless of color or race, was to her a means of bringing home the best concepts of religion. Hence it was that she became beloved, revered, and esteemed by everybody. She became a comforter when gloom entered a home, a Florence Nightingale where plague held sway—all this because she had faith in a better humanity.

One may question the doctrine of immortality, of a life beyond this. In Grandma's immortality is a verity and a reincarnation. She was a product of a Jewish home life at its best—such a life is an achievement reached by few—a legacy that enriched all who knew her. She lived long enough to pass through trials that tested her love, her patience, but they left no shadow behind, and today her personality comes to our mind when we look for a womanhood to guide us to that goal where strife and prejudice have no place.

Uncle Sam Ullman.

Rebecca Gratz

The Idol of Her Generation

During the ante-bellum period, Rebecca Gratz (1781-1869) was probably the outstanding Jewess in the United States. For reasons unknown to us, she never married. There is a family tradition that she was in love with a Gentile but refused to marry out of the faith.

Though she was very active in philanthropic work in the larger general community, much of her life was devoted to charitable organizations providing for Jewish women and children in her native Philadelphia.

In 1838 she founded what may well have been the first Jewish Sunday school in this country. It was fashioned after similar Christian Sunday schools, some of which had their origin also in Philadelphia.

Miss Gratz was a woman of considerable culture and a prolific writer of letters. The American Jewish Archives has copies of over a thousand letters which she wrote to her family and friends. Many of the literary figures of the North were her friends, among them Washington Irving. According to family tradition, she was the original of the Rebecca in Sir Walter Scott's Ivanhoe. There is, however, no authentic evidence to confirm this claim.

From the four portraits of her by Thomas Sully it is quite apparent that she was a very attractive woman. It is inevitable that this cultured, charming, socially acceptable person would exert a strong influence in her own circle, especially on the impressionable younger generation.

One young lady, a niece, had a "crush" on her "sainted" Aunt Rebecca. This was Sarah Ann Hays (1805-1894), who, in June, 1836, married Captain Alfred Mordecai, the distinguished ordnance expert. Consequently, Sarah's Recollections of My Aunt, Rebecca Gratz, by "One of Her Nieces" (Philadelphia, 1893) is a very subjective and sentimental sketch; nevertheless, it throws light on a woman who was very much admired in her day by many people.

The Recollections, which are reprinted here, were written in February, 1870, about six months after the death of Miss Gratz; they were not published until a year before the death of Sarah Hays Mordecai.

A Bright Ornament of Society

This little memoir was written twenty-two [three] years ago [1870], and has been hid from the light all that time, but now I feel that the time has come, if ever, for its use.

Those who knew my aunt, and were her friends and c[on]temporaries, have gone, one by one, to their rest, and I feel that my time is drawing near, and that no one will be left to record the memory of Rebecca Gratz, the gifted woman of her time, or to say her praise, as the original of Scott's Rebecca in *Ivanhoe*. . . .

I write this to save from oblivion and forgetfulness the memory of one of the brightest ornaments of society, one of the most useful and holy of the children of Israel, one who from my earliest day I was taught to consider *perfect*.

My beloved mother [Richea Gratz, born 1774] always looked up to her with affection and pride, and we, her children, were taught to share with her the love and reverence which my aunt inspired from all. Yesterday while listening to the prayer (*Eschabas*) said to her memory—"Who has found a virtuous woman, for her price is far above rubies"—I naturally enough began to think of my sainted aunt, Rebecca Gratz, and it was with feelings of almost horror that I thought, though my children knew her, my grand-children might never know that such a person existed. The memory of her will be forgotten, and that great light which shone upon us will leave no sign behind, and weak and feeble as my pen is, and unfitted to contemplate or tell of her perfections, I feel impelled to use it in trying to carry, for at least one generation, her beautiful character and pious ways. "The righteous are taken from the evil to come," but should their memory die with them?

She whom we all honored in life was full of years, having lived to the blessed age of eighty-eight; and as we are told that length of years is a heritage from the Lord, we may so presume that in that way he "blessed his hand-maiden," and gave her many years to perpetuate her life and be as a beacon and light to her generation and to her people, and to the people among whom she lived. As Abraham was a prince among the people where he dwelt, so was

273

Rebecca Gratz a princess among her own people, who looked up to her with pride for the position she held among her own people and among the "strangers" [Gentiles] by whom she was surrounded.

Born of Jewish parents, who brought her up in the strict faith of their fathers, she had but few associates among her own people in her early days, but I do not believe she was ever swerved from the religion of her fathers. She idolized her parents, particularly her mother, and to the latest day of her life she never ceased to reproach herself for one act of disobedience to her, which she never forgot or forgave herself for.

Her friends were very numerous, and among the Gentiles, among whom she dwelt, she had one, then living in New York, dearly loved and prized, and a constant correspondent. This friend died of fever, and our dear aunt, to show her grief and affection, wished to wear the garb of mourning. Her good, amiable mother opposed it, but she yielded to the wishes of her own heart and youthful friendship, and put it on. Before the year of black expired she had to deepen it for that beloved mother, and so tender was her conscience, so deep her self-upbraiding, that to the day of her death, forty years after at least, she would relate to me this act of *disobedience*, which she never could cease to reproach herself with. . . .

I have always admired my grandparents, as [Gilbert] Stuart [the painter] has represented them lifelike as they appear together over the sofa in their gilded frames. The sweet placidity of my grandmother [Miriam Gratz] with her folded white hands in her lap, her brilliant black eyes and intelligent face, mingled with sweetness, and a ladylike composure over the whole, which convinces you she was a sweet, quiet, gentle lady. My grandfather [Michael Gratz] was equally quiet and gentlemanly, with a degree of languor over him, which showed he had not the strength to battle with the ills as well as the prosperity of life, but nothing of weakness. [Sully, not Stuart, painted the Michael Gratz portrait.]

The subject of this little memoir was born on the fourth of March, and as long as I can remember back her natal day was celebrated by her nieces and nephews, and then by her great-nieces and nephews.

How well I remember her eightieth birthday [1861]! Draped in a handsome silk dress and new cap, she was seated in her comfortable, warm chair to receive her friends and her relations on this memorable day. She appeared to be fully aware of the great event, and her face was draped in smiles, and each gift and good wish she received with loving pride and affection. She had cakes and flowers, pincushions and little mats, the handiwork of her nieces, and every-one brought some little offering. She would rise and accept the gift with smiles and thanks, and, quite overpowered, exclaim: "You make me feel so humble with your gifts. I am not worthy of all this." . . .

SHE WAS SUCH AN ELEGANT WOMAN

When I was young I used to hear all my young friends and their mothers admire my aunt, "Miss Gratz." She was such an "elegant woman, so handsome, so refined." "She graced the ball last night. She and her brother, Mr. Hyman Gratz, were the handsomest people in the room." As a child I was flattered at this notice of my aunt, whom my beloved mother always taught me to revere, but it was not until after years that the greatness, and I may say nobleness, of her character dawned upon me. An acquaintance with the world taught me how far superior she was to those I mingled with, how quiet and unobtrusive in all her elegance, how modest when referred to and admired. How beautiful in thought and feeling her letters can only show, as they often did to all her relations, for to them she was always a ministering angel. Coming to them in sorrow, with affection in one hand and religion in the other, she always healed the wound she came to bind. Her soothing words came to comfort me once at the death of a little child, which I lost after a short illness. Her words soothed me more than any other; they appeared to reach the right place and give me ease. Words at that time appeared useless, but hers were inspired to me and I felt them. . . .

This is not a memento of statistics, but of *love*. I have not yet said where Rebecca Gratz was born, or in what year. She was born in Philadelphia, March 4th, 1781; died August 29th, 1869. I have not yet said where she was educated, what famous school she was edu-cated in, or what honors she took in it; but in those days education was very primitive and no school was famous.

I have heard her in late days tell an anecdote of her school, which sounded very amusing to my ears, and I will put it here. I have forgotten the name of the schoolmistress, but it was a large school, with rows of children sitting on benches the whole length of the room. She said that just as the clock struck twelve a short recess would be proclaimed and the door opened. A tall gentleman, the brother of the schoolmistress, would appear, dressed in the height of the costume of that day—cocked hat, powdered hair, queue, blue coat and metal buttons, short knee breeches and shoe buckles,

white stockings, ruffled shirt. He would walk up the row of benches
and girls to the platform, where the schoolmistress was, take off his
hat, bow over her hand and say: "Good morning." He would then
pull out a snuffbox, open it and ask her to take a pinch of snuff,
close it and walk back again through the girls to the door, and out.
This happened *every day regularly*. "I can see the old gentleman
now," she would add. "And did he never say anything more?"
"No, never; he disappeared just as he came, and never spoke to
anyone but his sister."

It has been said that women had less education in those days,
perhaps less in the "ologies," but my aunt was conversant with
Burns, and Pope, and Milton, and even to her last days would repeat the "Universal Prayer" [by Alexander Pope], "Edwin and
Angelina" [by Oliver Goldsmith], Scott's Ellen in the *Lady of the
Lake*, and many other poems. She also repeated beautiful snatches
of poetry and would say: "Where is that from, do you know?" And
I had often to confess myself at fault. One verse she particularly
dwelt upon. One day she repeated it so often that I retained it:

> Let me, like Israel, hope in God;
> This name alone implore,
> Both now and ever trust in Him
> Who lives for evermore. . . .

My aunt was always efficient, no matter where placed or by whom
called upon. A board of twenty-four ladies, of whom she was one,
were the founders of the Asylum for Orphans in Philadelphia
[1815], and for forty years she acted as secretary and member of
the purchasing committee. Those who have read her annual reports
may see the beauty of her language and the simplicity of her style.
Every succeeding year her reports were read with interest, and each
one differed from the other, and all were alike beautiful to my mind.
I have never read such beautiful language as hers. Her letters, and
she had many correspondents, are unparalleled—the flow of her
language so easy, her ideas new and brilliant, her words natural,
affectionate. Of all the famous letter writers whose letters have been
published, not one can compare to her.

She was always accustomed, from her childhood, to the best society, and, when a girl, the Ogdens, Go[u]verneurs, Hoffmans, Fennos, Washington Irving, James Paulding, Sam. Ewing, the choicest
wits of the time, were her intimates, and all admired and appreciated
her. She and her two beautiful sisters were the toast of the club and
of the day, as "The Graces," slightly altering "The Gratzes." They

were beautiful women, as two miniatures I have copies of by Malbone, which he took when they were about twenty years old, can testify; and they were good as well as beautiful.

As I am writing for those who come after me, I may as well tell them that Sir Walter Scott is said to have taken his heroine, Rebecca, in his *Ivanhoe*, from Rebecca Gratz, and truly he could not have chosen a nobler type of a Jewish maiden than she was. It is said, and I believe in good sincerity, that Washington Irving carried the memory of my aunt abroad with him. They had been sincere friends, and Mr. Irving had been in love and engaged to a sweet friend of hers, Matilda Hoffman, who died very young and left Washington Irving's life a lonely one ever after. Aunt Rebecca was her friend and his, and when he went abroad and visited the great novelist, Sir Walter Scott, Washington Irving told him, one day, sitting in his study, of the Rebecca who was a Jewess, and who was beautiful and brave in her faith, and adhered to the one only God, and he put her in his story of *Ivanhoe*. And then he sent the first copy to Washington Irving and asked him how he liked his Rebecca, which he had portrayed from his account of her.

There was some story of my aunt's struggles with love and religion, but duty conquered, as it always did with her, when opposed to inclination. My aunt, Rebecca Gratz, was an old maid, at least in the common acceptance of the term. True, she never married, but she was a mother to the orphan and destitute, to the friendless and oppressed, to those in poverty and want, and to the sinner and contrite.

LABORS OF LOVE

But it was among her own people she shone most conspicuously. There her labors were truly of love. She saw the young of her people growing up in ignorance of their faith, and she conceived and executed the idea of a "Sunday school," to be held in some room where the children would assemble to hear the word of God, to learn his commandments, and receive instruction in the religion of Israel. She, with other ladies, founded the institution [1838], and for years she was its president and head.

Every Sunday her steps were bent to the room appointed. Her majestic figure rose high above all there collected, a hundred scholars or more, to hear her mild and firm voice read a chapter of the Holy Bible, and then they, in unison, repeated a prayer written for them by herself, which combined "all prayer." She appointed and arranged all the teachers, and conducted the school with a dignity and modesty which pervaded all her works. The children looked up to her with reverence and admiration, their parents with gratitude and love. . . .

Her good works did not cease here. The [Female] Hebrew Benevolent Society [1819] was the work of her hands. She reared and fostered it, and cared and toiled for it and made it what it is, a society doing good to all our people, clothing the naked, feeding the hungry, and giving them assistance in every way.

The [Ladies' Hebrew] Sewing Society had its first impulse from her hands [1838]. The Fuel Society [1841] was also encouraged and benefited by her substantial aid, and, in truth, she assisted them all, not only by head and heart, but in more substantial ways.

Nor must I forget the Foster Home, for poor Hebrew children. She began [1855] and fostered that institution; she wrote its code and bylaws; she was its head and director, its manager for years. She gave the managers the experience of a life of usefulness, and they accepted her as a chief who would guide them with her knowledge and ability, and they delighted to follow where she led. It is surprising to think how many institutions she managed at the same time, and all with ability and energy. She was always an active member of all these societies, and her opinion was met with deference by all the ladies of the board. . . .

Of the large family my grandparents reared, five sons and five daughters, all tall and elegant, conspicuous for manly beauty and feminine loveliness, the youngest daughter, Rachel, was the most beautiful of all. She grew up in beauty and married Mr. [Solomon] Moses, of New York, who subsequently moved to this city [Philadelphia]. They had several children, but death took the lovely flower in its prime. I saw her in her coffin with her sleeping infant beside her. They were buried in one grave [1823]. My Aunt Rebecca then made a home for the motherless. The seven bereaved children and their father went to her home. She comforted and tended them in their days of mourning, and to the youngest, who was but a boy of two years old, she was a mother indeed. . . .

VISITING WITH AUNT REBECCA

My Aunt Rebecca was in the habit of visiting the fashionable watering place, Saratoga and Ballston Spa, for her health, and every succeeding summer she went attended by some of her nieces and brothers. She was the admired of all the beauty and fashion there. . . .

I went with her the year before I was married, in June, 1835, to visit her brother Ben, in Kentucky. There her reputation had preceded her, and on our first day Henry Clay, the hero of Ashland, came to see her and invited her to dine at Ashland. I went with her to that dinner party and saw the honors paid to her. Mr. Clay had invited a party to meet us, but he it was who took Rebecca Gratz in to dinner and placed her by his side, talked to her as great men talk, and after dinner gave her his arm and conducted her to see his farm, his sheep and his cattle, his dairy and his chickens.

From all the high men and women in Kentucky she received ovations of respect and attention; from all men and women of her day she was admired and praised; no matter how great expectation rose, no one was ever disappointed when they saw her; the beauty of her face and dignity of her form, the grace and ease of her manners, won all admirers.

I never shall forget when Washington Irving returned from Spain [1832], after an absence of fifteen [seventeen] years from his native country. I most fortunately was at Aunt Becky's when he called, immediately after his arrival, to see his old friend, Rebecca, and, with the familiarity of an old friend, she called him "Washington." He told her all about the book he was then publishing, *Tales of the Alhambra*. He spoke of the Alhambra with warmth and delight, expatiated on its courts and baths and wondrous splendors, said that Matio, who flourishes in his book, was a real character, and what struck me afterwards in reading his book was that he wrote precisely as he talked. I could hear his voice talking as I read. He dined the next day after his visit at aunt's, and I had the happiness to be invited to dine with him and sat next to him. . . .

LAST DAYS

It may not be out of place in this little sketch of my dear Aunt Rebecca to mention that during her life that unfortunate Civil War occurred, which shook this continent to its centre and almost dissolved these United States. She, like a true woman, stood firm and true to her country; as she had followed one true God, so she could know but one united country. She knew, as Mr. Webster said, "no North, no South, no East, no West"; all the United States were her country, and she could not divide them during the four years of bloodshed. She never doubted but that the government would be successful and never allowed herself to believe to the contrary. She was true to her country as to her religion, and in both was true to herself. . . .

Her latter days were feeble, and the time came when "the grasshopper was a burden," and the health which had sustained her in all her labors gave way. A slight paralysis of the throat made swallowing at times difficult, but when the attack was off she would forget it and ever welcome her friends with a smile of affection, and when you asked her how she was, "I'm well, thank God." . . .

Her family surrounded her in her last illness, her only surviving brother from Kentucky, the three nieces to whom she had acted a mother's part, and her nephew Horace [Moses], who was a son to her. One day I went in to see her and found her very sick; she was sitting up in bed, and after saying "good morning," I found her suffering. I asked her if she wanted anything. She looked around her; seeing Becky Nathan at the foot of the bed and Miriam Cohen on the other side, she bowed gracefully to me and, pointing to each of the girls, she replied: "What could I want, so surrounded?" . . .

Her last will and testament in this world began with these beautiful words: "I, Rebecca Gratz, of Philadelphia, being in sound health of body and mind, advanced in the vale of years, declaim this to be my last will and testament. I commit my spirit to the God who gave it, relying on his mercy and redeeming love, and believing with a firm and perfect faith in the religion of my fathers: 'Hear, O Israel, the Lord our God is one Lord.' "

This was the heading of her will, and so she remained ever steadfast to her God and her religion. Hers was truly a *noble* life; and may she rest in peace with all the daughters of Israel, and let us say, "Amen."

Rosa Mordecai

The Oldest Jewish Sunday School

Sarah Hays Mordecai's Recollections of her dear Aunt Rebecca Gratz were colored by the sky-blue spectacles of worshipful admiration. It is curious that four years after Mrs. Mordecai published her reminiscences—and three years after she passed away—her daughter Rosa also published her memories of the same woman. In 1897, in a Philadelphia Sunday school magazine, The Hebrew Watchword and Instructor, *she printed her "Recollections of the First Hebrew Sunday School," February-April (1897), No. 6, p. 5; No. 7, pp. 11-13; No. 8, pp. 4-5. They were reprinted by Dr. Joshua Bloch in the* Publications of the American Jewish Historical Society, *XLII (1953), 397-406.*

But what a difference in the approach! The daughter, Rosa, though she knew her grandaunt very well, described her sympathetically but realistically as she wrote of the Philadelphia Jewish Sunday school of the 1840's and the 1850's.

The description that follows of how and what Jewish children were then taught is probably the most detailed account that we have of the religious-school education of the Jewish child in the days before the Civil War.

For a number of years, Rosa and two of her sisters kept a private school for young ladies. They were equipped to do so, for the Mordecai girls were well-educated. Be assured that Major Mordecai saw to that. Good education was the core of the family tradition.

Like her mother, Rosa lived to a ripe old age; she died in her ninety-eighth year in the city of Washington.

She was a good Jewess, no doubt due to the influence of her pious mother. Though Rosa had no means and, apparently, was dependent on others for support in her last days, she had friends in the highest places. It is too bad that she did not write more about herself.

The Zane Street Sunday School

My first distinct impression of going to the Hebrew Sunday school was some years after it was organized by my great-aunt, Miss Rebecca Gratz, and while she was still its moving spirit (some time, I think, in the early fifties). The room which the school then occupied was on Zane Street (now Filbert Street) above Seventh Street, over the Phoenix Hose Company. This was prior to the days of the paid fire department. Before mounting the stairs, I would linger, as many of the girls and all the boys did, to admire the beautifully-kept machines, with the gentlemanly loungers, who never wearied of answering our questions. The sons of our most "worthy and respected" citizens ran after the Phoenix in those days. But I catch a glimpse of Miss Gratz approaching, and we all scatter as she says: "Time for school, children!"

The room in which we assembled was a large one with four long windows at the end. Between the centre windows was a raised platform with a smaller one upon which stood a table and a chair. On the table was a much worn Bible containing both the Old and the New Testaments (Rev. Isaac Leeser's valuable edition of the Hebrew Bible had not then been published), a hand-bell, Watts's Hymns, and a penny contribution box "for the poor of Jerusalem." [Leeser's Hebrew Bible was published in 1848; the English translation, in 1853.]

Here Miss Gratz presided. A stately commanding figure, always neatly dressed in plain black, with thin white collar and cuffs, close-fitting bonnet over her curled front, which time never touched with grey; giving her, even in her most advanced years, a youthful appearance. Her eyes would pierce every part of the hall and often detect mischief which escaped the notice of the teachers.

The only punishment I can recall was for the delinquent to be marched through the school and seated upon the little platform, before mentioned, under the table. Sometimes this stand would be quite full, and I was rather disposed to envy those children who had no lessons to say. But, her duties over, Miss Gratz would call them by name to stand before her for reproof, which, apparently

282

mild, was so soul-stirring that even the most hardened sinner would quail before it. She was extremely particular to instill neatness and cleanliness. A soiled dress, crooked collar, or sticky hands never escaped her penetrating glance, and the reproof or remedy was instantaneous.

The benches held about ten children each. They were painted bright yellow, with an arm at each end; on the board across the back were beautiful medallions of mills, streams, farmhouses, etc., etc.

The instruction must have been principally oral in those primitive days. Miss Gratz always began school with the prayer, opening with "Come ye children, hearken unto me, and I will teach you the fear of the Lord." This was followed by a prayer of her own composition, which she read verse by verse, and the whole school repeated after her. Then she read a chapter of the Bible, in a clear and distinct voice, without any elocution, and this could be heard and understood all over the room. The closing exercises were equally simple: a Hebrew hymn sung by the children, then one of Watts's simple verses, whose rhythm the smallest child could easily catch as all repeated: "Send me the voice that Samuel heard," etc., etc.

Many old scholars can still recall the question: "Who formed you, child, and made you live?" and the answer: "God did my life and spirit give"—the first lines of that admirable Pyke's *Catechism,* which long held its place in the Sunday school, and was, I believe, the first book printed for it. The Scripture lessons were taught from a little illustrated work published by the Christian Sunday School Union. Many a long summer's day have I spent, pasting pieces of paper over answers unsuitable for Jewish children, and many were the fruitless efforts of those children to read through, over, or under the hidden lines.

I could recall the names of many who sat on the long benches as scholars, or in the chairs as teachers, but they have all scattered, some to far distant homes, others to the eternal home. And those who are left are now all men and women, advanced in age, some of them grandfathers, some grandmothers of the present generation. Yet all still bear a grateful recollection of the Zane Street Sunday school, over the Phoenix Hose Company.

THE ANNUAL EXAMINATION

The Sunday school was removed in 1854 from Zane Street to the lower floor of the building of the Hebrew Education Society, then situated on Seventh Street, below Callowhill. This kindness has never been withdrawn, and the Sunday school has ever since enjoyed the free use of the rooms of the Society, wherever located.

Miss Gratz was still superintendent, president, treasurer and secretary—the powerful and most capable factotum. I, with many others, was soon promoted from the ranks of the scholars to the dignity of teacher, owing to the great increase of very young children. The room was by no means as suitable as the old one, having a very low ceiling and small windows, affording insufficient light and air in summer, while two large stoves at the entrance heated only a small area on a cold winter's day. But economy was most strictly observed by Miss Gratz in all her dealings, and it was very necessary in the management of such a limited revenue as the school has always possessed. The saving of rent, however, enabled her to spend more liberally for the growing wants of the school.

The benches were low and semicircular; the teacher, sitting in much closer contact with the pupils, was thus supposed to be able to maintain better order, and little restless feet were not so often seen dangling under the superintendent's table. The platform was much larger and had a kind of alcove behind, in which were seated the pupils of the graduating class, taught by Miss Sim'ha C. Peixotto, who struggled with the difficulties of Johlson's catechism until Mr. Leeser wrote his valuable *Catechism* for the school, and dedicated it to Miss Gratz. The articles on the table were also slightly changed; a handsome copy of Rev. Isaac Leeser's large edition of the Holy Scriptures replaced the old King James's version.

A roll book was added, and a fine gong bell rang for order, instead of the little tinkling one of the old schoolroom. Maps of Palestine, the Ten Commandments, and other more appropriate emblems adorned the walls, and resolutions of the members of the Phoenix Hose Company.

A few changes had also crept into the weekly routine. The psalm read one Sunday was repeated the next week by the older classes, a certain number of verses being assigned to each scholar. It sometimes happened that the succession would be broken by the absence of one or two pupils, but good marks, pretty cards, and a general desire to improve or get a prize made attendance very regular.

There were various devices used to amuse the very young children before Miss Rebecca Moss started her infants' class, attended with such marked success. Both Hebrew and English primers were resorted to, in the vain attempt to teach reading, but if the least progress was made one Sunday, it would be entirely forgotten before the next lesson; particularly as the books were not allowed to be taken home. . . .

About this time Miss Sim'ha C. Peixotto, of grateful memory, saved us the trouble of pasting over objectionable passages, by undertaking to write the scriptural questions, and published the first volume of her excellent catechism, which held its well-deserved place in the school for many years.

Pyke's *Catechism* was freely distributed, and instead of being taught, parrot-fashion, by the teacher, the tiny green books went home to many Jewish households, with a penalty of five cents attached if injured or lost; and this fee was strictly exacted by the young librarian, who was a great disciplinarian. Books were not very often allowed by him to be taken home, but were read, after the lessons were recited by the scholars, or aloud by the teacher, if it so happened that all her class studied in the same book, or the same lesson. Generally, however, owing to private reasons, kinship, or popularity, a class would be composed of eight or ten boys and girls of different ages and ability, and consequently these were taught out of several books, or even different parts of the same book.

Both Rev. Isaac Leeser and the Rev. Dr. (then Mr. [Sabato]) Morais were constant visitors. The former, with his strongly [pock-] marked face, gold spectacles and inexhaustible fund of ever-ready information, was a most welcome sight to the young teachers, puzzled by the questions of their big, clever scholars. He knew every child and teacher, called each by name, and nothing was too trivial or too intricate to claim his clear explanation.

Mr. Morais was then young, active, and full of enthusiasm, always ready to lead the Hebrew hymns or take the class of an absent teacher. Tradition says it was in Sunday school that he was first attracted to his beautiful young wife [Clara E. Weil], who was one of the most beloved teachers. Be that as it may, most certainly courting was openly encouraged both by Miss Gratz and Miss [Louisa B.] Hart, who, having never tasted the delights of matrimony, naturally wished all their young charges to enjoy connubial bliss. My own teacher has often told me since, how her husband was first drawn towards her by her gentle manners to her young pupils. Other successful and unsuccessful lovers will always retain pleasant memories of the old Sunday school, and of their walks to and from it.

The annual examination was held about Purim time [February-March]. Why at that time, I never could find out, as the work of the class had to be immediately recommenced, unless it was a sort of anniversary, as the school was first opened March 4th, which, by a curious coincidence, was Miss Gratz's birthday.

Can any of you recall the dear old Cherry Street Synagogue, on those March Sundays [when the annual examination was held]? I can see it so distinctly with its circular benches and deep gallery facing the large open space between the *Tebah* and the *Hechal* [the reading desk and the Ark], with its broad steps and light doors that raised like a window. It was with something like awe that on these anniversaries we women took possession of the ground floor. [Women were not allowed to sit with the men at the regular services.] A small table was placed in front of the reading desk for Miss Gratz. The classes were all arranged in the men's seats and were called up to stand and recite by Mr. Abraham Hart [the famous publisher], who presided at the desk, his own clever children invariably making the best recitations and carrying off the prizes. The classes were arranged in a semicircle, according to the part of the book they studied, the pupils returning to their seats when the limit of their lessons had been reached. One teacher stood in the centre, giving the questions, or, if the classes were numerous, walked gradually around the circle. Thus every child was really examined, and each book recited in whole or in part.

The monotony was varied by monologues and dialogues; then came the distribution of prizes, which were called out by Mr. Hart, giving the name of the teacher with the three best scholars. The first prize was always a Bible; or, rather, a Bible and two books were given to each class. These books were most carefully selected by Miss Gratz herself, and handed by her to each child with a kind, encouraging word, often with a written line on the flyleaf. As the happy children went out orderly by class, through the back door, each was given an orange and a pretzel.

Simple days of our youth, where are you now?

No More Oranges and Pretzels

In 1857, before the Jewish Foster Home was removed to its present handsome building in Germantown, the older children came to the Sunday school for instruction. I had in my class, together with children of my own personal friends and relatives, many of these bright boys and girls. It was a real pleasure to teach them from [H. Loeb's] *The Road to Faith*, the best work for the purpose. May I be pardoned for saying that I retain a personal interest in all the members of that class and that each boy and girl (most of them now with children of their own) has done credit to my instruction?

In 1858, Miss Gratz, after twenty years of untiring energy and admirable management of the school, though her "sight was not dim, nor her natural force abated," took Jethro's admirable advice to Moses by appointing "officers to assist her in her work"; so The Hebrew Sunday School Society was incorporated, with Miss Gratz as its first president. She was then seventy-seven years old, but she continued her weekly attendance several years longer until in 1864, when increasing infirmities gradually made the duties no longer possible, she resigned the presidency in favor of her devoted friend, Miss Louisa B. Hart.

Miss Hart's aim in carrying on the school was to maintain in every particular the high standard of her predecessor, and to continue as "Miss Gratz would have done" was her final decision in all matters. She entered heart and soul into her work, and was universally beloved by both pupils and teachers, whom she encouraged to meet every Saturday evening and on other occasions at her house on Lombard Street, and subsequently on Clinton Street. Those hours of innocent mirth, good cheer, and unstinted hospitality must still linger in the memory of her numerous "young friends," as she delighted to call them.

In 1871, Miss Ellen Phillips, a lady of much intelligence, kindly ways, and attractive manners, became the third superintendent of the Sunday school. She had been one of the original teachers and had served faithfully under both Miss Gratz and Miss Hart. She saw plainly that with the great increase of the foreign [immigrant] element, the school could no longer be conducted on its old basis. Changes and improvements were introduced, and in the following year the school was divided into Northern and Southern schools, and Miss Gratz's great-niece [my sister], Miss Laura Mordecai, inaugurated, at Twelfth and Chestnut Streets, the first radical change to a "Mission School."

About this time, cards with the thirteen articles of the Jewish creed were printed for the school, and others with the picture of Moses holding the Tables of the Law and the Commandments in rhyme beneath. The reciting of the psalm was discontinued. The superintendent read a chapter from the Holy Bible which was carefully explained on the following Sunday by the Rev. Dr. S. Morais, who never allowed inclement weather or other duties to interfere with this self-imposed task. Miss Hart and Miss Phillips both relied on Dr. Morais in many ways, and he always proved himself more than equal to their constant demands upon his time and great erudition, in explaining each holy festival, as it occurred, conducting the examinations, etc., etc. His devotion to the interests of the school has never flagged, and has become one of the many ways by which he has gained what the poet tells us should be the crown of old age, "honor, love, obedience, troops of friends."

Now, besides a religious school attached to every synagogue and temple in Philadelphia, the Sunday school has four large schools, each consisting of many hundred[s of] scholars, as you may read in *The Hebrew Watchword,* but which, I am ashamed to say, I have never visited, and must therefore leave to others to describe the good work done in them. At the time of the branching out of the schools, classes were arranged in accordance with the capacities of the pupils, and the lessons for each Sunday were clearly defined and explained in teachers' meetings after school, when "Work, work, work" took [the] place of "The Voice that Samuel heard"; when oranges and pretzels were superseded by theatrical performances and tableaux. I had already ceased to be a teacher in the Sunday school, thinking myself, even then, too old to learn new ways; but I am young again, in recalling for the benefit of the rising generation incidents which will make them smile at the changes which time has wrought.

I must say a few words to the teachers, as well as to the pupils, upon the birth, growth, and extent of the school, established in 1838. Miss Gratz was then fifty-seven, an age which most people would consider too advanced to attempt a new undertaking. Yet she lived to see it increase from a handful—fifty children and seven teachers, mostly of her own family and all of the Mickveh Israel Congregation —until, when she handed it over to her successor twenty-six years later, there were scholars from every congregation in this city, besides many foreigners among the 200 pupils.

Nor was all the good work done by this little "acorn." The "tall oak" whose branches extend near and far over our crowded streets and alleys into every corner of Penn's "Faire Towne" has yet stretched further, until at present, in almost every part of this vast country, South, North, East, West, the example first set by the Hebrew Sunday school of Philadelphia has been taken up, and Jewish religious schools are planted wherever there exists a settled Jewish community.

Haiman Philip Spitz

A Pioneer Merchant in Maine

Like some American Jewish worthies, Haiman Philip Spitz came to America via England. He left his native Posen, where he was born in 1816, and lived for five years in England. Obviously, the linguistic and business skills acquired in that country were to stand him in good stead on this side of the Atlantic. By the time he was twenty-four years of age, he had already landed in New York.

Spitz's memoirs help us to gauge the beginnings of the participation of the Jews in the garment industry. In the middle 1840's he was manufacturing clothing in the North for southern markets.

For a while he lived in New Orleans and, like many others in that city, was belligerently desirous of hastening the conquest of Mexico, documenting his bellicose sentiments by fighting in the army of General Zachary Taylor.

After the Mexican War he moved to Bangor, Maine, where he remained for about a decade, until the panic of 1856-57 crippled the lumber business and compelled him to seek greener fields.

Wandering about, always looking for larger opportunities to support his ever-increasing family, he found himself in 1859 in Baltimore, where he lived for a generation, before joining his children in San Francisco. While in the Maryland city, he engaged in the wholesale liquor and cigar trade, and when the Civil War broke out in 1861, he sold hats, caps, boots, and other clothing and garment supplies to the army. That type of business was not new to him; in 1845, the year before the war with Mexico, he had sold to the government summer suits for soldiers, at $6 apiece.

Spitz was interested in Judaism. It was in his house in Bangor that the first synagogue in Maine was called into existence—in 1849, not 1852, as he erroneously wrote in his reminiscences. In postbellum Baltimore he was, apparently, active in the congregation of Rabbi Benjamin Szold. Jewish traditions and ceremonies were observed in his home. At the Seder, the Passover feast, in his home in San Francisco in 1883, he sat at the head of the table and could

289

smile upon his wife, seven children, six grandchildren, two sons-in-law, and others.

Spitz died some time after 1886, the year in which he finished writing Haiman Philip Spitz, An Autobiography *(1886?). The following extracts are taken from that book, pp. 3-32.*

Posen to New York Via England

On the thirteenth day of April, 1816—in the Hebrew calendar, the ninth day of Nesan—Ernestene, daughter of Philip Lichtenstine, gave to her husband, the merchant Abraham Spitz, her first-born son; they named the child Haiman Philip Spitz. . . .

In 1834, my second sister, Rosa, married a gentleman named M. Levy. In that year I left Posen for Bromberg, in Prussia, took a place in a dry goods store, remained one year, and then went home again. I arrived in Posen in the month of April, before Easter, to be with my parents and brothers and sisters during the holidays. In June, 1835, I left home for England, arrived in London in September, took a situation in a French bazaar, with a small salary, not knowing the English language, which was hard in the beginning. I tried to learn, to better my condition, in which I succeeded.

The next year my firm sent me out as a "commercial traveler"—so-called in England. I worked hard and faithfully, and succeeded in getting good customers. My sales improving year after year, my salary was raised accordingly. After working several years with that house, and having saved some money, I concluded to go into business for myself, and established [settled] in Bath, England.

My brother, Peter, arrived in London; he came to work for me. I traveled to solicit trade and gain customers; my brother remained at home to attend to the orders. Finding that my brother was not the proper man for the place, we did not stay long together. I concluded to sell out my business to Mr. Joseph Samuel[s], of Bath. My brother having a desire to go to America, but not having the means necessary, I furnished him the passage money and $250 besides; my brother was a furrier. Then he and a gentleman named M. Marks, who was a capmaker, and who was worth $250, formed a partnership and left together for America in 1839, and I made preparation to go home, to Posen. . . .

I assisted the old folks, to make them comfortable. I went in the grain and wool business with my father, remained a few years with them at home, left the business with my father and started for England, June, 1840, arrived in London from Hamburg in July, went

291

to Bath to settle up my business with Mr. Samuels, went from there
to Birmingham, then to Liverpool, where I took the sailing ship
"North Carolina" for New York, [and] arrived in New York on
August 3d, 1840. Not being pleased with the new country, and my
limited amount of money getting less every day, and not having
enough to go into business with, I felt blue. My brother and his
partner were at the wharf when I arrived. We rode to his boardinghouse; we were pleased to see each other. I told him all the news
from home—of parents, brother, and sisters and their children—of
our entire family—which pleased all of us; told of the good time I
had at home.

The Pestilence in New Orleans

As stated before, I had no liking for New York, and made up my
mind to go to New Orleans. My brother paid me the money which
I loaned him in Liverpool, England. I purchased goods in New York
—caps from the firm of Spitz & Marks; sent the goods by a sailing
vessel to New Orleans. At that time we had no steamers on that road.
A few days afterward I went on board of the ship, accompanied by
my brother and Mr. Marks. I looked around the ship and found a
very rough crowd, cursing and swearing. I felt I must go, having paid
my money; but I felt I ought to stay when my brother bid me good-
bye. I went with them as far as the shore. My brother said: "Rush
back; the ship will go in ten minutes." "Let it go," I said. He said
again: "Go." I turned around to go on board. "Good-bye!" my
brother called. I turned again from the ship toward my brother, and
said: "By the help of God, I will not go with that ship," and went
home with him, losing my passage money.

A week after I left New York for New Orleans. I arrived at that
place, after a passage of thirty-two days, on September 25th, 1840.
I found the place deserted, and the yellow fever raging and a good
many people dying; black crape on so many doors, which I had
never seen before, that really I got frightened. It looked very discouraging. A week after my arrival I asked about that ship—when
it would arrive. To my horror I read in the paper that the ship was
lost, and with it the captain, the crew, and over 100 passengers. It
was a total wreck. I was very sorry for them, and thanked the Almighty for saving me.

A few weeks after my arrival the yellow fever checked, and a
great many people commenced to arrive in the city from the East
and the West. Everything began to look lively, and business was
good. I took a stand in the market with those goods I brought from

New York. I did a good business. Expenses of living were very high: $5 a day in a sailors' boardinghouse, and other houses, which were not fit to live in. Hotels rated high, and in private houses you were not safe. Such was the state of things in New Orleans at that time. No doubt there were many good people there, but they kept back from those who came from the East or West.

Things began to look satisfactory with me; I had good health and plenty of business. A man who came with me from New York (the father of five children) was taken sick in his boardinghouse, and was sent to the hospital. The next day I went to the hospital to inquire after his health and, to my great surprise, was told that he died that morning of yellow fever. I felt very sorry for him. I was also told that if I wanted his body, to do me a favor it would be given to me if I pay expenses; if not, it would be given to the doctors [for dissection]. I went to several of my countrymen, got the sum together, handed it to the man at the hospital, got the body, and had it buried in a Jewish burying ground.

A few days after this his wife, with two children, arrived, looking for her husband, but could not find him. She was told to go and see me. She came to my place of business, asked me what had become of her husband, whether he was dead or among the living. Seeing the situation of the poor woman, who was half crazy, I told her that he had gone into the country to peddle and would be back in a few weeks. I asked her: "Where are your children?" "On the ship," she said. "What made you come out so quickly?" She answered: "I cannot live without him." I went with her to the ship, got the children and her baggage, and took them to a boardinghouse. A week after, I told her that I had received a letter from her husband at Mobile, Ala., that he would go from there to New York. The poor woman believed all that! I showed her a bogus letter. I believed she would be better off in New York, and my object was to induce her to go there. She was anxious to go back. I engaged berths, paid for them, and gave her some money, which I told her I would charge to her husband. They arrived in New York. When there she found out her husband had died of yellow fever at the hospital. She wrote to me to let her know all the particulars, which I answered, and sent her the death certificate; also, in what Jewish burying ground he was buried, and the name of the congregation. It was no encouragement for me to like New Orleans—such a sickly place.

BUSINESS AND WAR

I attended to my market business, in company with a man of my age, born in the same place, in Posen; his name was J. Spiro. He was in the grocery business; I with Yankee notions. We had a small room rented, where we slept. Our market business commenced at five o'clock A.M., and closed at 1:00 P.M. The balance of the day I went peddling, making a little money. Thinking I could not make enough money to go East and back again (I had to go East for my goods, but my partner bought his groceries in New Orleans), I concluded to go to the country and peddle, to make more money. Besides, I did not like city life in the style in which it was conducted at that time —too much fun and devilment for me. So we parted. My partner left New Orleans for Rio de Janeiro, and I went by steamer with my goods to Natchez, Miss., bought a horse, and traveled the country—through Mississippi and Louisiana—and sold a good many goods. I have never heard of my partner to the present day.

The hardships in that country at that time were many, the country roads were bad, and we had to stand a good deal; the sales were small, but the profits were large; the people were economical, and there was not as much money in 1841 in this country as there is at the present day.

In April, 1841, I left New Orleans for New York, took with me $2,000, bought goods at auction and in several other houses, mostly for cash—a few on credit—some ready-made clothing and caps of the firm of Spitz & Marks.

September, 1841, I left New York and returned to New Orleans and sold my goods at good profit. In that year my brother Peter married in New York, dissolved partnership, and moved to Boston.

May, 1842, I left New Orleans again for New York. My capital having increased, I bought more goods, went to Boston to see my brother and his wife. He had established himself in the cap business. I gave up my fancy business, went to New York, and commenced making up clothing for the southern market. I bought some tailors' trimmings for tailors, and left for New Orleans, where I sold my goods. I continued in this business, going every year to New York to make up clothing for the South.

In 1845, business was remarkably good, and I had to order goods to be sent to me. At that time war broke out with Mexico, through the influence of a certain gentleman [John Slidell?] with whom I was acquainted, and what we called the "Filibusters." I was a member of that society. Its aim was to bring on a war with Mexico. It was a secret society, composed of Americans. I went to see Adjutant Gans and General Gates and received an order for 1,500 summer suits for the soldiers; sent to New York for them; received and delivered them; for which I received $9,000 in United States bonds, payable at the United States Treasury, Washington, but which I sold in New Orleans. I belonged to a military company called the "Harrison Grays."

One day the steamer "Galveston" arrived from Texas with the news that American blood had been spilt on American soil by Mexicans this side of Fort Brown, and that our country was in danger. They commenced drafting. All the city military companies were called out—our company among them—by General [Persifor F.] Smith. Speeches were made by several soldiers, and the question asked if all the companies present would volunteer to start with the steamer "Galveston" to Galveston, Texas, to the seat of war. To which we all said, "Yes," except two Spanish companies; they refused to fight against Mexico. Their swords were taken from them, and they were disbanded by order of General Smith. All the rest of the companies were sworn in and equipped. We put ribbons on our caps as volunteers, and with a band of music, marched through the streets to get more volunteers, in which we succeeded. We certainly were the cream of the city—merchants, doctors, lawyers, judges, mechanics. We marched down to the wharf to go on the steamer, greeted by the people all the way. We arrived in Galveston, and were put under General [Zachary] Taylor's command. Our company was sent out to watch bridges and reconnoiter.

We were not in any battles, except at Cerro Gordo and Resaca de la Palma [Palo Alto?], where Major [Samuel] Ringgold, from Baltimore, was killed. After that we were again sent to watch bridges. We had hard times. Several of our company were wounded by the Mexicans. We stole from the farmers all we could find and left them nothing. We had good times, plenty to eat, and we wasted the rest. Such is war!

During that time they were drafting in New Orleans and bounties given. Men were coming in large numbers from all parts of the United States. We were discharged and sent back to New Orleans. When we arrived the governor, mayor, city officials, and the citizens showed us great honor, for we were the first when our country was in danger. The city was in holiday attire. The military escorted us through the city. I feel good when I think of it sometimes.

BOSTON CLOTHIER

A few weeks after that I left New Orleans for New York. I went to Boston to see my brother, and while there looked around the city to find some business to settle in. I concluded to go in business with my brother Peter, the firm to be Spitz & Brother, wholesale and retail clothiers. We located on Hanover Street, with a branch house at New Orleans, which I was to attend to. The manufactory was in Boston under the management of my brother. He was married, while I was still single at that time, although four years older than he. He was active, and paid strict attention to business; I, also, to my branch, and everything went on satisfactory for a year or so. Here a mistake was made by my brother which nearly ruined our business.

A man came to my brother with the sheriff and asked him to go bail for him or else he would be ruined, at the [same] time crying bitterly. Brother knew the man, and believed what he said to be true; that his partner ran away and took all the money with him, and that he was arrested. My brother, being young, honest, and inexperienced, gave bail for him. He did not let me know, for I certainly would have refused, a mistake which he afterward found out to his sorrow. We owed the merchants with whom we were dealing, and they believed we were swindlers, also, on account of our bailing that man; so they attached the store in Boston, and also my business in New Orleans. I released my part of the indebtedness for one-half cash and notes for the balance, with my brother's endorsement, and continued business. Our credit then was not as good as it had hitherto been.

In 1846, we gave up our southern trade, and I returned to Boston. I settled our affairs with our creditors, continued the retail trade in Boston, and everything went on well again under my management. We had a good city and country trade.

On February 3d, 1847, I married in Boston, and ten months after, my wife gave birth to a son. We named him Samuel. He died when eleven months old and was buried in Boston, in 1848. After the death of my boy, which I took very hard, I became discouraged, and not seeing a good prospect for business, we dissolved partnership.

BANGOR, MAINE

I left Boston and went to Bangor, Maine, took a store on the Kenduskeag bridge, and again commenced the clothing business. In the beginning it was dull. The people there did not encourage newcomers until they became acquainted. It was an English custom. They generally asked to what church you belonged; they would patronize church members. It was a poor chance for me, being an Israelite. I found out I would have to become acquainted in order to make a living. I liked the place and the style of the people; so I tried to make friends. Being a Mason, I visited lodges; joined the Odd Fellows and other societies, and became a citizen of the United States; I became acquainted with their style.

My wife having been raised in this country, she made many friends; we were respected by those with whom we had dealings, my business improved, and we were perfectly satisfied with our surroundings. There were six Jewish families in Bangor: one kept a clothing store, two kept dry goods stores, and the others peddled. We visited our neighbors and places of amusement; we visited American families, and they visited us, and we were much liked. It was our spring of life, which we spent to our satisfaction.

In Bangor we found the people with whom we associated to be of a fine order. Myself and wife were happy and prosperous. I bought a fine house, formerly owned by a Mr. Jordan; it contained all the modern improvements, with a stable in the rear. . . .

In 1852 a congregation was established in Bangor. Mr. [Moses] Silber was president; H. P. Spitz [myself], vice president.

In 1856 and 1857 business became very dull; a panic prevailed all over the United States. Maine was a great sufferer, as nearly the whole trade was lumbering, which was entirely stopped. I kept a wholesale and retail clothing store and furnished the lumbermen with their outfit when going to, and returning from, the woods. As this trade was lost to me, and having a large family to support, I contented myself with the retail trade; but business getting worse and worse, and no prospect of it getting better, I concluded to break up business and leave Bangor with my family and go to Boston. We arrived there in 1858.

ON THE ROAD TO BALTIMORE

I took a house on Shawmut Avenue, and a loft on Milk Street, and sold liquors and cigars, at wholesale and retail. My trade was good; but Massachusetts passed a liquor law, making liquors contraband, and all such debts could not be collected by law. I had money out in the city and country, which was hard to collect, only at a sacrifice.

I collected all I could and left for the West. I took my eldest daughter on a visit to my sister, in Hartford, Connecticut. The child did not want to stay; took her with me to New York, Philadelphia, and Baltimore; left her with some relatives in Baltimore, and went to Cincinnati and several other places to find a place to settle in.

I could not be suited, so I went back to Baltimore, and after looking around for a week, found a house and store on Lexington Market; a four-story brick building with a store, a fine cellar, and a splendid yard; a suitable place for the business which I intended carrying on —a cellar large enough to hold 100 barrels of whisky. I went to the landlord, took a lease of the house and store for one year, with the privilege of three years more; took the keys, and was happy to think it would be a good place for business. I left my daughter in Baltimore and went to Boston to bring my family.

On arriving in Boston, I found my wife sick in bed, but my five children in good health. Imagine, dear children, how I felt—ready to start but having a sick wife on hand. My wife and children were all to me, and for their sakes I worked—looked out for their comfort and education. Although a merchant with limited capital, I managed just as well as any rich merchant. Thank God, I always had enough to be comfortable, and lived in style according to my income. I spent a good deal of money to have my daughters accomplished and my sons educated, so that they would be able to go into any branch of trade in which I had succeeded that might be offered to them. I always was in moderate circumstances; could always make as much as we needed, and even something more. Although I had chances to become rich, luck was always against me.

I was waiting until my wife got better to go to Baltimore. I wrote to the landlord to be excused for not coming, giving my reason, and stated that we would come as soon as she was better. In answer to this he said he would rent the house if I did not send him three months' rent in advance. I sent him the money, and he sent me a receipt. My wife getting better, I was a happy man again. We made arrangements to leave. We had the furniture, pictures, and all the household goods packed, and with my liquors and cigars, they were shipped by steamer to Baltimore. Mother, five children, and myself went also by steamer. Our passage by rail would have been much cheaper, but thinking it would be much better for our health, it being in July, to take a sea voyage, as they would become more acclimated upon arriving at Baltimore. When we reached there we all took some medicine, which proved to be good for the children and ourselves.

It was very hard for us to break up home and business in Boston, and part from brothers and sisters and friends; but such is life. We cannot have what we wish; only that which is ordained for us. When in Bangor, I had a photograph taken of the birthplace of our six children and of ourselves, of which they were very fond, and which we took along.

BALTIMORE DURING THE WAR

On July 22d, 1859, we arrived in Baltimore with six children; our eldest daughter, seven years old, and our youngest son, Jacob, fifteen months. I opened a wholesale liquor and cigar store. When our piano, furniture, and household goods arrived, which were many, we moved into our house. For our passage, stock, and furniture I paid $658.40. We had a nice yard for the children to play in, and we were again comfortably situated.

In the beginning my business was not as good as it should have been. I could not make a living or cover my expenses. I did not want to lose what little I had, so I concluded to try to get a situation which would enable me to attend to my own business at the same time I attended to another's. Such a situation I would have accepted. I visited the Masons' lodge, got acquainted with several brothers, told them my situation, and gave them references in Bangor; told them I was able to be a bookkeeper, or an assistant, or a salesman; would like to have a situation from 9:00 A.M. to 4:00 P.M.; and that I was willing to work. Two weeks after that a gentleman got me a situation to my wishes; it was to be assistant bookkeeper in a commission house, with a salary of $75 per month, and time from 9:00 A.M. to 4:00 P.M.; the balance of the day I could attend to my own business.

During my absence my clerk received orders, and when at home I attended to it myself. The first year, with my salary and hard work—attending two places of business—I made my expenses. The second year my trade improved, and I was obliged to give up my situation. My employers were glad that my business was improving. They sent me to a tailor to have a fine suit of clothes and an overcoat made for myself, as a present for faithful services, for which I thanked them. I left them in January, 1860. The war broke out. One partner [in the business I just left] was a Rebel; the other a Union man. They broke up business and retired. The Union man left the books and business under my charge to close. For salary I was to receive a percentage of all the money I collected. It came very handy to me; for business was very dull.

War had been declared; soldiers were gathering in all parts of the

United States to go to the seat of war (Washington), then to Virginia. The first regiment (the Sixth Massachusetts) arrived in the city of Baltimore. The citizens tried to prevent their landing and in doing so killed several soldiers. The people became terribly excited and rushed to the armories and took possession of all the arms. The bridges in the city were burned down by orders of Mayor Brown and Marshal Kane. The city was in a horrible condition; nothing could get in or out; business was entirely stopped; no work for mechanics or laborers; the poor were in great distress. Many enlisted to get the bounties, to prevent their families from starving. Such was the situation at that time.

The Union people had to keep still; all had to pretend to be Rebels. In order to be treated right in school our children were obliged to carry Rebel emblems. Afterwhile things began to look a little better, although hurrahing for Jeff Davis was heard everywhere. Our city was very hard to get through; but after a good many reinforcements had been sent to Washington by water, it became better regulated, and the bridges were rebuilt. The mayor, the marshal, and a great many Rebel citizens were arrested; martial law was declared; people began to breathe more freely; soldiers in great numbers were arriving day and night, and business began to improve. I put up a place at the Washington depot, on the Baltimore and Ohio Railroad, and opened a liquor and cigar store to supply passengers and soldiers, which proved to be a success. I still continued my other store, which I attended myself, while I employed a man to take charge of the one at the depot. But the government passed a law forbidding the soldiers to buy liquor and the merchants to sell it, as it was reported that it had been poisoned.

After taking the liquors out, so that I would be free from the law, I sold the place to a Mr. Morris, from Virginia; he had lost all he had except $6,000. He sold groceries. I gave him the lease of the house and store; his wife and son kept it, did a good business, and made money. Two years after he got sick and died, leaving a wife and eight children. The son who had charge of the business left it and went South, taking the money with him, which he spent in helping the Rebel cause. The woman sold her business. She lost nearly all she had, and had seven children to take care of. Myself and several gentlemen with whom she dealt helped to support her. She had property in Richmond, and after that place had been taken by the Union Army she went back with her family, and they are in good circumstances again.

My business then was good, although many restrictions were placed upon merchants in selling goods. I had lost some money before the war commenced. One day a Southern man came into my store and handed me $250 which had been sent to me by a gentleman living in South Carolina; he had been a school friend of mine in Europe. I sold him goods in Baltimore. He could not send the money at that time by mail or express.

A society was formed called "The Minute Men" to protect the city when in danger, of which I was a member. Several patriotic gentlemen of wealth sent me to army headquarters, near Richmond, with some goods for our officers and soldiers. Then I received a commission from the government and went to Norfolk, and from there to the White House, where I received some papers to go further. I went to Camp Lincoln, four miles from Richmond; arriving there, I delivered my papers to the provost marshal, General Porter; I was introduced to General McClellan and officers; disposed of the goods, and sent for more. This was on the Chickahominy River. The goods which I had were Kossuth hats, military caps, boots, underwear, and blue sacks, with U. S. buttons; also, shoulder-straps for generals, colonels, majors, captains, and lieutenants. . . .

I left . . . for Baltimore, where I arrived July 5th, 1862, still sick; it was nearly a year before I got well. I had contracted a Chickahominy River fever. I was not able to get back to the seat of war again, so remained at home and attended to my business, and managed to get along very well. Business commenced to be good all over the Union. I speculated in whisky and had bought a large stock, when the government raised the tax on all liquors. My health improved, and I enjoyed myself with my family. In 1863, my health was restored; my two daughters were in the high school, and my sons were advancing in their studies. I felt proud to know that my boys would be able to fill any situation that might be offered to them. Things went on very well in my domestic and business relations; my children were growing up to my heart's desire, and we were all blessed with good health. Our children had great desire to study, which pleased us.

William Frank

Pilgrim Father of Pittsburgh Jewry

William Frank was one of the three or four men who founded the Jewish community of Pittsburgh in the fall of 1846. His laconic autobiographical notes are of considerable interest. They accurately reflect the humble beginnings of the early immigrants, many of whom (like Frank, a weaver) were artisans. He became a peddler in eastern Pennsylvania and thence went further west. Probably because he lacked capital, he bypassed Pittsburgh and continued his trade in eastern Ohio.

In his autobiography, Frank mentions a number of friends and associates. A study of the occupations which they followed in Pittsburgh, where Frank later lived, shows that he and his brother-in-law, Ephraim Wormser, sold dry goods. His erstwhile partner, David Strassburger, and Nathan Gallinger opened pawnshops. The Meyerses were drovers, as was one of the Reis brothers; the other was a tailor, and Louis Jaraslowsky was in the clothing business.

In his later years, William Frank was a glass manufacturer in Frankstown, on the outskirts of Pittsburgh. It is thus probable, as he claims, that this town was named for him. Some historians believe, however, that the town received its name from the colonial portage town on the Kittanning Path.

Frank's notes were written after 1889, at which time they abruptly break off. The original German jottings were translated into English, probably by his son Isaac William Frank. The latter, a distinguished steel manufacturer, was for many years the president of the United Engineering and Foundry Company of Pittsburgh. William died on September 22, 1891.

The memoirs which follow are taken from the English copy in the possession of the American Jewish Archives.

A Wandering Journeyman

I was born the sixteenth day of April, 1819, or on the eighth day of Passover, which day I always celebrated as my birthday. I was born in Burgpreppach Township, Hopheim near Bamberg, Bavaria.

As early as ten years of age I was put to work to earn my living, bringing fish from Hassfurt, which was four hours from my village, and must return by daylight, and often carried 80 to 100 fish, on which I earned 2 to 3 kreutzer. When I was thirteen years old, I went with my father to market and fairs to sell goods. At the age of fourteen I was arrested by police, and was taken to the magistrate at Ehren [?] and was sentenced three days to jail on bread and water because I had not started to learn a trade.

After this I was apprenticed to a shoemaker. I was there two weeks when my master gave me a pair of stinking boots to mend. I threw the boots down and said: "If the farmers want their boots mended, they should do it themselves," and thereupon ran away. I was then apprenticed for three years to Solomon Selig, in Schweinfurt [Bavaria], as cotton goods weaver, for which my father paid thirty gulden for tuition. After completion [of my apprenticeship], I remained with my master six months as [a] journeyman weaver.

When I started to travel to the larger cities of Bavaria and worked as a journeyman, the first place [where I was] employed was in Bieberich, near Würzburg [Bavaria; there is also a Bieberich near Wiesbaden]. [I was hired] by a Christian with whom I had lodging, but ate my meals with Jews. I did not work on Saturdays and usually had my dinner with a Mr. Adler, who later went to Philadelphia and became president of Rodef Shalom Congregation in that city.

After working in Bieberich one year, I started out to travel as a journeyman and secured employment with Aaron Hess in Hallevich [?]. After six months [I worked in] Aschaffenburg, Frankfurt, Mainz, Worms, Darmstadt, Mannheim, Heidelberg, Landau, Speyer, and many smaller towns and villages. I saved more money out of my earnings this way than if I had worked at my trade. In all my travel[s] I did not eat *trefe* ("forbidden food") and was in excellent health.

Again I worked at my trade in Edenkoben, Rhenish Palatinate, with a Christian, and again had my meals with Jews. After six months I began to think of journeying to blessed America, going home to say good-bye to my parents and brother and sister.

After leaving home, I set out for Würzburg, where I had left my traveling journeyman's book [which served as a pass] with the police, who wrote in it permission to return to Edenkoben, with instructions that if I went farther, [the authorities were] to take the book and return it to Würzburg and to arrest me.

I went to Landau, which is in Rhenish Bavaria, where I had a cousin by the name of Abraham Frank. I told him I wanted to go to Weissenburg in France. I showed him my traveling journeyman's book, but he said he thought he could arrange it with the stage driver so that I would have no trouble. The driver put my "Wander-buch" [traveling journeyman's book] in his fodder bag and, when we reached the border, said to the officer that "I was a Weisburger," and he let me pass without further trouble.

On arriving at Weissenburg, I immediately went to the ship's agent and procured a ship's contract [ticket] from Havre to New York. Then journeying to Strassburg, Metz, Paris, where I remained three days, and to Havre. Going directly to the ship's office, [I] was informed that the ship had not yet arrived and that it would be thirty days. This was sad news for me, as French was only spoken, and I did not understand it, and anyway, had not calculated in the delay and did not have enough money to wait so long. I took lodging where I paid 15 sous, about 24¢, for sleeping only, without food.

I wandered about, finally discovering a store where German was spoken, and went in, which proved to be a hardware establishment. I asked for the proprietor and told him my predicament. He gave me credit for knives, forks, and spoons, and I was to pay him every night for my sales [as a peddler], which I did, and thereby earned my lodging and meals, also enough to purchase zwieback, wine, coffee, and tobacco and other necessary things for the ship's journey. The proprietor wanted me to remain with him and promised that I would have "America" in France, and had it not been that I had paid my ship's fare, I would have likely remained in Havre.

PEDDLER IN LANCASTER COUNTY

The ship, "The Great Eagle," a large sailing vessel, sailed at [the] end of thirty days. I was on the ship only one hour when I became violently seasick, which lasted three days, during which I wished many times that I had remained in Havre. I was quite well during the remainder of the journey, which was forty-nine days, landing in New York on May 1st, 1840.

Here again I had a cousin living by the name of Frank. I hunted him up and remained with him overnight. He loaned me $3 with which to reach Philadelphia, where my stepbrother, Phillip Frank, lived. He was a shoemaker and had several journeymen working for him. He had a nice business but was a poor manager, and his wife could spend more than three men could earn. He had made his start by peddling merchandise and had about four dollars' worth of odds and ends in a handkerchief, which he gave me to sell. I remained in Philadelphia seven weeks and purchased additional goods each day. [I] paid my lodging, $3 per week, to my sister-in-law. She did not want to accept it, but I told her I came to America to earn my own living, and if she did not take it, I would go to a boardinghouse.

During these weeks I made the acquaintance [of] and purchased goods from Blum & Simpson, who gave me credit for goods to the extent of $100, to go peddling out of the city. I peddled in Lancaster County [Pennsylvania] one year and sent my parents $700, for them and my sister Babet and brother Moses to come to America with. They came, but my sainted mother lived only six months after arrival.

Before the family came, I had gone in partnership with David Strasburger in Kilgore, Carroll County, O., where we kept store and "batchelor hall" for a time, when Strasburger married, and we moved to Franklin, Harrison County [Ohio?].

ROMANCE AND INTRIGUE

As was my custom to purchase goods, I made a journey to Philadelphia, traveling by steamer from Steubenville to Pittsburgh, then by stage to Harrisburg. During the trip my boots hurt me, and my feet were swollen, so I took them off and also lost my hat during one of the nights' travel[s]. We arrived at Harrisburg for breakfast, I carrying my boots, and hatless.

On the train from [to] Philadelphia sat a young man who, no doubt observing that I was a follower of Abraham, moved next to me and, during conversation covering many subjects, he said he could scarcely await the train's arrival in Lancaster, as he had been married six weeks before and had been away several weeks.

I told him that if I could meet a desirable girl, I would like to marry also. He said if I would stop at Lancaster, he would introduce me to his wife's cousin, who was living with them, and that he knew she would make a good wife. . . . I permitted myself to be persuaded and stopped over at Lancaster for one night, purchased a hat, and went with my new friend to his home to see the girl, who seemed to suit me.

Next day I started for Philadelphia, and with me her brother, Ephraim Wormser. They had one uncle, by the name of Rauh, a rabbi in Philadelphia, of whom I made some inquiries. [Moses Rauh was minister of Rodef Shalom Congregation in Philadelphia.] On arriving at my brother's home, my sister-in-law congratulated me on my engagement. I told her I knew of no engagement. She said she had met a man by the name of Katzenstein, who told her to tell me that his sister . . . had arrived from Germany in New York, and, that when I came, to tell me to go to New York to marry her, if I met with his approval. I told her I knew nothing of the affair and would not go to New York, but that I had other ideas and that I had seen a young lady in Lancaster, who suited me, and I think I can get her.

As it was *Rosha Shana* [New Year], I attended the synagogue, where I met Wormser also. After service he invited me, and we went to a saloon for a glass of beer. In the course of conversation he asked me: "What do you think of my sister?" I said: "I had made inquiries about her, and that if she would have me, I would be willing to marry her." He said [that] he had made inquiries concerning me, and that they were satisfactory, and believed that if I would write to his sister, that she would accept me.

I wrote a letter in that saloon. What it was, I am too modest to say, as I had never written a love letter before. As I was twenty-three years old and had to provide a living since my tenth year, no love affairs entered my mind. I received an answer the following day, and to my great luck, the answer was favorable. Fourteen days later Uncle Rauh married us on October 18, 1843, at Lancaster, Pa., Paulina Wormser to William Frank.

When we arrived at Franklin, Mr. Strasburger came to the carriage. I introduced him, saying: "This is my wife." He said he thought there was something of that kind taking place, as I had remained away so long. As we entered the room, I said to Mrs. Strasburger: "This is my wife," and she said: "But it is not my sister. We had written to Philadelphia that you should bring my sister." I said: "I had not received such a letter."

A few days later, I met a lawyer who said that my partner wanted to sue me for breach of promise for not marrying his sister-in-law.

The lawyer asked me if I had written, but I told him: "No. That Strasburger had written, unknown to me." So he said that Strasburger should marry her himself.

THE PARTNERSHIP DISSOLVED

After we had been home sometime, I left at times to peddle, as I was well acquainted and could dispose of considerable merchandise, and, during my absence, my wife went into the store and was a successful saleslady. But on [my] returning one time, she said she would not tend store unless I was at home, as she did not get along with Mr. Strasburger complaining. When she said to a customer the price was 18¢, he said it was 20¢, and other complaints. I did not blame her, but asked her to wait until we had paid our debts; then I would make short work of the partnership. One day Strasburger said to me: "You married a fine lady, but she would not attend sales any more." I told him she was right, as he disputed her sales and was otherwise disagreeable.

In the early winter we bought geese to hold and fatten. On a Sunday morning soon after, Mr. Strasburger knocked loudly at our door and said: "Frank, get up. We will kill the geese today." I said: "They are not fat yet, and we bought them for that purpose." He said: "You can keep yours and charge yourself with a bushel of corn they eat." This riled me, and I said: "I know of a better thing to do." "What?" said he. I said: "We will 'kill' partnership; then you can kill your geese when you want to, and I can do likewise." He asked me if I was in earnest, and I assured him I was. . . .

"Well," he said, "if you are in earnest, we will get at it at once." We agreed that we would divide anything that was dividable, and [for] the things not so, we would draw lots, which we reduced to writing. We carried out this plan until it came to the sign "Strasburger & Frank," which had cost $2. I said he could have my half for $1. He said: "No, we have divided all else; we will divide the sign also." So we sawed it in two, he getting "Strasburger" and I, "Frank."

From Franklin we moved to Jefferson, Harrison County [Ohio?], and opened a store there in the spring, and here our Hyman was born. The second summer there, we were visited by a young man by the name of Hart. We took a ride in the afternoon, and when we were near his home, our horse took fright and threw us out of the buggy, and my wife had her arm broken. It was quite serious, and she was laid up two months, and a month later our second son, Ephraim, was born.

PITTSBURGH MERCHANT

In March, 1846, we moved to Pittsburgh. We were there but six months when Ephraim died, and we buried him in the Troy Hill Cemetery, which Mr. Strasburger, Emanuel Reis, and I had recently purchased for the Congregation Bes Almon [Cemetery Society], of which we were the earliest members, it being the first Jewish congregation in Pittsburgh. Later, when the congregation became mixed, and Mr. Wm. Armhold (1854) was the reader, the Polanders [Poles] wanted a reader from Baltimore, who had a wife and children in Poland, and we wanted to retain Mr. Armhold.

I resigned as a member; then Wormser, Strasburger, Gallinger, Meyer, and others [resigned also], and by night we had organized a new congregation, which I named Rodef Shalom ("seek[ing] peace"), inasmuch as we desired peace. We retained Mr. Armhold until after the dedication of our temple in Hancock St. in 1861. We had previously engaged Josiah Cohen as an English teacher. [Josiah M. Cohen later became a judge of the Court of Common Pleas.] I was president of the temple when it was dedicated. . . .

In 1847, Louis Jaraslowsky and I started the Hebrew Benevolent Society, and it has been kept up under that name until this day. . . .

Immediately on arriving in Pittsburgh, I rented a store on Market St., between Third and Fourth Aves., where mother [my wife] assisted to good advantage for several years, when our growing family claimed all her time. . . .

Wormser and I were partners for nineteen years as dry goods merchants and glass manufacturers. The works were built at Frankstown, which was named after me, in 1858. I continued in the glass business with [my] sons Hyman, Sam, and Abe until 1876, when the factory burned and was not rebuilt.

What Do Women Want?

I want a red dress.
I want it flimsy and cheap,
I want it too tight, I want to wear it
until someone tears it off me.
I want it sleeveless and backless,
this dress, so no one has to guess
what's underneath. I want to walk down
the street past Thrifty's and the hardware store
with all those keys glittering in the window,
past Mr. and Mrs. Wong selling day-old
donuts in their café, past the Guerra brothers
slinging pigs from the truck and onto the dolly,
hoisting the slick snouts over their shoulders.
I want to walk like I'm the only
woman on earth and I can have my pick.
I want that red dress bad.
I want it to confirm
your worst fears about me,
to show you how little I care about you
or anything except what
I want. When I find it, I'll pull that garment
from its hanger like I'm choosing a body
to carry me into this world, through
the birth-cries and the love-cries too,
and I'll wear it like bones, like skin,
it'll be the goddamned
dress they bury me in.

Kim Addonizio

Louis Stix

Honesty Is the Best Policy

The New York Herald *for July 27, 1902, carried a list of American Jewish millionaires. Among the names was that of Louis Stix, who had died in New York City just two days before.*

Stix's beginnings, however, were certainly very humble. He was born in Demmelsdorf, Bavaria, in 1821. His maternal grandfather was the village teacher and "rabbi." When only a lad, young Louis was apprenticed to a glazier; later, but still before he was twenty, he became a journeyman.

An older brother of Louis Stix, Carl, came to Cincinnati in the 1830's. Because of Germany's intolerance toward Jews, because of American opportunities which beckoned, and because of his desire to help his parents, Louis joined his brother by 1841. His devotion to the family was strong. As soon as he and those of his brothers who were already in America were financially able, they brought over the rest of the family, including the parents.

Louis started out as a pack peddler and soon owned a horse and wagon. He hawked his wares in the neighborhood of Cincinnati, in southwestern Ohio, and in eastern Indiana. By 1843 he and his partners opened a little shop, although some of them continued to peddle. At one time, the partners owned general stores in Mason, Ohio, and Billingsville, Indiana. Willing to do anything to make an honest dollar, Stix also traded in country produce and hogs, and even sold carriages.

Not only was Stix willing to make an honest dollar, but he was distinguished for his honesty in dealing with his creditors. Because of losses incurred by his partner Victor Wallach, an inveterate gambler, the firm of Stix & Wallach was compelled to make a settlement in 1850. Fourteen years later Stix had paid off all the debts, with interest.

Some years before the Civil War, the new firm of Louis Stix & Company, dealers in dry goods, was founded. The business prospered to such an extent that in 1864 Louis Stix found it imperative to settle in New York as the firm's resident buyer. His younger brother Henry went into the wholesale clothing business of Stix, Krouse, &

Company. William, the youngest brother, settled in Memphis, where he helped establish the firm of Rice, Stix, & Company, which later moved to St. Louis.

During his years in New York, where he lived from 1864 until his death in 1902, Louis Stix devoted himself to the promotion of the Cincinnati firm, which was conceded to be one of the best-known dry-goods houses in the Middle West. He was also active in the social and philanthropic work of New York Jewry and of the general community, serving as a director of Mount Sinai Hospital for over a quarter century.

Stix married Yetta Hackes in 1851, and left ten children and numerous grandchildren. In 1901 he had the satisfaction of celebrating his golden wedding anniversary and of recording the silver anniversary of a daughter and the marriage of a granddaughter. Life certainly had been good to him.

About 1894, "The Infallible Louis," as his children jocosely called him, sat down to write his autobiography. The last lines were written but a few months before his death, after which his family printed the memoir for private distribution with the imprint: Louis Stix, Reminiscences Chronicled as a Recreation in His Later Years, 1821-1902. *The following extracts from this volume of 394 pages are taken from a photostat copy in the possession of the Director of the American Jewish Archives.*

The extensive memoirs are rich in detailed descriptions of the activities of peddlers and merchants. Numerous anecdotes throw light on the political, economic, and social life of the general community of southwestern Ohio in the days before the Civil War. For persons interested in post-bellum New York, there are many pages describing Stix's experiences as a businessman and philanthropist. The autobiography is an excellent source for the study of a successful American merchant. Unlike numerous similar works, Stix was relatively frank and straightforward in reciting his ups and downs.

Our Distinctive Family Name

THESE recollections are born of a long deferred purpose. The history of every life is valuable. Its struggles, its efforts, whether successful or otherwise, and even its mistakes, become beacons and landmarks, serving as a guidance to those who may find themselves in similar straits or difficulties.

It is needless for me to say that I am neither historian nor linguist. The all-absorbing cares of a life spent in mercantile pursuits have debarred me from the acquisition of attainments which would have made my task easier, and greatly improved the literary style of these recollections. Nevertheless, though thus hampered, and realizing in advance the impediments in my way, my naturally strong determination to carry out all I undertake has urged me on, and enabled me practically to bring to a conclusion these reminiscences. If I have succeeded in making them interesting to my posterity, I shall have brought to a happy termination my self-appointed task. My mention of figures and amounts must be received as only approximately correct. . . .

My father's family had no family name at the time of his birth. Nor do I know whether any of the family names . . . existed prior to 1813. Prior to that date, the custom prevailed, among European Jews, of giving to boys one name only, with the name of the father joined either with or without a connecting *ben* (which [*ben*] means "son"). Certain it is that my father, like all Jewish citizens (such designation is perhaps a liberty) of Bavaria, was compelled, under a law passed in 1813, to adopt a distinctive family name. Acting under this compulsion, he adopted the name Stix. I shall always feel grateful for that law and its enforcement. It prevented the complications and consequent confusion, arising from the repetition of names from generation to generation, which had prevailed to such an extent that neither postman, court officials, friends, nor foes, could insure a communication reaching its intended destination. It was moreover fortunate in securing for us an individuality of name, as my father, who always had an aversion to long and unpronounceable names, was thus enabled to legally make his own selection, and in so doing,

311

chose a name which has the merit of extreme brevity and entire orig-
inality. Though unknown when my father appropriated it, it has, I
have heard, during the last century, been adopted by several families,
both in this country and abroad. Yet it remained so rare that, in 1887,
a cablegram sent to me by one of my daughters, from Carlsbad,
Bohemia, addressed "Stix, New York," reached me without requiring
fuller address. May the name be transmitted in its original honor,
unsullied by any unworthy act, as I received it from my parents, and
hand it to my descendants, and may it continue to be esteemed no
less proudly than by those who bore it in my generation. . . .

ON THE ROAD TO CINCINNATI

The passage was uneventful. Forty-three days after leaving Bremer-
haven I landed at New York City [1841?]. My effects were examined and passed customs inspection without any duty being imposed.
The captain took me to his hotel and sought to have me remain and
return with him, promising me a position as soon as he dared con-
sistently to appoint me. But I had come to the United States to remain.

My companions and I passed the first day on shore in seeing the
sights of New York. We found friends and acquaintances and were
received by all of them with good will and hospitality. We were offered money, more than sufficient for our wants, by at least six different persons; among others by Meyer Wald. Among those friends
whom we found were our fellow-townsmen Abraham and Henry
Mack, brothers. After a brief sojourn in New York we started for
Cincinnati. Abraham Mack, who had been in the United States for
some years and spoke English, made all the arrangements for our
trip westward, and accompanied us to Cincinnati, at all times showing all of us that gentlemanly courtesy for which he was well-known.
From New York we went up the Hudson River to Albany by steamboat; from Albany to Schenectady we traveled by rail, and we made
our way from the last-named place to Buffalo by canalboat. The
captain of the canalboat had contracted with us to reach Buffalo to
make connection with a certain boat which was to convey us across
Lake Erie to Cleveland, but he failed to make the connection, and
we felt seriously inconvenienced by the consequent delay, and Mr.
Mack threatened to sue the captain. While waiting, however, for the
next boat, the news reached us that the boat which we had intended
to take had been, while crossing the lake, destroyed by fire, and that
most of its passengers, including many who had crossed the ocean

with us, as well as other immigrants, had perished. We deemed our escape almost providential, and did not sue the captain of the canal-boat. We took the next scheduled boat across the lake and, when we arrived at Dunkirk, an immense crowd met us, inquiring for friends and relatives. It was a heart-rending scene, these stricken mourners, grieving over the loss of fathers, mothers, and other dear ones. It was the saddest and most pitiful spectacle I ever witnessed. At every landing we made there was a repetition of misery.

From Cleveland we journeyed by canal to Portsmouth, Ohio, passing Chillicothe, where three stepbrothers of the only cousin we had on the maternal side were living. At Portsmouth, we met Mr. Kornblieth, a merchant whose destination was the same as our own, Cincinnati. We stopped at the same hotel as he did, and found his family very kind and hospitable. They did all in their power to make amends for the absence of our parents and supplied their place to the best of their ability. The friendship then established has been of lifelong duration.

THE PEDDLER WHO SPOKE FRENCH

Brother Carl and Martin Stadler [who also came from Demmelsdorf] were partners. They went through the country with a wagon, selling goods. Max Stadler and I also entered into a similar business arrangement, and with him I formed my first partnership. We went about on foot, visiting the rural districts. Max, who was very industrious and a hard-working man, sold more goods and carried a larger bundle than the writer. He took the liberty, without consulting me, of buying a horse. I at once insisted on a dissolution of the partnership. While he used every argument to persuade me to keep the firm together, I would not consent; so we parted, remaining friends. I outbid my partner when dissolving, so that a considerable profit accrued to the firm. Max was willing that I should become the owner of the horse, as he had already made up his mind to purchase a pair. With these, and a new wagon, he increased his business to quite an extent.

In 1841 I first crossed the state line from Ohio into Indiana. A merchant, named Mr. Johns, who kept a store not far from his residence, demanded to see my license. I pretended I did not understand his request, and kept on showing him my goods. Knowing that there were Germans in the neighborhood, I pretended to be French; whereupon he called his son, a young man just from college, to interpret my unintelligible jargon. The boy knew about as much French as I did, but, as I had a slight knowledge of Hebrew, I repeated some words to his great confusion. He assured his father that he could not understand my French, and that I must speak a dialect which was only used in a certain locality, and not universally recognized. Shortly after, Mr. Johns met me at Oxford [Ohio], and wanted me to accompany him to the professor's house, to whom he complained that his son's education was quite unsatisfactory in regard to his acquirements in foreign languages. The professor, who knew me, replied that although his boy had but little knowledge, yet he was perfectly confident that I had none at all. I met Mr. Johns after this interview, and acknowledged that my pretense was to avoid arrest and a fine for peddling without a license, which was a requirement in the state of Indiana.

The first goods which we found profitable in our business throughout the country were made of German silver, manufactured by Hall and Elton. I sold them on credit, and warranted that they would retain their bright color. Before long, however, they tarnished and looked like copper, and if left in any acid, were nearly ruined.

When I called upon my customers after six months or a year to collect the money due me, they showed me the goods, and although greatly disappointed that they had turned out so unsatisfactorily, yet, having sold them in good faith, believing them to be excellent metal as represented, I left it with my patrons to decide the value, and pay me whatever they considered a fair price. This course had the effect of increasing their confidence in my honesty, which I never abused.

A TALE OF TWO HORSES

While peddling, I bought a horse, seventeen hands high, and quite as beautiful as he was high. On my first attempt to hitch him to my wagon, I discovered that he was determined not to work. I tried every means to induce him to do so, but without success. He would throw himself upon the ground and refuse to rise. I was advised to put live coals under him, and was told that, under the influence of this stimulant, he would not only get up, but give up, and thereafter realize that I was his master and that he must obey me. I tried it and the plan worked to perfection. After driving him for a while, I found that the animal was so short-winded that, when pressed beyond a walk, he would puff and blow like a blacksmith's bellows. I was therefore tender with him, and the only time I drove him faster than a walk was upon entering a town.

One day I came to Monroe, Ohio, where Mack Bros. were keeping a store. As I pulled up at the door of their establishment, an old jockey, who with his eyes shut knew more about a horse than I did, or ever expect to, pretended that he had taken quite a fancy to my steed, and invited me to go with him to his farm on the outskirts of the town, doubtless with the intention of taking advantage of me. He began by proposing that he would trade horses. I asked him if he would warrant his mare sound, for I had noticed that she was blind in one eye. He guaranteed her as sound as a dollar, upon which I warranted my horse to be as sound as his mare. In trying to prevent me from discovering the blemish in his animal he kept aloof from my horse. We finally traded upon such terms that he gave me about $50 to boot; not a bad bargain for me, for I had purchased my horse at auction for less than the man paid me as the difference in value. We changed harnesses, and I obtained a much better animal, in spite of the loss of her one eye, which only affected her appearance, than the one I sold, which was wind-broken and of very little account outside of his huge size and generally fine appearance.

The jockey was caught in his own trap, and never drove the horse to town or spoke of me. He finally traded him to a wagon manufacturer, from Dayton, Ohio, who was taking some of his vehicles to market. He traded for one conveyance and about $50 in cash.

ADVENTURES OF A PEDDLER

In the year 1842, while I was driving in my wagon in the neighborhood of Newton, Ohio, a Mr. Williams [a Jew] met me and asked to be taken in. An immense freshet had recently swept everything before it, and in trying to cross the Little Miami at an old and heretofore perfectly safe ford, my horses unexpectedly lost their footing, and swam quite a long distance; the wagon upset and the goods were soaked with water. I at once put them in good shape and sold them to the best advantage I could. Mr. Williams returned to the city for the purpose of going to the temple to give thanks for his deliverance, as is the custom with Orthodox Jews when their lives have been spared from a threatening catastrophe.

About this time I called upon a man in that region to collect a debt, long since due me, of $100. He paid me the money but, as he did so, seemed deeply affected and shed tears. I asked him why he cried, and he replied that he had promised to send money for his parents, then in New York, to come on and live with him. Although my means were limited, and the amount due me was of considerable value, yet I returned it, and told him to use it for that purpose, and pay me when he could conveniently. He was not able for a long time to do so, yet finally he returned both principal and interest, and it always gave me much pleasure and gratification to see him with his parents, brothers, and sisters, and to know that I had been instrumental in giving him such pleasure. They all felt deeply grateful throughout their lives for the kindness I had extended to them.

In the year 1843 I stayed one night with a Mr. Montgomery, and went in company with Miss Montgomery and her uncle to an apple cutting [paring bee?], at the house of her sister, Mrs. Port. I took some other young lady home, not intending any incivility. Miss Montgomery's uncle took it for granted that I would be her escort back. Miss Montgomery, thus left without anyone, was escorted home by her nephew, who supplied the vacancy, and she bitterly complained to her father of my rude, ungentlemanly treatment. In the morning, on going after my team, Mr. Montgomery, in a rage at the indignity I had shown his daughter, ran after me with a hayfork. I had great difficulty in making him understand the mistake, and that no disrespect was intended—finally, after much explanation and apology, his anger was appeased, and I was allowed to depart in peace.

The next time I visited the place, I stayed with one of his neighbors, Mr. Dodd. After supper, I went out sleighing with his daughter, Mary. The sleigh upset, and the poor girl returned home minus some of her teeth. The next day, I found that my horse, that I had been out with the night before, had been so severely kicked by his companion in the stall that I was obliged to shoot him, there being no hope of his recovery. I next took Mary to a Masonic celebration at Cornersville [Connorsville?], Indiana. A Mr. Magnus kept a hotel there, and he had made a contract to furnish a first-class dinner to all who attended. His wife, an excellent milliner, had no idea how to feed such an immense army of hungry people. Wishing to treat them to some delicacy, she baked a kind of fritter, called *Schneeballen* in German. The more you ate of this food the more you required; your appetite was rather improved than diminished, and many left at once for neighboring places to appease their hunger, in quite an indignant state of mind. Dinner had been ordered for one thousand guests, and there were over five times that number waiting to be fed, and not half enough bread to supply their needs. All were annoyed, and Mr. Magnus was ignominiously expelled from the lodge. The officers were more to blame than he, however, for if they had calculated correctly there would have been no such disappointment. We then engaged to go together to the annual Masonic dinner at Eaton, Ohio, feeling assured that the lesson of the preceding year would be a salutary one to the brothers, and we might reasonably expect a fine entertainment. This one proved a grand success and I enjoyed the festivities exceedingly.

That same year I was returning to Cincinnati, from a trip to Logan County, Ohio, and I passed through West Liberty and sold some goods to one of the merchants. I carried quite a large sum with me in two wallets. By some unaccountable carelessness, I left one of those wallets on the counter. The merchant found it, and sent a young man after me to return my missing property. He mounted the first horse he could find and started in pursuit. I heard him following, and naturally supposed, as it was dark, that he had evil designs; so I drove faster and faster, fearing robbery, until I reached an inn, where I halted. Here he overtook me, explained his object, and restored the wallet, but refused all reward which I would willingly have given him, as I felt extremely thankful to him.

About this time, I employed a man to travel through the country and sell clocks for me on twelve months' credit. I had bought, as I supposed, excellent timepieces, so I guaranteed them for a year. But when the time expired, and collections were due, many complained and refused to pay, because the goods were not as represented. I had become quite a successful tinkerer by this time, so I fixed up a number of them to the satisfaction of the owners. Some of the notes I had received, however, were hard to collect. Stopping one night with Mr. John Beard, I traded four hundred dollars' worth of these notes for 120 acres of land near West Mansfield, Logan County, Ohio. At the same time Mr. Beard offered me more valuable land for additional notes, which proposition I declined, fearing to invest too much capital in property. Becoming a landowner, I went to see my newly acquired estate. I learned that Henry Clay was the proprietor of the adjoining tract of 640 acres, which was offered for sale at $1.25 per acre.

On my way home, I rented a store for a few days at Bellefontaine, selling goods at private sale in the daytime, and in the evening at auction. The business was not very remunerative, so I packed up and went to Urbana, Ohio, where I made quite a stir in the auctioneering line at night. I sold so much cheaper for cash than the old merchants did, who gave credit for twelve months, that they attacked me in the public press in a merciless manner. Weaver & Bros., an established mercantile house, denounced me in the papers as a swindler and a thieving Jew. I hardly understood the nature of this most serious accusation, but a gentleman of wealth and high social position benevolently came to me and brought with him a German to act in the capacity of interpreter. When the situation was duly explained to me, I was asked what action I intended to take to defend myself against those unwarrantable aspersions, so detrimental to my business interests, and derogatory to my character. Finding me helpless to cope unaided with so grave a charge, this kind-hearted philanthropist, Dr. Musgrove, who was either an Irishman by birth or born of Irish parents, offered to publish a reply for me free of charge, if I would bind myself to the following line of conduct as the only true and honorable course for me to pursue. I accordingly agreed to sell all my goods at a reasonable and fixed price. I was also to be truthful, obliging, and strictly honest in all my dealings—thus I would, he assured me, attain success in business and silence my enemies, while he would immediately champion my cause, which he did most thoroughly.

My gratitude toward this noble benefactor prompted me to follow throughout all my future career his wise and excellent advice. It established firmly within my soul the principles of probity and justice, which I have endeavored to make the basis of my character. I speak with all due consideration when stating that I have never taken any unfair advantage of any person. I had been taught uprightness at home, but Dr. Musgrove added the clinching nail to early influences and instructions, and I have ever honored and revered his memory.

I ran short of goods while in Urbana and employed a wagoner to go to Cincinnati and bring me a load of merchandise from there. I promised to be there in time to load the merchandise and to give him an extra price, provided he would carry no other goods but mine, which I just then wanted particularly for an approaching holiday, and so could not afford to take any chance of delay. To this the wagoner agreed, but, notwithstanding this agreement, he made a secret arrangement with my business rival, Weaver & Bros., who had attacked me in the press, that he would bring them part of a load. A day or so before I expected to start, Mr. Weaver, who knew my arrangements, left at midnight for Cincinnati. The hostler at the stable learned what was going on, and instantly came to my room, with information that Mr. Weaver had departed. He had heard some conversation which betrayed all the details of the scheme planned to circumvent me. Mr. Weaver, although a rich man, never failed to do a mean or dishonest act to obtain a business advantage, far preferring it to a straightforward action. Nevertheless, he finally learned to leave me alone, for I succeeded perfectly in defeating his plans.

In less time than it takes to write this page, I was on my way to Cincinnati, taking another route, although the regular and best one was through Dayton. Reaching Cincinnati about sundown, I found the wagon had arrived, and made the teamster stop at the Brighton House, an entirely out-of-the-way place. I sent my goods there with a drayman, and started the wagon back with its consignment, just as my opponent put in his appearance to purchase his merchandise. He soon learned that I had been there, and that the wagon on which he had relied had already gone, laden with my stock. He was bitterly disappointed when he discovered that I had outwitted him, in spite of his vigilance and midnight start. I received my goods some days before his appeared, and was thus enabled to supply a pressing want of some specialties. This gained me much popularity. . . .

KEEPING STORE IN OHIO

Unfortunately, we [I and three other partners] decided to move into the country, and started a general store at Mason, Warren County, Ohio [about 1844]. We were acquainted with this place and had many friends residing there. Here we did quite a lively business, building up a good trade and establishing an excellent reputation. Still, we barely held our own at first, for there were two other stores that, previous to our coming, had never sold any goods except at large profits. One of these immediately began selling at such reduced rates, that its proprietor declared it would only be a short time before we would be obliged to close up and move away. In this, however, he was mistaken. I had inherited some of my father's obstinacy, and instead of failure, our sales increased at lower prices.

The farmers in the surrounding country bought their goods of us. We had but limited room, and insufficient help for our business, and our customers bought only leading and bulky articles. We had all we could do to keep the goods which the farmers insisted on taking with them. We had no time, nor had we the room, to show fancy goods and therefore did not handle them. We sold twenty-eight pounds of sugar for $1, salt at 90¢ per barrel, saleratus [baking soda] at 5¢ per pound, and molasses for 18¾¢ per gallon. Indian head sheeting we sold at $1 for twelve and a half yards, and charged a similar price for the best prints, with a spool of cotton and a card of hooks and eyes thrown in. We offered a free conveyance to our customers to take them home.

In this connection I remember, and will narrate, the following incident. A gentleman was sitting in one of our opponent's stores. He took a handkerchief from his pocket, and the proprietor, observing it, remarked: "I will wager you paid much more in the Jew store than I ask, for the articles you bought there." Whereupon the farmer enumerated what he had bought and inquired: "What would you charge me for the same?" The storekeeper mentioned about one-half the price he had quoted a few days before, upon which came the ready response: "I will take them all, and please charge my last purchase at the same figure now given, as you will find you charged me double the price when I bought last week from you."

About the same time, a Mr. Holmes came into our store just as I opened it one morning. He made some trifling purchase, taking care, as he did so, to exhibit a very large and well-filled pocketbook. He had gone but a few moments, when he returned, stating that he had lost his wallet and asked if I had found it. As the wallet was not there, and I knew that no one but myself had entered the store since he left, as I had been engaged in sweeping the sidewalk, I followed him to his hotel, and induced some of my friends to interest themselves in my behalf. We obliged him to undress, and, when stripped, the missing money was found in his boots, whereupon I seized a chair and broke it over his head. He had me arrested. Squire Dodd fined me a mere trifle. As we left the office, I struck him again. I was immediately rearrested, and brought back to the justice, who bound me over to keep the peace, and gave me a lecture. This ended Mr. Holmes' conspiracy, and he found it convenient to leave the place. My opponent, Mr. Hogan, did not resort to such a scheme again. He undoubtedly hired this miscreant to injure my reputation, through jealousy of my great success in business. He believed my success was due to the large profits I made, but that was not true, as I discovered when I closed that business, and started in the city. . . .

I recall, too, as is usually the case, that my first proficiency in the acquisition of English was in the way of profane utterances, a fact which called forth the following rebuke.

There was a certain Miss Polly Thompson, a well-regarded maiden lady, who invited me one day into her parlor and, in a very kind and considerate manner, addressed me in a womanly fashion, as follows: "Mr. Stix, we all respect and like you. Are you aware that you wound our feelings by the frequent use of profane language?" While I was hardly conscious of having done so, I immediately promised her that from that moment I would refrain from all rude or inconsiderate remarks, and assured her that hereafter, if she ever caught me using any objectionable word, I would agree to forfeit a silk dress, as the penalty, on each occasion. Although she was never entitled to claim my self-imposed penalty, at least so far as oaths uttered in her presence were concerned, I showed my respect for her admonition, and my regard for the sterling worth of her character, by giving her carte-blanche to get anything she wanted at any time in the stores of the town where I used to live, and have it charged to my account. My brother Henry insisted upon sharing with me in this pleasurable act of benevolence. We were honored by being permitted to defray her funeral expenses, for she became quite impoverished in her old age. Few better women have lived than Miss Polly Thompson. She reached the ripe age of ninety and departed, beloved and respected by all who knew her.

While I have ever been thankful to "Aunt Polly" for her merited rebuke, it was not always easy to remember my promise. I recollect how, on one occasion in particular, my wagon was stalled in the mire. Although the load was not heavy for the strong, seventeen-hand horse I was driving, yet, do what I might, I found it impossible to induce the animal to pull. Nothing I could think of would make the horse draw. As a last resource I said despairingly that "if it were not for Aunt Polly, I would swear, for this is too much for flesh and blood to bear." I gave way at last and made good use of my whip, aiding its application with a due mixture of the words I vowed never again to use. It worked like a charm, and often afterwards, when business was dull, and I was asked: "How goes your trade?" I felt, and replied, that "if it were not for my promise to Aunt Polly, I would say it was——." . . .

I always enjoyed stopping at Dr. Rowl's house, as both host and hostess were charming people. Mrs. Rowl was a lovely lady, and the doctor's rank as a surgeon of high attainments was unquestionable. On one occasion, in 1845, while I was peddling about Indian Creek in the neighborhood of Oxford, Ohio, I was driving after dark to reach the Rowls, when a man came through the woods, into the middle of the road, and asked for a ride. He was about to stop my horses, when I drew my pistol, ordered him out of my way, and threatened to make short work of him. I snapped my whip simultaneously with the warning, and though my pistol was not even loaded, my action threw him off his guard. I afterwards learned that a young man of very suspicious character lived near the scene.

Some time after, on my way from Billingsville [Indiana] to the city [Cincinnati], while driving up a long hill, someone approached and addressed me by my name, in a very familiar style, asking for a ride. As I had considerable money about me, I did not stop. My interlocutor then gave a sudden bound and sprang toward the rear of my wagon. Quick as a wink, I gave the word to my horses, applied the whip to start them off, and soon distanced my pursuer. I realized that it was a preconcerted plan to rob me; that the man had gone on in advance of me, knowing I would start for the city, and had calculated to spring into the wagon, if I refused to hold up. Although I traveled back and forth on the same road many times afterward, I never again was accosted. . . .

In the Hog Business

One season, about the first of the year, I went to Billingsville to collect money, as was the custom. Farmers who enjoyed good credit paid every twelve months. I found that these farmers were holding back and not selling their hogs, and often, after they had sold them, they paid other debts first and settled their store bills by giving a note at twelve months. We could really not afford to wait so long a time. In this emergency, I proposed to my dear brother to buy the hogs in the neighborhood, particularly from those who owed us money. Nothing suited brother Henry so well as this enterprise, and variety gave zest to our undertaking.

The first man he called on was Squire Frazy, a near neighbor and special friend, who always had the finest hogs in the county. When he was made acquainted with our intention, he replied with great promptness: "Mr. Stix, if you go into the market to buy, no one shall have my stock but yourself." The price was agreed upon: so much a hundred [pounds]. Mr. Frazy asked brother Henry if he preferred scale weight, or if he would guess at the number of pounds. Brother Henry prided himself upon being an expert, and considered his ability somewhat underrated; so he replied that it was useless of Mr. Frazy to put himself to any trouble; he could readily determine. Cordiality and confidence were thoroughly established by brother Henry's decision, and when, to prove his skill beyond a doubt or question, he insisted upon having the hogs weighed and the difference was less than a pound on 300, the weight of each, his reputation was unquestionably settled.

His next attempt at determining weight was not so fortunate. Frazy's lot had been about ten heads, but McCoid's stock numbered seventy-five. This turned out to be a poor and unprofitable business speculation. McCoid was only too willing, knowing brother Henry's successful test, to leave the matter of weight for Henry to decide, which proved to be in this instance about one-tenth less than the weight named by Henry, and at which estimate he had closed the bargain. We lost on this transaction what we had gained on the former, and came very near not getting our pay at all. The house to which we had sold the hogs was on the verge of bankruptcy, and failed only a few days after I had secured the sum due us, through prompt and earnest effort. They owed many people who could ill afford to lose their money, and who were seriously inconvenienced by their inability to meet their demands.

Passing through Oxford, Ohio, in 1846, with a drove of hogs, many of them could, and did, succeed in outrunning my horse, which was by no means a slow animal. One of the heaviest gave out just in front of the Mansion Hotel. Squire Satan, lawyer Smith, the constable, and the hotelkeeper assisted me in lifting the hog into my wagon. The mud at the time was some inches deep, and it was hard traveling. At the last stopping place before we reached the city, I rode ahead to make arrangements for myself, my men, and the drove of hogs, to stay overnight. Among my help were some colored men. As we entered the dining room I was shown a separate table, which I declined. From this fact, I became known as an abolitionist, which was the actual truth, and which fact, when known, caused me the loss of a number of friends. . . .

One time, after a short absence, I found the hogs had entered the warehouse of our Billingsville store, and selected the supposedly fresh eggs, butter, and any other delicacy they considered a suitable relish. I scolded, and my good brother made countercharges, not without foundation. These eggs, it seems, brother Henry had sold to a manufacturer of liniment, who failed to call for them, and by now they had become putrid. Hence the eggs that remained after the swine had enjoyed their feast had such an unbearable odor that I hired a wagoner to haul them to an uninhabited section; the very memory of them now is nauseating and unendurable. Brother Henry is said to have kept this store in Billingsville, Indiana, but the fact would be far more correctly stated, if we said that the store kept brother Henry.

He was always a great admirer of the fair sex, and although industrious, he was somewhat irregular in his habits. But there was one marked exception to his deficiency. In correspondence he was punctuality and informality combined. His evident preference was for young ladies. But in order not to excite jealous feelings, he addressed letters replete with expressions of equal attachment to all, and he favored them all so equally, that if the name had been omitted from the letters, each might have been mistaken for the other.

Billingsville recalls an amusing experience. I was mounted on one of my horses, the other following like a dog, jogging toward home after a long trip. On my way I met a drover with cattle, who asked my assistance, as one of his hands had been taken sick. The gentleman took quite a fancy to me, and wanted to know if I would engage to work for him. I answered that I would consider his proposition. At the dawn of day, he asked me to take his place, while he rode ahead to make arrangements to stay overnight. As I rode up to the gate, the drover stood talking to the farmer, who had addressed me as "Mr. Stix," to the great astonishment of my new acquaintance. "Who is that young man?" he inquired. The farmer replied: "That is our merchant at Billingsville." I enjoyed the joke, regarding it as a compliment that he fancied he had met a good German boy. . . .

Trouble at the Tollgate

In the year 1847, I had an amusing experience while passing a tollgate. I drove quite rapidly, more to display the fine points of my team, than to save time. I had wrapped up in a piece of paper, which I threw to the keeper, some change which I thought would be the correct amount of toll. My calculation was at fault, because the government had recently passed a law of which I was not aware, and, consequently, the amount that I gave him was short one cent.

When I had gone about 100 yards, I heard the gatekeeper call out after me. I pulled up as soon as I could. The man was quite angry, and authoritatively demanded the extra cent. I asked pardon, when informed, for not knowing the new requirements and handed him a quarter of a dollar, expecting he would give me back the change without further delay. He took the quarter but insisted upon my driving back to the gate to receive what was due me, as a sort of revenge for the trouble to which he had been put by mistake. I did not propose humbling myself by acceding to the demand dictated by such a disagreeable spirit, so hastily replied: "All right, that pays for next time too." A short time after, I passed the gate from the west and called out as I rode through: "I paid you last time."

Whether my watchful friend was confused because I came from the same direction as before, or whether he failed to hear what I said, as he afterwards asserted, I do not know, but he mounted a horse and galloped after me, shouting at the top of his lungs, and commanding me to stop. I had a fine, fast team, so kept him within a hopeful, encouraging distance, giving him a lively chase for several miles. I could have distanced him completely without much exertion, but concluded to turn in at Beaver Tavern, to water my horses, and give my enraged pursuer a chance to overtake me. The landlord, who was an acquaintance of mine, was also one of the directors of the road, and when he heard my story, he reprimanded the tollkeeper for his conduct, and advised him in the future to use more common sense and act less officiously, so that his services would be more appreciated by both the officials and the traveling public. His horse was yet blowing from the race when I left him, a wiser, but a deeply disappointed man, since he had expected commendation. He learned a useful lesson, however, by this experience, for he never again annoyed the writer on any future occasion.

At another time, while collecting goods with my wagon and team, bought at different stores, I was holding the lines and a porter was lifting a box into the wagon when a shriek from a steamboat whistle startled the horses. They ran wildly, breaking the lines by which I held them, and never stopped in their headlong career until they brought up in a drug store with not a wheel left on the wagon. The police arrested me, but I proved to the court that the accident was no fault of mine, so I was released, and sent my wagon to the shop for repairs. This misfortune occurred on the second day of a [Jewish] holiday. Father and his good Orthodox friends considered that I had but received my just reward, and thought it a judgment. . . .

THE HAZARDS OF BUSINESS

Among the many occupations in which I have engaged is included that of auctioneering. At Urbana I sold goods in this way twice a week. I also disposed of the stock of a Mr. Watson in Billingsville, and our own at Mason [Ohio]. I did all the crying myself and made quite a fair success of it.

The Billingsville stock was sold on credit to a Matthew Lewis, who was highly recommended by some of our best friends. He removed the goods to Laurel, Indiana. When we became suspicious in regard to his movements, we employed a person to watch him, who reported that we had better come on at once, as he was packing up all his effects and evidently intended swindling us. Subsequently he sold out and ran away.

I reached Laurel the very evening that he left. After feeding my horse and taking my supper, I started for Cincinnati, where I hoped to overtake him. My idea was that he was most likely to try to dispose of his horses (with which he made his escape) in the city.

I left, intending to ride all night, as Laurel was about fifty miles from Cincinnati, expecting to reach that city by morning. In crossing the White Water River sometime after midnight on the ice, it unfortunately gave way. The river was too deep for me to touch bottom, and my horse swam to the opposite shore. At best, I could not swim, and with my heavy overcoat, gloves, and shoes, I was even less able to make a successful attempt. Throwing away my gloves and overshoes as useless encumbrances, I clung with desperation to the horse's tail, and finally managed to get upon his back, as he broke his way through the ice. During the ride, I was soon frozen to the saddle.

Near daylight, I reached a house whose illuminated window had invited me onward, and encouraged me to feel that warmth and shelter were not far away. I hallooed for some time; at last someone came to my relief. This man unfastened the saddle to which I was frozen, and carried me into the distillery on the outskirts of Matamoras, Indiana, where they doctored me up with whiskey both inside and out. When I had taken about half a pint, they sent to the house for dry clothing and a carriage with a bed in it, to take me to the hotel at Matamoras. There was no charge for anything in the way of service, excepting what I gave to the driver. I went to bed, sent back the borrowed garments, had mine dried, and by next morning was again on my way.

On reaching Cincinnati, I went directly to an auction stable, where I found Mr. Lewis' horses. I had them attached, and he ran away on hearing of my appearance on the scene.

After complying with the requirements of the law in advertising, and paying expenses, I received the little that remained. I heard nothing personally from Mr. Lewis. About ten years after, I received an anonymous letter, mailed from Missouri, informing me that this man had two pieces of property in his name. I sent my claim to a lawyer and, after a suit, bought the land at sheriff's sale. Mr. Shenklin, the lawyer, paid the taxes on the wrong land for some time. Other claims were made by the wife for her dowry, and so, after retaining the property for about twenty-five years, a Mr. Stein sold it for me, and I do not believe that I ever realized the money I had expended upon it in paying the sheriff and other charges. In fact, I am quite confident I was out of pocket besides, for expenses. My attorney alone made a good stroke of business out of this transaction. Although deficient in some things, he was never found to be so in this particular respect.

My Parents Join Me

Father had emigrated to America in 1844 by advice of his physician. He had accordingly sold his house and such possessions as he did not want to take with him, packed up his effects, and left his native land with four children. . . . [By 1844, four of the ten children were dead.]

Now our revered parents were with us in America and were surrounded by their six children, all of us anxious to do what we could for their general comfort, and happiness, and with one accord we tried to induce father to retire from active work. Mother, with her calm, strong, religious feeling, learned to be content and never murmured. It was such a blessing to see their dear faces smiling upon us again that, with united voices, we urged father to devote himself to rest for the balance of his life and to enjoy thoroughly seeing his wife so happy. He did indeed feel proud and satisfied. Nevertheless, the habits of years of industry and activity were still so strong within him that he embraced the first opportunity to be busy and useful, with that earnestness of purpose which always insured success. He provided his family with both necessities and comforts most liberally, and, in a short time, he owned his own house and occupied it—a better one than that in which I lived. He also never failed to aid those who needed assistance, for he was very benevolent and generous in supplying help to those whom he considered worthy. He was an excellent judge of character and was rarely deceived by any impostor.

Mother was exactly the reverse. She had never learned to refuse an appeal, and her reputation was thoroughly established for being easily imposed upon. So kind was her heart that, although duped as often as there were days in the week, when the swindler was exposed, she invariably remarked: "Well, I will never be imposed upon in that way again." The next time there was only a slight change in the form of the appeal but with the same result. The principle upon which she based her action was, "Better be cheated a hundred times than let one worthy person in need suffer from a refusal." Her maxim, often quoted, and always lived up to, was, "If charity is bestowed at all, give with a will at once, and you really give doubly."

The greatest and most satisfactory pleasure of her life was enjoyed when she asked her children for liberal contributions to cancel some promise she had made of assistance, on condition that our business had been good during the year. In 1878, I remember, she

asked me if we had been successful, and, of course, all was extremely
prosperous, if dear mother inquired. Thereupon she requested me to
give her $100, which I handed her most willingly, although my
share of the profits at our annual accounting were about $330 net.
My recompense was complete when I saw the pleasure she enjoyed
in dispensing gifts to her pensioners. From my purse many received
her bounty and never looked for it in vain. When she had but little,
she had to give sparingly; but as her means increased, so did her
charities multiply—she was never so poor as to be unable to give a
portion to those whom she believed to have less than herself. . . .

The following incident centered about mother. . . . We had but
one hydrant to supply the water which was common to all the six
families who occupied the neighboring dwellings. One of the tenants,
a German, who had imported his home-acquired prejudices, and had
not yet parted with them, annoyed my family in every conceivable
way, never losing an opportunity to be disagreeable. On one occasion, a certain young girl pretended to have use for the hydrant
and kept my mother waiting an unreasonable time for the water
she wanted to procure. Growing weary of seeing my mother thus
interfered with, I stepped forward and demanded of the young girl
that she should give my mother a chance. She declined, whereupon
I picked up the vessel, which had been filled to overflowing, and
discharged the contents without much ado over the troublesome
damsel. Though she only received a portion of the shower, while my
mother, who snatched the bucket, caught the greater share, she
brought suit against me. When the case came to trial, the judge
decided in my favor. I was defended by Judge Stallo, and our
opponents were obliged to pay the costs.

My Charming Business Partner

About this time [1848?] I made the acquaintance of, and became
allied in business with, a young man named Victor Wallach, who
came from an excellent family in Cassel, Germany. His brother was
engaged in the stationery business in New York, and was a prominent and respected man. Although Victor Wallach was an excellent
salesman, popular among the ladies, handsome, charming, highly
educated, possessing every qualification to make him a successful
businessman, yet he had never saved a dollar, had no credit, and
deserved none. This man made great promises and, as far as selling
goods was concerned, surpassed every expectation. He soon relapsed,
however, into vices, wickedness, and immorality. His passion for

gambling had been so long an indulgence, that he yielded to the temptation, and I realized, with deep regret, that our prosperous business, promising such a brilliant future, was doomed to disaster through the unprincipled conduct of this man, who was so gifted, amiable, and fascinating that he was both trusted and beloved.

It was indeed a sad awakening, when my suspicions became confirmed, and failure seemed inevitable. As a salesman, my partner was the best I have ever met. I could not compare with him in this respect. Although hard at work all day, he was no less busy every night after he left the store, gambling without any conscientious scruples as to the manner in which those extravagant debts were to be paid. So card playing was his financial ruin. His favorite game was poker, and, to make good his losses, he not only stole money but resorted to all kinds of deceptions and treachery. He had accomplices who took goods which were bought with this purpose in view. When I found myself involved in such intricacies, seeing no means of escape [because he was my partner], I consulted some of my heaviest creditors, among whom was Mr. John W. Ellis, and inquired what would be the best course for me to take. They advised me to diminish my indebtedness as much as possible, and when the time came, they would help me to get rid of Mr. Wallach, and if possible, try and keep up the business.

Amid all these difficulties and complications, I was compelled to be absent, in order to attend to personal affairs requiring immediate attention. It was my purpose, when leaving, to be away several days, but returning home unexpectedly in the evening, I found the cash short a very large amount. Early next morning, one of my creditors, who had been playing in the game with my partner the previous night, sent for me to let me know that he had seen Mr. Wallach give a large check of several hundred dollars to one of the party, and so notified me in order that I might stop its payment. I did so, and again consulted Mr. Ellis, who proposed I should close the store and put the key in my pocket. One friend directed me to an attorney whose special legal practice was in settling up business difficulties of this kind. His counsel was that I should sell out my store to my father, and, at any cost, get Wallach to sign with me, giving me to understand that this was the only thing I could do under the circumstances. I paid him his charges and decided to look up another attorney, who did not attend exclusively to failures and bankruptcy.

A friend accompanied me to his lawyer, John Kebler. After explaining the matter to him, he remarked: "If you are one-half as honest as you appear, I will get you a settlement with your home creditors before you go to bed this night." He sent for them at once, to find out their intentions. They showed no opposition, and proposed that all whom we owed should meet, and they would agree to act fairly. Mr. Kebler called the meeting that very evening. I offered them all I had, if they would release me. My keys, books, and money had been taken out of the bank, so as to make it doubly certain that the check given by my partner the evening before, amounting to nearly $1,000, should not be paid. Wallach had overdrawn to a large amount. Still, his attorney would not give up the assets to me, nor to our creditors, even under the promise of releasing him from all liabilities, but demanded the sum of $5,000 to yield his interest in the firm. By the advice of my lawyer and creditors, I gave him about one-half this sum, and within a few days he lost at gambling nearly all he had received from me, and insisted that I should furnish him with sufficient money to take him to California. Our creditors agreed to accept 50¢ on the dollar. In making such compromise, I had agreed to furnish my creditors who asked for it an endorser; but many of them did not want any. Among this number were friends with whom I had grown up from childhood. . . .

Trauenstein & Co., and Stix, Krouse, & Co. volunteered their signatures for all I required. Later on the firm of Trauenstein & Co. was ruined by endorsing to a large amount for the liquor house of A. Louis. I came forward, remembering their kindness and generosity to me, and acted as security for a portion of their settlement, remarking that I would reciprocate their favors to me, even if I had to pay their obligations myself, to the amount of my endorsement.

My chief delight was in selling goods. I must have proved a success, for many of our best customers preferred to have me wait upon them. This, however, was only after my separation from Mr. Wallach, as I was not nearly as popular with the ladies as he was. We were very busy from the time we opened our retail dry goods store on Fifth Street [in Cincinnati], and after that I started anew with determination and energy, the odds all against me. I worked late and early, practicing the strictest economy. I was under little or no expense, paying neither board nor washing, as I lived with my dear parents.

I smoked no cigars nor pipe, drank not even a glass of beer, and blacked my own boots. I do not believe that my personal expenses were as much as $10 a year after our failure. I became quite appreciated by the trade; business gradually increased, and my reputation for a cheap and honest house was my biggest card.

A short time before my marriage, one of my lady friends presented me with a white embroidered vest. She afterwards became the wife of Mayor Harrison of Cincinnati. I made it my life study to do what was right, and my religious duty to do to others as I would have them do to me. My word was my bond, and I never, to my knowledge, went back upon it. When I review this portion of my past life, I remember that many of my opponents prophesied my failure. Nevertheless, I overcame the many obstacles by which I was surrounded, and when I quit the retail, and commenced the jobbing business, my neighbors were my first and best customers. If it had not been for my partner, Mr. Swarts, I should never have changed, as I always liked the retail business, and found it hard to give it up. . . .

Upon the occasion of my sister's wedding, I had promised all my employees a holiday to enable them to attend the ceremony. To protect our property during our absence, father had engaged a German woman to watch the house and the store beneath it. About midnight I received word that my establishment had been robbed. It seems that the store door had been opened with a key of which the thief in some manner had obtained a wax impression. He had been very successful, for upon examining the stock, we discovered that no less than one thousand dollars' worth of silk had been carried off.

Upon consulting the woman whom we had employed to guard the premises, she acknowledged that she had heard someone moving about downstairs, but that she had been so frightened that she not only had failed to give the alarm, but had hidden herself and remained concealed until I had entered the store.

On discovering our loss, we went immediately to the police station, where we were agreeably surprised by finding not only the goods that had been stolen, but also the thief who had stolen them.

At the time of our dissolution [1850], I was sued by a merchant tailor, Mr. Holliday, for a large amount due for clothes made for Mr. Wallach. At the time I was thoroughly despondent and wearied, so my attorney advised me to settle with him in order to save me from further annoyance. At the same time he did not see how I could be held responsible for my partner's private accounts for personal expenses. I offered to pay the tailor in goods from my stock, as he had often bought merchandise from us, but he refused my proposal and sued for the money. Mr. Force, afterwards General Force, who had just commenced practice as partner of my friend Mr. Kebler, was my attorney. He asked Mr. Holliday if he had brought his books into court for consultation and confirmation of his claim. They were sent for, and he was required to swear to their correctness. Then Mr. Force asked to see the entry of Stix & Wallach's indebtedness. The charge was against Victor Wallach, whereupon Mr. Force told me to go home, as the court and witnesses had made a mistake, and I was not the person referred to in the entry, and in no respect liable for the debt. He bade the squire adieu, and so ended Mr. Holliday's suit. Undoubtedly he left his claim to his descendants for collection. . . .

PREJUDICE, LUCKY NUMBERS, AND A SMART ALECK

In 1849 I went with my clerk, Mr. McCullough, to a German masked ball. He was a young American, blonde, and six feet tall. As we entered the room, someone made the discourteous remark: "What business have you here? We do not want Jews." Mr. McCullough thereupon gave the person a severe thrashing. After this unpleasant scene one high in position advised me to leave and return home, offering me his carriage, as he knew that trouble was brewing. We thought it prudent to heed his warning and to retire from the festivities. I had no idea that in free America such narrow-minded prejudices had been imported from the mother country, which I had been glad to leave on this very account.

The next day the offending person came to my store and threatened to sue Mr. McCullough. The latter gave him distinctly to understand that nothing would please him better than to be sued in such a cause, for that would have meant ruin to the prejudiced German's business, as his drugstore was right in the Jewish quarter, and fully half his patrons and friends were of the Jewish faith, and they would certainly have found him out most effectually.

That same year, some ladies who were interested in a charitable purpose called upon me, requesting a donation for a fair they proposed organizing. I had already contributed money, but besides they wanted a liberal gift of something upon which they could make a profit. I entirely approved of the object, a most worthy one, and heartily acceded to their wishes. I presented them with a patchwork quilt worth $50, with this proviso, that they would not raffle it off for less than $100, making 100 chances at $1 each. I was to have one chance in my own name, one for my mother, and another for my sister. Shortly after, the committee waited upon me to inform me that mine was the lucky number, and they wanted me to sell the quilt to them. I repeated my last arrangement. Again I was favored by a visit. This time they desired to buy my three chances. I offered them my chance of $1, but was unwilling to dispose of my mother's and sister's, and was particularly positive in stating that if I won the quilt, it was not for sale. They then acknowledged that I was again the winner. We still have the quilt in our house. . . .

One day, while standing in front of my store, I observed a young lady passing out and I heard her rebuke one of my clerks, remarking: "You had better keep your French *meshoves* ["junk"] yourself." Inquiring into the cause of offense, I learned that one of my salesmen, after waiting upon her most attentively for a long time, had failed to make a sale, and, as she was leaving, Cranny, another salesman, asked if he could not show her some new French *meshoves* which had just arrived. She understood what he meant perfectly well. I cautioned Cranny that a repetition of such conduct would result in a loss of his position.

I Get Married

Although I had withdrawn from ladies' society, unconsciously I had learned to respect and honor, above all others, the one whom I afterwards loved and married for the many virtues she possessed. Although we were neighbors, I had given so little expression to my real sentiments that, when I asked her for her hand, she was much astonished, and so were my dear parents, and her brother and uncle. I, however, objected to the attentions of her brother to my sister.

One morning, dear mother came to me quite annoyed, complaining that dear father had learned that brother Henry was engaged and he would not tell her to whom. This proved to be only a conjecture. To enable her also to have a secret, I informed her, under promise of keeping the intelligence entirely confidential, that I was engaged to Miss Hackes. No doubt she meant to keep her promise, but she could hardly wait to see dear father, and was quite unhappy until she could communicate the good news, and enjoy it with him. My parents never regretted my marriage, for they gained a lovely daughter, and her goodness was always appreciated and reciprocated by them. By her lovely disposition she has strengthened the affection and harmony that has ever existed in the Stix family, and I know of no household as large as ours, where there has never been a misunderstanding among the many additions to it by marriage and by birth. May our children ever follow the example of which we are proud and justly so!

Soon after our engagement, Miss Hackes moved with her folks to Western Row, at present called Central Avenue, between Fifth and

Sixth Streets. I visited her nearly daily, after my store was closed, which was never before ten o'clock, and at the latest left her house about midnight. Just at this time she felt her loss of a loving father most keenly, as she had waited on him through a long and lingering sickness.

From the date of our betrothal, September, 1850, we made many plans as to our future. We each determined to be frugal. On the eleventh of March, 1851, we were married in the Masonic Hall at corner of Third and Walnut Streets. The day was clear and bright, as beautiful a one as we could desire. The wedding was a double one: Jacob Krouse and myself each paying in proportion to the number of his invitations. My wife, on her way to the ceremony, as she passed the store, by special arrangement, let me know that it was time for me to close the store, as I had promised my help that I would do so to give them an opportunity to go to my wedding. The store was more crowded than ever; I hardly knew what to do. I finally informed the customers that they could take such goods as had been bought and pay for them, or come back tomorrow, as all my help had been invited to see me married at the hall. Any of the customers who wished to join us were then invited to do so. My dear parents' carriage was waiting for me.

Everyone who cared to attend marched to the hall, and many considered this also an invitation to the table. There was plenty of room, and I asked the landlord to have a lot of fruit and, particularly, a few boxes of oranges at my expense. He refused and would not allow me to do it. To punish him for his stubbornness I did not order a drop of anything to drink, although 250 persons were sitting at the dinner table. . . . I gave them an order to get all the drinks and cigars at the bar below at my expense, the same standing good all night, without tickets. Mr. Krouse, who had by far the fewer guests, could not well do otherwise, so our wedding was the first temperance wedding among our friends. I told Mr. Reitzenberger right there and then, that should I have a half dozen more weddings, never would I have another one at Reitzenberger's. Nevertheless, many of my lady customers who marched to the hall were more than pleased to see the ceremony of a Jewish wedding, and thanked me cordially, as it was all new to them. Subsequently, I received a valentine, beautifully decorated, with two doves making love to one another. It was a most dainty, exquisite design and, as usual, anonymous. I afterwards learned that a young Welsh lady, an heiress, who owned more than twenty houses and stores in New York City, had thus favored me. . . .

Just here let me say that I am about to enter into the details of an occurrence where, I must confess before beginning my story, I was entirely in the wrong; but, as I have committed myself to the truthfulness of all these narrations, I must, as ever, be candid in my acknowledgments, even though they should prove me to have been both hasty and inconsiderate.

We were seated at the table, my wife and I, beginning our breakfast. She had boiled four eggs, the usual number, and the first one I opened appeared stale, which destroyed any further appetite I might have had for eggs; at least for the time being. I did not attempt a second one, although my wife opened the second one for me. I did not care for it after my recent experience, as may well be supposed, but took it simply to please her, while she ate the third one. This, of course, left but one egg, which she insisted I must take. This I refused to do; and to let her understand that once "No" meant "No" decidedly, I continued to resist all the eloquence and persuasion which she brought to bear to compel my acquiescence.

Our controversy finally reached a point where, losing my temper, I flung the egg out of an open window which faced my seat and was temptingly near. While my wife did not utter a word, her face spoke volumes. I admit there was no excuse for my acting so hastily; but it was not without some good effect, and from that day to this, I have never been urged to give up my views for her ideas, nor have I ever had occasion to let my temper get beyond my control; at least so far as the egg question is concerned. To prevent any similar occurrence, we buy only eggs whose origin is thoroughly known, and whose purity can be warranted, and usually pay double price, since we have learned the difference. . . .

A Lively Episode

During the same year [1851], I had quite a lively episode with a Mr. James McCully, an Indiana merchant, who did business at Liberty. He was very far behind in his payments, and paid no attention whatever to our requests for a settlement. After repeated, ineffectual efforts to have him come to some honest, satisfactory understanding, I finally decided to see him personally. I also took the claim of Stix, Krouse, & Co. with me, and found that McCully was on the verge of failure. He tried to put me off by promises which he never intended to keep, and only made for the purpose of effecting a delay, the better to arrange for his anticipated financial difficulties and gain whatever advantage was possible. I consulted my friend, a lawyer, named Mr. Yearyon, as to the best course to adopt to prevent this swindle, and he advised me to take whatever I could manage to secure, as he expected any day to get a judgment against him for an eastern creditor, and he did not believe he would succeed in collecting over half the amount which was due. Returning to McCully, I found that the best arrangement I could succeed in making, even after threatening him, was 50¢ on the dollar, payable in goods. I was forced to accept this proposition; but the prices he charged were outrageous, and seeing no redress by any fair or honorable adjustment, I determined to set a trap for him.

I offered him a big price to take me to Oxford in time to catch the stage for my return home. In the haste of our departure, he hitched up his team and threw the goods into the wagon without requiring the receipt. He took his jewelry box with him, expecting to trade watches on the way. When we arrived at Oxford, Ohio, he put his horses in the stable, and I called on Squire Sertain to make out an attachment that my attorney, Smith, had furnished. The constable, who was my friend, only awaited my word to do his duty. I called Mr. McCully into the parlor and informed him as he was now out of his state, I would have an attachment in the hands of the officer served at once upon him if he did not pay me. He was forced into compliance, as he found himself in the same predicament in which he had placed me but a short time before, when I was in his state and at his mercy. I agreed to allow him a reasonable time to redeem his property without any expenses attached, and furnish him with enough money to hire a conveyance to return to his home. He never redeemed his pledge and threatened to shoot me if I ever told how he had been trapped and circumvented—while in Indiana, he had me at his mercy, but in Ohio, I was master of the situation. I have never been a good collector, and have often felt hurt when people tried to rob me deliberately, but in this instance I made quite a success.

McCully failed shortly after this experience, and not many weeks following, again bought goods of our house for cash . . . .

My Conscience Rewards Me

I had in my employ for ten years or more a good, trustworthy man by the name of John Jones. He became dissatisfied [about the year 1854] after some other house had promised him a large advance in salary, and acted in an unbecoming manner, quite the reverse of his usual gentlemanly conduct. I told him that if he wished to go, I would not stand in the way of his advancement, and although his time was not up, his salary would be paid him up to the hour he left. He accepted the new position, which was only guaranteed on his promise that his trade would follow him. In this respect he signally failed and consequently lost the situation. Being out of work, he was forced to accept a very poor place in a shoe store, which he kept only a short time. He commenced drinking, got in debt, and although an excellent, reliable man while in our employ, could no longer support himself nor his family, and sank lower and lower from day to day. His wife, who was always a lady, came to me, knowing that in the heat of temper he had insulted me, and begged me to take him back. I promised to do so if he would ask my pardon. She went away perfectly happy, and the next morning he came prepared to carry out the arrangement I had made with his wife. I told him that his willingness to do right was as good as the deed, and that he might go to work and feel at home as in the past.

Soon I noticed someone following him from morning till night. I insisted upon being informed in regard to his business and learned that he was the broker of a life insurance company, that Mr. Jones's dues were now thirty days past due, and that he had persuaded the company to be lenient, promising that if he secured his position, he would pay up. I advanced the money for a year, instead of paying quarterly as he had been in the habit of doing, and I told him he could commence to pay it back to me when his other debts were all discharged. He died soon after and his wife followed him shortly. They left three children, who, of course, were benefitted by the insurance, and who would have been quite destitute without it. The church trustees paid me the premium I had advanced and thanked me for what I had done in this respect for my old clerk, while my conscience rewarded me as well for the kindness I had extended. . . .

IT'S A WISE SON WHO KNOWS HIS OWN FATHER

Once, upon returning from one of my business trips in the East, having been away about a month, I entered a saloon in the evening and, in a fit of absent-mindedness, sat down at the same table with my father, without observing him. This made him so indignant that he vowed he would not enter my house for a year. Then I told him that I would go all the more frequently to see him, but I would not allow my children to visit him while he remained from under my roof. It would have been a deprivation to father not to see his grandchildren daily, so he was much perplexed as to what to do. In his extremity he went to Dr. [Isaac M.] Wise [the rabbi] for counsel, who told him that he must not adhere to his resolution, that such vows should never have been made, and certainly were better broken than kept. The same delightful visits we so thoroughly enjoyed were then resumed, without any further interruption. I tried to cure myself of this absent-mindedness which had caused this trouble. Sometimes when my thoughts were upon other matters, my wife used to send someone to watch for me when I was expected, as I frequently passed the house without realizing that I had gone beyond it. . . .

I Was an Opponent of All Involuntary Serfdom

From the day I first landed in this most glorious country, until the present time, my principles have never undergone any radical change. I was then, as I am now, an outspoken opponent of all involuntary serfdom, and against the acquisition of any new territory to perpetuate this unfortunate evil. I have always advocated a gradual emancipation, and an indemnity to be paid by the government to our Southern neighbors for their pecuniary losses in parting with their slaves. I could never understand how any good man could feel or think otherwise. My open opposition to slavery had cost me the goodwill of many Southern customers, and at no time before the war was it considered safe for me to venture south of Mason and Dixon's line. I was fortunate enough to hear Abraham Lincoln speak in Cincinnati, and I shared all his opinions. He spoke to thousands, and, in addressing our Kentucky neighbors, claimed no more right to interfere with their slaves than with any other property they might possess. He cautioned them against any unlawful acts.

A short time before the war [1861] I was in New York. I went with brother Henry to his boardinghouse for dinner, which was kept by a lady whose name was Mrs. Weil. Her table was one of the best, and her boarders were about equally divided between North and South. In a general conversation, a coreligionist and brother merchant living in the South, whose riches about equalled my own when I came to America, remarked that Southerners could not live without slaves. I replied to this by a very uncalled-for remark not at all flattering to our race who were living in the South. As this was at the dinner table, the Southerner, who had learned to look on us Northerners as "dough faces," as they called us, drew his pistol to compel me to take back my words. A gentleman from Cincinnati, who was at the table, also drew his pistol and offered to meet the Southerner in any way he desired. The latter was only too glad to get away, and I hope has since learned to do without slaves, or has returned to the place from which he came, where he was almost a slave himself.

While I was buying goods in New York at this time, the most exciting news was received of the firing of the Confederate soldiers on Fort Sumter, and the surrender of our troops. I have never seen a community so disheartened and distressed. The staunchest and strongest cried like children. All good citizens felt the calamity and feared the worst. I left with the first train for home. On the journey all sorts of plans for the future came into my mind. One was to pack up our stock of goods and move them to the country, which idea I soon abandoned, when I made a calculation upon the number of carloads they would make. I figured that at least twenty cars would be required. At that time that was the greatest number a locomotive could draw. Then I thought it would be impossible to secure the requisite number of packing boxes and cases, and I would find it difficult, if not impossible, to get any insurance. When we arrived at Commonsville [Cumminsville, near Cincinnati] most of the passengers alighted, but I went directly to the city as all my dear ones were there, and I preferred to be with them.

On my way home from the depot to my house, I was escorted by some home guards, who immediately enrolled me among them. I was satisfied with this arrangement, as it put me in the same company where my brothers and friends belonged, and I was particularly pleased to be under the command of Judge Storer as captain. My first act of service was to stop a gentleman on the street and demand his pass, or oblige him to prove that he belonged to some military organization. I had a band around my hat lettered "Storer's Home Guard," and I carried a Sharp's rifle. The man would not answer me, nor did he give me any satisfaction. I accordingly brought him to headquarters. The officer commenced laughing and told me that the prisoner was deaf and dumb. . . .

Some time after this experience, I was released from duty, having taken a government contract to make certain flannel undergarments. Any person thus employed was permitted to remain at home to attend to the details of the manufacturing and delivery of the goods. For this reason I had agreed to furnish the garments at a very low figure, but when they were ready the material had advanced fully one hundred percent so I really had offered them at a losing price. They were not accepted, however, the excuse being given that they were not up to the required standard. I asked the officer if he would cancel my contract, which he willingly did, and I sold the goods the same day for fifty percent more than I would have received for them from the government had all been satisfactory. But singular as it may appear, the same party who bought them from me at an advance actually disposed of these rejected garments to the government for about double the amount I was to have received originally for them. I did not hesitate, when I learned of this transaction, to express myself very freely in reference to the management of the officials, and I received word that if I did not keep my mouth closed on that subject not another dollar would be given to any Cincinnati firm on a contract from that time forward. Moreover, the provost marshal informed me personally that he was afraid of me, and he frequently refused to furnish me with permits for shipping any merchandise southward, when other firms, for some unknown reasons, had no difficulty whatever in obtaining them when business requirements made it necessary. Why this distinction was made in their favor, I never knew—excepting that bribery and corruption had made such inroads that it was difficult for those who rejected all such means to have any favors extended, or even to have their just rights without being interfered with. . . .

MY WIFE'S MOTHER

Shortly before we moved to New York [about 1863], my wife's mother was taken very ill. The doctor gave her up, and she was not expected to live another day. A set of women called at our house [the female branch of the Holy Brotherhood], whose occupation it was to wait on the dying and pray for them, according to the amount of pay they received. This custom I objected to most seriously, as women of this stamp could really have no true feeling for the patient and could only consider the dollars they received. I looked upon their services as heathenish, savage, and inhuman, and, without hesitation, forbade their entering the sickroom, as I knew that my mother-in-law had no use for such hypocrites, and felt exactly as I did about them. When I refused them admission to her, they had the impertinence to tell me that they would not put their hands on the corpse if mother should die. She rallied, however, that very night, and recovered; whereas, if I had permitted those ceremonies, they would probably have hastened her death. Mother moved with us to New York, and passed away the second year after we left Cincinnati. While in every way a noble woman, she died as she had lived, without any religious ceremony—nevertheless a good and model woman.

As illustrative of her strong sense of right, I recall the following humorous incident. A certain vagabond, who had the advantage of knowing most of the Hebrews in our city, made swindling and lying his occupation. He started out with the intention of getting what he could from [my mother-in-law] Mrs. Hackes and my wife, to help support him in idleness. Although he was known to be an impostor, yet nearly everyone seemed willing to be victimized by the eccentric beggar, and to contribute a certain share to his assumed necessities. He had a brother, who was a very respectable man, doing a good business, but who found it impossible to influence him to give up the wretched way of living to which he had taken a fancy.

On one occasion, determined to make a haul, he told [my brother-in-law] Mr. Hackes he was going to see his mother and sister, to endeavor to get something out of them for his personal assistance. When he reached our house, he said he had been sent by [my brother-in-law] Mr. and Mrs. Hackes, who had helped him for a long time. Then he told a pitiful story of a sick wife and children, and of other sorrows and afflictions, which he fancied would aid him in making an impression and in securing the money he wanted to collect. My wife and her mother gave him quite a sum, and promised him some old clothing the day following if he would call for them. That evening we went to [my brother-in-law] Mr. Hackes' house, and he also, it seemed, had been favored by a visit from Mr. Small, who entered his office smoking a fine Havana cigar, and bragged of his success in gaining all he required for his immediate use.

Mr. Hackes told his mother that she had been duped by this rascally fraud. She kept quiet, however, fully convinced that he would return the next day for the garments. When he put in his appearance, as she had anticipated, with some horrible additions to his previous story, she made good use of the broom that she had purposely placed in a convenient position, so he departed, not quite so well satisfied with his reception as he had been on the former occasion, and totally disinclined to publicly boast of the broomstick so successfully brought into requisition. From this time forward, he no longer counted my wife or mother-in-law among his patrons.

While perfectly aware of his shortcomings, I nevertheless contributed to his support, by giving him a yearly amount, for which he gave a receipt as per contract, keeping his accounts as well-balanced as if he was a bookkeeper in a regular, legitimate business. What became of him later on in life I have never ascertained, as he never sought me out; but when I knew him, he was a young man with many years apparently before him in which to continue this idle, wretched calling which he had adopted. He always dressed in the height of fashion, and lived on the fat of the land. His good education served him only to carry out more successfully his fraudulent practices and impositions. . . .

Charity for the Wives of Soldiers

In the days when charity was being solicited for the wives and children of our soldiers, some of my brother merchants called to see me, and complained that one of my partners had not responded in such an amount as it was supposed he was able to contribute. They hoped that I would increase this donation. I at once declined to interfere, but promised that I would make good the deficiency at the first opportunity which offered itself. Subsequently, a lady in a carriage called at the store and asked to see one of the firm. I told her that I was one of its members. She then handed me a small subscription book with various sums promised, none of which exceeded $5. I signed on the proper line and subscribed $100. Any bookkeeper would have understood the figures. I told her to let the committee collect it. The lady, whom I did not know, as she failed to introduce herself, was Mrs. [George Hunt] Pendleton, and she felt insulted and told her husband about it, and he reported our interview to the dry goods committee, of which he was one of the officers. He objected to my audacity very strongly in telling Mrs. Pendleton to have the committee collect the $1 which I had signed as a contribution. The subscription book was then shown to establish the amount of my contribution, when one of the members, on looking at it, remarked: "Gentlemen, this does not mean $1; it means $100, as it here appears."

Mr. George McAlpine and Mr. Pendleton were then appointed to call on Louis Stix & Co. to collect the amount therein mentioned. Mr. McAlpine met me and said: "Will you please pay your subscription?" and added: "Why did you request that the committee call personally to collect it? Do you think yourself so much better than the rest?" I excused myself on the ground that I did not know the lady, and my contribution being $100, I thought she would be pleased, rather than dissatisfied. Mr. Pendleton, who afterwards ran for the Presidency, was then presented as the husband of the lady who had called upon me. He very warmly thanked me for what I had done, fearing his wife had failed to do so, having been under the impression that the amount I had promised was but a dollar, and that the committee must come for it. I afterward met Mrs. Pendleton at a fair, and she expressed her personal gratification to me.

Jesse Seligman

The Making of a Financier

David Seligman, of Baiersdorf, Bavaria, had eight sons, all of whom migrated to the United States in the 1830's and 1840's. Joseph, the eldest, and the real founder of the family fortunes, came in 1837; Jesse arrived in 1841, at the age of fourteen.

Most of the brothers were peddlers and then followed the common pattern of shopkeeping. The Seligmans, unusually successful, turned to clothing manufacturing and, finally, during the Civil War, to banking. The magnitude of their clothing business may be gauged by the fact that in 1862 the United States government owed the firm $1,000,000 for garments which had been supplied to the armed forces.

During the crucial Civil War days, when the French and English were not eager to buy American bonds, the firm of J. & W. Seligman & Company, through its Frankfort-on-the-Main office, sold close to two hundred million dollars' worth of United States bonds in the German market. It has been said that those sales were almost as important as the victory of the Battle of Gettysburg.

In 1891, fifty years after his arrival in this country, a dinner was given in honor of Jesse at Delmonico's in New York. In the speech that he made on that occasion, Jesse told the story of his early days and of the beginnings of the family fortunes. That autobiographical address, most of which is reprinted below, was included in the memorial volume which was published after his death in 1894: In Memoriam, Jesse Seligman (New York, 1894), pp. 5-16.

The career of Jesse Seligman and his brothers was not typical of the German Jewish immigrant. Jesse began as a peddler and left a fortune which was estimated—by the newspapers!—to be anywhere from $10,000,000 to $30,000,000. He was very much admired in his days, not only for his integrity and his numerous philanthropies, but for his financial success which confirmed the popular belief that America was the land of unlimited opportunity. The Philadelphia Record of April 24, 1894, summed up the fond hopes of that generation in the following sentences:

Jesse Seligman, of New York, who died yesterday at Coronado Beach, California, was a prominent and most admirable representative of his race in America. From the most humble beginnings, a friendless boy carrying a peddler's pack, he rose to become the head of one of the greatest banking houses in the world, and an unofficial but trusted adviser of the Government in some of its important financial operations. Mr. Seligman's career was an exemplification of the opportunities afforded under a free government to the most lowly of its citizens to attain a high and influential position.

Forty Days and Forty Nights from Shore to Shore

I was born in a small village called Stadt Bayersdorf, Bavaria, where my ancestors, dating back over 200 years, are buried. My parents were good, honest, noble, and charitable. Their family consisted of eleven children, eight sons and three daughters. My eldest brother, Joseph Seligman, having graduated from the university in Erlangen, thought that he would do well to seek his fortune in the new country, the United States of America, and on his arrival here, in the year 1837, he obtained employment as cashier with Mr. Asa Packer [a Pennsylvania businessman]. Encouraged by his success, my next two older brothers, William and James, followed in the year 1839. I was then at the gymnasium [high school], making preparations to enter the university at Erlangen. After receiving glowing letters from my brothers in America, I asked permission of my parents to go to the new country also.

They assented, and on May 1, 1841, I started for Bremen, and, after reaching there, I learned that the vessel that was to carry me across was a small ship bearing the name "Johan Georgic." When on board, I inquired for my cabin, and one was accordingly assigned me. I found it was also to be occupied by three other passengers. The interior decorations of the cabin were not of a very high order, viewed from an artistic standpoint. The ceiling and walls were covered with whitewash, which had evidently been laid on in liberal quantities, judging from the transformation undergone by one's wearing apparel after coming in contact with it. The bed, while not a bed of roses, consisted of a soft wooden board, with a blanket to cover the occupant while he enjoyed his peaceful slumbers.

The menu could scarcely be said to rival that prepared under the supervision of Delmonico's chef. It was made out daily and consisted one day of pork, beans, and a cup of water; the next day, of beans, pork, and a cup of water; and the following day, of a cup of water, pork, and beans; and so on throughout the voyage, which occupied forty days and forty nights, from shore to shore.

On the last day of that voyage, which was fifty years ago, on the fourth of July last, when I awoke, I beheld Staten Island in all its beauty. My first thought was to offer a fervent prayer to the Almighty God for having brought me over safely to what I then regarded as paradise itself, and my second thought was to swear allegiance to the government of the United States. Whether I have been steadfast in that allegiance, it is not for me to say.

At that time the island looked picturesque and charming, and the houses were painted white, which, gentlemen, must be evidence to you that I had never visited the place; otherwise the island would have been "painted red," to use an expression with which, no doubt, some of you are not altogether unfamiliar.

New York on a Shoestring

It was on a Monday morning that I landed at Castle Garden, and at a time when immigrants were in great demand. I soon learned that the government had sent an official to me for the purpose of seeing whether my wooden box (Saratoga trunks or Gladstone bags not being fashionable in those days) contained anything that would be subject to the payment of the duties provided in the then "McKinley Tariff Bill."

After ransacking the contents of my humble box, I observed that the official made a very serious face, and, fearful that he had discovered something that would compel him to retain it, I asked him the cause of his annoyance. He stated that he felt very much disappointed, indeed, in not finding a dress suit among the contents of my wardrobe. I told him that in my haste to get to this land of liberty and freedom, I had overlooked it.

I then applied to him to direct me to a good hotel where I could stop at the rate of one dollar per week, knowing that my means at that time would not allow me to stop at either the Windsor or the Fifth Avenue. I was too modest, however, to make known this fact to him, and I assigned as a reason for not seeking these high-priced hotels that I was awaiting the arrival of my traveling letter of credit, which I had also forgotten in the hurry of my departure.

He directed me to a hotel in Division Street, where the clerk at the desk, knowing that I would like to obtain a fine view of the city, instructed the hall boy to conduct me to a room on the top floor, or, to be more candid with you, to the garret, which I found I could reach without being obliged to use the elevator.

After remaining in this city for two weeks, I found that my supply of cash was diminishing very rapidly, and that I had just sufficient money left to take me to Lancaster, Pa., where my three older brothers, Joseph, William, and James, were then in a small business. I remained in Lancaster a few weeks, during which time I learned the English language to some extent, and, at the same time, mastered the science of smoking penny cigars.

My brothers consulted as to what was the best course for our future, and as brother James, in the year 1840, was a pioneer in the South, going there and remaining during that year, and returning with a net profit of about $800, we concluded to take the advice of this purse-proud nabob—that we would better our condition by removing to that section of the country.

THE MOSQUITO SERENADE

The four of us came on to New York and took passage in a schooner, which took six weeks to make the trip to Mobile [Alabama]. During the voyage we encountered a very severe storm, and at one time expected that the schooner and all on board would be lost. In fact, it was reported that we were lost, but he who is born to be hanged can never be drowned.

On our arrival in Mobile, we immediately sought out a boarding-house; and as we had been nearly starved on our voyage, I need not assure you that our appetites were whetted to do justice to our provender when we reached the dining room. The report quickly spread that four foreigners had arrived, and, when we retired for the night, we were honored by a serenade, the musical part of which consisted chiefly of humming sounds, with which our ears were not at all familiar.

We soon discovered that this beautiful concerto came from a swarm of mosquitoes (any one of which would have looked with scorn upon the Jersey mosquito) that hovered around our beds. Notwithstanding their musical turn of mind, they were out for blood, so to speak, and it was not until early in the morning, after they had sampled us very freely, that they consented, much to our relief, to take their departure.

IN THE CHAIN STORE BUSINESS

Our capital was small, and would not permit us to open a business in a large city, such as Mobile was at that time. We therefore thought it advisable to go to some interior town, and Selma [Alabama] was selected as the place where we should pitch our tents. We opened a small store, and while brother Joseph remained in charge, William,

James, and myself went on a tour of inspection of the surrounding country, to be absent four weeks, at the expiration of which time we were all to meet in Selma again and compare notes.

The traveling salesmen of that period did not enjoy the luxuries that men of that vocation now expect, and as it was not customary to have a porter to carry your grip or parcel, we were obliged to perform that task ourselves. We were so much encouraged by the result of our first trip, that we concluded to make another for four weeks, and we found that our supply of merchandise was diminishing very rapidly.

Our capital, however, was increasing at such a rate as to enable us to open more stores, which we did, brother James leaving for New York City in order to make purchases for the amount of cash he had, and "running his face" [buying on credit] for the rest. We opened stores in Greensboro, Eutaw, and Clinton [Alabama. All close together]. At the age of fifteen, I was the possessor of my own store and had clerks in my employ.

We continued to be prosperous until the year 1848, when we thought that we might better our condition by coming north. Joseph Seligman and William left early in the spring, and brother Henry, who had then come out from Europe, and myself remained to wind up the business. At this point, I desire to say that I shall always feel grateful to the people of the South for the kind and cordial manner in which they treated us during our stay there.

On reaching New York, in the summer of 1848, I found that my elder brothers had already established an importing business. Brother Henry and myself started a business in the beautiful town of Watertown, Jefferson County. Here, with the assistance of the ladies, always partial to me, we soon increased our business.

At Watertown, I had the pleasure of learning to know and esteem the great and illustrious General [Ulysses S.] Grant, who was then a lieutenant at Sackett's Harbor. On our acquaintance we immediately became friends, and from that hour until his death I know of no one who was entitled to greater love and respect from not only his own immediate friends, but from the people of the entire country.

ON THE TRAIL OF THE FORTY-NINERS TO SAN FRANCISCO

In 1850, when the "gold fever" broke out in California, I determined to leave the store in the hands of my brother Henry, so that I might venture out there to ascertain whether we could not still further improve our condition. I took with me quite a large quantity of merchandise, and got it over the isthmus [of Panama] as far as Gergona.

Here I found that there were not mules enough to carry all of my wares to Panama in time to enable me to reach the steamer, so I was obliged to wait for two weeks, when I boarded the "Northerner." There were quite a number of steerage passengers and only sixteen cabin passengers, many of whom were stricken down with the Panama fever, and before we reached San Francisco eight of them were buried at sea.

My brother Leopold, who accompanied me on this trip, was also stricken with the disease, but, fortunately, before we reached Acapulco [Mexico], it turned into chills and fever, which was the means of saving his life.

Arriving in San Francisco, in the fall of 1850, I landed near Sansome and California Streets, the bay reaching as far as that in those days.

I at once searched for a store for the purpose of offering my merchandise, and the only one that there was the slightest prospect of securing was on Commercial Street. After being there for only a short time, I found that very high winds prevailed at times throughout the city, and knowing that there was a scarcity of water, and that the houses were frame structures (with the exception of a few that were built of iron), I saw that there was great danger of a conflagration.

Learning of a brick building that was in course of erection by Messrs. Hassler, Bains, & Co., in California Street, I at once applied for one-half of it when it was ready for occupancy. It was the only brick building in the city of San Francisco at that time.

FIRE, SHIPWRECK, AND POLITICS

After being there a short time, a fire broke out on the third of May, on what was known as the Plaza. I at once went there to assist some friends in removing their merchandise, but soon found that it had gained such headway that it would probably sweep the entire city. I immediately returned to my own building and found that the Damaha Hotel, a building adjoining the one I occupied, and kept by Captain Jones, was guarded by a number of his waiters, who were covering the roof with wet blankets, and who also stood in readiness with buckets of water.

I at once explained to Captain Jones that if my house were to take fire, nothing could save his hotel from destruction, as it was built of wood, and I suggested that he transfer a number of his men to my roof, so that, in the event of my success in fighting the fire, his hotel would also be secure. He acted upon my suggestion; and it was well that he did so, for the Customhouse, on the corner of Montgomery and California Streets, took fire, and swept everything before it, with the exception of the building that I occupied and Captain Jones's hotel.

Howard Fire Company, No. 3, did me great service during the fire, and I joined the company that night, serving and running with the machine for several years, so that I am now an honorably exempt fireman. Of all the dealers in merchandise, I was the only one whose house was saved, and as I had many articles that were needed at that time, I soon disposed of much of my stock, though I made no attempt to increase or reduce my prices.

Shortly thereafter, the affairs of the city became so disorganized that it was unsafe for anyone to walk in the streets without being well-armed, for there was no telling at what moment one would be attacked by the thieves, thugs, and desperate characters that had overrun the city. It was, therefore, found necessary to organize a vigilance committee to suppress this lawlessness and rid the town of bad characters. I became a member of the committee, and remained so until perfect order was restored. . . .

Upon my return to San Francisco, the famous Committee of Twenty-one was formed, with the object of nominating and electing such candidates as would give clean and honest government in both the municipal and state offices. I had the honor of being one of the members of that committee, a fact which I have never had cause to regret, for in the fall of 1857 I had engaged passage for myself and my family to come on east, but the committee insisted upon [my] remaining until the ticket was elected. This I finally decided to do, a decision which in all probability saved my life and the lives of my family, for the "Central America," which was the ship upon which I had engaged passage, went down at sea, and many of her passengers were lost. So much for serving one's country.

In concluding this narrative of my career in California, I will say that I look upon that state as still offering great opportunities to the youth of our land, and, with her rich soil, salubrious climate, and energetic people, she is fast becoming a dangerous rival to some of the older states of the Union.

HIGH FINANCE

Arriving in New York in the fall of 1857, during the great panic, I attended to my California business, which was continued for some years after my departure from San Francisco. We found that our capital could not be invested to advantage in dealing in merchandise, and, therefore, my senior brother, the late Joseph Seligman, upon whom we looked more as a father than as a brother, and whose advice and judgment were cheerfully accepted by us, went to Europe for the purpose of establishing a banking house there, and also with the object of placing the United States bonds on the Frankfort [Germany] Bourse [stock exchange]. He was successful in enlisting the sympathy and support of the capitalists of Germany in behalf of our government, at a time when such sympathy and support were necessary to sustain its credit, and the result has proven that it was not without profit to the investors, for United States six-percent bonds were sold in Frankfort as low as thirty-nine in gold.

Since then we have been identified with every syndicate that has placed the United States bonds, and, more particularly, with the issue of four-percent bonds, which were floated when John Sherman was Secretary of the Treasury [1877-81]. These negotiations have had the effect of establishing the credit of our government, and today it stands higher than that of any government in the world, for we have been able to extend our four-and-a-half-percent bonds at the rate of two percent.

In 1864, other houses were established in Europe: the London house, Messrs. Seligman Brothers, which was headed by Isaac Seligman; the Paris house, Messrs. Seligman Frères et Cie., headed by William Seligman; the Frankfort house, Messrs. Seligman & Stettheimer, the head of which is Henry Seligman; and later houses were established in Berlin, Amsterdam, New Orleans, and San Francisco.

It is useless for me to tell you that during these many years great temptations have beset us, and that we have had to encounter many financial storms; but, thanks be to God, he has guided us through all these difficulties, and, no matter in what position we have been placed from time to time, we have always striven to retain our honor and good name.

Now, only a few words more about myself. My success, whatever it has been, gentlemen, I attribute, first, to the fact that I had the good fortune to become a citizen of this great Republic, under whose beneficent laws the poor and the rich, irrespective of race or creed, have equal opportunities of education and material prosperity; secondly, to the fact that I have always endeavored to extract something good rather than evil from everything that has come before me (which has had the effect of making lighter the cares and tribulations of this life) ; in the next place, to the great assistance of my good brothers, to the companionship and advice of a loving wife and children, and, above all, to a kind and merciful God.

Henry Seessel

Typical German Jewish Immigrant

Henry Seessel (1822-ca. 1911), like other Rhineland Jewish immigrants whom we have learned to know, migrated to New Orleans [ca. 1843], via Paris and Havre.

It is interesting to follow his career after he arrived. He went north to Natchez, and, before he finally settled down for life in Memphis in 1857, he had worked and done business also in Vicksburg, in Cincinnati, in Lexington, Kentucky, in New Orleans, and in Richmond and Milliken's Bend, in the state of Louisiana. In between he had fought for a year in the Mexican War as a member of Cassius M. Clay's company in the Third Regiment of Kentucky Mounted Volunteers (1846-47). Seessel calls his autobiography Memoirs of a Mexican Veteran, *but he exhausts the narrative of his army service in the one sentence: "I will not relate the incidents that happened during the year that I belonged to Uncle Sam, as it would take up too much time and space." If all memoir writers were as considerate about "time and space" as Seessel, historians would have precious little material for their books.*

Seessel was in many respects the typical Jewish émigré from Central Europe. That is why he is significant. His is not a tale of progress from rags to riches; his is not a Jewish Horatio Alger story. For years he was an itinerant merchant, peddling clothes and jewelry; he quarreled with his family; he was a trunkmaker, a storekeeper, a stock raiser, a saloonkeeper, and a butcher. The yellow fever struck his family and his employees, and hurt him in business, making it difficult for him to keep what money and possessions he had acquired by dint of hard labor and great effort.

His close identification with the synagogue is documented by the simple statement that during the yellow fever epidemic of 1873 in Memphis, "I acted as warden of our burial ground and buried close on to 100 of our people."

The following extracts from the Memoirs of a Mexican Veteran *(Memphis, 1891), pp. 1-30, are a true reflection of the problems, hardships, and modest successes of the average Jewish immigrant in the days before the Civil War.*

A Greenhorn Peddler in Mississippi

In the spring of 1891 I suffered with rheumatism and went to Hot
Springs, Ark., to be cured. While there I felt lonesome, and in order
to kill time I decided to write a history of my life, which, I trust,
will be interesting to my children and at the same time give them
some idea of what I had to suffer and how different I was brought
up from them.

I was born on the nineteenth of March, 1822, in the city of Speyer-
on-the-Rhine. My mother died when I was four years of age and left
my father with nine children—six girls and three boys. One year
after my father again married, his second wife being a widow with
three children. A child was born one year later, and father took sick
and died, leaving us in poor circumstances. A few days after father's
death the child also died. Then the children separated. Our stepmother took her three children and the others were distributed
among relatives. All household furniture and everything of value
was sold at auction, and our poor stepmother started to keep house
for herself and children. . . .

Now, towards the end of the fourth year [in Paris], I received a
letter from my brother, who at that time was living in Natchez, Miss.,
asking me if I wanted to come over to this country; if so, that he
would send me the money to come with, provided I had none myself.
I answered and asked him to send the money and I would come. Then
about three months afterwards I received a draft for 100 francs, or
$19, with which I was to come over to this country. This sum I was
afraid would hardly be sufficient. I remained another month in
Paris, as I had a good job, and saved a little more money to help
along.

Finally I made up my mind to go. Then I got everything ready
and told all of my friends farewell, and, with a heavy heart, left for
Havre by steamer as far as Rouen and from thence to Havre by rail.
The reason I went by steamer to Rouen was I bought my ticket all
the way through to New Orleans from an agent in Paris, and all the
emigrants were shipped that way. I do not remember how much I
had to pay, but it was not much. There were no steamers then from

Havre to New Orleans, therefore I had to go on a sailing vessel. I arrived at Havre without accident, and found out that we were to set sail the following day. I had to buy my provisions for the trip. I soon found some emigrants who went by the same vessel, who assisted me in getting what I needed, but I soon found out that my money would not reach, and was compelled to dispose of a new suit of clothes and some other articles, for which I got very little, but I managed to get enough to buy what I needed and had a small sum left.

The vessel's name was "Laffitte à Geyer." We had 300 steerage passengers and a few cabin passengers. The captain and the other officers and crew were all French. We left in time, had a good voyage, and crossed the ocean in thirty days, which was a fast trip, and we had fine weather all the way.

On landing at New Orleans I was met by a young man who was looking for me, who was in the employ of a large wholesale clothing house by the name of Jonas Brothers, with whom my brother was dealing, and whom he had instructed to look out for me. They asked me many questions of how I was provided with clothes. Of course, I told them that I had to sell the best I had, to raise money enough to buy provisions at Havre. They also had instructions to furnish me with what I needed, which they did. I arrived at New Orleans early one morning, and the same evening the old steamer "Missouri" left for Natchez. I was shipped on deck for $2.

The first parties I met on the steamer were two old friends of mine from Speyer, by the name of Adler and Schott. Adler was the father-in-law of Schott. They also lived in Natchez, and had bought a small amount of goods, as Mr. Schott was a peddler. They also traveled on deck and were kind enough to let me sleep with them, as I had nothing myself to sleep on. From them I found out that my eldest brother had died a few months previous to that time. I did not even know that he was in this country, but my friends told me that he came over with my brother's betrothed, whom he married soon after they arrived.

The steamer was only two days going to Natchez. My brother was expecting me and met me on the boat, and, of course, was glad to see me. His wife, also, was seemingly glad, but, alas, it did not last long. My brother was also peddling at that time. There were a great many young men peddling, all of them making their home at Natchez, and they were stopping at Adler's, who kept at that time a boardinghouse for peddlers.

My brother had at that time one child. There were also some fam-

ilies living there from home, all of whom I knew when I was a boy
at home, and all were glad to see me. All of them had left Speyer
long after I had left, and none knew what had become of me. (Very
few of those that were peddling out of Natchez at that time are living now. Some of them have become large merchants, while some
others never did much good for themselves. I don't think that, besides myself, there are four out of about thirty living.)

After I had remained in Natchez about one week my brother and
myself started on our first trip together. We had a horse loaded
down with three large packages of dry goods and clothing. Both of
us walked, and I had to lead the horse. This was an entirely new
business to me. I had to learn a good deal. I knew nothing whatever
about handling goods, nor did I know how to handle a horse. I had
to learn how to curry a horse, which I had to do morning and evening. Instead of my brother making the negro, where we stopped
overnight, clean our horse, he made a negro out of me and made me
do the dirty work. Of course, I thought then, as green as I was, that
it was my duty to do it, but I soon found out different.

I did not relish the work of peddling at all. Every time we stopped
at a farm to sell goods I had to pack the heavy packages in and out
of the houses, and while my brother was selling goods, I stood and
watched on the outside, so no one would steal anything.

It was very easy in those days to sell goods. There were no stores
at every crossroad. There were stores only in the towns. The eating
did not suit me, as I was not used to eating American dishes, such
as hot bread, turnip greens, and pork. The walking of from ten to
twenty miles per day I did not relish, either. In fact, I would have
rather worked at my trade, which I learned in Paris, for twelve hours
every day for all the time than to peddle for only one day. We made
our first trip and sold out in two weeks. I suppose we had no less
than five hundred dollars' worth of goods; besides, my brother carried a jewelry box, out of which he sold a good deal.

After resting a few days and replenishing our goods, we started
on our second trip. This time it went a little easier with me. I saw
that there was no other chance, and by degrees I got used to it, but I
never fancied it. This time we went further than the first time and
stayed out four weeks, and again my brother must have made a paying trip. He always got good prices for his goods. We made a third
trip of four weeks and sold out again.

Now, for those three trips that I made, during which time I had
to do the work like a slave, I received no pay. My brother said I
had to do the work to pay him back the money he sent me to Paris,

and for the clothing he had to buy for me on my arrival; but that
from that time on he would give me one-third profit; that is, of the
net profits, after paying expenses, when we were out together, or half
profit when I went out alone, but I would have to pay board when
at home. We made two more trips, and my share out of same
amounted to about $50.

The first trip I tried alone he hired a young man to go with me,
but after the first day I made him go back home, as I did not like
his company. He was too impertinent with the people. I got along
pretty well for a "greenhorn" on this my first trip alone, but after
being out two weeks I went back home, nearly sold out, making a
nice little sum for myself.

Every time I came to Natchez after being out from two to four
weeks, a dozen or so of the peddlers met and generally had a little
fun together, but my brother did not like for me to have any pleasure.
He, in the first place, was not on good terms with the Adlers, who
kept the boardinghouse where all the other peddlers stopped, although we hailed from the same place in Europe. He thought himself above the others, he always being very proud, and, furthermore,
he wanted me to help his wife in her housework at home, but to all
this I seriously objected.

I made two more trips alone on half profit, but on this last trip
I traded goods for a lady's gold chain. There was at that time a great
deal of old jewelry in the country among the farmers, for which the
peddlers traded goods. Now, this chain for which I traded, some other
peddler had traded for once before me, but brought it back to the
party from whom he got it, saying it was brass. The first peddler had
it guaranteed to him for good gold, but when I traded for it the
gentleman would not guarantee it any more, but he said it was sold
to him for gold in New Orleans when he bought it and paid $50 for
it. I thought I could not lose much, and kept the chain.

This is hardly worth relating, but I only wish to show how my
brother treated me, and why I did not remain long with him. When
I returned from that trip, and after settling up with him, I showed
him the chain. It had been agreed that I was to get half profit from
all old jewelry that I bought. As soon as he saw the chain he pronounced it brass. Of course, he would not stand half the loss; at
least he said as much. It did not cost me more than $3. I said noth-
ing, put the chain in my pocket, and all was satisfactory.

In the afternoon I went downtown, and, passing a jewelry store
on Main Street, I went in and showed my chain, offering to sell it
for old gold, but on first looking at it they also pronounced it brass.

I insisted that they should try it with acid. They cut one of the links in two and then dipped it in a little acid, and to their astonishment the chain stood the test of the acid and proved to be good gold. They then bought it of me for $22. I then went home and told my brother of my good luck. He claimed half the profit, to which I objected. We had a quarrel over it, and then I told him that I would no longer remain with him. I packed up what little belonged to me and moved to Adler's boardinghouse, and this ended our friendship. Everybody that heard of the affair said I acted right, and also said that my eldest brother, who died before I came to this country, who also peddled for my brother, had been treated no better at his hands.

I had some money of my own. I bought myself a cheap horse, and with the rest of my money bought a small stock of goods and commenced to peddle on my own account, but made up my mind that it would be better for me to try some other section of the country. I therefore took all my belongings and traveled as far as Vicksburg, selling goods all the way there. It took me about two weeks to make the trip, and I sold nearly all I had by the time I reached there. I found several old acquaintances there from Speyer, and many young men from our section of the country, who were mostly peddlers. Among them were the firm of Schulz & Sartorius, who had a large wholesale dry goods and clothing store, where the peddlers laid in their supplies.

After remaining a few days to rest, I also bought my goods and started out alone. I soon got acquainted among the people in the country. I also made rapid progress with the language. I learned it much sooner than many others. The reason was because I spoke French fluently.

Trunk Making, Clerking, and Peddling Up North

After making several trips out from Vicksburg (this was during the summer of 1844) I took sick with chills and fever. It seemed that I could not get cured of them. I therefore made up my mind to go farther north. I sold out my goods and also my horse and started for Cincinnati. I had the bad luck to get onto an old boat, and it took us two weeks to make the trip, but we arrived there in safety. I soon found a place to stop, not far from the steamboat landing. A man by the name of Pfau kept a boardinghouse, with whom I stayed for the time being.

On the following day after my arrival I hunted for a situation as clerk in some store. I thought I would try that for a change. I soon found what I was hunting for with a man who kept a retail clothing store by the name of Weiler. He was to pay me on trial $25 per month, with board and lodging, as stockkeeper. I worked to his satisfaction the first day. On the second day, there being nothing to do on the inside of the store, he told me to stand on the outside and ask people as they went by to come in and buy goods.

The very first man I stopped to get him inside the store happened to be some ruffian from the country. He looked at me for a moment and then with a curse knocked me out into the middle of the street, calling me a "damned Jew dog." This was a little too much for me to stand. I went inside the store after I had gotten up and told Mr. Weiler that I would not stay another moment in his house for any price; that I thought too much of myself to be treated in that style. He paid me for what work I had done the day previous, and I then went back to the Pfau's boardinghouse.

This Mr. Pfau was a very clever man and seemed to take a liking to me. He asked me if I knew no trade. I told him that I was a trunkmaker, which I had learned in Paris. He knew of an old man by the name of Cohen, not far from his place, who was making what was called paper trunks. They were small boxes pasted over with paper, then the paper was painted black and then iron bands put around them and a lock put on, also some fancy paper pasted on the inside. This was easy work for me. He took me to the place, and I had no trouble to get work, for Mr. Cohen was only too glad to give me work, as he himself was old and feeble and wanted a cheap man to help him. I made a bargain with Mr. Cohen for so much per dozen and went to work at once, remaining with Mr. Pfau for boarding and lodging.

This Mr. Cohen was an old bachelor, a very nice old man. I worked there for about three months, being well pleased. During that time I made a good many friends and also found some of my home people, especially one family by the name of Lyons, from Grunstadt, whom I knew at home. They had a large wholesale clothing store, where I often went to spend my evenings. All of a sudden Mr. Cohen took sick and died a few days afterwards. Again I was without work. There was no stock on hand; what little was left did not amount to anything, and I did not feel myself able to carry on the business on my own account, being a mere stranger in the city and having no capital.

About that time a cousin of Mr. Lyons', of the same name, who had a business at Lexington, Ky., came on a business trip to Cincinnati to buy goods. This Mr. Lyons needed a young man as clerk.

I had no trouble to engage myself to Mr. Lyons, who seemed to be a very nice gentleman. I made no price with him as to what salary he was to pay me until he could see what I knew about the business. As soon as he got through with his business we left together for Lexington, and I went at once to work. I soon found out that we were getting along well with each other. A few days after I had commenced to work, Mr. Lyons proposed to pay me $40 per month and lodging, but no board, he being a single man and sleeping in a room back of the store. Board being cheap, I accepted the offer. We got along very well, and I remained with him until the spring of 1846. I saved all the money I could, as there was no chance to spend much in an inland town, and only paid $12 a month for board.

I JOIN THE ARMY TO FIGHT THE MEXICANS

About that time the war with Mexico broke out, and one morning, in the beginning of the month of April, 1846, old Gen. Lesley Combs, on horseback, with drum and fife in front and a string of men in the rear of him, were marching by our store, calling for volunteers to go and fight the Mexicans. I at once took the fighting fever, and went into the store and told Mr. Lyons that I would volunteer also. He laughed at me and would not believe it, but I joined the company that was forming in front of the store, where Gen. Combs made a fine speech, which stirred my blood still more. I followed the company until we reached the court house, where other men made more speeches, and we all had to promise to assemble at the city hall that night for the purpose of electing our officers, as we had enough men to make up a company.

When I came back to the store, Mr. Lyons tried very hard to keep me from going, but I was obstinate. My mind was fully made up. I said to him that I had nothing to lose; I had no one that cared for me. My brothers and sisters did not even know where I was, and even if they did, none of them took any interest in me. Therefore, I could only lose my life, which I did not value a great deal, and should I get crippled in a battle, I knew that the government would take care of me; but getting wounded never entered my mind. I thought that if I ever should get into a battle, I would either get killed or get out of it safe and sound.

We selected our officers that night, and Cassius M. Clay [later minister to Russia], a very noted man at that time and a very rich man, was chosen captain. We were to go as infantry. On the following day the captain went to Frankfort, the capital [of Kentucky], to enter our company, but the regiment being already filled, he either had to enter as cavalry or not at all. He telegraphed this fact to the first lieutenant, who called a meeting of the whole company and stated the fact to them. Of course, there was no dissenting voice, and the captain was instructed to enter as cavalry. The only trouble that arose was, as the government did not furnish horses to volunteers, and about half of the company had not the means wherewith to buy horses, who should buy them?

When our captain came back from Frankfort, he took all the men who did not have the means to buy their own horses, of which there were about thirty, and bought horses for them, with the understanding that they should pay him a certain amount in cash each month from their pay, but as I had the means, I bought my own horse and also my uniform. When all were ready we went on horseback to Louisville, where the regiment met. There we were duly mustered and sworn in, and after remaining there a short time we went by boat to a point opposite Memphis, where we received our arms.

Each company was furnished by the government with a baggage wagon; besides, there were forty wagons to haul provisions. On the eleventh of August we took up the line of march through Arkansas and Texas, a stretch of 1,300 miles, to the Rio Grande, on the line between Texas and Mexico.

I will not relate the incidents that happened during the year that I belonged to Uncle Sam, as it would take up too much time and space.

In the spring of 1847 our time had expired for which we had volunteered. We were sent by water by way of the Gulf of Mexico to New Orleans, where, after a few days, we were discharged. The rest of our pay amounted to $95, and, besides, each of us got a land warrant for 160 acres of land, which we could locate wherever there was government land, but most of us sold our warrants, myself among them, for $65. There were speculators ready to buy them up at that price. Out of that amount of money I then had I owed some to the sutler, which had to be paid, leaving me about $100, out of which I bought a trunk and filled it with all kinds of clothes.

MY SISTER DIES OF YELLOW FEVER

While in New Orleans I met with two of my sisters. They came from Europe during the time I was in the army. They were certainly rejoiced at seeing me. They had been living a short time with my brother in Natchez, but, not being able to agree with his wife, went to New Orleans, where I found them both at work, one as house-keeper in a rich family, the other in a millinery establishment. Both were well contented. I remained in New Orleans about one week. My sisters wanted me to remain there, but I longed to return to Lexington, where I was well acquainted and had many friends. My youngest sister was engaged to a very nice fellow by the name of May. I tried to get them both to come with me, but they declined. I therefore got ready to leave, but before going I made them promise that if at any time they wished to come to me they would let me know, and I would send the means to come, provided they needed it.

Finally I told my sisters farewell and left per steamer for home. I called Lexington home, as I had more friends there than anywhere else, and, besides, the most of my comrades in arms were living there. I arrived home without any accident and at once went to my old employer, Mr. Lyons, who was expecting me. He offered me my old place again, but I gave him no definite answer about it. Before I left for the war I made the acquaintance of a young man from Cincinnati who was peddling jewelry in that section of the country, who had told me that he was making a fine living and money besides, and offered to take me as a partner at any time that I felt inclined to accept the offer. But after inquiring for this party I was told that he had left the country.

I took a notion to try my luck alone, and told Mr. Lyons of it. He told me he thought I could do very well; that the country was very rich and the people very liberal. Mr. Lyons was kind enough to give me a letter to his cousin in Cincinnati to assist me all he could, and to try to get me credit as much as I wanted. I therefore went to Cincinnati. Mr. Lyons did all he could for me, assisted me in buying, as he knew more about what I could sell than myself, as he had been peddling in the same country some years previous to that time.

After I had completed my purchases I returned to Lexington and soon started on my first trip. I returned about the first part of August. A few days later I received a letter from one of my sisters in New Orleans, informing me that yellow fever had broken out there, and that she was going to Biloxi, and that she would come to me at once if I would send her money. I at once sent her a draft, which I am sorry to say she never saw. She got ready to come to me and had to go back to New Orleans to buy some things she needed. She took the fever and died before my money could reach her. The money I sent in care of a Mr. Coleman, who was a friend of hers, and no doubt he used it towards paying her funeral expenses, as I never heard anything more of it. I have her letter which she wrote to me in my possession, and intend to keep it as long as I live, as that is all that is left of her. My other sister remained in New Orleans, but never took the fever, and married soon after that time. What became of the man to whom my sister was engaged, I could never learn. I never heard anything of him any more. Perhaps he also died, as I really believe he did.

I was so broken up about the death of my sister that I could not do anything for several weeks, but in the latter part of August I started out peddling again and worked hard through the whole of the fall months and all winter. By the beginning of spring, 1848, I had made about $1,000 clear money, and did not owe anything.

MARRIAGE IN EUROPE

The thought of my dear sister dying so young, in the full bloom of her life, worried me so much that I had no rest anywhere. I made up my mind to go at once to Europe, to find out what my other four sisters were doing there. I never tried to do anything in all my life that, when once my mind was made up, but what I went right ahead and did it. So I made one more trip in order to sell all I could, and after returning to Lexington I sold what I had left to other peddlers. I also sold my horse and everything that I had no use for, told all my friends farewell and started for New York. On arriving there I found that a sailing vessel was to leave the next day, and I at once bought a second cabin ticket and moved my trunk aboard the vessel. The vessel went to Liverpool, which was somewhat out of the way, but not knowing anyone in New York, I thought best to leave at once rather than to remain. We left at the appointed time, and after a trip of twenty-two days we landed safely at Liverpool. . . .

I remained a few days with my sisters [in Otterberg, in Rhine Bavaria] and went on to Speyer. I went to the only Jewish hotel there, which was kept by a Mr. Rose. I did not know where else to go, although my uncle, at whose house I was so well treated for four years, was living there. I did not care to stay at their house. Right here I must state that I did not make the trip to Europe with any intention of getting married. I only went, as stated before, to find out what my four sisters were doing. But when I saw my wife, who was then a girl, the niece of Mr. Rose, just seventeen years old, and knowing the whole of her family from my childhood, I at once made up my mind to ask her to become my wife, and come with me to this country. She was also an orphan, and one of a family of four sisters and one brother, and besides, like myself, she was not very tenderly cared for. . . .

Our wedding was to be private. Our party and my wife's relatives were to be present. I returned to Speyer the day before we were to be married, but to my sorrow I found out that the government officials were looking for me, because they said that I was subject to military duty, as I had never received my discharge from the government. There was then but one way for me to do, provided I could carry out my plan successfully, and that was to slip away unnoticed and get into France at once by the shortest road, and then let the rest follow me and get married in Strausberg [Strassburg], which was the nearest city in France. I accordingly told them all good-bye, and in company with my stepbrother walked as far as Bruchsal, over the Rhine from Speyer, nine miles from there. We had to wait but a short time, when the train from Mannheim on the way to Carlsruhe came along. I took the train, and my brother returned home after promising me that he would come with the party to Strausberg and be present at my marriage.

I arrived safely at Carlsruhe that night and early on the following day took the train for Strausberg, where I arrived on the same day. Once there I breathed easy, as I was a free man. Had I not done what I did, I might have been arrested and would have had to serve six years in the army. There was then a brother of my wife's grandfather with a very interesting family living in Strausberg, who also kept a Jewish hotel. I had no trouble in finding his place. Of course, I was a stranger to them, but my wife's uncle gave me a letter of introduction to them in which he stated the whole affair.

After I had been in Strausberg two days our whole party arrived by boat, namely, my intended, her uncle and aunt, my brother, and my three sisters. My brother, with my intended's granduncle, went the following day to the chief rabbi to see about our marriage, but he refused to marry us unless we had a certificate from the police authorities that everything was all right, but as I did not have the same, he refused to marry us. Then my intended's uncle had to engage the services of an old rabbi, who was at the head of a Jewish college, and in company with a half dozen of his pupils and all of our party went across the Rhine in a large omnibus to a town named Kehl [Germany], and there we were married according to the old Jewish custom, our marriage certificate being written in Hebrew, which I hold to this very day. We returned to Strausburg as soon as the ceremony was over, and after paying the old rabbi ten francs in gold, which satisfied him, we had a good dinner at my wife's relatives, and after dinner we made our arrangements for our departure for Paris on the following day, which we had to travel by stage. In the morning we told one another farewell. Our party left for Paris, and the others left on the next boat for their homes in Speyer.

We had a pleasant trip to Paris, after thirty-six hours travel, but arrived there very much tired out, being cooped up for so long a time. I selected a good hotel, being pretty well-acquainted in Paris, and remained there for a whole week, during which time I took my wife and sisters around and showed them the most interesting parts of the city. At the end of the week we left for Havre. On arriving there we found a sailing vessel getting ready to sail for New Orleans, in which we engaged passage, and on the following day departed. After a pleasant voyage of forty-eight days we arrived safely at New Orleans, where I intended to make our home. . . . [But he soon decided to go to Vicksburg, where there seemed to be more opportunity.]

Peddling and Keeping Store along the Mississippi

We took a boat and, after bidding our friends good-bye, left for Vicksburg. After a four-days journey we arrived there in safety. I at once went to the store of Mr. Sartorius, who was at that time living near the steamboat landing. He also invited us to come and stay at his house until I could find something to do. Mr. Sartorius was a goodhearted man and assisted me all he could. I soon found a place on the outskirts of the city where a party kept a grocery, which he offered for sale, and which Mr. Sartorius assisted me in getting. We moved again and started into business. In the meantime, Mrs. Sartorius engaged my oldest sister to work for them, my other two sisters remaining with us. I had very little luck in our new place and did not remain there very long, but before leaving there our first child was born to us.

I sold out again and started to peddling, first in Mississippi and sometimes in Louisiana. I found the latter place more profitable to work in and did not return to Mississippi. I soon got acquainted in that country and after a while was induced to move there and open up a store at the parish [county] seat, a town by the name of Richmond. On returning home from my last trip I told my people about it, but they asked me to wait a while, as both of my sisters were in the meantime engaged to be married, and they thought it best for them to get married before I moved away. Then, after remaining a short time longer in Vicksburg, both of them married.

It was about the year 1853 that we moved to Richmond, La. I rented a store and went to New Orleans and bought a nice stock of goods and opened up and sold a good many goods. About six months later I again went to New Orleans to lay in a fresh supply. I at first started on a cash system, but other stores doing a credit business, I soon found out I had to do it also or lose trade. I therefore went, to my sorrow, into a considerable credit business, and soon found out I had no goods and no money either. On top of that, an overflow came and drowned out all the crops, and I could not collect anything. I wrote to my people in New Orleans, stating the facts to them, and asking for time to pay. They gave me a few months' time, but I soon found out it was useless to try to keep on. I therefore gave up all the goods and accounts I had on hand, and with the little money I had left moved and bought a small place at Milliken's Bend, right on the river.

In the meantime, a brother and sister of my wife's had come over from Europe. The sister remained in Vicksburg, and the brother came to live with us. The following year another sister and her husband came over and came to live with us. All this happened while we were yet in Richmond. We kept a kind of boardinghouse in Milliken's Bend, and myself and brother-in-law traded in beef cattle, which we drove out and sold in Vicksburg; besides, we did some butchering. We lived in this place until 1857. In the meantime, my brother had moved to the city of Memphis, and with a Mr. Simon kept a wholesale dry goods and clothing store. He invited me to come on a visit, which I accepted. On arriving there, I stopped at my brother's house a few days, when I returned home again.

I MAKE MY HOME IN MEMPHIS

The following year I took a notion to move to Memphis, thinking it would be a better chance in a large city to get into some better business, and my wife also approved of it. In the meantime, my wife's sister got married in Vicksburg, and her brother, who was living with us, went to St. Paul to live. We therefore got ready to come to Memphis. I sold my place and some livestock I had on hand, and on the last day of August, 1857, landed in Memphis with five children and all of our household goods. We had to go to my brother's house at first, but on the third day after our arrival I bought out a beer saloon which had been well established. We kept this place for about eighteen months, and during this time we had the misfortune to lose one of our children. The saloon business was too confining for me; besides, we had very little room for our family, having but two rooms that we could use.

I again sold out, and on looking around for something else to do, I finally drifted into the butcher business. I would have done well, had I not had the bad luck to go into a co-partnership with a no-account man, who was highly recommended to me. This man robbed me of all we made during the nine months that we were together. Then I started alone, and did well, being by that time up to the business, and having gotten acquainted, and by hard work. I had a place leased with eight acres of ground upon which I built a slaughterhouse. We were doing a good and paying business when in '61 the war broke out. As soon as Memphis was taken, two regiments of Federals went into camp in the rear of where we lived and soon commenced to rob us of everything we had. They tore down all our fences and often annoyed my wife during the time I had to go to market. I then rented a house in the city, to which we moved, leaving two employes in our place to take care of what was left, which the soldiers could not take away. During the year we lived in the house we moved into, I bought the house where we are now living. From the time we moved into our own house we did very well. I had bought four slaves for our own use, for which I paid $3,100 in good money, all of which we lost during the war, but I still kept on making money and soon bought another piece of property, on which I built a house.

August Picard

Militant Artisan

*August Picard was an Alsatian, born in a village in the Depart-
ment of Haut-Rhin in the year 1812. At the age of eighteen he left
home and wandered off to Paris to make his fortune. Though a
butcher by trade, he was willing to do anything to make an honest
franc, but was not particularly successful in the various jobs to
which he turned his hand.*

*In 1834 he was drafted to serve in the French Army and, in a
modest fashion, made quite a career for himself. But he was hot-
headed and brooked insults from no one. After he had been in the
service some time, he killed a man in a duel. In 1840, his abilities
and his manliness earned for him the coveted stripes of a sergeant
major, but that same year he had to flee for his life after he had
severely wounded a commissioned officer in a duel. The officer, a
captain, had made a slurring remark about Jews.*

*In England, where Picard had taken refuge, life was anything but
dull for him. He was always in the middle of things. He was be-
friended by the son and the daughter of an English lord; he succeeded
in borrowing £5 from one of the Rothschilds—no mean achievement.
He refused to join Louis Napoleon in his descent on France, and
had an almost disastrous affair with an English girl. To escape the
consequences of his love-making and the young lady's threats, he
fled once more, this time to the United States. The year was 1841.*

*While in England, Picard had learned another trade: making
springs for women's bonnets. With this skill at his finger tips but no
cash in his pocket, he went to work in New York City.*

*In the following pages, translated from the French, Picard re-
counts* The History of My Life *in this country from 1841 to 1848.
The original manuscript, a copy of which is in the American Jewish
Archives, carries the story to 1857. This memoir was written that
year.*

*Though Picard's narrative is largely spiced with his amorous
adventures, he still found time to record his struggles to make a
living as an artisan and to portray his difficulties as a storekeeper
in metropolitan New York. Unlike most other memoir writers, he*

described his social life, thus enabling us to know what the immigrant of that day did with his leisure.

In later years he traveled to South America, but finally settled in the South, in New Orleans. Apparently, he attained some degree of affluence as a shopkeeper, for he sent one of his sons to a European university. His latter years were spent in Vicksburg, Mississippi, where he joined a married daughter. He died in 1872.

A Stranger and Penniless

The ship on which I was to sail was the "Clifton," under Captain Ingersoll, an American. The night before I was to leave I was robbed of everything I had: my trunk, my personal effects, and my money, and another trunk belonging to a lady who was a fellow-passenger. There remained of all I owned only a half-crown, 55 sous [about a half dollar]. I was in despair. I had worked so hard to amass this money. It represented my savings for eighteen months. Heavens! How many sleepless nights did I spend working for this money, only to lose it all in a single day!

That was just too much! I went to see the French consul, and then on bended knees I begged the captain to delay the ship for several hours, but it was of no avail. The money and everything that was inside the trunks was forever lost.

The next afternoon around 6:00 P.M., it was growing dark. We were already at sea. I was in such deep despair over this great loss and over the thought of arriving in a new country a stranger and penniless, that I resolved to throw myself into the sea at the first opportunity. But, apparently, the captain had noticed something, for just as I was about to jump into the sea, I felt someone grabbing my coat collar, swearing profusely. He took me to the nearest cabin and said: "Listen, young man, I have a simple question to ask you. What did you bring with you when you came into the world?"

"Nothing, captain," I answered, smiling.

"Well, then," he said to me, "make believe you came into the world yesterday. You've got a trade, you give a good appearance. Losing money doesn't mean that much. You can make a great deal of money in the United States. You're still young and it's a new country." With that he left me.

Those words on the captain's part seemed unusual to me. They represented new ideas for me. I had never heard such an argument before. But the idea wasn't bad. As a matter of fact, I followed the captain's advice and took courage. I often said to myself after this event: "I am certainly not permitted to take my life. Almighty God has given me life, and when he deems it necessary to take it away, I will be ready. He is the Master."

MAKING SPRINGS IN NEW YORK

After traveling fifty-six days, we arrived in New York on November 12, 1841. I shall never forget how terribly cold it was that day. I went down with some other passengers to a shabby-looking hotel. It was located at No. 17 Front Street, and its landlord was a Mr. Rucastel. Although the weather was cold, I had no suit to put on. Those which I had when I left for New York were half worn out on the ship, and since, as you know, my best things were stolen from me at Liverpool, I had no shoes to put on my feet, and the ones I did have were practically worthless. But Almighty God, in whom I placed all my hopes, had not abandoned me.

I had tried for a week to obtain an order to make springs, which were new in this country. Everywhere I was told that this was not at all a good time for marketing, that it was the slow season. If I came back after the first of the year, they might possibly give me an order. There were others who said that they were not buying anything at the moment, because they were taking inventory.

There was at this time a French-Swiss named Rouislot, who made springs, which he sold for as much as $30 a gross, while I used to sell them in London for the price of six shillings (or 7.50 [francs] in French money), and was quite happy with my profit. Nevertheless, by searching from morning to night to get an order to make springs, I found a man named W. M. Pinio, who at this time was living at the corner of William and Ciedar [Cedar?] Streets. This generous American took pity on my unfortunate position and gave me an order for twenty gross of cap springs at $4.50 a gross.

Who was happier than I? But to fill this order, I needed money to buy steel, and I had none at all. I didn't know anyone in New York whom I could ask for any, even for a few days only. Moreover, I couldn't ask Mr. Pinio for money, who didn't know me. I was highly embarrassed. I had an old black coat, already a little worn, which was worth $2 at the most, but I needed at least $5 to buy the steel and fill this order. I went to No. 1 Division Street. There was a pawnshop in that building at this time.

I asked to speak to the proprietor of the business. "I am the proprietor," said an older gentleman about fifty years old.

"Sir, would you be so good as to lend me $4 for this item?" I said, showing him my old, worn coat. "It is only for several days. I will [pay] you back gratefully," and as I said this, tears came to my eyes. I was crying like a child, because it was the first time I had to go to a pawnbroker.

This man had pity on me and lent me the $4 I asked him for, saying: "I have good faith in you and in your word. I am lending you $4, but, truthfully, your coat is worth no more than [$]2."

With this money, I bought some steel, or rather a steel thread. Mr. Rouislot, who also made springs, did not know the secret. He had to cut each thread with heavy scissors, spring by spring, while I bought steel thread and made it come out to the desired number.

Three days later I brought ten gross of springs to Mr. Pinio, saying: "I confess to you without shame that you are doing me a great service in advancing me the money for these ten gross, since I have no more to complete the order." I told him what had happened to me at London and at Liverpool.

"Poor fellow," he said to me, "you should have told me the first time you were here. I would have advanced the entire sum to you."

I thanked him for his generosity, telling him that I would never forget the service he performed for me.

"How can you wear a light coat?" he went on, "in such cold weather, when I am not warm in a heavy coat?"

When I showed him the ticket I had received from the pawn-broker, then he insisted that I accept the money for the whole order, that is, for twenty gross at $4.50, $90.

I accepted, and went at once to see the old gentleman who had my coat in pledge. When he saw me come into his office, he said right away: "I was sure you would come back. I am rarely mistaken in my judgments, and you have the face of an honest man."

I then went to purchase the necessary clothing, and five days later brought the rest of the springs to Mr. Pinio, who was well-satisfied with their quality. Even today whenever he sees me, either at home or elsewhere, he breaks into a smile.

JANE

On the twenty-fifth of December of the same year, 1841, I changed lodgings to stay at No. 33, Bowery, in an American boardinghouse run by a man named Nuel, for $4 a week. In this house I met the most charming little creature you could possibly see, a girl named Jane Miller. Born in New York of Irish parents, she must have been about seventeen or eighteen. She was the niece of Mrs. Nuel, the landlady.

I believe it is useless to detail her charms, but that it is enough to say that I became madly in love with her although I was twenty-nine years old. I didn't dare declare my passion for her for fear of being scorned by her, but, little by little, I came to be rather familiar with her. Now I took her to the theater with her aunt; another time it was a party in the fields; still again we went to the ice cream parlor to eat sherbet. All of this amusement went on for about four months. I was making as much money as I wanted; I had days when I made as much as $30. It was a beautiful country for a workingman.

The springs were sold as soon as I made them, and sometimes even, they were sold before they were made. I sold them at insane prices; I sold them as high as $18 a gross. That lasted until the beginning of the month of June, when the price was [$]5 a gross. I was not sorry for this slack time, because I was tired. I was working eighteen hours a day and sometimes, when I was very busy, I worked whole nights without going to bed.

My passion for Jane had become stronger and stronger, even without response on her part. It was stupid. One Sunday afternoon I found myself alone in the living room with her. I made her a full declaration of love, to which she listened without anger. I depicted my passion in the most heated terms. Jane saw no designs in the thing, however, because this love was a sort of plaything for her.

When I had finished, she answered me: "Mister Picard, I have known for a long time that you love me. But I will never belong to a man without loving him also." Then she went out of the parlor.

I said to myself often: "Jane is wrong. She was an orphan with good fortune. Her education was neglected, and she was her own mistress at an age when reason is not yet formed. She has managed to be compromised by giddiness. Perhaps I am wrong, yet I have well understood that Miss Miller doesn't have the courage to admit love for me, but I believe she has belonged to another."

This thought revolted me. I believed her so pure that I found a certain spotlessness in her beauty. Jane was in love; for this severity which she had for me, she took off for another. For I had already noticed several times that she had preferences for a young man, a humbug actor named Ruisselet. All these intrigues lasted just about until August, but I still loved my pretty Irish girl.

It was impossible for me to bear such a burden any longer. That very day I knew what to do: I would go to her and ask her firmly how I stood. For to live this way in uncertainty was impossible for me.

In the afternoon I met Mrs. Nuel. I asked her for a moment's talk, but before I could open my mouth to tell her what I wanted to talk about, she broke in: "I know, my dear sir, what you want to say to me. I am Jane's aunt; she has lived with me since her parents' death. Her conduct to you is incomprehensible for all of us in the house. She has nothing. Really, this girl gives us a lot of worry. Next, she does nothing in the house. You know that I am the mother of a large family, and I am not rich, or I wouldn't keep a boardinghouse."

The next day, around 9:00 A.M., Jane came into my room, where I was working. I was very astonished to see this proud young lady coming into my workshop. She told me: "Mister Picard, you complained to my aunt about my treating you hardly and coldly, as you call my conduct to you. Well, I find you Frenchmen extraordinary. As soon as they see a girl that suits them, they want to know at once just where they stand. But remember, Mister Picard, that if such is the style in your country, it is different in this country. People are colder in order to better judge people. Give me at least some time to get acquainted with you, and, after that, we shall see."

In spite of this word spoken in a severe tone, I did not retain any less hope. Oh, heavens, she was beautiful with her feelings aroused. Her slightly pale cheeks became pink, and as she spoke she looked at me once in a way that gave me hope.

While I am in the process of outlining the passion which I had for Jane Miller, as well as I can write reasonably (since she charmed me so from our first meeting), I will see if it is possible to give an idea of her beauty. Jane was blonde, but one of these medium blondes with blue eyes. There was in her beauty a kind of poetry that my pen is not gifted enough to present completely. A brush would be better. Her eyes spread love, reverie; her mouth, with its pink lips and pearly teeth; her head, which she carried slightly tilted because the luxuriant mass of her hair had wearied her when she was little; her figure, graceful and suave; her throat, white as alabaster. This is Jane Miller physically. No one should be astonished that I loved her so.

Yet behind so many charms, there were many treacheries, many hypocrisies. She was only eighteen, but she knew as much as a woman of thirty. For I must tell you that, for all the love and patience I held for her, she pretended little by little to be less severe toward me. But I found it was only for the purpose of better deceiving me.

At this time Jane left her aunt's house to go live uptown at the home of one of my countrymen, who was a worker in a cap factory. He was Jacob Galinger. Through this Galinger, I learned later that she was in love with a young cutter in the same factory with her, named Samuel Riche, of Polish origin.

At the same time, Jane made me believe that she loved me, and that the ice was about to melt, while actually she was getting ready to marry this young hat-cutter. The proof that she had promised love to two men, but marriage to my rival, actually came after a month, when they told me that Jane was married to Samuel Riche.

As for me, as soon as the market for springs went off, at about the end of November, I left the United States on a sailing ship bound for Havana, named "Hellespont," to forget my unfortunate love affairs. Two weeks later, at one in the afternoon, we entered the port of Havana, the city famous for its cigars. I went to stay at an English hotel for $3 a day.

The city of Havana itself is very poorly built. The streets are so narrow that two vehicles cannot pass in the same street, for lack of room. The houses are very tall, and with only two floors. All the ground floor windows are decorated with an iron grill, and most of them have no panes.

But when you go out of the city, the picture changes. The view is magnificent. You notice the beautiful theatre of Dacon, then beautiful, decorated roadways on each side of the main road. Banana groves, fig trees, and orange trees, all of which give forth a delicious odor.

After a month's stay in Havana, I fell in love with the landlady of the hotel. She was a widow, a charming woman with a great deal of wit, and had a $40,000 fortune—200,000 francs and the hotel. She was not a young girl any more, but was about twenty-nine or thirty, very likeable and passably pretty.

At the end of a month of sighing on the part of both of us, we were in love with each other, without ever having said so. I would have perhaps married Mrs. Alexander Morrison but for the difference in religion. She was a Protestant, born in Edinburgh, Scotland, while I was a descendant of Moses.

After I had been in Havana five months, that is, at the end of April, my sweetheart told me one morning: "Now, my dear Auguste, it is time for you to leave for the North, for the yellow fever will soon begin its ravages."

I made a few objections, in spite of which, deep in my heart, I was glad to be going back to the city of New York.

She promised me that she would soon come to join me in New York and spend the summer there.

Several days later I departed for New York on "La Barque Rapide," under Captain Ward. After ten days I disembarked at New York. Although I had made a lot of money, when I checked my accounts upon my return, I was not richer than I had been when I left six months before. I obtained lodging at No. 37, Frankfort Street, in a French boardinghouse run by a man named Cole.

The next day I called on my washerwoman, Mrs. Allen, who lived at this time on Second Avenue near First Street. The first person I saw as I went into the house was Miss Jane Miller, or rather, Mrs. Riche. My heaven, how she had changed in so short a time! This was not the girl fresh as a rose whom I had known a year before. Her eyes were marked with blue spots; she was thin and worn-out; in short, I hardly recognized her. Apparently, while I was in Havana, after one month's honeymoon Mr. Riche became weary of his dear other half, and one fine day he boarded a ship bound for Hamburg, without so much as a by-your-leave. As soon as Mrs. Riche saw me, she ran into another room.

The following day my washerwoman came to get my soiled linen from my trip. Mrs. Allen gave me all the details of the great poverty Jane Miller was in, how she had neither a dress to wear nor shoes to put on, and that Mrs. Nuel had forbidden her from her house. Knowing that Mrs. Allen was a good woman, and not having any child, Jane begged her to give her hospitality until she could find a job working in a cap factory. I answered Mrs. Allen that, if she was willing to be discreet, I would give her some money for Mrs. Riche, provided she didn't say where it came from.

I had begun to make springs again, and although the season was already well along, I still could sell all I made for two months.

One fine morning, at about seven o'clock, someone came knocking at my door. What was my surprise on seeing enter my house Jane Miller, that proud young lady I had loved so much. She threw herself at my knees, saying: "Generous man, you don't know how God has punished me, I admit it, for having acted badly toward you, because I did not appreciate a heart like yours. I see that it is too late now. I will regret all my life having denied the most generous and noble of all men. For you have always acted like a father and a brother toward me, with a husband's devotion, while I treated you so as to repay you with the blackest ingratitude.

"I am coming back," she went on, with tears in her eyes, "to beg you to do one last noble deed, the last time, for me. It is one service to add to the others you were willing to do for me at first, when you had the goodness to pardon the evil I did you. I beg you to do me a last favor, which I shall never forget. And I will pray to the Lord to grant you happy days and a long life so that you will be repaid as you deserve."

"Tell me, Mrs. Riche, what can I do for you?"

"Generous man, you can do me a grand favor in lending me the little sum necessary for furnishing a little room I rented uptown at Twenty-seventh Street near Second Avenue. I pay a dollar a week. Furthermore, I will obligate myself to pay you back this sum later, for I have found work in a cap factory on Twenty-sixth Street, at the place of Charles King's, the manufacturer."

"Mrs. Riche, I promise you I will grant this last favor which you ask. It is no longer the sentiment of a year ago, because my heart is dead for you forever. I will grant your wish, but not out of love; it will be because of former acquaintance."

She thanked me with tears in her eyes, and left me.

As it happened, I went the same day to Chatham Square and sent her a bed, a little dressing table, four chairs, a little table, and a mirror. All that cost me $28.56. She wrote me several days later in thanks and at the same time invited me to come the following Sunday to see her in her new dwelling. She said she was expecting me.

This invitation startled me greatly. Could she believe I had fallen so low as to accept the leavings of others? Or did she think she could still enjoy perfect love with me as before? But you will see that this invitation had a purpose. The following Sunday, out of pure curiosity, I went to see Mrs. Riche on Twenty-seventh Street between Second and Third Avenues. She received me very gladly, trying always to talk about past times. But it was about lost times, too; my heart was closed for her. And so, after this last visit, I went back no more.

In the same house, I had met a compatriot named Galinger, an Alsatian like me. I learned later from him that Jane had met a young man, named Bouché, of her own type. I even learned that she was expecting, and intended to attribute the baby to me if it really came. That is how I was repaid for all the goodness I showed for Jane. But in spite of everything, she did not follow up her threats. I haven't heard any more about her, except that about five years later I met one of her neighbors named Fisher, who told me that she was very wretched, and that Bouché, her husband, beat her every day.

FANNY

I met a countryman of mine at this time, a man born at Metz, in the Department of Moselle. He was in business on Read[e] Street. Mr. Morange, for this was his name, kept a bar and billiard hall. On Saturday my friends and I often went to see Mr. Morange to play a game of billiards. Well, one Friday evening, when I was going

down Read[e] Street to see Mr. Morange with the intention of playing a game of billiards, how great was my surprise when I entered
the house and saw a pretty girl, a charming creature about nineteen
or twenty years old. She was of medium stature, with curly, chest-
nut-brown hair, brown eyes, well-rounded shoulders, well-made waist
and arms, small, white teeth, a child's hands, a small foot, and finally, an alabaster white throat. In spite of the fact that her throat
was a little large, it suited her very well. This evening she wore a
green wool dress, which looked very well on her, and a little, black
tulle shawl that concealed her charms. This young lady was named
Fanny Levy. She was born in a village in the kingdom of Württem-
berg, Obe[r]ndorf.

She seemed so noble and gracious that she made an impression
on me from our first meeting. I couldn't sleep the whole night thinking of her; I had fallen desperately in love with her.

I must tell you that this was my first true love. I am not deceiving
myself in saying that. I don't mean my first affairs, my first intrigues.
I had given so little of my heart to the others that I found it all to
devote to this girl.

The next day, which was a Saturday, I visited my compatriot
Morange on Read[e] Street. My first question was: "Who was that
charming young lady that I saw here last evening?"

"The devil take it, my friend! As you were going in, you saw this
girl for the first time last night, and you then come right away to ask
information. My faith, I am sorry not to be able to satisfy you, but
she has been in New York too short a time. She is the maid of the
house, but I can assure you that, if she ever becomes your wife, you
can flatter yourself for having the right sort of woman. Several of
my customers already have wanted to meet her, but she sent them all
away. I promise you that if Fanny ever becomes your wife, you can
congratulate yourself on being a fortunate man."

In the afternoon, when I had an opportunity to see her again, she
appeared to me still more beautiful than on the night before. Imagine my happiness in learning from her own mouth that she was free,
and had made the acquaintance of no young men, that she distrusted
men and especially Frenchmen, who are still more deceitful than
the others.

"How wrong you are judging me, Miss Levy! All men are not
alike. Read more deeply into my soul. I have had the pleasure of
knowing you only a short time, and yet I have now only one thought,
one goal, one desire. Do I need to tell you that I love and respect
you at the same time, and that since yesterday evening, when I saw

you for the first time, your beloved image has not left my heart, nor my memory? I will love you forever, Miss Fanny, because my love is sincere, for you are the first to make me experience a true sentiment. Oh, tell me only that you love me a little! It is before God the Almighty that I make here the oath to love you always and to make every effort possible to make you happy, if you will accept me as your husband."

"Mr. Picard, I will be very happy and very proud to be your wife. I have a great deal of confidence in the words, because I believe they are sincere, and I hope you will not deceive me."

Several days later, we called on the sister of my fiancée, who was married to a German named J.[ulius] Hornthall. Being a merchant, or rather a peddler, he was away from home for ten months out of the year. My future sister-in-law lived at this time at 17 Orchard Street.

My fiancée leaned on my arm, her long hair flowing over her gown. She walked thoughtfully, with a light step which she adjusted to mine. From time to time she looked at me with her soft eyes, so pure that you read there not only a woman's virtue but a girl's innocence, too. She introduced me to her sister, who greeted me cordially. She was two years older than my Fanny, a charming woman full of coquettish wit like all pretty women. She had beautiful, soft, black eyes, beautiful teeth, and curly black hair. Taller than my fiancée, she was named Matilda. Toward evening I took Fanny back to Read[e] Street to Mr. Morange's. After that day, few passed when I did not go to see my beloved.

I discovered new qualities in her every day. She had a very sweet temperament; she had a good heart. And so I loved her sincerely, fervently, and respectfully. This was not love, it was adoration. I was content to admire her, nor did I desire more in my platonic love. I passed happy times near her, especially in the evening. We were so happy with each other that we thought of nothing else. Often we built castles in the air.

Two weeks later my fiancée was to go stay with her sister, where I went to see her almost every evening. Several months later they [people] began to gossip, telling my dear Fanny: "So you believe this young man will marry you as soon as possible! Don't you see that he is making fun of you, that he is only amusing himself with you?" Others told her I was very wicked, and once married I would beat her; or I would leave her to go to another country. But my Fanny knew that these were lies intended only to blacken me in her eyes.

But all these rumors amounted to nothing, for on the twenty-fifth of September, 1844, we were married in New York at No. 202, William Street, by the Reverend Mister Hescht [Jonas Hecht?]. Mr. Ely Weil was my witness, and Julius Hornthall was my wife's witness. Just ten months later, on the seventh of August, 1845, my dear son Henry was born at 85 Chatham Street. I became the happiest of husbands, the happiest of fathers.

Nevertheless, we had many reverses of fortune. I was too good, too confident, too stupid, too clumsy, and not shrewd enough to succeed in New York.

On the fifteenth of May, 1847 [1846], my brother-in-law, Selegman Hirsch, came to New York, accompanied by his wife and two children. Mrs. Hirsch was a beautiful woman four years younger than my Fanny. I had a little store at No. 80 Chatham Street. It was a haberdashery with a big room behind, which I had taken for my workshop. My wife, and a boy of sixteen or seventeen years who served as clerk [also worked in the store]. I had as my only capital about $900 in merchandise. When my brother-in-law, who came from a town in Mississippi, saw I was not doing badly with a small stock of merchandise, he said to me one evening when we were together in a family group: "I don't see why you don't try to enlarge your shop."

"My shop is long enough and wide enough for all the merchandise I have in it," I said.

"But, my dear fellow, you don't understand. I mean that if I put $2,000 more in merchandise into it, you will sell a lot more. If you want us to be partners, each half of the partnership will profit, and at the end of the week, each one will draw out of [the] shop $20 for necessary weekly expenses."

"By golly," I said to him, "I believe that this will be much better. Indeed, the more merchandise you have, the more you will sell. Besides, I like to have the shop filled with goods."

On the fourth of July, 1846, we were very surprised to receive news that my wife's father and mother and four sisters had arrived. We hastened to go down to the vessel, whose name was, if I am not mistaken, "St. Denis du Havre."

You can imagine how thrilled my wife and I were to see her parents again for the first time after more than six years. My wife's four sisters seemed distinguished, although they were dressed like peasant women. The eldest of these four sisters, a girl named Nancy, was a very friendly person, small, and not very pretty. She was wise and good to a rare degree. The second of my sisters-in-law was named Adeline. About sixteen or seventeen years old, she had a magnificent build, tall and well-proportioned, a graceful, unpretentious walk, brown, curly hair, pearly teeth, and a lot of wit. She was not beautiful, but there was something in her face which attracted, which pleased. The third sister was named Julia, a beautiful, fresh girl of thirteen or fourteen. And the youngest was named Theresa. She was the smallest and very roguish, and gave promise of becoming a beautiful girl. She had that noble and distinguished walk which one rarely encounters.

My Fraudulent Partner

There were several young men who had come from Germany with my father-in-law. There was one of them from the same town, a man named Jacob Goodman, about twenty years old, and very intelligent. He had learned to keep books at Mannheim in Germany. He spoke a little French. I took this Goodman, then, to be my clerk and to keep books at the time when, my brother-in-law having added $2,000 to my shop, sales were going much better. And also expenses were much heavier. Each one took $20 a week, while at other times I had enough for the expense of the house of $6.

As for me, I rarely busied myself with my shop, for I worked all day making springs. My brother-in-law Hirsch did all the necessary duties of the shop. Toward autumn, my brother-in-law left to go back to his town in Mississippi, Satartia.

I was left alone, then, in the shop with my clerk Goodman. In December, when affairs began to stagnate, Goodman and I took stock of the shop. We found that we were $400 in the red, instead of having $2,900 worth of merchandise. I certainly understood nothing about it, for sales were good; we had always made enough to pay expenses. I thought we would be $500 ahead. I was really disappointed. But Goodman, who was a distant relative of my wife, told her one day that my brother-in-law had cheated me; for each time at the end of the week, when my brother-in-law and he had made the accounts of what he had bought and paid for, if he was short $20 or $30, he would tell Goodman to put it on the cash merchandise book, of merchandise which was constantly bought.

I assure you that this pained me deeply. "How could that be?" I said to myself. "Here was a man declaring himself very rich, who came north knowing I was poor. He took advantage of me, who believed him the most honest man in the world. How is it possible? I would not have believed it if the evidence was before my eyes. My God, is it possible that there are such perverse, deceitful men?"

That caused me a lot of trouble. I had bought nothing for more than two weeks, but when December came, near Christmas, I began to buy a lot of fancy things for New Year's. And so I bought a large quantity of toys for Christmas, and I even had the back room set up for a grand display of children's toys that I had bought cheaply. But not having any gas in the back room, I had a lamp to light this large space.

I was speaking of the arrival of my wife's dear parents. The second of the girls who came to New York was named Adeline. She was an intelligent girl, and very likeable; often she worked my press. (I had forgotten to mention that after I had been in New York for some time, I met a skillful mechanic whom I got to make a press to round out and pierce the springs from many pieces in a single blow. That worked very rapidly.) She understood at once how to work the press. In the first place, a lot of attention was necessary because there was a needle attached to a little screw. She worked well, and I was satisfied with her. So I often bought her either a dress or something else; I often walked with her either to go eat sherbet or to the theater.

THE FIRE

On the twentieth of December of the same year, there was a dance. My dear Fanny had gotten a ticket for $2, and she required me to go to the dance with her sister Adeline, because there wasn't anyone there who knew her. I was obliged, then, to go with her. She danced better than I had ever seen anyone dance before, light as a gazelle, and as gracious. And so everyone admired her. But at around eleven o'clock I was waltzing with her when I glanced at the door and saw my wife, pale as death, asking for me. I ran over at once [to] where she was.

"My God, what is the matter?" I said, alarmed.

She was crying and she spoke so that I couldn't understand anything of what she was telling me, and her words were even more indistinct because of the noise people were making and the music playing. However, after a second, she made me understand and explained to me that there was a fire in the shop. I didn't let her finish; I got my hat and ran at top speed. But what horror awaited me at the front of the shop! The fire was out, but all my beautiful goods were soaked, especially in the front room, where the fire did not reach, because the fire came from the interior. I spent the night at the shop to see that no one stole anything, because the door could not be closed, as it was off its hinges.

The next day I went to see the insurance companies. I forgot to observe that we were insured by the City Company for $1,500 and by Hartford Protection for $1,000. These gentlemen said they would send someone to verify the disaster. About four o'clock in the afternoon, the president of the City Insurance Company, with Mr. William H. Carry, agent, from 186 Pearl St., came. George Price, the president, asked to see my books. He even noticed that William H. Carry's name was on them. I was not far from them and I thought I could hear the latter say to the president that he had known me for a long time, always as an honest man. Then the president called me and said: "Mr. Picard, I see, most unfortunately for you, that your loss is great. So I offer you a check for $1,200, and you will keep the damaged merchandise." I answered that I would go to see him the next day.

The next day, at ten o'clock, I presented myself at the City Insurance Company, where the president greeted me cordially. After having talked a little, I agreed to accept the offer he had made to me the day before. At once he told a clerk to make out a check for $1,200 in my name.

But at the other insurance company, the Protection of Hartford, the president was not as generous as the president of the City Insurance Company. First, they looked for tricks, and for the fact that we had closed the shop too early, since, until Christmas, it was usual to keep the store open till midnight. In short, I asked: "What decision will you make?"

The president told me: "Mr. Picard, I offer you $500, and you will keep the spoiled merchandise, but this offer is actually more than [the stuff] is worth. For we sincerely believe that there was a great deal of negligence on your part and on the part of these women."

I told him: "Sir, I cannot accept this offer because I was insured for more than $500." But if he were willing to do as the City Company did, I would come to an agreement with him.

Then he said: "Mr. Picard, this is our last word."

Thereupon I left him and went to see a friend of mine, I. A. Dettenhoffer [Isaac Dittenhoefer?], who kept a big store for wholesale novelties. He was an honorable and respectable man. I told him in a few words the subject of my visit. "My dear sir, what do you expect me to say? Go see my lawyer, who lives at 20 Nassau Street, on the third floor. Ask to speak to George Richard. He will tell you what is best to do."

I went to 20 Nassau Street. I met Mr. Richard and repeated to him what I had said to Mr. Dettenhoffer, and how my settlement was made with the City Insurance Company. Then he said to me: "Sir, wait ten minutes for me here. Their office is quite near here. I will be back in ten minutes." He went out and several minutes later returned.

"Well," I said, "were you more fortunate than I?"

He said to me: "They are rascals, Mr. Picard. Go get a notebook of paper and write in it all the goods that were soaked in your shop, burned or not burned, and when you are finished, bring this notebook here. After that, we will see. But you will not be able to sell any of your things before you are settled with your insurance."

"To do what you tell me, Mr. Richard, would take me at least two weeks, because there are at least 5,000 different articles." Then I asked him: "Mr. Richard, Mr. Dettenhoffer recommended me to you, knowing well that you are an honest man. I ask you sincerely, as a friend, what is the best thing for me to do?"

"In the first place," he said to me, "if this case comes before the court, and there is the slightest evidence against you, you will be further obliged to pay the expenses, and you will lose the $500 that they offered you. And if I were in your place, I would accept. When you are dealing with faithless people, the sooner you get settled the better."

I answered: "I believe I will take your advice." I gave him the policy and several minutes later he came back with a check for $500. This business cost me $10 with Mr. Richard.

The next day I opened the shop and spread out all the soaked goods outside. Most of it sold well. We were busy all day, and during ten days we made sales of $750, which, combined with the $1,700 from the insurance, made $2,450. I put $2,000 in the bank on reserve for my brother-in-law. If he came back in the spring, I was going to pay him back his money, saying that if I ever fell for taking another partner, someone could box my ears. I still had $450 in cash and some goods that we had set aside, worth about $200.

On the evening of this last sale, at supper, I said to Fanny: "Dear, we have very little left to begin again with, for of the money I have on hand, half must go to repair the shop and have it painted again." Mr. Chappman, the landlord, required that I replace the shop just as it was before the fire, but I observed to him that he had drawn insurance money and should be satisfied. Then he told me my lease was up. I still had [a] fifteen months' lease, and the rent was cheap. "Mr. Chappman," I said, "we have been good friends and neighbors for two years. It is not worth it now to quarrel."

My Wife Was a Good Manager

One morning I said to Fanny that maybe she could borrow $300 or $400 to renovate the shop. Then she said: "If you need $300, I can give them to you without borrowing them."

"What?" I cried. "Where did you get this money?"

"Oh, it is easy to say how I got it. I saved it." And she went to get $350 in gold.

I was very happy, and said to myself: "That is what it means to have a good manager." Then I began to work again, and after two weeks, I opened the shop with a new assortment of goods. I sold a lot to peddlers, but with little profit.

On the fifteenth of March, 1847, my son Nathan was born. He was a great joy to the house.

At the end of April, 1847, my brother-in-law, Hirsch, came to New York to bring his family and at the same time to settle his account with me. But when he came to the shop on the day of his arrival, he said to me: "The devil take it, how come you have such a small stock of merchandise?"

"Listen to me: don't fear for your money; it is in good hands. The little stock of merchandise you see belongs to me; I don't owe a cent to anyone."

"What? You don't owe a cent? Then I see you are a fool. How can you think you are smart because you have no debts? Well, my dear brother-in-law, I think the opposite to be true. The more a man owes, the more he shows he is a businessman and that he knows at the same time how to work his own finances, so that when bills come that he cannot pay, the creditors can wait."

This, indeed, was somewhat novel to me. I could see the biggest thief and the biggest swindler are considered shrewd fellows. But as soon as I gave him a check for $2,000 he gave me a receipt and left.

At the end of August, my sister-in-law, Mrs. Hirsch, went back to her home, which was a town named Greenville, on the Yazoo River. Her departure grieved my wife greatly, for this dear sister Bertha was her favorite sister. Morever, they had made the crossing together when they left Europe.

On the fifth of March, 1848, my son Julius was born. We were thrilled in spite of the fact that he seemed thin and very delicate. He was a pretty little boy. For godparents he had Ely Weil and Justine Weil, his wife.

O, how well I still remember those happy days which passed so quickly, and how good a mother my dear Fanny was! My second son,

Nathan, had at this time what they call in this country the summer complaint; that means generally a sort of diarrhea in the second year. Many die of this sickness, and my little Nathan had a serious case of it. This was in 1848. I had a little shop on Grand Street. My wife was very useful about the shop, either to go buy what was needed, or to pay a bill, or at the auction. But in spite of all the observations I made to her, there was no way to keep her at the house, because Doctor Williams kept telling her that if she wanted the baby to survive, there absolutely must be a change of climate. As it happened, two days later she left by steamer for the city of Albany, on the Hudson River, about 150 miles from New York. She came back a month later with a joyous heart because she had saved the child's life.

THE FRENCH FLAG AND THE NEW YORK MILITIA

At this time there were some French residents, citizens of the United States, who were not satisfied because there was a law that each United States citizen must serve either seven years in the militia or seven years as fireman, or to be eligible for jury duty until the age of sixty. One day I saw in the *Courrier Française,* a daily paper, an announcement of a meeting of all citizens of French origin. The meeting was to take place at Mr. Delmonigoti's, at the Hotel Française.

As soon as everyone was arrived, they got to work. First, after the president of the assembly had discussed this question, we resolved to form a company of the New York Militia. At once, we organized ourselves to elect officers, under-officers, and corporals. Preference was made for all those who had already served in France. We named as captain a man named Lunady; as first lieutenant, Auguste Picard; and as second lieutenant, Antoine Manoin. The uniform of the company was completely French, except that the officers wore a red silk sash. The name of the company was the Lafayette Guard.

Captain Lunady went to Albany to see His Excellency, the governor, to ask him to incorporate us into a regiment of the New York State Militia. The governor answered Captain Lunady that he would write to General Sandfort [Charles W. Sandford], who commanded the First Division. Several days later we were incorporated into the Twelfth Regiment under Colonel Stebbins.

The duties were light: going out three or four times a year on parade. But in spite of this, we were busy. The time chosen for

weekly drill sessions was Thursday night, from eight to ten. The
hall chosen for training was Mercer House. There was also, twice
a year, target practice. Then, on General Lafayette's birthday, there
was a great family celebration. We went out in full dress with the
French flag, either to Hoboken or to St. Johns's (?) Park, led by
a fine band. Each time we had a lot of fun until night.

The first such affair we celebrated was grandiose. There were
ninety-five men present. We left at 8:00 A.M. to go to Hoboken. We
performed several maneuvers, and then the wives of company members arrived, with their children and friends, at three o'clock. It was
time for dinner. Several days in advance we had arranged with a
restaurant for dinners at $2 per person, with a bottle of wine for
each included. After des[s]ert there were toasts. The first was to
France; the second to the United States; the third to General Lafayette, whose birthday we were celebrating; the fourth was to the
ladies present; the fifth for the governor of New York; [the] sixth
to General Sandfort; next to the general of the Fourth Brigade; then
to Colonel Stebbins; finally, to the officers of the company. All
these toasts lasted just about until dark. Next I formed the company
into battle rank, ordered: "By the right flank, quick time, march!"
and we returned to New York.

The next day General Sandfort sent for me to report to him at his
house. When I came, he showed me into his office and said: "Captain Picard, I had you come expressly to give you a reprimand for
a grievous fault you have committed against the military discipline
of New York State. You went out yesterday with a French flag. I
point out to you, you are no longer French. You have sworn to be
loyal to the United States and to the American flag. You must not
believe that I am an enemy of the French; on the contrary, I have
always loved the French nation because it is to them in great measure that we owe the liberty of our dear republic. I pardon you this
time, but in the future, when you take your company out alone, you
may not go out with your French flag, but only with the American
flag."